'This urgent, compelling and carefully curated volume is a vital corrective to the field of queer and trans migration studies. By decentring an emphasis on legal regimes, Euro-American perspectives and South-North migration trajectories, *Queer and Trans African Mobilities* fills gaps in knowledge and understanding that have existed for decades. As a whole, the essays in this book invite readers to expand their thinking on migration narratives, securitization regimes, belonging, and what it means to think about queer Africa. This book should be mandatory reading for anyone teaching about queer and trans migration, gender and sexuality on the African continent, and the necessity of geographically specific analyses of transnational mobilities.'

–**Karma R. Chávez, Associate Professor, The University of Texas at Austin, USA**

'This gem of a collection thoroughly reorients our understandings of queer and trans migrations, mobilities and movements within and from the African continent. It reframes how African nations, and queer and trans migrants, are imagined, conceptualized and engaged. The authors provide innovative methodologies, epistemologies and key questions for scholarship, activism and policy-making. Read this groundbreaking book.'

–**Eithne Luibhéid, Professor and Director of Graduate Studies, Department of Gender and Women's Studies, University of Arizona**

'*Queer and Trans African Mobilities* is bold and transformative in its challenging of our understanding of the intersections of gender, sexuality and mobility in Africa. From a variety of disciplinary perspectives, the book is a worthwhile provocation and powerful reminder of how queer and trans mobilities on the continent are and should be imagined and theorized. The essays in this book push back against rigid interpretations of Africa and its peoples and the monolithic view that queer and trans Africans only move to the Global North to find more accommodating spaces. The book makes important contributions to the conceptions of border regimes as well as local, regional and global responses to queer and trans mobilities. *Queer and Trans African Mobilities* is a tour de force and a timely contribution to queer migration studies and queer African studies.'

–**Gibson Ncube, Stellenbosch University, Co-Convenor of Queer African Studies Association**

'*Queer and Trans African Mobilities* crucially intervenes in queer migration studies and politics by fully accounting for the journeys of queer and transgender Africans on the African continent, to different continents and countries, and on digital platforms. By centring queer and trans Africans' experiences with migration, mobility and travel, this timely book demonstrates how migration studies and queer African studies can enrich one another.'

–**Ashley Currier, author of *Politicizing Sex in Contemporary Africa: Homophobia in Malawi* and *Out in Africa: LGBT Organizing in Namibia and South Africa***

'*Queer and Trans African Mobilities* is an exciting and relevant collection of essays exploring the limits and possibilities of migration, asylum and diaspora. The various essays exfoliate the layers of cultural, emotional and political issues that confront these minoritized subjects who cross various virtual and geographic borders in their attempt to find home, solace and safety amidst the tribulations of the contemporary world. Among its various valuable interventions is the complicating of the directionality of migration, which is typically portrayed as movements from South to North. By offering studies on South-South mobilities, this work enables a new cartography and an expansive way of understanding the travails and travels of African queer and trans subjects.'

–Martin F. Manalansan IV, University of Minnesota, Twin Cities, USA

'Camminga and Marnell have produced a rare edited volume whose value far exceeds the sum of its parts. Not only does it offer original insights into the lives of people often hidden in plain view, but bravely charts a research agenda at once provocative and respectful, poignant and political. It unsettles migration studies' geographic and conceptual centre. But more than that, it does the same for queer, trans and gender studies. It introduces authors many will not yet know, sites that rarely feature in dominant accounts, and lifecourses that only a few will imagine possible. It sets the bar for collaborative, generative research that broadens and deepens through contributions to both scholarship and social justice.'

–Loren Landau, Professor of Migration and Development,
University of Oxford, UK

QUEER AND TRANS AFRICAN MOBILITIES

Migration, Asylum and Diaspora

B Camminga and John Marnell

ZED

LONDON · NEW YORK · OXFORD · NEW DELHI · SYDNEY

ZED BOOKS
Bloomsbury Publishing Plc
50 Bedford Square, London, WC1B 3DP, UK
1385 Broadway, New York, NY 10018, USA
29 Earlsfort Terrace, Dublin 2, Ireland

BLOOMSBURY and Zed Books are trademarks of Bloomsbury Publishing Plc

First published in Great Britain 2022

A catalogue record for this book is available from the British Library.

Library of Congress Cataloging-in-Publication Data
Names: Camminga, B, editor. | Marnell, John, editor.
Title: Queer and trans African mobilities : migration, asylum and diaspora
/ [edited by] B Camminga and John Marnell.
Description: New York : Zed, 2022. | Includes bibliographical references and index.
Identifiers: LCCN 2021056547 (print) | LCCN 2021056548 (ebook) |
ISBN 9780755638987 (hardback) | ISBN 9780755638994 (paperback) |
ISBN 9780755639007 (epub) | ISBN 9780755639014 (pdf) | ISBN 9780755639021
Subjects: LCSH: Sexual minorities–Africa–Social conditions. | Sexual
minorities–Legal status, laws, etc.–Africa. | Sexual minority
immigrants–Social conditions. | Africa–Emigration and immigration.
Classification: LCC HQ73.3.A35 Q84 2022 (print) | LCC HQ73.3.A35 (ebook)
| DDC 306.76096–dc23/eng/20211117
LC record available at https://lccn.loc.gov/2021056547
LC ebook record available at https://lccn.loc.gov/2021056548

ISBN: HB: 978-0-7556-3898-7
           PB: 978-0-7556-3899-4
         ePDF: 978-0-7556-3901-4
        eBook: 978-0-7556-3900-7

Typeset by Integra Software Services Pvt. Ltd.

To find out more about our authors and books visit www.bloomsbury.com
and sign up for our newsletters.

We dedicate this collection to the memories of Sarah Hegazi and Chriton Atuhwera (Trinidad).

CONTENTS

Part III
THE DIGITAL AND THE TRANSNATIONAL

Part IV
BORDERING IN ACTION: IDENTITY, BELONGING AND WELLBEING

CONTRIBUTORS

Yara Ahmed *is an Egyptian queer feminist researcher wandering the geographies of becoming and dreaming in a precarious world.*

Caio Simões de Araújo *is a postdoctoral research fellow at the Wits Institute for Social and Economic Research (WiSER), University of the Witwatersrand. He is a grantee and collaborator of the Governing Intimacies Project, based at the same university.*

Godfried Asante *is an assistant professor of Communication, Difference and Disparities at San Diego State University. His research focuses on social identities such as race, class, gender and sexuality in transnational and mediated contexts.*

B Camminga *(they/them) is a postdoctoral fellow at the African Centre for Migration and Society, University of the Witwatersrand, South Africa. Their first monograph,* Transgender Refugees and the Imagined South Africa *(Palgrave 2019), received the 2019 Sylvia Rivera Award in Transgender Studies (with Aren Azuira) and an honourable mention in the Ruth Benedict Prize for Queer Anthropology from the American Anthropology Association. They are the co-convenor of the African LGBTQI+ Migration Research Network (ALMN).*

Florent Chossière *is a PhD student in geography at Université Gustave Eiffel (France). His doctoral research deals with lived experiences of migration and asylum by SOGI applicants in France. He is also a fellow of the French Collaborative Institute on Migration.*

James Maingi Gathatwa, *a graduate student at Mount Kenya University, has extensive experience on LGBT issues. His research interests include social justice, economic empowerment and health, especially of marginalized populations.*

Marien Gouyon *has a PhD in anthropology. After three years as postdoctoral researcher at the University of Angers and one year as a teacher-researcher in China, he is now a research engineer at the Aix-Marseille University. He has published* 'Ana Loubia': Ethnographie des homosexualités masculines à Casablanca *(Vulaines sur Seine, 2018). He is currently working on gay male migration in Morocco and the United Arab Emirates.*

Verena Hucke *is a researcher at the chair for Sociology of Diversity, University of Kassel, where she is pursuing her doctoral thesis on the negotiation of sexualities in the migration regime in South Africa. Her research interests include gender* *studies and feminist theory, critical migration and border regime studies, and queer migration studies.*

Margaret Jjuuko *is an associate professor in the School of Journalism and Communication, University of Rwanda. Her research areas include, among others, environment communication and social justice in developmental contexts.*

John Marnell *(he/him) is a doctoral fellow at the African Centre for Migration and Society, University of the Witwatersrand, South Africa. His most recent publication is* Seeking Sanctuary: Stories of Sexuality, Faith and Migration *(Wits Press 2021). He is the co-convenor of the African LGBTQI+ Migration Research Network (ALMN).*

Agathe Menetrier *is a doctoral candidate at the Max Planck Institute for Social Anthropology (Halle) and the Ecole Normale Supérieure (Paris). Her PhD project explores LGBT asylum in West Africa, for which she conducted fieldwork in Dakar, Banjul and Nouakchott. Agathe is the volunteer coordinator of the Africa team at Asylos.*

Emmanuel Munyarukumbuzi, *a faculty member at the African Leadership University, Rwanda, holds a Master of Communication from Bond University, Australia. His research interests include communication for development, social justice and ICTs in communication.*

Gonca Şahin *has an MA in International Migration and Ethnic Relations. She is currently coordinating the migration program of a women's NGO in Turkey, working for the economic empowerment of Syrian women and Turkish women through women's cooperatives. Her current research interests focus on queer migration.*

Charlotte Walker-Said *is an associate professor of Africana Studies at the John Jay College of Criminal Justice, City University of New York. Her work examines Christianity, human rights, migration, and gender and sexuality in Africa. She is the author of* Faith, Power and Family: Christianity and Social Change in French Cameroon *(James Currey 2018) and, with John D. Kelly,* Corporate Social Responsibility? Human Rights in the New Global Economy *(University of Chicago Press 2015). She is currently working on a history of non-state militaries in Central Africa through the twentieth century.*

ACKNOWLEDGEMENTS

The editors gratefully acknowledge the financial support of the National Research Foundation of South Africa.

We would like to thank our colleagues at the African Centre for Migration and Society, University of the Witwatsrand, for their guidance and encouragement. In particular, we would like to recognize the support of Jo Vearey, Thea de Gruchy, Lenore Longwe and Kwandakwethu Ndaba.

A special thanks goes to Siv Greyson, who provided invaluable assistance as we prepared the final manuscript.

We would like to express our gratitude to Anne Begg for allowing us to reproduce an edited version of Asante, G. (2018), '"Where Is Home?" Negotiating Comm(unity) and Un/Belonging among Queer African Migrants on Facebook', Borderlands, 17 (1): 1–22.

We must also acknowledge Duke University Press for granting permission to reproduce the epigraph on page 21. The text is taken from Garcia, A. (2017), 'Heaven', in J. Biehl and P. Locke (eds), Unfinished: The Anthropology of Becoming, 111–29, Durham: Duke University.

This publication would not exist without ZED/Bloomsbury. In particular, we want to thank our commissioning editors, Melanie Scagliarini and Olivia Dellow, for believing in the project and for their conviction that scholarship on this topic deserves a global audience.

Thank you to the exceptionally talented Audrey d'Erneville for allowing us to reproduce the beautiful cover image. Please check out her work and support where possible.

We would like to recognize and celebrate the extraordinary efforts of our contributors, some of whom conduct research in difficult and even hostile conditions. We also owe a debt of gratitude to our wonderful peer reviewers who were so generous with their time, feedback and encouragement.

We must thank all of the queer and trans migrants, refugees and asylum seekers who courageously shared their experiences, thoughts, memories, hopes and desires with the authors, often at great personal cost.

Last but not least, we would like to thank our incredible partners, Ruth Ramsden-Karelse and Bernard Moshabane, for their endless love and support.

FRAMING QUEER AND TRANS AFRICAN MOBILITIES: ABSENCES, PRESENCES AND CHALLENGES

B Camminga and John Marnell

On 15 November 1884, the major European powers met in Berlin to carve up a continent. They haggled over 'ownership', made claims to territories and peoples, and debated how best to 'trade' resources. By the end of the conference, they had inscribed borders that remain to this day. While the 'scramble for Africa' lasted less than a century, its legacies can be seen in a wide range of legal, political and cultural structures. These inherited modes of social regulation are perhaps most visible in the fervent use and expansion of colonial-era penal codes to punish those perceived to transgress sexual and gender norms – be it through their identities, intimate relationships, sexual practices or expressions of self (Rao 2020; Namwase, Jjuuko and Nyarango 2017). Political, cultural and religious leaders often exploit anxieties over social disintegration to position anything outside the bounds of heterosexuality as 'unAfrican' (Currier and Cruz 2020; Thomann and Corey-Boulet 2017; M'Baye 2013; Awondo, Geschiere and Reid 2012; Epprecht 2008). This highly emotive discourse provides the moral justification for punitive actions intended to reproduce the heteronormative social order (Marnell 2021). The strategic use of incendiary rhetoric, often coupled with state-sanctioned violence, has led to a new phenomenon in Africa's long history of migration: the movement of people fleeing persecution due to their sexual orientation and/or gender identity and expression.

The ongoing persecution of sexual and gender minorities is frequently cited by Western commentators as evidence of Africa's inherent and inescapable barbarism. In turn, colonial notions of the 'savage continent' are repackaged for the twenty-first century. Although there is a growing body of research challenging reductive and neo-colonial portrayals of queer and trans migration (e.g. Camminga 2018; Murray 2016; Aizura 2012; Jenicek, Wong and Lee 2009; Manalansan 2006), there remains a paucity of scholarship emanating from, or even concerned with, the Global South. The limitations of this geographical orientation are increasingly acknowledged, yet little has been done to meaningfully address the issue.

It is here that *Queer and Trans African Mobilities* makes its intervention. In showcasing Africa-centred research, this collection challenges how the continent is imagined, conceptualized and spoken about. Some chapters confront this tension head-on, while others offer more indirect critiques of the Euro-American bias haunting queer migration studies, but all push back against narrow renderings of Africa and its peoples.

It is not easy to introduce such a diverse body of work. The research collected here is situated within disparate epistemological, methodological and theoretical traditions, and interrogates migration and displacement from various standpoints. Rather than present a standard overview of chapters in sequential order, we want to locate each one within broader interdisciplinary debates. Our goal is to map out thematic and analytic linkages, thereby exposing how the chapters speak to one another and to existing scholarship.

Some of these linkages are visible in how the content has been curated. The chapters are categorized according to four crosscutting themes – complicating migration narratives; barriers to protection; the digital and the transnational; and bordering in action – each of which reflects an established line of inquiry within queer migration studies. This arrangement allows us to highlight resonances between specific chapters, while also gesturing to the major knowledge gaps being addressed by this volume. Yet, while section headings serve as useful signposts, they can limit how work is perceived and interpreted. In the discussion that follows, we attempt to trouble our own curatorial decisions. We do so by placing the chapters within an analysis of queer migration studies and queer African studies and by reading them in light of pressing questions about research practices, disciplinary challenges and future priorities.

Re/orientations

As noted, queer migration studies is overwhelming focused on South-North trajectories, implying that this is the primary – if not the only – direction in which queer and trans people move. The preoccupation with South-North movement not only perpetuates racist tropes of Africa – alongside similarly harmful stereotypes about Asia (Yue 2012), Latin America (Mayers 2018) and the Middle East (Masri 2017) – but also reduces individuals with complex lives, identities and emotions to stock characters (Marnell et al. 2021). Accounts of queer and trans migration – no matter their form or intent – remain organized around 'a narrative of movement from repression to freedom, or a heroic journey undertaken in search of liberation' (Luibhéid 2005: xxv). Such a framing contributes to homonationalist discourses (Puar 2007) and neo-colonial practices (Jung 2015) by suggesting that states in the Global North are better equipped to 'save' queer and trans people.

Florent Chossière, in one of the few chapters in this collection to take Europe as its starting point, pushes back against this tendency, disrupting well-worn discourses of 'liberation' and 'freedom' in a bid to reframe queer migration scholarship. Although anchored in France, Chossière's analysis complicates Global North exceptionalism by showing how asylum and immigration systems exclude rather than protect. In addition to critiquing the political categories used to classify people on the move, Chossière pushes back against notions of passivity and victimhood by documenting transnational solidarity practices between refugees and asylum seekers in France and those who remain on the African continent.

The scholarly fixation with host states in the Global North has led to a concerning myopia, one that continues to shape how queer and trans migration is approached, including who we imagine queer and trans migrants to be, where we think they are going and how we understand their motivations, aspirations and experiences. The need to rethink popular assumptions is explored in detail by John Marnell in his chapter on the politics of representing queer and trans Africans on the move. Drawing on an arts-based project conducted in Johannesburg, South Africa, Marnell calls for research, writing and publishing practices that are more critical and diverse. In particular, he underscores the importance of providing migrants, refugee and asylum seekers with opportunities to curate their own self-representations. Marnell's chapter offers a powerful reminder that the research methods we deploy inevitably shape the stories we tell, which in turn has consequence for academic, legal, policy, humanitarian and activist responses.

The way in which knowledge on queer and trans migration is currently produced and disseminated does a disservice to those whose lives we seek to document and understand. Approaching research from a Global North vantage point not only perpetuates certain readings of people and place, but also stifles the possibility for more nuanced theorizations of local, regional and global responses to queer and trans mobilities. Similarly, the limited attention afforded to migration within queer African studies means that a whole raft of socio-political dynamics, discursive practices and lived experiences are being overlooked. When queer and trans people move, they carry with them ideas, beliefs and language, inevitably coming into contact with other systems for knowing, describing and expressing gender and sexuality. At the same time, queer and trans Africans in the diaspora are projecting new identity formations and signifying practices back towards the continent. Thus, there is an urgent need to consider the influence of migration practices on local responses to sexual and gender rights, and vice versa. It is our hope that the scholarship collected here expands queer African studies by drawing attention to mobility and related issues. In many ways, this volume represents a natural progression within the discipline, given its investment in theorizing contestation over identities, rights, archives, histories, oppressions and legal systems, and in marking various forms of resistance, resilience and survival.

Tentative steps have been taken towards addressing migration within queer African studies (e.g. Koko, Monro and Smith 2018; Nyanzi 2013). While certainly a welcome development, this work is indicative of another geographical bias that deserves unpacking. Research to date has overwhelmingly focused on South Africa (e.g. Marnell 2021; Beetar 2020; Bhagat 2018; Camminga 2017; Palmary 2016; Dill et al. 2016), with a few notable exceptions (Broqua et al. 2021; Pincock 2021; Camminga 2020; McQuaid 2020; Menetrier 2019; Moore 2019; Nicholas 2017; Pierce 2016; Rosenberg 2016; Millo 2013). South Africa's overrepresentation in the literature can be explained by its widely lauded human right mechanisms, including formal recognition of queer and trans refugees (although, as the literature cited above argues, progressive laws do not always translate into meaningful protection). The need to look beyond South Africa was something we were acutely attuned to when approaching this collection. Our goal was to capture the breadth of queer and trans movements on the continent. Put another way, we wanted the collection to be a snapshot of key developments, trends and issues, not only moving beyond South Africa as a geographic, theoretic and epistemic focal point but also challenging the preference for legal and procedural analyses.

On language and visibility

As is evident from the varied research in this volume, there is no single story of African queer and trans migration. There are very real specificities of experience that emerge when migration and asylum interact with different political, discursive, ideological and ontological formations linked to gender and sexuality. For this reason, the authors in this collection have been intentional in their use of language, both in how they refer to research participants and how they frame the stories centred by their work. For example, Verena Hucke's study of cisgender lesbian migrants and asylum seekers in Johannesburg, South Africa, reveals the complex ways in which gender, sexuality and mobility intersect to produce particular lived experiences. Adding to a growing body of work exploring lesbian women's experiences of migration (e.g. Tschalaer 2020a; Luibhéid 2020; Moore 2019; Lewis 2013), Hucke argues that when one approaches research from the perspective of lesbian women – rather than, say, 'LGBT' or 'queer' people – one is immediately confronted with a striated border regime. In this case, Hucke explores how multiple geographical and sociological borders shape access to labour rights and places of worship, thereby shifting attention to everyday negotiations of being and belonging.

The need for precision in language is also reflected in each author's efforts to trouble the political categories associated with people on the move, such as 'migrant', 'refugee' and 'asylum seeker'. This is particularly important when writing about the African continent, where compounded barriers prevent queer and trans individuals from being officially recognized as refugees, despite meeting the eligibility criteria listed in domestic and international law (e.g. Mudarikwa et al. 2021). This reality is further complicated by the self-identification practices of research participants, many of whom claim migration categories in ways that differ from official legal definitions. Much has been written about the politics of naming in relation to border regimes, especially in Global North contexts (e.g. Crawley and Skleparis 2018), but greater critical attention is required if we are to untangle the murky relationship between identity categories linked to gender and/or sexuality and the lexicon of migration. We hope the scholarship presented here provokes others to think more deeply about the geopolitical, neo-imperial and neoliberal dynamics lurking within hegemonic naming practices, especially in relation to those moving on or from the African continent. What does it mean, the authors in this collection ask, when words like 'migrant', 'refugee' and 'asylum seeker' rub up against 'queer', 'trans' or 'LGBT', particularly in contexts where individual and group rights are fiercely contested?

As editors, we were deliberate in our use of 'queer and trans' in the title. We recognize that 'queer' holds particular global currency and 'takes into consideration diverse desires, experiences and cultural practices' (Matebeni 2019: 3), yet we also remain cognizant of the dangers of uncritically adopting such terminology. Scholars such as Keguro Macharia (2015), Sylvia Tamale (2014) and Sokari Ekine and Hakima Abbas (2013) have done vital work tracing the neo-colonial impulse behind the exportation and imposition of Global North identity categories. We draw from a wealth of thinking in queer African studies on the importance of distinguishing between queer as a *verb* and queer as a *noun*. Stella Nyanzi (2014) powerfully describes the concept's potential as a verb:

> [Queer can stand] in the way of restrictive forces of gender binarism, rigid heteronormativity and heterosexism fuelled by patriarchy and colonial impositions. In this version, queer can be used as a destabilising tool, creating not only uncertainty but also possibilities.
>
> (3)

As a noun, 'queer' is understood to encompass a diversity of non-heteronormative sexualities and an ever-expanding array of gender identities, including those captured by words like 'gay', 'lesbian', 'bisexual' and 'transgender', but which is capacious enough to move well beyond them.

Umbrella terms such as 'queer' may offer convenience and flexibility, but vigilance is required when using them, especially in reference to contexts where they are not fully recognized, embraced or understood (Marnell et al. 2021). Despite our best efforts, gay men remain overrepresented in this collection, as they do in queer migration studies more broadly. What is refreshing is how our contributors have made clear, as best as possible, the focus of their research through their use of language. This helps readers understand whose narratives are being told and whose experience they might speak for. We also acknowledge the implicit tension when talking about 'queer' in relation to migration. 'Queer' does not carry as much traction as 'gay' – the former has less value when it comes into contact with asylum systems that prefer terminology linked to stable, clear-cut identities. Furthermore, as many critiques point out, the established vocabulary of academia and activism in the Global North differs, sometimes drastically, to the language taken up on the African continent (Camminga 2019; Oloka-Onyango 2015).

Bearing this in mind, we still believe 'queer' holds value, especially when considered in light of its amendments, appropriations and applications within African knowledge production. It is also broad enough to capture the ways in which varied identities speak to and infuse one another, while simultaneously engaging with questions of class, race, nationality and culture. In this regard, we are inspired by Vasu Reddy, Surya Monro and Zethu Matebeni's (2018) reading of queer in relation to the continent: 'African non-heterosexual sexualities and gender diversities are ... neither static nor uniform; rather, they are dynamic, multifarious and resilient' (1).

Our decision to add 'trans' to the title was motivated by similar concerns over the politics of language and visibility (Jobson et al. 2012). Again, this was intentional. While many trans people identify as queer, not all do. In fact, many reject this label because of its insistence that gender categories are slippery, unstable and fluid. Some trans Africans feel strongly that their gender is fixed and defined. The 'and' in our title creates room to explore this tension without erasing specificities, ignoring self-identifications or downplaying contestations. Our primary intention is to underline how transgender experiences of migration differ from those of cisgender lesbian, gay and bisexual people. Conflating or dismissing these differences is as dangerous as the geographical and conceptual biases flagged above.

It is equally important for us to acknowledge what is not in our title: intersex. This, too, was deliberate, but not in the sense that we wanted to disregard particular identities, experiences or needs. Rather, we felt it disingenuous to suggest that this collection deals meaningfully with intersex issues. We acknowledge that African intersex people not only exist but also face unique challenges (see Kaggwa 2011), not least of which are migration and asylum. It would be remiss of us to ignore the continued absence of intersex people in migration scholarship, both in this collection and in the literature more broadly. Indeed, a lack of attention towards these issues persists despite emerging visibility of intersex migrants and asylum seekers, such as in the recent application *L.B. v France (Fifth Section)* (2021). This case, which deals with an asylum claim by a Moroccan intersex person, was the first time the European Court of Human Rights had considered the relationship between sex characteristics and asylum.

Rather than silently omit intersex issues or deceptively fall back on the LGBTI acronym, we want to highlight the acute need for research in this field. The little literature that does exist indicates a pattern of resettling African intersex children and their families to Nordic countries, where it is believed they will be offered better healthcare (Breen 2012). There is insufficient space here to consider the long-term implications of these cross-border movements, but we must still note this history of facilitated migration and recognize that medical resettlements affect how intersex Africans are seen, known and understood. It remains to be seen whether the surgical interventions linked to these movements were consensual and medically necessary.

This concern over the resettlement of intersex children brings us to the challenge of youth more broadly. With the advent of digital communication and social media, increasing numbers of young people are embracing their identities and seeking active online engagement. Why would it be any different on the African continent? Yet, the age of interlocutors is rarely flagged as a concern within queer migration research. In focusing so heavily on the end points of migration, it is easy to lose sight of the individuals – often young people – who are unable or unwilling to move between continents, perhaps because of an absence of documents, a lack of funds (be it for smugglers or plane fares) or an inability to access formal migration pathways. For many young queer and trans Africans, moving within the continent is their only viable option. As an example, the number of unaccompanied queer and trans minors arriving in Nairobi, Kenya, tripled between 2015 and 2017. This growing cohort of minors was more diverse in its constitution than the adult queer and trans refugee population, most of whom came from neighbouring Uganda (Moore 2018).

This trend is reflected in Emmanuel Munyarukumbuzi, Margaret Jjuuko and James Maingi Gathatwa's timely contribution to this volume in which they interrogate barriers to mental and sexual wellbeing for refugee youth living in Nairobi. Drawing on rich qualitative research with young people from Burundi, DR Congo, Ethiopia, Uganda, Somalia and South Sudan, the authors show that refugee youth face particular difficulties owing to their age, nationality and documentation status. These challenges are further complicated by Kenya's current legal formulations, which can make the provision of health and social services a criminal act (outreach activities targeting queer and trans people can be classified as 'promoting homosexuality'). This results in an increased risk of exploitation, victimization and negative health outcomes.

Thinking queer migration, or Africa is a country

By curating this body of scholarship according to its geographical focus, rather than emphasizing thematic or disciplinary linkages, we hope to shift how 'Africa' is viewed within queer migration studies. Existing scholarship tends to elide the cultural, linguistic and social differences of those seeking asylum, homogenizing disparate experiences and backgrounds under the broad category of 'queer asylum seeker'. Countries of birth are largely presented as inconsequential, as narrative elements rather than critical considerations. This provides little clarity on the specificities of leaving any one place, and even less of an understanding about the relationship between places left behind and those where asylum is sought.

As Charlotte Walker-Said argues in her chapter, greater attention needs to be paid to countries of origin if we are to accurately track migration catalysts, understand how asylum systems operate and theorize the social, legal and political functions of violence. In Cameroon – the focus of Walker-Said's chapter – state, family and community forms of violence are not only inextricably linked but are also deeply associated with patriotism. This causes problems for those seeking refuge, in that most determination procedures recognize only limited forms of violence as persecution. Understanding the intricacies of violence in specific African contexts, especially those where public and private forms of violence cannot be easily distinguished, is critical if asylum systems are to respond to the needs of queer and trans applicants. Walker-Said makes references to the US and the UK asylum systems, using these case studies to call for sexuality-based asylum claims to be recast as political-based asylum claims. By contrasting the two jurisdictions – both of which have set key legal precedents and influenced how other states understand and respond to sexuality-based asylum claims – Walker-Said is able to identify entry points for challenging existing protocols. Her argument echoes the work of African queer theorists, many of whom push back again generalized accounts of 'African homophobia':

> 'Africa' is not singular but instead a heterogeneous geopolitical entity with multilayered complexities of transnational contexts, represented by a diverse set of identities of its peoples. In other words, African countries vary considerably in the ways that gender and sexuality are constructed, with postcolonial and neo-colonial relations, local subjectivities, traditionalist patriarchies, and nationalist homophobias intertwining with human rights frameworks and activist interventions.
>
> (Reddy, Monro and Matebeni 2018: 2)

Reading queer and trans mobilities through a geographical lens allows us to identify and make sense of different practices and trends. What does the significant number of queer and trans people from Southern Africa, including countries such as Botswana and Zimbabwe, applying for asylum in Australia between 2016 and 2018 tell us about the desirability of Australia as a safe haven, considering the prohibitive cost of travelling there from the African continent?[1] The presence of asylum claimants from North Africa in Spain seems logical, especially when one considers historical links between the Maghreb and the Iberian Peninsula, but how are we to read the presence of those from Kenya, Nigeria and Ghana?[2] How do we make sense of South Africans seeking asylum despite their home country's progressive laws?[3] Or the increasing number of queer and trans Africans coming into visibility in Latin America?[4]

Similar questions lie at the heart of Gonca Şahin's chapter, which draws on extensive fieldwork in Turkey. Şahin contrasts the experience of Ahmad – a 27-year-old gay man from North Africa diagnosed with a life-threatening illness – with those of her Iranian interlocutors, teasing out survival strategies deployed by people with different levels of access to community support. By focusing on Ahmad's experiences in a country not considered a regular transit point for queer Africans, Şahin challenges queer migration scholars to look beyond networks of care based on ethnic, national or linguistic ties, suggesting that queer community bonds can supersede these. Her work illustrates how analyses of migrant networks can (inadvertently) overlook the experiences of 'hidden' individuals and dismiss less obvious forms of solidarity.

Perhaps the most significant intervention offered by this collection is its reorientation towards South-South movement, a phenomenon that continues to receive scant critical attention within queer migration studies. Caio Simões de Araújo's contribution explores movements between Mozambique and South Africa. His nuanced portrayal of shifting mobility patterns over more than a century complicates popular narratives about how, when and why queer and trans people migrate. His chapter explores an archive of movement, tracking flows and counterflows but also challenging readers to consider the social, political and affective dimensions of mobility. He shows that desires and aspirations – be they romantic, economic or political in nature – are multifarious, working in multiple directions at once and leading to various forms of movement. The most important takeaway from de Araújo's contribution might be his reminder that a search for 'freedom' and 'safety' is not always the dominant force in queer and trans migration.

The need to push beyond reductive notions of migration also drives Yara Ahmed's contribution. She beautifully illustrates that being queer, being African and experiencing migration are not always about a transition from point A to point B. Ahmed, like many of the authors featured here, argues for more expansive conceptualizations of migration, noting that traditional forms of mobility remain out of reach for most Egyptians. Disrupting the received logic that kinetic movement is an essential component of migration, Ahmed foregrounds the spatio-temporal, affective and subjective dimensions of mobility. By delving into her interlocutors' dreamscapes, Ahmed reminds readers that while many queer and trans people desire to move, to seek safety elsewhere, to escape the here and now, most are unable to relocate easily. Critically engaging with the imagination, she argues, allows one to think beyond linear notions of time and space and to recognize how various potentialities shape and are shaped by one's context. Her interlocutors are all too aware of what life in the Global North could mean for their futures and their families. Contrary to popular belief, a move from the Global South to the Global North can – as it does here – invite a sense of 'stuckedness' (Hage 2009).

This reading of migration as more than kinetic movement flows throughout the collection and is particularly useful for rethinking the relationship between physical and digital mobilities. For many queer and trans Africans, the borderless world of the internet presents opportunities to form interpersonal connections and intimate relationships, while also facilitating the transmission of ideas, discourses and representations. Indeed, digital technology plays a key role in queer and trans migration, allowing not only for the formation of transnational solidarity networks but also for the exchange of resources. The internet serves as a bridge between those in the diaspora and those still at home, while also serving as a linking point for those needing community and support. This is certainly the case for Godfried Asante's interlocutors. Focusing specifically on queer African men living in North America and the United Kingdom, Asante deftly explores how these individuals use social media to explore their identities, forge a sense of belonging and create deterritorialized safe spaces. In this case, closed Facebook groups serve as a digital 'home' in which connections are made, knowledge is shared and ideologies are contested.

But not all aspects of the digital are positive. As well as offering space for knowledge dissemination and network building, the internet serves as a repository for stereotypical representations and a medium through which misinformation is channelled. The question of how scholars might ethically approach, write about and respond to harmful digital materials is at the heart of B Camminga's chapter. Specifically, they consider the emergent digital archive of Nigerian refugee Miss

Sahhara, asking what travels and what returns, and how one might address that travel and return. Crucially, the chapter contains a letter of instruction from Miss Sahhara herself, in which she outlines her wishes for how this digital archive is to be used. Camminga's chapter questions the use of deadnames by transgender studies scholars, while also considering what trans existence in the diaspora tells us about the travel of language and identity. In doing so, Camminga exposes overlaps between migration studies, archival studies, communication studies and queer African studies, challenging readers to hear the whispers of queer and trans mobility echoing through different disciplines and to consider how uncritical usage of sources can do more harm than good.

Reflections on power, privilege and positionality

In circulating the call for this collection, we hoped to address some of the imbalances and gaps outlined above. We believe passionately that migration between and from African countries deserves critical attention, especially as national borders become securitized and externalized. It is vitally important that scholars consider what such movements look like, what is driving them, what their impacts are and how they relate to other migration practices. It was our interest in these questions that motivated this collection. However, the need for a publication like this should never come at the expense of honest and open conversations about individual positionality, unequal funding mechanisms and academic structures that reward Global North scholars. It is not lost on us that we, the editors, are both white and situated in South Africa. Though we are transgender and queer (B) and cisgender and queer (John), we have access to and benefit from systems of power courtesy of our skin colour. These privileges are not available to any one of the migrants, refugees and asylum seekers referenced in this collection, nor are they shared equally among the contributors. For this reason, we made every effort to prioritize the voices of Global South researchers, activists and practitioners and to provide mentorship opportunities for emerging and/or marginalized scholars. The call for submissions was sent out in English, French and Portuguese, with an explicit commitment to funding translation costs for those not working in English. We also relied, as much as possible, on subject matter experts from the Global South as peer reviewers, in an effort to reverse dominant trends in academic knowledge production.

Our commitment to making space for Southern voices is reflected in the authors featured here, though the final contents list does not tell the whole story. We must acknowledge those scholars – both authors and reviewers – who expressed interest in this project but were unable to submit final chapters or meet the demands of our production schedule. It is undeniable that deep structural inequalities exist within the global academe and that these have dire consequences for those working in the Global South. Some hopeful contributors were overwhelmed by existing work commitments or had to prioritize other projects for financial reasons, while others struggled emotionally to revisit research linked to personal trauma. All of these obstacles – whether they were overcome through dedicated support or not – had an impact on the finished product. We make this point both as a way to acknowledge the many scholars who contributed to the project but whose names do not appear in the contents list and as a reminder of the structural impacts that persist in the research sector, all of which have been intensified by the Covid-19 pandemic.

There are also specific barriers to producing knowledge on queer and trans issues that deserve attention. Criminalization in many African countries not only makes fieldwork a challenge but also complicates access to resources and materials. In extreme cases, searching for or possessing literature marked by certain terms ('LGBT', 'transgender', 'homosexuality', etc.) can be dangerous, even more so now that the internet is being tightly regulated and monitored in some countries. It can also be difficult to have queer African scholarship published. Many Africa-focused journals reject submissions on queer topics because they do not consider them serious or rigorous enough, or because they are unable or unwilling to mentor those working in emerging research fields. For scholars in the Global South – many of whom already work under precarious conditions – writing on sexual and gender diversity can threaten job prospects, career progression and even economic survival, while also provoking tensions with colleagues and university administrators. To this end, we are humbled and inspired by the response we received to our call and by the immense commitment of our authors.

One of the practical ways in which we tried to mitigate these barriers to publication was to develop peer-review guidelines (see appendix). These did not impose specific rules, but rather reminded reviewers of the intersecting inequalities that block certain scholarship from reaching a global audience. We asked reviewers to offer unbiased critique based on their expertise while remaining mindful that our prospective authors are from diverse linguistic and national backgrounds. For many, English is their third or fourth language, and some work in under-resourced and potentially hostile contexts. Given this, we encouraged reviewers to supply recommended readings, to focus on the quality of argumentation rather than minor grammatical issues and to be constructive when writing comments, bearing in mind the potential for existing socio-political inequalities to be reinforced. Overall, the guidelines were well received, and we remain grateful to the scholars who so eagerly and willingly shared readings, thoughts, comments and support.

Critical considerations about race, power and resources were not limited to editorial decisions. The benefits, challenges and ethical conundrums of whiteness within migration work cannot be downplayed, and we are pleased that these tensions are explored across the collection. As elucidated in Agathe Menetrier's chapter, and hinted at in Marien Gouyon's, whiteness continues to be associated with access, influence and possibility. For Menetrier, undertaking field research meant being read by her interlocutors – gay Gambian asylum seekers in Senegal – as a mediator to Dakar's white 'expatriate' network and to international organizations that might provide assistance. At the same time, she found herself thrust into the role of 'expert witness' by the UNHCR and overseas benefactors, with her whiteness considered proof of her ability to testify to the veracity of asylum claims and requests for support.

In Gouyon's chapter, the strength of white privilege is made stark. One of his interlocutors – a gay Cameroonian migrant living in Morocco – notes the different treatment he and his white European boyfriend receive. Gouyon uses this anecdote to interrogate 'occidental privilege', a set of provisions that allow Western 'expatriates' to exploit economic and social advantages while abroad. For Amélie Le Renard (2019), occidental privilege is distributed according to the social positions occupied by Westerners. It constructs the mysteries of Western-ness by instrumentalizing the relationships of gender, sexuality, class and race. This is evident not just in this interlocutor's experience but also in asylum regimes more broadly (see Güler, Shevtsova and Venturi 2019).

The way in which geopolitical and social hierarchies seep into the operations of international protection mechanisms is disturbingly captured by Gouyon. He argues that the UNHCR branch in Rabat is unable to provide meaningful protection, is suspicious of many queer and trans applicants (believing them to be economic migrants) and is staffed by people who may hold discriminatory views about sexual and gender diversity. These prejudices are reinforced by a wider culture of criminalization in Morocco. At the same time, locals facing homophobic/transphobic persecution struggle to access protection because of current formulations of asylum. Such obstacles are the direct outcome of a global structure that has only ever imagined protection being offered by the North.

The international system: Failures and evolutions

There is, we believe, a direct link between the circulation of people, ideas and identities and the emergence of legal challenges and reforms. Expansions of refugee law and its application have as much to do with those actively seeking protection as it does with reception states, with the former often motivated by the latter's shortcomings. It is crucial that this dynamic is acknowledged, not just in relation to refugee law but also in the development of human rights more broadly: '[t]hat human rights law offers an important bolster to refugee law is widely-acknowledged. However ... refugee law has its own progressive dynamic, which leads human rights law just as much, if not more, than it follows human rights law' (Costello 2016: 209).

Many important legal and procedural challenges have come from Africans, including pressure to broaden notions of gender and sexuality as they pertain to asylum. A key example is asylum claims involving non-binary persons, with recent cases involving applicants from Somalia and Tunisia (Tschalaer 2020b). Likewise, questions have been asked about whether refugee protection should be extended to cisgender men in heterosexual relationships with transgender women. One such case, heard by the Dutch Immigration and Naturalisation Service, involved a Moroccan man who argued that his relationship opened him up to homophobic persecution, even though he does not identify as gay or understand his relationship in such terms (Middelkoop 2013).

The failure of global protection mechanisms to respond adequately to queer and trans refugee populations in Africa, or to recognize the contributions made by these individuals to such structures, is another area where this collection makes an intervention. It is undeniable that the present guidance provided by the UNHCR and its partners is concerned with South-North migration, implicitly suggesting that the North is driving efforts to protect people escaping homophobic/transphobic persecution. Yet, it is actually the claimants themselves who have led the charge, pushing for more expansive understandings of identity and persecution, often at great personal cost. It is undeniable that Global North countries have benefited from these advocacy efforts and legal challenges. What is often left unsaid is the resistance of Global North states to attempts by queer and trans Africans to secure protection, or the intentional moves of these states to keep vulnerable populations in the Global South. The result is growing numbers of queer and trans asylum seekers stuck in countries that offer protection through the UNHCR but that continue to criminalize specific sexual practices and/or prosecute 'indecency' or 'unnatural vice'. This creates a paradox in which queer and trans asylum seekers are simultaneously protected and criminalized, relegated to a realm of illegibility and precarity (Camminga 2021). Examples of this can be seen across the continent, including in Kenya, Senegal, Tanzania and Uganda.

Conclusion: New directions and perspectives

The Global South remains host to the 'vast majority of the world's queer refugees, many of whom remain undocumented' (Lewis and Naples 2014: 916). It is also worth remembering, as Guy S. Goodwin-Gill (2007) points out, that African countries offer the 'full spectrum' of refugee movements, in that they function as both refugee producers and hosts. It is vital, then, that queer and trans migration in and from this part of the world receives greater scholarly attention. Recent shifts in global migration governance, including significant decreases in third-country resettlement, make this need more urgent than ever before. If space is not made for African queer and trans mobilities – along with similar phenomena from other Global South locations – then queer migration scholarship will remain blind to key dynamics, practices and trends. Research in this field must move beyond the assumptions and stereotypes that dominate thinking on African queer and trans lives. If nothing else, we hope this collection points to the disparate catalysts, experiences and outcomes associated with queer and trans migration on and from the continent. These movements are not unidirectional, nor can they be reduced to a singular oppression-to-liberation narrative. We must also be open to the possibility of African states being sites of becoming and belonging as much as they are locations marked by violence and insecurity.

Queer migration scholarship records the experiences of people from all over the globe, but this diversity is lost when the unit of analysis remains structures of asylum in the Global North. This framing also limits our ability to recognize specificities and divergences or to map less obvious migration trajectories. The decision to leave one's home is hardly ever simple, and for many queer and trans individuals it is one of necessity. The same applies to transits and arrivals, neither of which are straightforward. These realities are reflected in this collection, which documents a wide range of movements and all of their attendant benefits, difficulties and complexities. The traces, forms and impacts of these journeys are tracked through narrative, gossip, tabloid press, digital media, zine-making, Facebook posts and Grindr messages, indicating a delicate web of queer and trans connection across the African continent. The ways in which gender and sexuality shape migration are never uniform and are not easily captured by concepts like 'queer' or 'trans' or 'Africa', even when these terms are placed alongside one another.

In troubling the imagined dichotomy of Global North states that benevolently 'save' refugees and Global South states that violate rights and produce refugees, we hope this volume opens up new avenues for analysing queer and trans mobilities. The work presented here invites readers to reconsider what it means to be a queer or trans migrant from Africa and to rethink how intersections of gender, sexuality, mobility and asylum give rise to particular experiences. In doing this work of decentring – which is not equivalent to getting things right all the time – this collection poses a challenge, not only to present literature but also to current humanitarian, activist and policy responses. By pivoting attention towards Africa, we wish to prompt critical conversations about the meaning of protection, as well as how and where it might be extended.

Migration is many things. It is memory. It is dreamscape. It is investment, insurgency, desire, displacement, planning, protection, provocation and perception. It is movement in forms yet unknown. It is paperwork and interviews and bureaucracies. It is being transferred from one government department to another, from one refugee camp or global NGO to another, from one permit type to another. It is seemingly endless bags, bodies, dresses, boats and borders. For queer and trans people from the African continent, it can mean exhausting efforts to create a home and forge a sense of belonging, while potentially leaving behind loving families and friends. Indeed, queer and trans Africans who move are not always escaping vicious or hateful relatives, even if they do face oppressive social systems.

This volume, we hope, offers some fullness to these journeys, lives and desires, while at the same time charting new inroads for queer African studies and pressing for greater nuance in queer migration studies. There is much that both fields can gain from new perspectives and positions. The scholarship featured here pushes us to think differently about what happens when borders, laws, customs, religions and global systems come into contact with queer and trans Africans. We are optimistic that these interventions will inspire more research in this field, as well as additional resources and opportunities for those working on the continent.

Notes

1 For an overview of countries of origin for queer and trans asylum seekers in Australia during this period, see Jaz Dawson (2019).
2 For information on the demographics and experiences of African asylum seekers in Spain, see George Freeman (2017).
3 As an example, see Refugee Status Appeals Authority (2010).
4 Numerous studies mention queer and trans asylum seekers from Africa seeking protection in Latin America (e.g. Theodoro and Cogo 2019; Andrade 2018).

References

Aizura, A. Z. (2012), 'Transnational Transgender Rights and Immigration Law', in A. Enke (ed.), *Transfeminist Perspectives in and beyond Transgender and Gender Studies*, 133–51, Philadelphia: Temple University Press.

Andrade, V. L. (2018), 'Gay African Refugees in Brazil: A Diaspora?', in H. S. Majhail and S. Dogan (eds), *World of Diasporas: Different Perceptions on the Concept of Diaspora*, 86–91, London: Brill.

Awondo, P., P. Geschiere and G. Reid (2012), 'Homophobic Africa: Towards a More Nuanced View', *African Studies Review*, 55 (3): 145–68.

Beetar, M. (2020), 'Bordering Life: South African Necropolitics and LGBTI Migrants', in S. Clisby (ed.), *Gender, Sexuality and Identities of the Borderlands*, 43–55, London: Routledge.

Bhagat, A. (2018), 'Forced (Queer) Migration and Everyday Violence: The Geographies of Life, Death, and Access in Cape Town', *Geoforum*, 89: 155–63.

Breen, D. (2012), *The Road to Safety: Strengthening Protection for LGBTI Refugees in Uganda and Kenya*, New York: Human Rights First.

Broqua, C., G. Laborde-Balen, A. Menetrier and D. Bangoura (2021), 'Queer Necropolitics of Asylum: Senegalese Refugees Facing HIV/AIDS in Mauritania', *Global Public Health*, 16 (5): 746–62.

Camminga, B (2017), 'Shifting Borderlands: (Trans) "Gender Refugees" Moving to and through an Imagined South Africa', *Dutch Journal of Gender Studies*, 20 (4): 359–77.

Camminga, B (2018), '"The Stigma of Western Words": Asylum Law, Transgender Identity and Sexual Orientation in South Africa', *Global Discourse*, 8 (3): 452–69.

Camminga, B (2019), *Transgender Refugees and the Imagined South Africa: Bodies over Borders and Borders over Bodies*, Cham: Palgrave Macmillan.

Camminga, B (2020a), 'Encamped within a Camp: Transgender Refugees and Kakuma Refugee Camp (Kenya)', in J. Bjarnesen and S. Turner (eds), *Invisibility in African Displacements*, 36–52, London: Zed Books.

Camminga, B (2020b), '"Go Fund Me": LGBTI Asylum Seekers in Kakuma Refugee Camp, Kenya', in C. Jacobson, M. Karlsen and S. Khosravi (eds), *Waitinghood: Unpacking the Temporalities of Waiting and Irregular Migration*, 131–48, London: Routledge.

Costello, C. (2016), 'The Search for the Outer Edges of Non-Refoulement in Europe: Exceptionality and Flagrant Breaches', in B. Burson and D. J. Cantor (eds), *Human Rights and the Refugee Definition: Comparative Legal Practice and Theory*, 180–209, Leiden: Brill.

Crawley, H. and D. Skleparis (2018), 'Refugees, Migrants, Neither, Both: Categorical Fetishism and the Politics of Bounding in Europe's "Migration Crisis"', *Journal of Ethnic and Migration Studies*, 44 (1): 48–64.

Currier, A. and J. M. Cruz (2020), 'The Politics of Pre-Emption: Mobilisation against LGBT Rights in Liberia', *Social Movement Studies*, 19 (1): 82–96.

Dawson, J. (2019), 'Past and Present: From Misunderstanding Sexuality to Misunderstanding Gender Identity in Australian Refugee Claims', *Australian Journal of Politics and History*, 65 (4): 600–19.

Dill, L. J., J. Vearey, E. Oliveira and G. M. Castillo (2016), '"Son of the Soil … Daughters of the Land": Poetry Writing as a Strategy of Citizen-Making for Lesbian, Gay, and Bisexual Migrants and Asylum Seekers in Johannesburg', *Agenda*, 30 (1): 85–95.

Ekine, S. and H. Abbas (eds) (2013), *Queer African Reader*, Dakar: Pambakuza Press.

Epprecht, M. (2008), *Heterosexual Africa? The History of an Idea from the Age of Exploration to the Age of AIDS*, Scottsville: University of KwaZulu-Natal Press.

Freeman, G. R. (2017), *Unveiling the Unspoken Lens of Reality*, Barcelona: Pride Equality International.

Goodwin-Gill, G. S. (2007), 'International and National Responses to the Challenges of Mass Forced Displacement', in J. Handmake, L. A. de la Hunt and J. Klaaren (eds), *Advancing Refugee Protection in South Africa*, 11–27, New York: Berghahn Books.

Güler, A., M. Shevtsova and D. Venturi (eds) (2019), *LGBTI Asylum Seekers and Refugees from a Legal and Political Perspective: Persecution, Asylum and Integration*, Cham: Springer.

Hage, G. (2009), *Waiting*, Melbourne: Melbourne University Press.

Jenicek, A., D. Wong and E. O. J. Lee (2009), 'Dangerous Shortcuts: Representations of Sexual Minority Refugees in the Post-9/11 Canadian Press', *Canadian Journal of Communication*, 34 (4): 635–58.

Jobson, G. A., L. Theron, J. Kaggwa and H. Kim (2012), 'Transgender in Africa: Invisible, Inaccessible, or Ignored?' *SAHARA-J: Journal of Social Aspects of HIV/AIDS: An Open Access Journal*, 9 (3): 160–3.

Jung, M. (2015), 'Logics of Citizenship and Violence of Rights: The Queer Migrant Body and the Asylum System', *Birkbeck Law Review*, 3 (2): 305–35.

Kaggwa, J. (2011), 'Intersex the Forgotten Constituency', in S. Tamale (ed.), *African Sexualities: A Reader*, 231–4, Cape Town: Pambakuza Press.

Koko, G., S. Monro and K. Smith (2018), 'Lesbian, Gay, Bisexual, Transgender, Queer (LGBTQ) Forced Migrants and Asylum Seekers: Multiple Discriminations', in Z. Matebeni, S. Monro and V. Reddy (eds), *Queer in Africa: LGBTQI Identities, Citizenship and Activism*, 158–77, Oxon: Routledge.

L.B. v France (Fifth Section) (ECtHR). (2021). Available online: https://www.sogica.org/database/l-b-v-france-fifth-section-2021-ecthr/?fbclid=IwAR3vY8fvUuu13-gO4vn5x NqaRKIpS4KNrTr0bQdNrugqM1UeTuqHhWa0CdY (accessed 26 April 2021).

Le Renard, A. (2019), *Le privilège occidental. Travail, intimité et hiérarchies postcoloniales à Dubaï*, Paris: Presses de SciencesPo.

Lewis, R. (2013), 'Deportable Subjects: Lesbians and Political Asylum', *Feminist Formations*, 25 (2): 174–94.

Lewis, R. A. and N. A. Naples (2014), 'Introduction: Queer Migration, Asylum, and Displacement', *Sexualities*, 17 (8): 911–18.

Luibhéid, E. (2005), 'Introduction: Queering Migration and Citizenship', in E. Luibhéid and L. Cantú, Jr. (eds), *Queer Migrations: Sexuality, US Citizenship and Border Crossings*, ix–xlvi, Minneapolis: University of Minnesota Press.

Luibhéid, E. (2020), 'Migrant and Refugee Lesbians: Lives That Resist the Telling', *Journal of Lesbian Studies*, 24 (2): 57–76.

Macharia, K. (2015), 'Archive and Method in Queer African Studies', *Agenda*, 29 (1): 140–6.

Manalansan, M. F. (2006), 'Queer Intersections: Sexuality and Gender in Migration Studies', *International Migration Review*, 40 (1): 224–49.

Marnell, J. (2021), *Seeking Sanctuary: Stories of Sexuality, Faith and Migration*, Johannesburg: Wits University Press.

Marnell, J., E. Oliveira and G. H. Khan (2021), '"It's about Being Safe and Free to Be Who You Are": Exploring the Lived Experiences of Queer Migrants, Refugees and Asylum Seekers in South Africa', *Sexualities*, 24 (1/2): 86–110.

Masri, H. (2017), 'A Liberated Life? Thoughts on the Paradoxical Binds of Queer Refuge', *Kohl*, 3 (1): 37–40.

Matebeni, Z. (2019), '*Ikapa Lodumo* – An Introduction to the Infamous Cape Town', in B Camminga and Z. Matebeni (eds), *Beyond the Mountain: Queer Life in 'Africa's Gay Capital'*, 1–9, Pretoria: UNISA Press.

Mayers, L. (2018), 'Globalised Imaginaries of Love and Hate: Immutability, Violence, and LGBT Human Rights', *Feminist Legal Studies*, 26 (2): 141–61.

M'Baye, B. (2013), 'The Origins of Senegalese Homophobia: Discourses on Homosexuals and Transgender People in Colonial and Postcolonial Senegal', *African Studies Review*, 56 (2): 109–28.

McQuaid, K. (2020), '"There Is Violence across, in All Arenas": Listening to Stories of Violence amongst Sexual Minority Refugees in Uganda', *The International Journal of Human Rights*, 24 (4): 313–34.

Menetrier, A. (2019), 'Using Social Networking to Decipher Gender Stereotypes at Refugee Intake Points', *Hermès, La Revue*, 83 (1): 177–85.

Middelkoop, L. (2013), 'Normativity and Credibility of Sexual Orientation in Asylum Decision Making', in T. Spijkerboer (ed.), *Fleeing Homophobia: Sexual Orientation, Gender Identity and Asylum*, 154–76, London: Routledge.

Millo, Y. (2013), 'Identity and Integration in Israel and Kenya', *Forced Migration Review*, 42: 52–3.

Moore, H. K. V. (2018), *Disaggregating LGBTIQ Protection Concerns: Experiences of Displaced Communities in Nairobi*, Cambridge: Refugepoint.

Moore, H. K. V. (2019), 'The Atmosphere Is Oppressive: Investigating the Intersection of Violence with the Cisgender Lesbian, Bisexual and Queer Women Refugee Community in Nairobi, Kenya', in A. Güler, M. Shevtsova and D. Venturi (eds), *LGBTI Asylum Seekers and Refugees from a Legal and Political Perspective: Persecution, Asylum and Integration*, 323–36, Cham: Springer.

Mudarikwa, M., M. Gleckman-Krut, A-L. Payne, B Camminga and J. Marnell (2021), *LGBTI+ Asylum Seekers in South Africa: A Review of Refugee Status Denials Involving Sexual Orientation & Gender Identity*, Cape Town: LRC.

Murray, D. (2016), *Real Queer? Sexual Orientation and Gender Identity Refugees in the Canadian Refugee Apparatus*, London: Rowman & Littlefield.

Namwase, S., A. Jjuuko and I. Nyarango (2017), 'Sexual Minorities' Rights in Africa: What Does It Mean to Be Human and Who Gets to Decide?', in S. Namwase and A. Jjuuko (eds), *Protecting the Human Rights of Sexual Minorities in Contemporary Africa*, 2–12, Pretoria: Pretoria University Law Press.

Nicholas, O. (2017), 'Life in Purple: An Exploration of Moroccan LGBT Identity and Migration', *Independent Study Project (ISP) Collection*, 2536. Available online: https://digitalcollections.sit.edu/isp_collection/2536 (accessed 21 May 2021).

Nyanzi, S. (2013), 'Homosexuality, Sex Work, and HIV/AIDS in Displacement and Post-Conflict Settings: The Case of Refugees in Uganda', *International Peacekeeping*, 20 (4): 450–68.

Nyanzi, S. (2014), 'Queering Queer Africa', in Z. Matebeni (ed.), *Reclaiming Afrikan: Queer Perspectives of Sexual and Gender Identity*, 65–8, Cape Town: Modjadji Books.

Oloka-Onyango, J. (2015), 'Debating Love, Human Rights and Identity Politics in East Africa: The Case of Uganda and Kenya', *African Human Rights Law Journal*, 15: 28–57.

Palmary, I. (2016), *Gender, Sexuality and Migration in South Africa: Governing Morality*, Cham: Palgrave Macmillan.

Pierce, S. (2016), '"Nigeria Can Do without Such Perverts": Sexual Anxiety and Political Crises in Postcolonial Nigeria', *Comparative Studies of South Asia, Africa and the Middle East*, 36 (1): 3–20.

Pincock, K. (2021), 'UNHCR and LGBTI Refugees in Kenya: The Limits of "Protection"', *Disasters*, 45 (4): 844–64.

Puar, J. (2007), *Terrorist Assemblages: Homonationalism in Queer Times*, Durham: Duke University Press.

Rao, R. (2020), *Out of Time: The Queer Politics of Postcoloniality*, New York: Oxford University Press.

Reddy, V., S. Monro and Z. Matebeni (2018), 'Introduction', in Z. Matebeni, S. Monro and V. Reddy (eds), *Queer in Africa: LGBTQ Identities, Citizenship, and Activism*, 1–16, Oxon: Routledge.

Refugee Status Appeals Authority (2010), *Refugee Appeal No. 76484*, New Zealand Refugee Status Appeals Authority, 19 May. Available online: https://www.refworld.org/cases,NZL_RSAA,4c1f87e12.html (accessed 16 September 2020).

Rosenberg, J. S. (2016), '"Like a Stray Dog on the Street": Trans* Refugees Encounter Further Violence in the Cities Where They Flee', *LGBTQ Policy Journal at the Harvard Kennedy School*, VI: 76–88.

Tamale, S. (2014), 'Exploring the Contours of African Sexualities: Religion, Law and Power', *African Human Rights Law Journal*, 14 (1): 150–77.

Theodoro, H. and D. Cogo (2019), 'LGBTQI+ Immigrants and Refugees in the City of São Paulo: Uses of ICTs in a South-South Mobility Context', *Revue française des sciences de l'information et de la communication*, 17. doi: 10.4000/rfsic.7053.

Thomann, M. and R. Corey-Boulet (2017), 'Violence, Exclusion and Resilience among Ivoirian Travestis', *Critical African Studies*, 9 (1): 106–23.

Tschalaer, M. (2020a), 'Waiting for LGBTQI+ Asylum Seekers in Germany: A Form of State Control and Resistance', *Association for Political and Legal Anthropology*, 15 September. Available online: https://politicalandlegalanthro.org/2020/09/15/waiting-for-lgbtqi-asylum-seekers-in-germany-a-form-of-state-control-and-resistance/ (accessed 16 September 2020).

Tschalaer, M. (2020b), 'Between Queer Liberalisms and Muslim Masculinities: LGBTQI+ Muslim Asylum Assessment in Germany', *Ethnic and Racial Studies*, 43 (7): 1265–83.

Yue, A. (2012), 'Queer Asian Mobility and Homonational Modernity: Marriage Equality, Indian Students in Australia and Malaysian Transgender Refugees in the Media', *Global Media and Communication*, 8 (3): 269–87.

Part I

COMPLICATING MIGRATION NARRATIVES

Chapter 1

LABYRINTHINE WANDERINGS: QUEERING MOBILITY IN IMPOSSIBLE GEOGRAPHIES

Yara Ahmed

'Becoming involves a basic tension – or perhaps alchemy – between destruction and creation.'

(Garcia 2017: 113)

In 'The Garden of Forking Paths', a 1964 short story by Argentine writer and poet Jorge Luis Borges, the protagonist, Doctor Yu Tsun, is faced with the mystery of a long-lost labyrinth, supposedly created by his ancestor, Ts'ui Pên. We learn that Ts'ui Pên left his job as a politician in order to write a novel and construct a labyrinth. Having died before finishing his novel, Ts'ui Pên left behind an 'indeterminate heap of contradictory drafts' and a cryptic letter stating, 'I leave to the various futures (not to all) my garden of forking paths' (36).

Borges' story is a conglomeration of fragmented spatio-temporal planes, where the author and his characters wander labyrinthine paths, drafting and redrafting their pasts, presents and futures. Along the way they engage in various life-making projects, each leading to a different self. The plot features endless possibilities, a web of potentialities knitted together from multiple threads of desire, hope and fear. It moves forward hesitantly, unexpectedly, unravelling in infinite directions; what is and what is yet to become are blurred.

In this chapter, I draw on Borges' metaphor of the labyrinth to explore how precarious queer bodies in Egypt navigate their life-worlds. Like Borges' characters, my interlocutors straddle multiple time-spaces: they imagine, wait, move and feel stuck. By adopting a spatio-temporal approach, I seek to open up the borders of inquiry and to expand current theorizations of mobility. Specifically, I draw on processes of dreaming to rethink time-space as it relates to queer migration. I approach movement not only as a kinetic faculty, but also as an affective and imaginative one. The movement I am concerned with here is related to shifts in the imagination, to people's dreams of what is yet to come and their efforts to construct alternative time-space. What happens when precarious queer bodies aspire for a 'somewhere else'? What are the politics that surround their dream-making projects? How does the constant desiring of other life-worlds reflect in the way that people move?

In analysing how my interlocutors engage with migration potentialities, how they make and unmake different tomorrows, I hope to *queer* normative conceptualizations of mobility. Like Judith Butler (2016), I understand queerness less as an identity category and more 'as a movement of thought and language contrary to accepted forms of authority, always deviating, and so opening up spaces for desire that would not always be openly recognized within established norms' (17).

There is a specific urgency in how queer bodies move within and from the context engaged with here. This has to do with the particular socio-political conditions that unfolded in Egypt during my fieldwork, conditions that continue to frame such bodies as undesirable and unwelcome. The state's understanding of what is 'moral' or 'traditional' is arbitrary and often relies on heteronormative frameworks of gender and sexuality. What is legal is often conflated with what is virtuous, courtesy of a violent strategy to 'secure' and 'protect' the state. The government's campaign to 'preserve' society's moral fabric not only positions certain bodies as threats to the 'natural' order but also ties discourses of citizenship, rights, peace, prosperity and territoriality with paramilitary forms of state control (Amar 2013). Furthermore, as a predominantly Muslim society, Egypt's militarist-national discourses are imbued with a sense of religiosity. What is *haram* (sinful) and what is *halal* (permissible) intertwine with what is 'legal' and what is 'illegal'. The regulation and persecution of queer bodies allow the apparatuses of the state 'to "perform" a discourse of national security through which national sovereignty … [is] (re)produced and political order … [is] maintained' (Pratt 2007: 129). One such incident unfolded during my fieldwork: a crackdown against 'alleged homosexuals' following a concert by Lebanese band Mashrou' Leila. The Egyptian state justified its actions as a necessary step for maintaining social order and 'family values'. Within this socio-political context, migration was increasingly seen as a 'way out' of the status quo for queer people in Egypt, even if leaving was not always viable or possible.

But migration is not where I want to start this chapter, nor where I will end it. I begin instead with the imagination. Movement in this chapter is understood as blurring the lines between reality and fiction. My interlocutors' dream-making projects are evidence of their attempts to establish a sense of relationality and homeliness within a geography that has persistently forced them to the periphery. Queerness here translates into a reorienting of the body's capacity to imagine other life-worlds, other attachments, other selves, other time-spaces.

The research that informs this chapter is largely dependent on processes of movement that are slippery: people imagining, experimenting, feeling disorientated, retracing their steps, reconfiguring. Thus, it is difficult to define my field of inquiry or my theoretical starting point. Categories, concepts and borders give a semblance of fixity, yet they remain incomplete and slippery: 'Egypt', 'Cairo', 'queerness', the 'state', the 'body'. What is clear is that this chapter draws on fieldwork conducted between March 2017 and July 2018 with and around mostly cisgender queer women and men in Cairo (early twenties to mid-thirties), all of whom were aware – at least to some extent – of terms like 'LGBT+', 'queer', 'gay', 'lesbian' and 'non-binary'. My fieldwork was a concoction of interviews and field notes from when I hung out with and listened to my interlocutors, in the process witnessing multiple dream-making projects take shape. These projects translate to a crafting of paths, a labyrinth of potentialities, as my interlocutors navigate the possibilities and impossibilities of crossing borders, moving out of a parent's house, confessing an infatuation, getting out of bed in the morning, or imagining a life that is somewhere or something else. Using these dream-making practices as my entry point, I argue that the *potentiality* for mobility is key to our understanding of queer migration. After all, it is the imagination – the ability to wonder and hope – that animates our desire for a better life. It is in the fragmented, labyrinthine pathways of the imagination that becoming happens.

Illegible imaginariums

Positivist approaches to knowledge dismiss the imagination as unreliable or 'not real'. At best, it is regarded as a secondary form of knowledge, akin to myths, anecdotes and fictions. The ambiguity and slipperiness inherent in the imagination are often negatively contrasted with 'rational faculties of understanding and reason' (Schlutz 2010: 4). Modern conceptualizations of subjectivity – most of which are built on the Enlightenment conceit of a 'rational and autonomous individual subject' (Schlutz 2010: 6) – rarely engage with the imagination, at least not directly. Instead, subjectivity is positioned as a set of rational and relational articulations that bounce off of each other, as opposed to the 'meshwork of entangled lines of life, growth and movement' (Ingold 2011: 63) associated with the sensory-planes of the imagination.

The received wisdom that the *rational* and the *imaginative* are diametrically opposed deserves troubling. Engaging the faculties of dreaming can shift the way we look at subjectivity, and by extension the way we understand processes of becoming. In considering the imagination, philosophers like René Descartes and Immanuel Kant recognize its indispensability to the constitution of the self. However, in both Cartesian and Kantian readings, according to Alexander Schlutz (2010), imagination remains a 'willingly subservient handmaiden' (141) to the faculties of rationality. For these philosophers, the existence of an absolute and autonomous 'subject' is only possible if the explicability of the rational self is guaranteed. The instability of the imagination, with its oscillating, variable limits and endless capacities, makes it unmappable and therefore dangerous to conceptualizations of the self as real and knowable. Yet, it is these very features that make the imagination indispensable to rethinking becoming.

Schlutz (2010) suggests that we think of imagination 'as a dynamic force' (10) that intersects and intertwines with many other variables to create the self. In his reading, subjectivity is produced through an endless process of becoming and therefore does not have 'a stable organizing center' (Schlutz 2010: 10). In other words, subjectivity is indeterminate and always in flux. The imagination is a key player in this process, in that its articulations are a form of narrating the self.

Moreover, it is only via the imagination that we can engage in the poetic process of thinking the impossible.

We can also look to queer studies for alternative readings of subjectivity. In recent decades, queer scholars have tracked how bodies orient themselves temporally and spatially, extending these theorizations to ask what it means to dwell, migrate, become, belong and feel at home (e.g. Merabet 2015; Muñoz 2009). Sara Ahmed's (2006) object-oriented ontology, following Graham Harman and Edmund Husserl, considers the impressions that inhabiting time-space leave on the body from a phenomenological perspective. Migration in Ahmed's work is a process of orienting and reorienting, of re-inhabiting space through navigating objects of familiarity and unfamiliarity as one moves towards an affective experience of homeliness. For Ahmed (2010), objects and their promises are always 'ahead of us'. People tend to orient their bodies towards 'happy objects', but when this orientation is threatened, when bodies are not able to 'extend into space, they might feel "out of place"' (Ahmed 2006: 12). While Ahmed's work is grounded in phenomenology, it also gestures to the role of the affective in ontological processes and how these shape how a body occupies space.

Dream-making takes place through a meshwork of images, ideas, words and memories, a constellation that is constantly making and remaking itself, extending its grasp onto our senses, our paintbrush, our pen, our movement, our 'becoming'. We dream all the time, creating other selves and other time-spaces. Our imaginations are not only a site in which desires and aspirations can be mapped, but also where our affective expressions of hope and hopelessness coalesce. It is where our fears and nightmares incarnate themselves, and where we construct and destroy our life-worlds.

Existential mobility: Time-space becoming

On 22 September 2017, more than 35,000 people gathered in Cairo's affluent Fifth Settlement to watch three bands play: Mashrou' Leila (Lebanon), El-Morabba3 (Jordan) and Sharmoofers (Egypt). Mashrou' Leila, whose lead singer is openly gay, is known for exploring themes of sexuality, politics, faith and other social issues in its songs. Several concertgoers at the Cairo performance held up rainbow flags. In response, the Egyptian state initiated a swift and severe crackdown on 'alleged homosexuals'. This included mass arrest, incarceration and/or home detention; entrapment through dating applications and websites; and forced searches of mobile phones during arbitrary stops (Human Rights Watch 2017). The crackdown primarily targeted concertgoers whose pictures had been posted online and people closely associated with these individuals, but also extended to those beyond the limits of heteronormativity (e.g. visible trans people, gay men and sex workers). In response, queer and trans groups rapidly increased their security precautions, including closing online pages and postponing activities. Some individuals even fled the country.

The 2017 incident was not the first of its kind. Egypt's state police has a long history of targeting, harassing and arresting people suspected of 'homosexual conduct' (Human Rights Watch 2004). Queer individuals are considered to be *shezoz*: an anomaly. The *Almaany* Arabic dictionary defines *shaz* (singular of *shezoz*) as 'abnormal', 'someone who is outside of the group/community' or that which 'deviates from the rule or the standard'. In common usage, *shaz* is a derogatory term for anyone or anything that violates gender or sexual norms.

One of the most well-known crackdowns occurred in 2001, when the state police raided the Queen Boat, a queer-friendly floating nightclub moored on the Nile in Cairo (Awwad 2010). In total, fifty-two men were arrested. Homosexuality is not explicitly criminalized in Egypt, but laws against 'debauchery' and 'scandalous acts' are regularly used to prosecute those who transgress heteronormative standards. According to Article 9(c) of Law No. 10/1961 on the Combating of Prostitution, *fujur* (debauchery) and *di'ara* (prostitution) are punishable by 'imprisonment for a period not less than three months and not exceeding three years' and/or a fine (Mendos 2019).[1]

In the wake of the Mashrou' Leila concert, the Egyptian state implemented a series of violent measures to curb queer visibility and, it hoped, the very existence of queerness. More than sixty people were detained on charges of 'inciting debauchery' in the two months following the concert (Hamid 2017). One person who escaped arrest was Karim,[2] whom I met through a friend in January 2018. Since raising a flag, Karim was in perpetual fear of being arrested or forcibly disappeared. He believed there were only two choices available to him:

> Anyone who is in a position where they feel endangered all the time, even if there is nothing that is actually threatening them, spend all their time dreaming. They are faced with two choices: either to start fixing where they are, or just dream [of somewhere else] all the time. And even if they chose to fix where they are, they are fixing it because they dream of that somewhere else, where they aren't worried about anything anymore.

The crackdown prompted Karim to put into action a long-contemplated plan: seeking asylum. The only prospect that staying in Egypt could offer was eventual arrest. He spent months unable to shake the feeling of being surveilled, convinced the authorities were coming for him. Karim isolated himself from friends and family, changed his phone number, closed all of his social media accounts and hid out at a friend's house. He also spent most of his time researching possible futures, trying to remain incognito as he did so: 'You open Google Maps and ask yourself – *where?*' It was in these moments that he laid the building blocks for a movement that was both an escape from being stuck and a movement towards a potential somewhere else. We spoke while Karim was awaiting the outcome of a visa application. He reflected on the emotions this process had produced:

> It has been a month, and I don't think I can stay here anymore. I spent so much time researching online, building a life somewhere else, down to every

detail: the rent of the house where I will be living, what I will be eating and drinking, the streets, the world. My life in Egypt is over. I look at the houses and I feel nothing. Leaving the country won't be a big deal. I can't live here anymore. I spent the two months after the concert, October and November, in fear. I am leaving behind one of the worst experiences [in my life], and I am leaving with a lot of hate for this country.

Karim's sense of being trapped, of having no real options or places to go, can be read as a form of 'existential immobility' (Hage 2009). Karim's detachment from 'here' – his family, his friends, his life-world – is his way of creating space for what may come. He inscribes his desires onto an imagined somewhere, a country on Google Maps that offers the potential for renewed possibility, a territory where mobility and becoming are possible. His desires are oriented towards a future temporality, an imagined time when fear, hiding and waiting are no longer the defining features of his daily life. For Karim, staying in Egypt translates into 'stuckedness' (Hage 2009): 'If I stay in Egypt, I will be seventy and I will still be afraid of the same thing.' The impossibility of Karim's position became a visceral sensation of being stuck. Every aspect of his here and now was experienced as a fear of detention – walking down the street became overwhelming; even hanging out with friends posed a threat to life. Only in his imagined future could he dream of a life that offered other potentialities.

What Karim refers to as 'fixing' is his way of transitioning from a detained self to a mobile self, of finding space for his body and his dreams. Imagining 'somewhere else' is a process of regaining the mobility that has been stripped from his current life. By mapping his dreams onto another country, Karim is seeking a landscape for his existential mobility. Ghassan Hage (2009) contends that existential mobility is a 'type of imagined/felt movement' (98) and considers it to be the affective foundation for mobility.

Looking at the implications of these imaginaries on our understanding of time-space leads us to Ernst Bloch, whose work on time and temporality continues to influence thinking on potentiality. In *Principles of Hope*, Bloch (1995) explores how we understand the past, present and future. Breaking away from dominant narratives that posit time as linear, Bloch contends that people's relationship to the future is informed by the practice of 'venturing beyond', a sort of wandering into an imagined spatio-temporal landscape. Venturing beyond is 'a mode of temporality, a cognitive and affective relation to time and a way to approach the relationship among historicity, presentism and futurity' (Weeks 2011: 186). For my interlocutors, the past, present and future coexist simultaneously, bound up in 'a relation of transmission or exchange' (Al-Saji 2004: 207). Seeking 'somewhere else' is more than simply looking towards the future – it interplays with other planes of what has been and what is. It involves a complex relationship with hope, memory and desire.

To understand where we are, we need to be more attuned to the relationships we have with our pasts, how we relate and imagine them, as well as the attachments we have to our imagined futures. Bloch's theories help us reconceptualize dream-making practices and their relationship to movement by destabilizing the conceptual hierarchy separating what is real from what is fiction (i.e. dreams, imagination, myth, etc.) and by troubling orthodox understandings of time-space as neatly structured and fixed.

Migration might be the symbolic 'launching pad' for reorienting the body (Hage 2009), but it is existential mobility – as the affective foundation of potentiality – that fuels the desire for movement (see also Ahmed 2006). For Karim, fear not only manifests as his remaining in Egypt, but also in the feeling of 'stuckedness' (Hage 2009). The sensation of being trapped extended beyond the immediate threat of the Egyptian state. Despite wanting intensely to leave 'here', Karim was afraid of not knowing what to do once 'there'. He also expressed concern over what he would have to give up: 'I don't want to lose [what I have here].' Migration does not necessarily signal 'the way out' of stuckedness, but rather represents an imagined existential mobility. Karim's desire to move towards a somewhere else does not necessarily mean he wants to detach himself from the 'here', however fragmented and infested by fear it may be. Both the 'here' and the 'there' retain possible features of stuckedness.

Two months after the Mashrou' Leila concert, I talked to Omar. He had just graduated from university and was working as a sales assistant in a mall. He also expressed a desire to leave the country, but did not have a destination in mind. Omar told me that his dream was to move out of his parents' house and rent a place of his own, a space where he could 'be himself'. He expressed frustration and exhaustion from the constant pressure to perform as someone else: 'I want to go somewhere else ... instead of pretending to be someone I am not, or acting like something I am not just to please them [his parents], just because I am afraid.' His existential immobility was experienced in his inability to inhabit space; his most prominent fear was being stuck in what he called his 'fake life'.

In *Queer Phenomenology*, Ahmed (2006) elaborates on the idea of disorientation:

> If orientation is about making the strange familiar through the extension of bodies into space, then disorientation occurs when that extension fails. Or we could say that some spaces extend certain bodies and simply do not leave room for others.
>
> (11)

Ahmed talks about sexual orientations as a 'matter of residence', defined by who and what we inhabit space with. She engages with queerness as a practice of extending the body. To make things queer for Ahmed means disturbing 'the order of things' in a world that is already 'organised around certain forms of living – certain times, spaces and directions' (161).

Omar felt that he was constantly being questioned about the way he dressed, talked and walked – in other words, how he inhabited space. These questions came from all directions, including relatives, schoolmates, colleagues and strangers. In Ahmed's (2006) lexicon, Omar did not fit with the 'skin of the social' (20). Bodies like Omar's find it hard to move because they persistently encounter 'stopping devices' that question their right to belong: 'Who are you? Why are you here? What are doing?' (Ahmed 2006: 139). These disruptive encounters inevitably create a sense of disorientation, of being out of place.

To reorient, one must align one's body in space by moving towards reachable objects. For this reason, Ahmed sees migration – including movements *towards* migration – as an attempt to re-inhabit space, to reshape the 'body surface'. For both Omar and Karim, the idea of moving – be it from Egypt to another country or from the family home to one's own space – was bound up with a sense of potential, a feeling that movement, becoming and belonging were possible. For Omar, existential mobility was irrevocably linked to 'not living as someone else and not leading a double life'; for Karim, migration was the 'launching pad' towards an indeterminate time-space that promised a 'better life'. These interlocutors' labyrinthine wanderings are reflected in acts of 'searching for space where the quality of their "going-ness" is better than what it is in the space they are leaving behind' (Hage 2009: 98).

Between 'here' and 'there'

Julie Chu's (2010) *Cosmologies of Credit* offers a conceptual framework for understanding the affective tensions between 'here' and 'there'. While these terms imply an oppositional relationship, locations that are distinct, mappable and clearly defined, their spatio-temporal architecture is actually malleable; the binary disintegrates the moment it comes into contact with the everyday. In her book, Chu explores the lives, subjectivities and desires of Fuzhou's hopeful migrants, tracing their perpetual pursuit of departure, their aspirations for mobility and their navigation of stuckedness against the backdrop of modernity's promises. She tells the story of Deng Feiyan, a young woman who is both Chu's friend and her interlocutor, who dreams of leaving Fuzhou's countryside for a 'better life' in New York.

Like Deng Feiyan, my interlocutors' everyday lives are infused with dreams of the somewhere else, a 'sense of imminent departure … enchant[ing] every move' (Chu 2010: 3). For example, Karim, who was attached to objects within his 'bodily horizon' (Ahmed 2010), went about his life entertaining the dream of leaving. Like Feiyan, Karim has not been able to leave, yet his narrative is imbued with a mobile force, a longing for and reimagining of movement.[3] A constant reorienting of the affective architecture of the imagination around the 'here' and 'there' occurs. Feiyan's everyday life is experienced as a state of transition, in which she remains 'constantly at the cusp of departure' (Chu 2010: 3). Karim's and Feiyan's sense of movement is tied to their existential mobility – the felt potentiality of movement and its imagined possibilities fuel their becoming. The 'here' and the 'there' are not premised on an actualized kinetic transition, but rather on the affective reterritorialization of possibilities and impossibilities.

Territoriality, in these instances, is not bound by geographies that conceive of space-time as autonomous. It is pronounced not through lineage or nationality, nor is it conceptualized as an essentialized feature of belonging, but rather oscillates between wanting, dreaming and their agitative capacities. Neil Brenner (1999) takes on a Lefebvrian approach, contending that capitalism and globalization drive a continuous fragmentation and rearrangement of space, or what he calls reterritorialization. He sees space as a political, social and economic product, rather than a static realm fixed in time-space. Although grounded in an analysis of space, Brenner's theory can be extended to encompass the temporal aspects of territoriality, specifically how one's experience of space-time emerges out of a specific political, social and economic configuration. In the context of this discussion, I am interested in how my interlocutors felt, navigated and imagined time-space.

My interlocutors mainly spoke of 'here' and 'there' as separate points on a map, yet the constant reterritorialization of these spatial and temporal points means that they wash over each other, muddying the distinction between the two. As imagining 'somewhere else' became part and parcel of the everyday, 'here' and 'there' became blurred – sometimes the concepts became irrevocably enmeshed, sometimes they stretched farther and farther apart, and sometimes they fragmented to the point of incomprehensibility. It was in the constant playfulness of these categories that my interlocutors' bodies narrated themselves.

The metamorphosis of detention

I sleep endlessly, I run away endlessly, I am afraid endlessly. I feel as if I am a newborn! But my birth today is different from the one before it! My birth today is a birth from the womb of agony! A birth from cruelty! I am not able to distinguish night from day – nothing is clear – the spider passes near me. He is my friend in this cell. A spider looking for a way out! Damn it, damn it! Maybe this insect, too, is a prisoner, detained! Why not? They bear enough irrationality, fear and cowardice to prosecute even insects, for whatever reason. Maybe that spider disturbed the detective. Maybe he disturbed one of the government officials. Or maybe it was an insect that lost its way and is looking for its people, just like me! I don't know my friend, I don't know.

(Hegazi 2018)

The arrest of activists Sarah Hegazi and Ahmed Alaa in the wake of the Mashrou' Leila concert garnered considerable media attention, both locally and internationally.[4] They were charged with 'joining a group formed in contrary to the law', 'propagating that group's ideas', 'promoting sexual deviancy and debauchery' and 'illegally procuring foreign funding' (Hamid 2017). After their arrest, Hegazi and Alaa were held in remand detention for fifteen days, pending investigation. As is often the case with Egyptian juridical processes, the period of detention and 'investigation' was stretched out. Every fifteen days, the court announced the menacing news that Hegazi's and Alaa's detentions were renewed. Reports of the violence to which Hegazi, Alaa and other detainees were subjected while in custody began to circulate. International outrage, spurred on by news coverage, pressured the Egyptian government into releasing the pair early, on bail while pending trial. However, other detainees facing similar charges and mistreatment remained stuck in a vicious cycle of remand detention, or were hastily sentenced to between one and six years in prison (Human Rights Watch 2017).

The concert was a moment in which fear and anxiety reterritorialized themselves onto the queer body. Day-to-day life became haunted by the dispositifs of control (Foucault 2010). The threat of imprisonment halted processes of becoming. The event and its aftermath triggered a collective experience of stuckedness. Shock at the speed and severity of the crackdown left many with a depleted imagination; potentialities and hopes for the future were replaced with a crisis of surviving the present moment, of getting by, of asking *Where do I go from here?* One young queer woman in her twenties posted the following on social media:

> I'm tired of being constantly worried. I want to come back [to Egypt] but I am scared of coming back as well. I keep telling myself that I'm too insignificant to be arrested. I don't pose any threat of any kind. I also feel stuck. I hate feeling stuck and incapable of doing anything.

This experience of stuckedness is part and parcel of the machineries of hopelessness that a neoliberal, securitized state creates. In *Revolutions in Reverse*, David Graeber (2011) explores the projects of hopelessness accumulated in the arenas of capitalism and argues that 'large heavy objects' manifest in the structural violence of the state. He argues that the construction of prisons, the expansion of armies and the maintenance of intense security apparatuses (military, police, propaganda engines, etc.) are a determinant of capital structures. He contends:

> Hopelessness isn't natural. It needs to be produced. If we really want to understand this situation, we have to begin by understanding … the construction of a vast bureaucratic apparatus for the creation and maintenance of hopelessness, a kind of giant machine that is designed, first and foremost, to destroy any sense of possible alternative futures.

(31)

A reimagining of the self occurs when heavy objects are encountered. Ahmed (2006) describes this process as the disorientation and reorientation of the body. After her release, Hegazi posted snippets of the journal entries she had written while in prison on Facebook and her blog. In recalling being sent to prison, Hegazi describes something akin to a rebirth – a 'birth from the womb of agony'. The shock of the encounter reterritorialized the labyrinths of possibility and impossibility, infesting the imagination with heavy objects. In such encounters, the body senses its precariousness and transforms its conceptual understanding of itself, blurring the boundaries between the imaginative, the real and the symbolic. Hegazi (2018) was acutely aware of this process, as is evident in her writing. The paragraph below is an extract of a conversation she had with a spider in her cell, which she posted on Facebook:

> I, too, am an insect, and anyone who is like us is an insect. All who stray from the herd are insects. We are insects – they look at us with disdain and discontent like they look upon insects. That is how Kafka described it in his novel *The Metamorphosis*, those who stray from the herd, wake up to find themselves metamorphosed into insects. But, it is okay – we are going to make peace with it!

Ahmed's queer phenomenology sheds light on the experience of metamorphosis to which Hegazi refers. In a sense, Hegazi is experiencing disorientation, the process of becoming 'oblique' (Ahmed 2006: 92). Impossibility inscribes an encounter with unfamiliar and heavy objects that pose a threat to the body's extension in space. Ahmed likens disorientation to 'losing a grip', a 'slipping away' of what was imagined to be reachable (162).

For Hegazi, the geographies of impossibility were reterritorialized when her body collided with the prison system. As a jailed body, Hegazi found it near impossible to suspend the heavy objects in her vicinity; her body was violently forced into an insect-like existence through the dehumanizing gaze of the state. The heavy objects at the state's disposal – the cuffs, the cells, the walls, the prison, the police officers – decreed a new sense of being and in doing so initiated a process of metamorphosis. Disorientation was violent and sudden, bringing with it a rapid reterritorialization of the body, mind and subject.

Precariousness in this sense is distributed differently according to the frames that measure the value of the body (Butler 2009). As Hegazi notes, 'those who stray from the herd' are relegated to the periphery of existence, marked with labels like 'vagabonds', 'thugs', 'illegal' or '*shezoz*'. A person's socio-economic background, gender, sexuality, race and ability often determine the level of mobility open to them. Those frames of value are multiple and coalesce in a variety of ways. Socio-economic capital alone does not always translate into a greater sense of mobility, but it intersects with a number of other zones of management that bodies are forced to navigate, creating a complex terrain of attachments, impossibilities and heavy objects.

The Egyptian state co-opted social anxieties by transforming them into practices of governance and control. As it strengthened its security apparatuses, it promised deliverance from precarity and uncertainty; the 'better life' was packaged as neatly wrapped gifts of civilization that manifested in heavy objects. The contradiction of state power is incarnated in its ability to 'unleash fear to control fear' (Graeber 2011: 11). Progress and development are sold as antidotes to unrest, instability and moral deprivation. Managing those who are deemed undesirable entails managing the social, economic, temporal and spatial aspects of everyday life – 'your politics, your affiliations, your nightmares, your ideology, your rights, your friends and neighbours. Your dreams' (Mohaiemen 2010: 90).

Temporary people, temporary dreams

Uncertainty is an important aspect of dream-making, in that it reiterates the precariousness of space-time and forces constant re-evaluations and revisions. As plans are imagined, they get reshuffled time and time again. A sense of temporariness permeates the life of my interlocutors – the temporariness of an unstable and hazardous politico-economic sphere, the uncertainties that heavy objects bear and the fragility of attachments. Even though the desire to leave saturated the immediate time-space of my research, the 'there' of people's dreams was rarely pinned on a map or marked on a calendar. At best, places and times were used as examples, signalling a possibility rather than a certainty. Almost immediately after a 'there' was pinned down, it moved again, with a pause, a stutter, a rethinking, a reimagining: *Well, perhaps not X, but Y instead.*

My interlocutors always spoke in maybes. Mazen is a university student who identifies as gay. Being highly active on social media and vocal about queer rights made him vulnerable to arrest, especially after the Mashrou' Leila concert. He had already been considering migration pathways prior to the concert, but his plan was constantly changing. He told me that he might wait until graduation and then travel on a student visa, or lodge an asylum claim after an upcoming internship in Europe, or arrange a marriage of convenience with a friend in another country, in the hope that this would facilitate citizenship. He told me that he found it hard to plan too far in advance and that he felt more comfortable with short-term goals. Anticipating what is yet to come brought him a lot of anxiety.

Uncertainty is neither an inherently negative nor an inherently positive element of queer dream-making, but it does precipitate a particular kind of affective movement and can generate multiple responses. Investing in a dream-making project involves reorienting oneself within a spatio-temporal architecture that is continuously negotiating the borders between possibility and impossibility. The term 'architecture' usually implies a fixed infrastructure, but the kind of architecture I am referring to here does not emerge from a blueprint. Rather, it is endlessly shifting, evolving and responding – it is 'infinitely saturated with invisible persons', to borrow Ts'ui Pên's words. Movement towards somewhere else does not necessarily have to materialize as cross-border migration. It could, for example, be the forging of a potential lifeway that leads towards imagined others.

Recognizing the nebulous terrain of queer movement stops us from thinking about it in terms of success or failure. Instead, we might recognize that queer movement lends itself to infinite almosts. The future is always suspended (Abourahme 2014). Looking at the spatio-temporal labyrinths of mobility challenges homogeneous understandings of migration and allows us to consider mobility not only in terms of the kinetic or the material, but also in terms of the affective. Movement does not have to register as a leap, nor as migration from one place to another. Conceptualizing movement in terms of the affective and the imaginative can reveal as much about queer mobility as more traditional theorizations of migration.

When Omar spoke of his aspiration to move from Egypt to a place where he could be 'himself', he enumerated all of the obstacles latent in this act of dreaming: getting through his compulsory military service, raising sufficient capital, finding a job so as to gain work experience, learning a new language and so on. At each of these checkpoints, Omar needs to reach what he calls a 'necessary' threshold. In waiting for the dream to come to fruition, Omar must maintain hope that such obstacles will be passed, even as new obstacles appear on the horizon. Moreover, in deferring his dream, Omar must allow this and other potentialities to exist simultaneously, to collide, coalesce and evolve in an endless process of dream-making that intersects with his emergent self. He told me of other dreams that did not seem as laden with heavy objects: moving out of his parents' house, living with his partner, pursuing his knack for designing clothes – all acts of re-envisioning the self. Things that are not yet there, but which are on the cusp of becoming. As urban sociologist AbdouMaliq Simone (2010) contends, 'the pursuit of survival involves actions, relations, sentiments, and opportunities that are more than survival alone' (38).

In the precarity of temporariness, people spend a lot of time waiting. Sometimes they wait for one thing and then another, getting stuck in an endless loop of almost becoming. Some wait for obstacles to melt, or for paths to open up. Some wait but move in their waiting. Others wait but forget that they are waiting. And sometimes waiting is violent: people are 'kicked around' the borders of possibility and impossibility, where they experiment with one life-world and then another in their imagination.

Hage (2009) looks at the politics and power geometries around waiting and contends that 'we all wait for futures' (1), especially in the advent of late neoliberalism, where futures are gushing with the promises of the modern:

> In general terms, waiting occurs on the boundaries between the time-saturated worlds or social imaginaries and the everyday experiences of subjects. Waiting is the tension of subjects as they exist on a boundary between a present (or even a past) world that they cannot leave and a future one that they cannot automatically or immediately enter.
>
> (45)

In this sense, waiting can entail a sense of temporariness that echoes a peripheral existence. Karim was already waiting long before the Mashrou' Leila concert. He told me that before that night, as he went about his everyday life, he could not shake the idea that he was going to have to leave the country. He felt that the waiting for change was endless. There was always a sense of temporariness in his staying in Egypt. This only became heightened after the concert. He expressed his frustration at being 'stuck here', of having no idea where he was going and what he was doing:

> A lot happened in the two months following the concert. It was almost like I wanted to get rid of everything I had here. I wanted to put an end to everything that was good, to fight with [my parents] and have them kick me out of the house …

I couldn't hide my fear ... Dawn was horrific for me; I couldn't sleep for the first two weeks ... I couldn't handle anything that was going on at home. I didn't talk or hangout much with my friends. I didn't go out much ... I was literally leaving behind everything I had here and I spent my time constructing a life elsewhere.

Karim's in-between state can be read as a temporary relation with the everyday; he walks the margins of being and belonging like a stranger, all the while engrossed in a future that seems just out of reach. As his relationships with family, friends and others are tested and stretched – sometimes intentionally, but often through circumstances beyond his control – he begins to build the foundation for another life-world, one that is located in an imagined but unknown time and space. Waiting is an expression of power. It tells us something about time and value, about the subject in waiting and about the things or people for which they are waiting (Auyero 2012). Although Hage (2009) foregrounds the stuckedness and uncertainty of waiting, he rejects the idea that it is an inherently passive activity: 'waiting indicates that we are engaged in and have an expectation from life' (1). The sense of stuckedness experienced by Karim does not necessarily entail stillness or stagnation. Rather, Karim invests in an existential movement, imagining other life-worlds and the connections, sensations, emotions and potentialities that come along with it: the street, the food, the place, the apartment he will sleep in. These objects of desire become emblematic of a reorientation, of movement, of becoming in an imagined time-space.

Conclusion

My interlocutors' labyrinthine wanderings made way for imagining different possibilities of being and becoming. These individuals are constantly forced to navigate hopelessness, a sense of impossibility and various apparatuses of surveillance and control. To do so, they conjured up dreamscapes of a better 'there', of a life in an imagined somewhere and sometime else. They exchanged stories, aspirations, tactics of mobility and ways to circumvent state regulations, with the intention of straddling the boundary between legality and illegality. As Brian Massumi (2015) contends, 'the ability to move forwards and transit through life, isn't necessarily about escaping from constraint' (12). In some circumstances, movement is 'walking as controlled falling' (12), where a person moves along with constraint, constantly playing with possibilities as they try to regain their footing.

My interlocutors understood a lot of their dreams to be 'impossible'. Yet, these imaginings, while not yet realized, indicate an engagement with life, a becoming, a movement. In dream-making processes, we never go into the 'mere vacuum of an In-Front-of-Us' (Bloch 1995: 4). In other words, we never look exclusively towards the future. Dream-making is productive because it is *not* 'confined within the finalities of any particular project' but rather moves endlessly 'without beginning or end' (Ingold 2011: 6). In that sense, dream-making fuels processes of becoming.

The queer geographies of dream-making I explore here pull at bodies and push against the skin: an intimacy, a friendship, a home of one's own, an affective experience of safety. Some dreams are pursued and written onto the body, while others are left and forgotten. They almost always change and shift with the constellations of attachments and heavy objects that people encounter: securitization, policing, censorship, surveillance and so on. We structure and suspend our bodies in our imaginations. We shift from imagining a self that is immobilized by heavy objects to imagining a self that is mobile.

As I engaged with different people and their stories, with the different ways that desires and dreams play out, I found myself wandering my own labyrinth, one that always seemed to be in the process of becoming. Whenever I sensed a pattern in my fieldwork, the feeling of certainty and clarity would inevitably slip away. It was those moments of loss and confusion – moments when I would ask, *Where am I, and what am I doing here?* – that best reflect the fragmented ways in which the imagining of different life-worlds happens and from which the potentiality for mobility emerges.

Notes

1   In most cases, prison sentences are extended to between eight and twelve years. Although the Egyptian penal code decrees that defendants be charged with one penalty for one act, even if it constitutes multiple crimes, the courts have sentenced some defendants to multiple penalties for a single action, which explains the lengthy prison sentences (Egyptian Initiative for Personal Rights 2016).

2   Pseudonyms are used throughout this chapter to protect participants' identities. Interview quotes and social media posts have been translated from Arabic by the author.

3   Since completing fieldwork, I have learnt that Karim has left Egypt. He had not made concrete plans when we spoke and so I analyse his words through the lens of potentiality, rather than actual experience of migration.

4   Sarah Hegazi and I talked during the early stages of my research, prior to the Mashrou' Leila concert. Her arrest, imprisonment and later exile in Canada made it difficult for us to continue our conversation. Sarah's determination to make visible her experiences of state repression means that there is now a rich online archive documenting her experience of incarceration and exile and its impact on her mental health. I draw on her blog and social media posts throughout this chapter as a way to centre her voice and to recognize the critical contribution she made to queer visibility in Egypt. Sarah died by suicide on 14 June 2020.

References

Abourahme, N. (2014), 'Ruinous City, Ruinous Time: Future Suspended and the Science Fiction of the Present', *City*, 18 (4/5): 577–82.

Ahmed, S. (2006), *Queer Phenomenology: Orientations, Objects, Others*, Durham: Duke University Press.

Ahmed, S. (2010), *The Promise of Happiness*, Durham: Duke University Press.

Al-Saji, A. (2004), 'The Memory of Another Past: Bergson, Deleuze and a New Theory of Time', *Continental Philosophy Review*, 37 (2): 203–39.

Amar, P. (2013), *The Security Archipelago: Human-Security States, Sexuality Politics, and the End of Neoliberalism*, Durham: Duke University Press.

Auyero, J. (2012), *Patients of the State: The Politics of Waiting in Argentina*, Durham: Duke University Press Books.

Awwad, J. (2010), 'The Postcolonial Predicament of Gay Rights in the Queen Boat Affair', *Communication and Critical/Cultural Studies*, 7 (3): 318–36.

Bloch, E. (1995), *The Principle of Hope* – Volume 1, Cambridge: MIT Press.

Borges, J. L. (1964), *Labyrinths: Selected Stories & Other Writings*, Massachusetts: New Directions Publishing.

Brenner, N. (1999), 'Beyond State-Centrism? Space, Territoriality, and Geographical Scale in Globalization Studies', *Theory and Society*, 28 (1): 39–78.

Butler, J. (2009), *Frames of War: When Is Life Grievable?* New York: Verso.

Butler, J. (2016), 'Rethinking Vulnerability and Resistance', in J. Butler, Z. Gambetti and L. Sabsay (eds), *Vulnerability in Resistance*, 12–27, Durham and London: Duke University Press.

Chu, J. Y. (2010), *Cosmologies of Credit: Transnational Mobility and the Politics of Destination in China*, Durham: Duke University Press.

Egyptian Initiative for Personal Rights (2016), 'Outrageous Prison Terms for So-Called "Debauchery Cases": Orchestrated Vice Police Campaign against Gay and Transgender People Continues', press release, 30 April. Available online: https://eipr.org/en/press/2016/04/outrageous-prison-terms-so-called-%E2%80%9Cdebauchery-cases%E2%80%9D-orchestrated-vice-police-campaign (accessed 19 April 2021).

Foucault, M. (2010), *The Birth of Biopolitics: Lectures at the Collège de France, 1978–1979*, New York: Picador.

Garcia, A. (2017), 'Heaven', in J. Biehl and P. Locke (eds), *Unfinished: The Anthropology of Becoming*, 111–29, Durham: Duke University Press Books.

Graeber, D. (2011), *Revolutions in Reverse: Essays on Politics, Violence, Art, and Imagination*, New York: Autonomedia.

Hage, G. (2009), *Waiting*, Melbourne: Melbourne University Press.

Hamid, D. A. (2017), *The Trap: Punishing Sexual Difference in Egypt*, Al Qahirah: Egyptian Initiative for Personal Rights.

Hegazi, S. (2018), 'Sarah Hegazi', Facebook, 26 July. Available online: https://www.facebook.com/sarah.hegazi1 (accessed 27 July 2018).

Human Rights Watch (2004), *In a Time of Torture: The Assault on Justice in Egypt's Crackdown on Homosexual Conduct*, New York: Human Rights Watch.

Human Rights Watch (2017), 'Egypt: Mass Arrests amid LGBT Media Blackout', 6 October. Available online: https://www.hrw.org/news/2017/10/06/egypt-mass-arrests-amid-lgbt-media-blackout (accessed 2 February 2020).

Ingold, T. (2011), *Being Alive: Essays on Movement, Knowledge and Description*, London: Routledge.

Massumi, B. (2015), *Politics of Affect*, Cambridge: Polity.

Mendos, L. (2019), *State-sponsored Homophobia* (13th edition), Geneva: ILGA World.

Merabet, S. (2015), *Queer Beirut*, Austin: University of Texas Press.

Mohaiemen, N. (2010), 'Otondro Prohori: Guarding Who? Against What?', in M. Narula et al. (eds), *Sarai Reader 08: Fear*, 81–90, Delhi: Centre for the Study of Developing

Societies. Available online: http://archive.sarai.net/files/original/8d0f60754aa7f07dd3b 1a218837935d.pdf (accessed 15 May 2021).

Muñoz, J. E. (2009), *Cruising Utopia: The Then and There of Queer Futurity*, New York: New York University Press.

Pratt, N. (2007), 'The Queen Boat Case in Egypt: Sexuality, National Security and State Sovereignty', *Review of International Studies*, 33 (1): 129–44.

Schlutz, A. M. (2010), *Mind's World: Imagination and Subjectivity from Descartes to Romanticism*, Seattle: University of Washington Press.

Simone, A. (2010), *City Life from Jakarta to Dakar: Movements at the Crossroads*, New York: Routledge.

Weeks, K. (2011), *The Problem with Work: Feminism, Marxism, Antiwork Politics, and Postwork Imaginaries*, Durham: Duke University Press.

Chapter 2

TELLING A DIFFERENT STORY: ON THE POLITICS OF REPRESENTING AFRICAN LGBTQ MIGRANTS, REFUGEES AND ASYLUM SEEKERS

John Marnell

As lesbian, gay, bisexual, transgender and queer[1] (LGBTQ) migrants, refugees and asylum seekers[2] become an increasingly visible population, their experiences of suffering and persecution are beginning to reach a wider audience. Although produced with the best of intentions – for example, to spotlight the gross inadequacies of existing protection mechanisms – academic, journalistic and activist depictions of LGBTQ migration tend to reduce their subjects' lives to a singular narrative of victimhood (Giametta 2020). Those coming from African countries are particularly susceptible to this treatment due to the pervasiveness of the 'homophobic continent' trope in the Western imagination (Thoreson 2014). In presenting LGBTQ migrants as simultaneously helpless and heroic – that is, as innocent yet courageous victims whose survival depends on outside intervention – mainstream portrayals reinforce a geopolitical dichotomy that imagines 'savage' Africa in opposition to the 'progressive' West (Rao 2020).[3] There is also a recognized tendency to replicate colonial or homonationalist logics when discussing Global North efforts to protect LGBTQ Africans (Kinsman 2018). This can be seen in a recent *Washington Post* article that contrasts the 'violent homophobia' of Uganda and Kenya with the joy of dressing up for a night out in Canada (Bearak 2020). What this journalist fails to mention is the neoliberal politics governing Canada's border regime and the documented challenges that LGBTQ refugees face upon being resettled there (Murray 2016).

Increased visibility of LGBTQ migration is undoubtedly a positive development, in that it places both countries of origin and countries of reception under scrutiny. What is concerning is the prominence of the 'single story' of African homo/transphobia within these depictions (Marnell 2014; Ndashe 2013). By perpetuating a simplistic oppression-to-liberation narrative, scholars, journalists and activists downgrade individuals with complex lives, identities and motivations to stock characters. Recognizing this propensity is vital if we are to more accurately theorize the socio-political conditions that compel LGBTQ Africans to leave their homes and the adverse conditions they encounter at various stages of their migration trajectories.

In this chapter, I share findings from an arts-based research project with LGBTQ migrants living in Johannesburg, South Africa. In analysing the project's creative outputs, I argue for a more expansive reading of LGBTQ movement within and from the African continent. The textual and visual materials that emerged from the project suggest that LGBTQ migrants are eager to counter dominant assumptions about their identities and experiences. Such depictions do not diminish the horrors of homo/transphobia, the arduous journeys that LGBTQ migrants make or the deplorable living conditions they often find themselves in. Rather, they remind those who engage them that LGBTQ migrants are multifaceted individuals with complex histories, needs and desires. This is evident from participants' self-depictions as spiritual, nurturing, erotic, resilient and family-orientated, even when their lives are marred by pain and hardship.

As well as probing specific creative works, I pose a more general question for those researching LGBTQ migration: how do the methods we use shape the stories we tell? In interrogating this question, I underline the value of providing LGBTQ migrants with the tools to craft their own stories. In making this argument, I do not mean to suggest that analyses centred on homo/transphobic persecution or procedural shortcomings are unnecessary. Such work has been, and will continue to be, urgently required. However, by limiting our critical focus to specific concerns – normally those that align with Global North political interests – migration scholars do a disservice to those whose lives we seek to document and understand.

Research context: Intersections of homo/transphobia and xenophobia

South Africa has long served as a reception country for LGBTQ persons seeking safety. Its reputation as a desirable destination stems from both its rights-based legislative framework, including a constitutional protection against sexuality- and gender-based discrimination, and its self-representation as the continent's most diverse and tolerant society (Camminga 2019). In order to comply with the constitution, South Africa's Refugees Act explicitly recognizes persecution on the basis of sexuality and/or gender as legitimate grounds for refugee status, making it the only jurisdiction on the continent to offer formal protection to LGBTQ persons fleeing persecution.

Despite these impressive legal provisions, LGBTQ people in South Africa continue to face institutional prejudice and high rates of violence, often in extreme forms (Gandar 2021). This is typically attributed to lingering misconceptions about sexual and gender diversity, specifically the belief that any deviation from heteronormativity is unnatural, un-African and ungodly (Vincent and Howell 2014). In many ways, this belief is a legacy of South Africa's history of colonial occupation and racial segregation, both of which were characterized by intense anxieties over sexual 'purity' and featured punitive laws intended to reproduce the heteronormative social order (Marnell et al. 2021).

Susceptibility to discrimination is heightened for those who identify as both LGBTQ *and* a migrant, courtesy of widespread xenophobia in many parts of the country (Beetar 2016). Although ostensibly driven by fears over 'escalating' immigration rates, anti-foreigner sentiments in South Africa can also be attributed to long-term governance failures, specifically the state's inability to address mass unemployment, wealth disparity and unequal access to land, resources and services (Landau 2019). It is for this reason that xenophobia is often directed at those viewed as competitors for socio-economic opportunities, rather than at foreigners across the board. LGBTQ migrants – the majority of whom are poor, black and from elsewhere on the African continent – represent a double threat, in that they fail to meet the minimum standards of heteronormativity and nationalism. In spite of this, South Africa continues to be regarded as a safe haven, attracting significant numbers of LGBTQ persons fleeing violence and persecution (Dill et al. 2016).

The drivers and impacts of homo/transphobia on the African continent are widely documented. Scholars convincingly argue that anti-LGBTQ crackdowns need to be situated within a historical and social context if they are to be properly understood, noting the influence of colonization, globalization, neoliberalism and other factors on local contestations over sexuality and gender (Hendriks and Spronk 2020). Although couched in the vocabulary of morals, traditions and family values, anti-LGBTQ rhetoric is best understood as a political manoeuvre (Msibi 2011). In denouncing LGBTQ identities as unnatural and immoral, social elites are able to produce a new form of patriarchy embedded in distorted religious/cultural norms (Tamale 2014). The widely held view that LGBTQ identities were imported to Africa through Western imperialism can be read as both a pushback against global power imbalances and an effort to bolster the status and authority of political leaders (Youde 2017).

Despite this critical work on the political, historical and discursive dynamics of homo/transphobia, scholars, journalists and activists continue to fall back on oversimplified accounts of anti-LGBTQ policies and practices. This has led African scholars like Zethu Matebeni (2014), Stella Nyanzi (2014) and Sokari Ekine (2013) to critique the neo-colonial impulse within much of the literature and to question the categories at the heart of Western ontological and epistemological traditions. While this chapter is itself a product of said traditions, it seeks to complicate hegemonic portrayals of sexual and gender rights on the African continent by exposing their dissonances and complexities.

Bodies and borders: The queer turn in migration studies

Interest in LGBTQ mobilities has intensified in recent decades, with scholars challenging the default conceptualization of the migrating subject as heterosexual and cisgender, not just in academic literature but also in policy responses, humanitarian interventions and bureaucratic practices (Mole 2021). Research has overwhelmingly concentrated on the ways in which asylum regimes disadvantage LGBTQ claimants, especially the difficulty they face in 'proving' their identities and related persecution (Güler 2019).

This fixation on barriers to legal protection extends to research on South Africa. Data suggests that 'implementation of [the country's] progressive legislation is fraught with inconsistencies' (Dill et al. 2016: 86), resulting in LGBTQ migrants being unable to exercise the rights guaranteed to them. A number of studies highlight failings within the Department of Home Affairs (DHA) – the state entity overseeing immigration and asylum – including discriminatory behaviours by state officials, egregious misapplications of law and endemic corruption (Mudarikwa et al. 2021; Koko et al. 2018). Ali Bhagat (2018) notes that navigating institutions like DHA 'poses particular challenges to queer asylum seekers where their race, class, and sexuality intersect to create tiered dimensions of discrimination' (160). He reads these experiences as evidence of a 'politics of abandonment' (159), asserting that the state is a complicit actor in violence against LGBTQ migrants. The heteronormative logic governing South Africa's asylum regime has also drawn criticism, with B Camminga (2019) tracking multiple ways in which the system fails transgender and gender-diverse migrants.

In addition to these legal and bureaucratic hurdles, LGBTQ migrants in South Africa face widespread prejudice. Studies point to multiple challenges, including social exclusion, community harassment, and physical, sexual and emotional violence (Beetar 2016). Many of the struggles faced by LGBTQ migrants mirror those of their cis-heterosexual counterparts, but are compounded by a perceived transgression of sexual and gender norms: 'Queer migrants do not experience homophobia/transphobia in one place and xenophobia in another, but rather live both concurrently. It is from the intersections of these (and other) forms of oppression that specific vulnerabilities emerge' (Marnell et al. 2021: 5).

By exposing obstacles to accessing and exercising rights, the literature cited above provides an important foundation for analysing the political, social and cultural dynamics shaping South Africa's response to LGBTQ migration. However, in centring narratives of institutional discrimination, existing studies perpetuate a one-dimensional reading of LGBTQ migrant lives, even if they do so unintentionally. They also imply that LGBTQ mobility is best theorized in relation to bureaucratic practices. For research situated in the Global North, it is usually homo/transphobia within countries of origin that is emphasized. As Eithne Luibhéid (2005) observes, accounts of LGBTQ migration – regardless of form or intent – remain organized around 'a narrative of movement from repression to freedom, or a heroic journey undertaken in search of liberation' (xxv). This narrative arc is also present in research on Global South contexts, although here there is likely a parallel focus on homo/transphobia within transit and reception countries. Considerable effort has now gone into debunking this oppression-to-liberation framing (Akin 2019; Raboin 2017), yet even this work continues to place state responses at the centre of any analysis. What is absent is the possibility of Global South countries being sites of belonging and survival, even if simultaneously marked by violence and insecurity.

While I recognize the importance of exposing the heteronormative underpinnings of asylum systems, I also believe there is great value in expanding the analytical frames used to make sense of LGBTQ mobilities. As the data presented in this chapter attests, LGBTQ migrant lives are complex: they can be joyful, intimate and optimistic as much as they can be sorrowful, despairing or lonely. LGBTQ migrants in South Africa and other locations encounter regular homo/transphobia, but they also build communities, develop livelihoods, form relationships and engage in social activities. In pivoting attention towards the quotidian aspects of my participants' everyday realities, I aim to build on Martin Manalansan's (2014) critical work on 'mess, clutter and muddled entanglements' (94) in LGBTQ migrant lives in the United States. Like Manalansan, I seek to challenge the necrophilic vein running through LGBTQ migration research by showing that *aliveness* can be present even within contexts marked by neglect and violence. I hope to show that my participants' lives – like those of other African LGBTQ migrants – are 'not always about misery, complete desolation, and abandonment but can also gesture to moments of vitality, pleasure and fabulousness' (Manalansan 2014: 100).

Creative methods: Participatory storytelling in action

Arts-based research (ABR) is increasingly recognized as a useful tool when investigating everyday lived realities and is particularly noted for its 'capacity to access and communicate sensuous, affective, tacit and embodied aspects' of human experience (Nunn 2017: 4). As well as fostering collaborative, participant-centred meaning-making, ABR has the potential to evoke strong cognitive and emotional responses, both for those involved in the research process and for those who engage with any outputs. This is because ABR 'enables a diversity of experiences to be communicated in ways that disrupt "common sense" understandings and act as a reminder that there are possibilities for things to be otherwise' (Foster 2016: 1). Creative methods can be particularly useful when engaging marginalized or 'hidden' populations because they not only foreground the lived experiences of research participants, but also validate those individuals' self-representations and signifying practices (Kihato 2009).

However, while creative techniques can open up new channels for generating and sharing knowledge, they are not innately 'empowering', nor are they free of the ethical dilemmas plaguing other forms of social research (Ellsworth 1992). Indeed, many creative research practitioners caution against overblown claims, especially the notion that ABR can 'give voice' to those who are silenced (Walsh 2014). There is also a risk of romanticizing ABR's epistemological foundation, specifically the idea that 'people are transparently knowable to themselves'

(Gallacher and Gallagher 2008: 502) and therefore the only ones truly capable of analysing their lives.

As a proponent of creative methodologies, I remain cognizant of these limitations, but I also recognize that ABR provides useful opportunities for exploring complex social phenomena. As Elsa Oliveira (2016) argues, ABR approaches, when used appropriately and responsibly, can 'unveil a wealth of information that other more traditional methods are unable to offer', while also creating the possibility for 'transformative moments for all involved – researchers, participants and public audiences alike' (276).

Project summary: Zine-making with LGBTQ migrants

The data presented here emerged out of an intensive storytelling workshop with eight LGBTQ migrants from the Southern Africa region. It is part of a larger corpus of work known as the MoVE: Methods|Visual|Explore Project at the African Centre for Migration and Society.[4] Grounded in the practices and pedagogies of popular education theorists like Paulo Freire, Orlando Fals Borda and Augusto Boal, the workshop used creative expression to facilitate deep thinking about the political, social and cultural issues shaping participants' experiences. Over four weeks, participants were introduced to a range of expressive modes, including applied drama, visual art, narrative writing and symbolic/spatial map-making. These techniques were then used to interrogate and analyse participants' memories, emotions and hopes.[5]

The workshop culminated in the creation of individual zines based on participants' stories. Zines are self-made, low-budget publications that usually deal with controversial or niche topics (Oliveira and Vearey 2016). They often employ unpolished layouts and DIY designs that can be easily reproduced. For Barbara Guzzetti and Margaret Gamboa (2004), zines represent 'an act of civil disobedience; a tool for inspiring other forms of activism; and a medium through which [their creators] effect changes within themselves' (411).

In order to protect privacy, participants were encouraged to publish their zines under pseudonyms, although some opted to use their real names since this information was already on the public record. Participants were also free to decide which identifying details would be included in publicly accessible materials, including academic papers. Thus, countries of origin are only specified here if participants gave explicit permission.

Complex narratives: When LGBTQ migrants tell their own stories

The discussion below draws on both creative works and spoken reflections. Because of space limitations, I restrict my analysis to the final zines, as participants considered these to be their most important workshop outputs. As well as searching out key themes within written texts, I look to interactions between different communication modalities, including visual, verbal and interactional narratives (Vacchelli 2018). In other words, I examine not just the content of creative artefacts – that is, the placement of words and images – but also the embodied, subjective, contextual and structural factors that shape the production of meanings (Riessman 2008). My interpretation takes into account behaviours observed during the workshop, comments made during feedback sessions and the intended audiences for the zines.

Agency and resilience: Rethinking migration catalysts

As anticipated, participants' cross-border movements were viewed as significant life events. Each person's migration story – from initial thoughts about leaving through to arrival in Johannesburg – was unpacked on multiple occasions using a range of expressive modes. This allowed participants to analyse their motivations, aspirations and experiences in ways they might not have done previously. While the decision to feature migration stories in the zines was not unexpected, the ways in which participants framed their journeys demonstrate their commitment to expanding mainstream narratives. Participants emphasized the compounding factors informing their decisions to move, challenging the assumption that sexuality/gender is the sole reason that LGBTQ persons migrate. There was also noticeable pushback against victim narratives, with participants highlighting their agency even within oppressive social environments.

Jonso, a transgender migrant, was adamant about foregrounding the economic circumstances precipitating his migration. He describes his father's death and the uncertain economic position in which this left his family, as well as his desire to contribute financially by sending remittances home from South Africa. While Jonso's sexuality – at the time of migrating he identified as lesbian – was a motivating factor, albeit one not openly discussed with his family, he felt it would be deceptive to suggest it was the sole reason. Furthermore, Jonso did not want his zine to play into the stereotype that Zimbabwean society is homogeneously homo/transphobic. Reflecting on his decision to migrate in a post-workshop interview, Jonso stressed that he made choices under difficult circumstances, rather than being forcibly exiled due to homo/transphobic abuse: 'Yeah, things are bad in Zim[babwe], but it's not like people think, [not] for me anyway. My family didn't do anything bad. I wanted to help them. That is why I moved.'

Hotstix, a lesbian from Zimbabwe, shared Jonso's desire to diversify existing representations. Her zine, aptly titled *Survival of the Fittest*, features a lengthy account of her illegal border crossing and her daily struggles as an undocumented migrant in Johannesburg. Without glossing over the dangers she encountered on her journey or the struggles she has faced, Hotstix highlights her fortitude and determination, believing this to be a more accurate representation of her character. Scattered throughout the main text are bolded words and phrases – 'BRAVE', 'TOUGH' and 'STANDING TALL' – which Hotstix regards as her defining attributes. In a post-workshop interview, Hotstix explained her decision to present her experiences in this way: 'These words here [on the page] are me – I'm strong, I'm brave, I do what I need to do. I wanted that to be part of it, you know? I deal with shit, but I'm still a survivor.' As this reflection makes clear, Hotstix was not interested in appearing as a victim. Instead, she proudly and unambiguously asserts her capacity to endure. This can be read as a declaration of her 'right to the city', in that she lays claim to both physical space and social belonging (see Beebeejaun 2017).

In presenting these alternative narratives, I am not suggesting that LGBTQ migrants do not flee horrific situations. Zines from this very workshop highlight the urgency with which many LGBTQ persons leave their countries of origin, as well as the fear and trauma they carry with them. In Mike's zine, for example, he shares a distributing account of state-sponsored persecution, including being arrested and detained after an LGBTQ event. However, when read as a body of work, the zines push back against simplistic readings, revealing LGBTQ migrant lives to be about more than suffering and alienation. They gesture to their creators' ability to survive within ambivalent, often hostile social locations, not by sheer luck but because of various coping strategies they deploy.[6] The social, political, economic and legal conditions in which LGBTQ migrants find themselves certainly constrain their choices, yet these individuals continue to assert some level of agency (Mai 2018).

Subversive sexualities: Erotic encounters as sites of belonging

Participants' desire to trouble hegemonic representations is perhaps most visible in their stories about sex, love and relationships. Tino, a gay asylum seeker from Zimbabwe, was resolute that his sexual escapades occupy a prominent position in his zine. He refused to present a sanitized or palatable version of his erotic life, arguing that to do so would deny a core aspect of his being. In the following story extract, Tino presents a detailed account of group sex:

> One day I was with two of my friends and we decided to invite some guys to come over. That day it was all get naked, legs up, let the flow be in control. Our motto was whatever happens here remains between us. The following morning I felt so exhausted. When I looked around, I could see torn Health4Men condom wrappers scattered around the room. The smell of poppers, lubricant, cum, weed and cigarettes had mixed to form a new sort of smell that is different to anything else on the planet. I forced myself from the bed, opened the window and started to clean up all the mess.

Tino's insistence that this story be included, despite protests from other workshop participants, testifies to a deep pride in his sexuality. There is a clear lack of shame or embarrassment in his language, which he revised multiple times to better convey his meaning.

It must be acknowledged that this anecdote forms part of a larger narrative about Yeoville, a low socio-economic suburb with a sizeable migrant population.

The group sex scene follows a description of homophobic taunts and physical violence, thereby juxtaposing moments of inclusion and exclusion within the same geographical zone (Figures 1 and 2). In his post-workshop interview, Tino clarified his intention:

> Yeoville can be very dangerous, but it was also home for many years. Here [referring to collaged visual elements] I wanted the pictures to show pain. It's the fear of being attacked. When you feel alone and afraid, you know? This stuff is about fun [referring to the pictures on the opposite page]. These cute guys, the condoms, the weed, the poppers – they represent fun things. I have sex. I like men. I don't feel ashamed about being gay. Yeoville is both these things. It's hard because of the violence and the police and the *tsotsis* [gangsters], but I have so many good memories. There have been hook-ups, parties, shagging, chilling with guys. It was a place where sometimes I felt unsafe and sometimes I was happy.

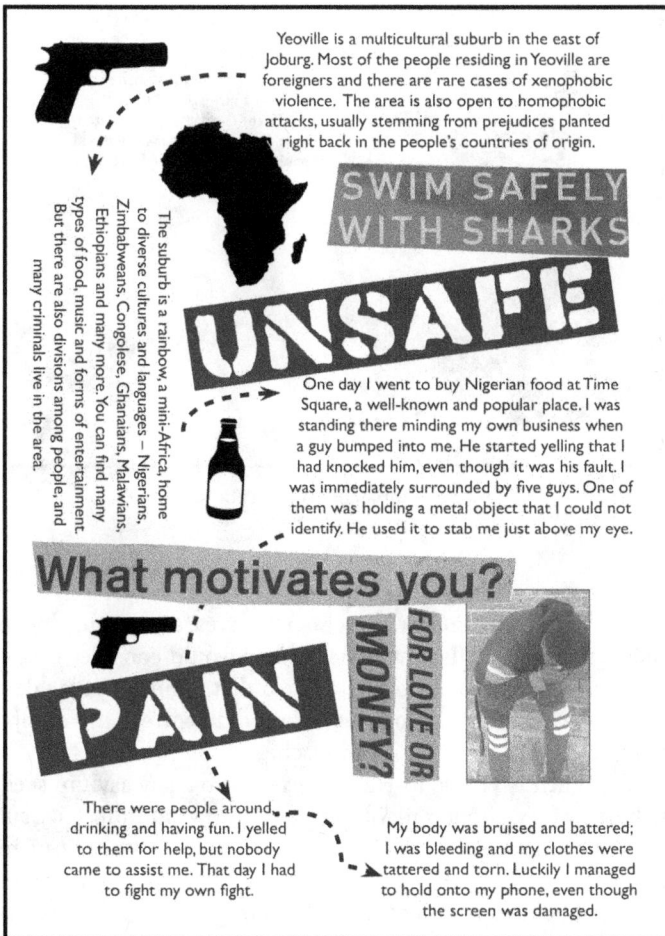

Yeoville is a multicultural suburb in the east of Joburg. Most of the people residing in Yeoville are foreigners and there are rare cases of xenophobic violence. The area is also open to homophobic attacks, usually stemming from prejudices planted right back in the people's countries of origin.

SWIM SAFELY WITH SHARKS

UNSAFE

The suburb is a rainbow, a mini-Africa, home to diverse cultures and languages – Nigerians, Zimbabweans, Congolese, Ghanaians, Malawians, Ethiopians and many more. You can find many types of food, music and forms of entertainment. But there are also divisions among people, and many criminals live in the area.

One day I went to buy Nigerian food at Time Square, a well-known and popular place. I was standing there minding my own business when a guy bumped into me. He started yelling that I had knocked him, even though it was his fault. I was immediately surrounded by five guys. One of them was holding a metal object that I could not identify. He used it to stab me just above my eye.

What motivates you?

PAIN

FOR LOVE OR MONEY?

There were people around, drinking and having fun. I yelled to them for help, but nobody came to assist me. That day I had to fight my own fight.

My body was bruised and battered; I was bleeding and my clothes were tattered and torn. Luckily I managed to hold onto my phone, even though the screen was damaged.

Figure 1 First half of Tino's zine spread about Yeoville.

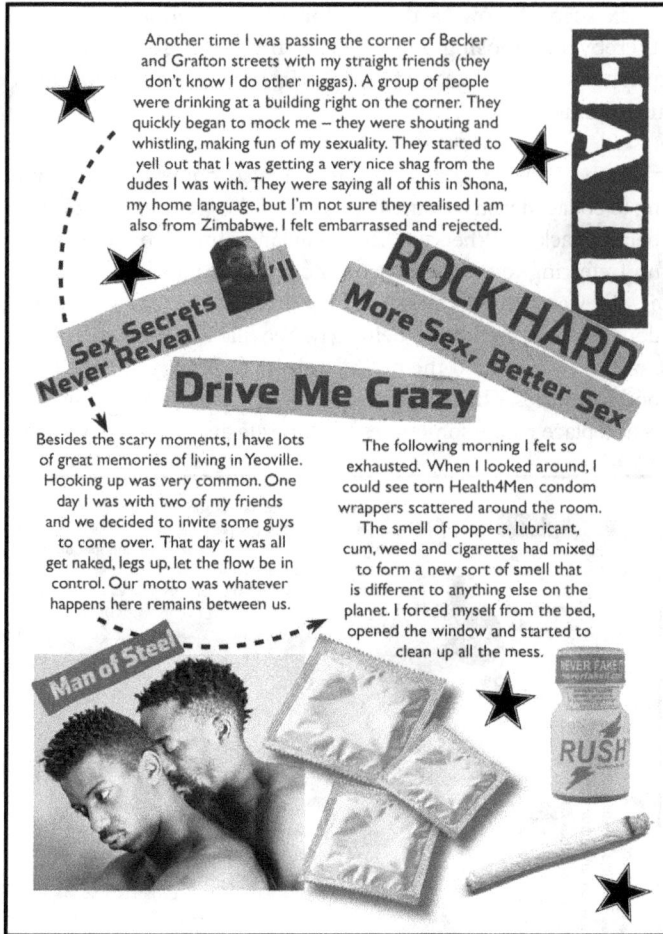

Another time I was passing the corner of Becker and Grafton streets with my straight friends (they don't know I do other niggas). A group of people were drinking at a building right on the corner. They quickly began to mock me – they were shouting and whistling, making fun of my sexuality. They started to yell out that I was getting a very nice shag from the dudes I was with. They were saying all of this in Shona, my home language, but I'm not sure they realised I am also from Zimbabwe. I felt embarrassed and rejected.

HATE

Sex Secrets Never Reveal

I'll

ROCK HARD

More Sex, Better Sex

Drive Me Crazy

Besides the scary moments, I have lots of great memories of living in Yeoville. Hooking up was very common. One day I was with two of my friends and we decided to invite some guys to come over. That day it was all get naked, legs up, let the flow be in control. Our motto was whatever happens here remains between us.

The following morning I felt so exhausted. When I looked around, I could see torn Health4Men condom wrappers scattered around the room. The smell of poppers, lubricant, cum, weed and cigarettes had mixed to form a new sort of smell that is different to anything else on the planet. I forced myself from the bed, opened the window and started to clean up all the mess.

Man of Steel

RUSH

NEVER FAKE

Figure 2 Second half of Tino's zine spread about Yeoville.

Tino refuses to capitulate to conservative social mores, as signified by his decision to unashamedly feature details that some readers would consider explicit. This is a radical departure from the 'innocent' figures that haunt popular depictions of 'LGBTQ Africa'. By placing his erotic life front and centre, Tino complicates the view that LGBTQ migrants simply await rescue.

A similar approach is visible in Henry's zine. Also a gay asylum seeker, Henry chose to include a story about a night out in Hillbrow, an inner-city suburb with a reputation for crime. Like Tino, Henry disrupts the notoriety of his setting, identifying it as a site where pleasure is a genuine possibility. The brief narrative describes his joy at being out with other LGBTQ migrants and features a flirtatious encounter:

A guy came up to me and pulled me aside. 'You really like dancing, hey?' he said with a deep voice. 'I have been watching you since I got here.'

Set among pictures of beer bottles, musical notes and dancing figures, Henry's narrative offers a counterpoint to experiences described elsewhere in his zine, such as struggles around employment, documentation and housing. By including this party scene, Henry reminds readers that he and his fellow LGBTQ migrants enjoy drinking, dancing and flirting. These activities, when undertaken in oppressive social contexts, may even be read as acts of resistance, in that urban spaces linked to division, neglect and oppression are reconfigured as sites of eroticism, joy and agency.

The examples above might seem frivolous, but they actually provide significant insights into how their creators experience desire, navigate relationships and forge a sense of belonging. Intimate encounters can be more than a simple physical exchange, as shown in other studies. For example, Yener Bayramoğlu and Margreth Lünenborg (2018) find that online dating platforms offer possibilities for LGBTQ migrants to access information and develop coping strategies. Henry's and Tino's narratives may not reference digital communication, but they do suggest a connection between the erotic sphere and survival tactics. For individuals with limited social or economic capital, erotic encounters may provide a means for expressing identity and establishing linkages. What is most apparent, however, is the centrality of sex to Tino's and Henry's sense of self.

Chosen families: Building networks of care

Other participants opted for a different approach, choosing to showcase their lives in ways that would be recognizable and relatable. For these individuals, it was important to portray themselves as upstanding and constructive members of society. One way this was achieved was by foregrounding piety and devotion. This was done in the hope of countering harmful stereotypes, such as the widespread belief that LGBTQ individuals are promiscuous, immoral and demonic (Kaoma 2018).

Zee, a lesbian migrant, wrote of her involvement with the LGBT Ministry at the Holy Trinity Catholic Church. She contrasts negative experiences in conservative religious institutions with her joy at finding an affirming faith community:

I had been told countless times by my mother that I would never be accepted by the Church, that God does not love people like me. So how did this place [the LGBT Ministry] exist? Since joining the group, I have learnt that I am loved by God, that He never makes mistakes, that I am a human being. I have found a family away from home and it has become my saving grace. I have a profound love for the LGBTI group: the support that is showered upon each of us, the unity of our chosen family, the respect that is shown towards all sexualities.

To communicate the strength of her faith, Zee illustrated her story with large crosses: 'They show that I'm a Christian, that I believe in God. ... I want people to know we [LGBTQ Christians] are here in Africa.'

Dee Jay, a lesbian asylum seeker from Zimbabwe, is also a member of the LGBT Ministry. She explores the group's role in her life through a collage that combines visual and textual elements (Figure 3). Over a photograph of the church's façade she placed a series of bolded and capitalized words, including 'SUPPORT', 'HOPE', 'OPPORTUNITIES', 'FAITH' and 'LOVE'. She titled the page 'My chosen family', indicating that her fellow group members are more than casual acquaintances. In a post-workshop interview, Dee Jay spoke of her pride at belonging to the LGBT Ministry and the positive role that Christianity plays in her life. In particular, she indicated a desire to show LGBTQ persons as active and dedicated members of faith communities (Marnell 2021; van Klinken 2019).

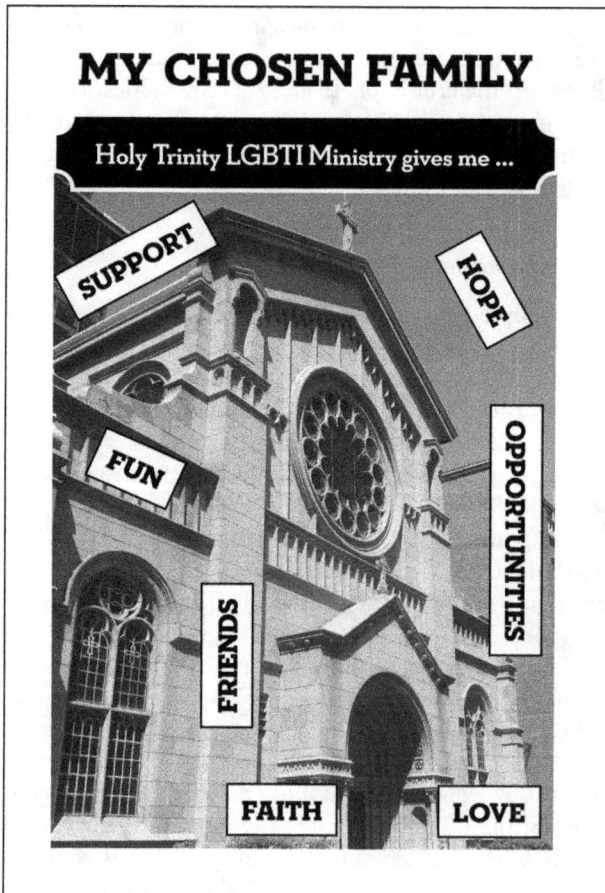

Figure 3 Dee Jay's 'Chosen family' collage about the LGBT Ministry.

Zee and Dee Jay were intentional in how they portrayed their religious lives, explaining that they wanted to depict LGBTQ migrants as devout, committed and organized. Both women have forged key relationships through the LGBT Ministry and continue to invest their time, energy and resources into the group so that others can receive similar support. By dedicating space in their zines to this facet of their lives, and by employing iconography with which readers would be familiar, Zee and Dee Jay challenge exclusionary religious discourses about LGBTQ persons.

Everyday life: Beauty in the banal

Participants agreed that the discrimination they experience is at least partially attributable to misrecognition, in that pervasive misconceptions make it difficult for locals to view them as brothers and sisters in need. They hoped their zines would underline commonalities, such as humans' shared need for love, sustenance, shelter and connection. Many participants chose to depict their daily struggles, noting that these are strikingly similar to the challenges facing other marginalized communities in South Africa. Jonso, for example, wrote of his battle to find employment, explaining that 'everything in South Africa costs money – without a job, it is difficult to secure accommodation, buy food or just survive'. Later in his zine, he recounts a four-month period of homelessness, describing the experience as 'hurtful and humiliating'.

Interestingly, Jonso decided to contrast these social challenges with the more pleasurable aspects of his life, such as evenings spent dancing with friends or sharing food: 'When I am at home, I enjoy cooking pork bones and *pap* [maize meal]. They are my favourite foods because they remind me of my father. Sometimes I invite friends over for dinner.' In South Africa, a country riven by unemployment, homelessness and poverty, Jonso's struggles may seem unremarkable, but it is exactly this ordinariness that he wished to communicate. By presenting the minutiae of his everyday life, Jonso hoped to dispel the misconception that LGBTQ migrants are unfamiliar and illegible.

Context matters: On potential misreadings

While the stories analysed here speak to the value of diverse representations, they run the risk of being misinterpreted or romanticized. The level of agency that marginalized populations actually wield continues to be debated. On the one hand, scholars like James Scott (1998) speak of 'everyday forms of resistance', which he defines as 'quiet, disguised, anonymous, often undeclared forms of resisting' (37) deployed by those with limited access to public power. On the other hand, Benedict Kerkvliet (2009) cautions against hurried assumptions about seemingly subversive activities: 'These are typically things people do while trying to "cut corners" so as to get by. Although they may approach becoming, or seem at first glance to be, forms of everyday resistance, they are not' (237). Julian Reid (2018) extends this critique by questioning the scholarly preoccupation with resilience. This once useful concept, he argues, is now little more than a cliché, bandied about with little critical reflection or interpretative clarity. While the current analysis is not framed in these terms, its focus on the politics of representation necessitates some level of engagement with these debates. Indeed, to overstate the positive aspects of LGBTQ migrant lives can simply reverse existing trends without interrogating their causes or impacts. How, then, does one interpret participant-generated stories without exaggerating claims to resistance or resilience?

Like any data, the zines need to be situated within a broader context; individual anecdotes are best read alongside competing or contradictory narratives, be they from the same project or external sources. Participants in this workshop were eager to portray different strands of their lives, but were also cautious about minimizing the challenges they face. Many chose to write about difficulties in accessing care or support, particularly discriminatory encounters with state institutions. Dee Jay, for example, chronicles her battle to survive on temporary asylum permits, which she has done for more than a decade and a half. As well as recounting dangerous nights spent outside Refugee Reception Offices and the frustration of having her case file repeatedly lost, Dee Jay recalls being mocked and humiliated by DHA staff:

> The man looked at me with disbelief and didn't waste time judging me. I remember him saying, *'Habe nahku umhlola wami kanti na Zimbabwe!'* – 'I don't believe there are gays in Zimbabwe!' I was the joke of the centre. I felt so humiliated. Within a few seconds, the room was filled with other employees who were called to see the lesbian from Zimbabwe. One even asked me if I had ever been with a man before. If these people knew what I had gone through, I thought to myself, they wouldn't be making a joke of my sexuality. Anger and hate brewed within me, and my eyes filled with tears.

This account echoes findings in other studies, reaffirming the degree to which stereotypes and misconceptions permeate South African state institutions (Marnell 2021; Mudarikwa et al. 2021; Bhagat 2018).

Hotstix also used her zine to spotlight institutional discrimination. She writes about two times she sought assistance from the South African Police Service, only to be confronted with prejudice and incompetence. She goes on to describe the horrific outcomes of these oppressive practices: 'LGBT people are being killed like flies, but the police turn a blind eye to our community.' Reflecting on this story in her post-workshop interview, Hotstix emphasized her desire to educate readers:

> Some of the challenges I face – like not having enough money to eat every day – are common, they are everywhere; there are lots of poor people. But other things I actually experience differently just because I'm a lesbian Zimbabwean. Like going to the police station, where you expect to be helped, but they don't help. … I chose to tell this story to enlighten people about the bad service people like me receive … These pages are about going to the police station and being rejected. It's about not being helped when you're in need. The pictures show how

I actually felt when this happened to me. I was broken, crushed, just like the plates in the picture. ... Even if someone has been killed, they won't do anything unless you give them money. It makes me angry, but I'm not going to hide who I am when I go there.

Yet, rather than dwell on these negative encounters, Hotstix opted to represent the full spectrum of her experiences. She was adamant that readers know about the hardship she endures as a lesbian migrant, but she also wanted to share more positive memories. Hence we see narratives of pain and injustice sitting alongside stories of love and community. It may be tempting for academics or journalists to zoom in on certain aspects of Hotstix's life – most likely her encounters with state-sponsored violence – but her zine pushes back against this myopic impulse, demanding instead that its creator be seen as a multifaceted individual.

Hotstix concludes her story about the police with an emotive plea: 'My greatest wish is to be appreciated and accepted, but most of all to be respected as a HUMAN BEING.' While these words are directed primarily at those who undermine Hotstix's safety and wellbeing, they also carry a warning for others. They remind the reader, including those of us pursuing scholarly ends, that the categories we use to describe people are never neutral; the analytic frames we deploy inevitably determine the stories we tell.

Cover art: Framing stories for public consumption

Participants regarded their zines as physical artefacts, objects to be held and flicked through, perhaps even passed from person to person. It is not surprising, then, that participants put considerable time and energy into their covers and titles. Participants refined their thinking by sharing prototypes and inviting feedback from the group. This iterative process allowed participants to think carefully about how their zines might be received and interpreted by readers.

Diverse visual techniques were employed to entice readers and signify meaning. Tino used collaged photographs of himself to illustrate the myriad challenges he faces, a message reinforced by his title: *The Trials of Tino*. Interestingly, while this cover elicits a palpable sense of danger and violence, its primary message is complicated by Tino's use of text. Overlaying the collage are the words 'Hard times don't kill you but make you stronger' – an unambiguous declaration of defiance and grit.

Jonso's back cover features a self-portrait overlaid with cut-out phrases, including the bold exclamations 'I'm happy', 'Zimbabwean' and 'Still strong!' Jonso later explained that he wants readers to look into his eyes and see that he is not ashamed. This message is reinforced by the pronouncement '100% STABANE' on the inside back cover. Here, Jonso pushes back against anti-LGBTQ discourses by reappropriating a derogatory term in isiZulu. When read together, these textual and visual elements communicate Jonso's deep pride in his identity and heritage.

One of the most evocative covers belongs to Hotstix (Figure 4). The back of her zine features a hand-drawn image within an outline of the African continent. It is unmistakably the Johannesburg skyline, indicated through famous landmarks such as the Hillbrow Tower. Feeding into the skyline from above are branches of a tree, each bough inscribed with a word, including 'Zimbabwean', 'lesbian', 'love' and 'accept' (among others). Underneath the skyline are the words 'Our home too' – another unequivocal avowal of LGBTQ migrants' right to the city. In a separate text box, Hotstix shares a short assessment of Johannesburg that includes the phrase 'Stigma and stereotypes are everywhere, but you have to focus on your own life and forget what people expect you to be.' This statement encapsulates the potential of diverse representations to complicate mainstream representations. Hotstix's desire to confront stereotypes also comes through in her opening statement: 'I want to educate those who don't know about these things and also share my feelings with the world so at least people might look at me differently.'

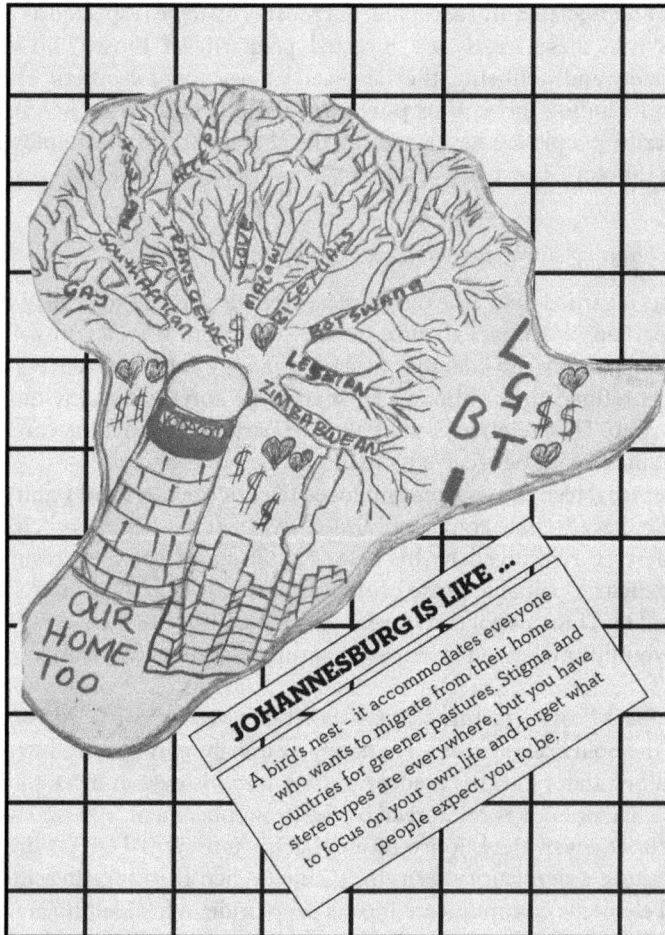

Figure 4 The back cover of Hotstix's zine.

Beyond the single story: On the value of diverse narratives

Many of the stories produced during the workshop were unsurprising. Participants felt compelled to document experiences of interpersonal violence, institutional discrimination and border crossings, both in a geographical and sociological sense. Participants also recorded their emotional traumas and everyday challenges, including the seemingly relentless struggle to carve out sites of belonging. Yet the zines are testament to the wide range of experiences that constitute participants' lives. Covering everything from the quotidian to the spiritual, the zines force readers to witness LGBTQ migrant lives as tangled, messy and manifold. Most importantly, they remind us – as academics, journalists and activists – that nuance and context are critical when documenting and analysing migration narratives.

It may be tempting to dismiss the more joyful or mundane anecdotes as outliers, as the experiences of a lucky few, but they are actually key threads in the larger tapestry of LGBTQ mobilities. The fact that LGBTQ migrants face harassment, discrimination, exploitation and violence is now well established, both here in South Africa and in other contexts, and it hardly bears repeating that research and advocacy on these topics must continue. But this cannot be our sole focus. The fact that participants in this study were so eager to expand the range of narratives about their lives raises pertinent questions about how LGBTQ migrants themselves want to be regarded. These individuals were eager to let people know about the bureaucratic and material obstacles they face, but they were equally committed to showcasing moments of connection, belonging and pleasure.

It must be acknowledged that this conviction evolved over the course of the workshop and was in many ways a product of the methodology employed. As well as introducing various storytelling techniques, the project offered participants an invaluable resource: time. Being part of a multi-week workshop allowed them to interrogate disparate experiences and to think critically about how, if at all, these should be framed and presented to public audiences. Unlike most research engagements, the workshop provided space for participants to consider how they wanted their narratives to be consumed. The vast majority of stories produced in the workshop did not make it into the zines. Sometimes this was because a story was deemed too private or emotional, while other times participants were content to share a narrative within the confines of the workshop venue. There were also moments when participants indicated boredom with particular themes/ topics because these had been covered elsewhere. Having curatorial control meant a lot to participants and they happily executed this responsibility, including making decisions about how I could interact with specific narratives (participants sometimes flagged stories as off-limits to me as a researcher, even though I had already seen, heard or read them).

While it is undeniable that creative methodologies foster opportunities for diverse narratives, it is unrealistic and impractical to suggest that all research adopt such an approach. These methodologies often require specialized skills, as well as significant financial and material resources. There is also hubris in assuming that certain types of research produce 'more authentic' forms of knowledge. Instead, this project foregrounds the necessity of plurality, both in a methodological and an empirical sense. The single story of LGBTQ migration is not the result of poorly executed studies or sloppy researchers, but rather stems from a commitment to exposing the interconnectedness of different regulatory regimes. Yet, in pursuing this aim, journalists, activists and scholars – myself included – determine which stories can and should receive attention. For us to see LGBTQ migrants differently, as Hotstix so eloquently implores us to do, we need to not only ask new questions but also create opportunities for LGBTQ migrants to engage meaningfully with their own narratives. Storytelling, in any of its forms, is one way this can be achieved.

Notes

1   Although none of the participants self-identified as 'queer', I include the term here as a way to acknowledge the ways in which cis-heteronormativity was challenged by participants during the project. I also wish to emphasize the murky politics circulating around Western ontological categories, such as their complicity in propagating particular notions of identity (i.e. as fixed, coherent and ahistorical).
2   Moving forward, this article uses 'LGBTQ migrants' as an umbrella term for LGBTQ migrants, refugees and asylum seekers. This is done in recognition that established legal categories do not always align with lived experiences or reflect individuals' self-identifications. In South Africa, for example, barriers to accessing the asylum system push some individuals who may be eligible for refugee protection into the immigration system or force them to remain undocumented. The 'correct' legal terms are used when clarification is needed or when referencing specific individuals.
3   Similar neo-colonial impulses have been detected in other geopolitical regions. For example, Hana Masri (2017) notes the lingering orientalism in depictions of LGBTQ migrants from the Middle East, especially the insinuation that such individuals must be 'rescued'.
4   Information about MoVE can be found at www.migration.org.za/move.
5   Given the limited space available, I am unable to provide a detailed overview of the workshop itself. For a discussion of theories and methods, see Marnell (in press). For practical information on individual activities, see the *Creative Resistance* toolkit (Marnell and Khan 2016).
6   While there is little data on how LGBTQ migrants tolerate hostile environments and possibly transform them into sites of belonging, it is illogical to assume that such processes are absent. I am thinking here of Don Mitchell and Nik Heynen's (2009) concept of a 'geography of survival', in which marginalized individuals invent coping strategies within locations marked by alienation, violence and surveillance.

References

Akin, D. (2019), 'Discursive Construction of Genuine LGBT Refugees', *Lambda Nordica*, 3/4: 21–46.
Bayramoğlu, Y. and M. Lünenborg (2018), 'Queer Migration and Digital Affects: Refugees Navigating from the Middle East via Turkey to Germany', *Sexuality and Culture*, 22 (4): 1019–36.

Bearak, M. (2020), '"We Were So Ready": LGBT Refugees in Kenya Live in Fear as Global Resettlement Is Put on Hold', *Washington Post*, 26 May. Available online: www.washingtonpost.com/world/africa/kenya-coronavirus-lgbt-refugees-resettlement/2020/05/26/3550cd0c-83ef-11ea-81a3-9690c9881111_story.html (accessed 15 December 2020).

Beebeejaun, Y. (2017), 'Gender, Urban Space, and the Right to Everyday Life', *Journal of Urban Affairs*, 39 (3): 323–34.

Beetar, M. (2016), 'Intersectional (Un)belongings: Lived Experiences of Xenophobia and Homophobia', *Agenda*, 30 (1): 96–103.

Bhagat, A. (2018), 'Forced (Queer) Migration and Everyday Violence: The Geographies of Life, Death and Access in Cape Town', *Geoforum*, 89: 155–63.

Camminga, B (2019), *Transgender Refugees and the Imagined South Africa: Bodies over Borders and Borders over Bodies*, Cham: Palgrave Macmillan.

Dill, L., J. Vearey, E. Oliveira and G. M. Castillo (2016), 'Son of the Soil … Daughters of the Land: Poetry Writing as a Strategy of Citizen-Making for Lesbian, Gay and Bisexual Migrants and Asylum Seekers in Johannesburg', *Agenda*, 30 (1): 85–95.

Ekine, S. (2013), 'Contesting Narratives of Queer Africa', in S. Ekine and H. Abbas (eds), *Queer African Reader*, 78–91, Cape Town: Pambazuka.

Ellsworth, E. (1992), 'Why Doesn't This Feel Empowering? Working through the Repressive Myths of Critical Pedagogy', in C. Luke and J. Gore (eds), *Feminisms and Critical Pedagogy*, 90–119, New York: Routledge.

Foster, V. (2016), *Collaborative Arts-Based Research for Social Justice*, Oxon: Routledge.

Gallacher, L. and M. Gallagher (2008), 'Methodological Immaturity in Childhood Research? Thinking through "Participatory Methods"', *Childhood*, 15 (4): 499–516.

Gandar, S. (2021), 'Bodies Pile Up as the Hate Crimes Bill Gathers Dust in Parliament', *Daily Maverick*, 27 April. Available online: https://www.dailymaverick.co.za/article/2021-04-27-bodies-pile-up-as-the-hate-crimes-bill-gathers-dust-in-parliament/ (accessed 20 May 2021).

Giametta, G. (2020), 'New Asylum Protection Categories and Elusive Filtering Devices: The Case of "Queer Asylum" in France and the UK', *Journal of Ethnic and Migration Studies*, 46 (1): 142–57.

Güler, A. (2019), 'Refugee Status Determination Process for LGBTI Asylum Seekers: (In)consistencies of States' Implementations with UNHCR's Authoritative Guidance', in A. Güler, M. Shevtsova and D. Venturi (eds), *LGBTI Asylum Seekers and Refugees from a Legal and Political Perspective: Persecution, Asylum and Integration*, 117–39, Cham: Springer.

Guzzetti, B. and M. Gamboa (2004), 'Zines for Social Justice: Adolescent Girls Writing on Their Own', *Reading Research Quarterly*, 39 (4): 408–36.

Hendriks, T. and R. Spronk (2020), 'Introduction: Reading "Sexualities" from "Africa"', in T. Hendriks and R. Spronk (eds), *Readings in Sexualities from Africa*, 1–17, Bloomington: Indiana University Press.

Kaoma, K. (2018), *Christianity, Globalization and Protective Homophobia: Democratic Contestation of Sexuality in Sub-Saharan Africa*, Cham: Springer.

Kerkvliet, B. (2009), 'Everyday Politics in Peasant Societies (and Ours)', *The Journal of Peasant Studies*, 36 (1): 227–43.

Kihato, C. (2009), 'Migration, Gender and Urbanisation in Johannesburg', PhD dissertation, University of South Africa, Pretoria.

Kinsman, G. (2018), 'Policing Borders and Sexual/Gender Identities: Queer Refugees in the Years of Canadian Neoliberalism and Homonationalism', in N. Nicol et al. (eds),

Envisioning Global LGBT Human Rights: (Neo)colonialism, Neoliberalism, Resistance and Hope, 97–129, London: Institute of Commonwealth Studies.

Koko, G., S. Monro and K. Smith (2018), 'Lesbian, Gay, Bisexual, Transgender, Queer (LGBTQ) Forced Migrants and Asylum Seekers: Multiple Discriminations', in Z. Matebeni, S. Monro and V. Reddy (eds), *Queer in Africa: LGBTQI Identities, Citizenship and Activism*, 158–77, Oxon: Routledge.

Landau, L. (2019), 'What's behind the Deadly Violence in South Africa? The Attacks on Immigrants are Neither Irrational Nor Spontaneous', *New York Times*, 16 September. Available online: www.nytimes.com/2019/09/16/opinion/south-africa-xenophobia-attacks.html (accessed 4 January 2021).

Luibhéid, E. (2005), 'Introduction: Queering Migration and Citizenship', in E. Luibhéid and L. Cantú, Jr. (eds), *Queer Migrations: Sexuality, US Citizenship and Border Crossings*, ix–xlvi, Minneapolis: University of Minnesota Press.

Mai, N. (2018), *Mobile Orientations: An Intimate Autoethnography of Migration, Sex Work and Humanitarian Borders*, Chicago: University of Chicago Press.

Manalansan, M. F. (2014), 'The "Stuff" of Archives: Mess, Migration, and Queer Lives', *Radical History Review*, 120: 94–107.

Marnell, J. (2014), 'Imagined Worlds', *Overland*, 216: 12–18.

Marnell, J. (2021), *Seeking Sanctuary: Stories of Sexuality, Faith and Migration*, Johannesburg: Wits University Press.

Marnell, J. (in press), 'Radical Imaginings: Queering the Politics and Praxis of Participatory Arts-Based Research', in S. Kindon, R. Pain and M. Kesby (eds), *Critically Engaging Participatory Action Research: Praxis, Paradox, Potential*, London: Routledge.

Marnell, J. and G. H. Khan (2016), *Creative Resistance: Participatory Methods for Engaging Queer Youth*, Johannesburg: GALA.

Marnell, J., E. Oliveira and G. H. Khan (2021), '"It's about Being Safe and Free to Be Who You Are": Exploring the Lived Experiences of Queer Migrants, Refugees and Asylum Seekers in South Africa', *Sexualities*, 24 (1/2): 86–110.

Masri, H. (2017), 'A Liberated Life? Thoughts on the Paradoxical Binds of Queer Refuge', *Kohl*, 3 (1): 37–40.

Matebeni, Z. (2014), 'How (not) to Write about Queer South Africa', in Z. Matebeni (ed.), *Reclaiming Afrikan: Queer Perspectives of Sexual and Gender Identity*, 61–4, Cape Town: Modjadji Books.

Mitchell, D. and N. Heynen (2009), 'The Geography of Survival and the Right to the City: Speculations on Surveillance, Legal Innovation, and the Criminalization of Intervention', *Urban Geography*, 30 (6): 611–32.

Mole, R. (2021), 'Introduction: Queering Migration and Asylum', in R. Mole (ed.), *Queer Migration and Asylum in Europe*, 1–12, London: UCL Press.

Msibi, T. (2011), 'The Lies We Have Been Told: On (Homo)sexuality in Africa', *Africa Today*, 58 (1): 55–77.

Mudarikwa, M., M. Gleckman-Krut, A-L. Payne, B Camminga and J. Marnell (2021), *LGBTI+ Asylum Seekers in South Africa: A Review of Refugee Status Denials Involving Sexual Orientation & Gender Identity*, Cape Town: LRC.

Murray, D. (2016), *Real Queer? Sexual Orientation and Gender Identity Refugees in the Canadian Refugee Apparatus*, London: Rowman & Littlefield.

Ndashe, S. (2013), 'The Single Story of "African Homophobia" Is Dangerous for LGBTI Activism', in S. Ekine and H. Abbas (eds), *Queer African Reader*, 155–64, Cape Town: Pambazuka.

Nunn, C. (2017), 'Translations-Generations: Representing and Producing Migration Generations through Arts-Based Research', *Journal of Intercultural Studies*, 38 (1): 1–17.

Nyanzi, S. (2014), 'Queering Queer Africa', in Z. Matebeni (ed.), *Reclaiming Afrikan: Queer Perspectives of Sexual and Gender Identity*, 65–8, Cape Town: Modjadji Books.

Oliveira, E. (2016), 'Empowering, Invasive or a Little Bit of Both? A Reflection on the Use of Visual and Narrative Methods in Research with Migrant Sex Workers in South Africa', *Visual Studies*, 31 (3): 260–78.

Oliveira, E. and J. Vearey (eds) (2016), *The Sex Worker Zine Project*, Johannesburg: MoVE/ ACMS.

Raboin, T. (2017), *Discourses on LGBT Asylum in the UK: Constructing a Queer Haven*, Manchester: Manchester University Press.

Rao, R. (2020), *Out of Time: The Queer Politics of Postcoloniality*, New York: Oxford University Press.

Reid, J. (2018), 'The Cliché of Resilience: Governing Indigeneity in the Arctic', *ARENA*, 51/52: 10–17.

Riessman, C. K. (2008), *Narrative Methods for the Human Sciences*, Los Angeles: Sage Publications.

Scott, J. (1998), 'Everyday Forms of Resistance', *Copenhagen Papers*, 4: 33–62.

Tamale, S. (2014), 'Exploring the Contours of African Sexualities: Religion, Law and Power', *African Human Rights Law Journal*, 14 (1): 150–77.

Thoreson, R. (2014), 'Troubling the Waters of a "Wave of Homophobia": Political Economies of Anti-Queer Animus in Sub-Saharan Africa', *Sexualities*, 17 (1/2): 23–42.

Vacchelli, E. (2018), *Embodied Research in Migration Studies: Using Creative and Participatory Approaches*, Bristol: Policy Press.

van Klinken, A. (2019), *Kenyan, Christian, Queer: Religion, LGBT Activism, and Arts of Resistance in Africa*, Pennsylvania: Penn State University Press.

Vincent, L. and S. Howell (2014), '"Unnatural", "Un-African" and "Ungodly": Homophobic Discourse in Democratic South Africa', *Sexualities*, 17 (4): 472–83.

Walsh, S. (2014), 'Critiquing the Politics of Participatory Video and the Dangerous Romance of Liberalism', *Area*, 48 (4): 405–11.

Youde, J. (2017), 'Patriotic History and Anti-LGBT Rhetoric in Zimbabwean Politics', *Canadian Journal of African Studies*, 51 (1): 61–79.

Chapter 3

ALONG THE PINK CORRIDOR: HISTORIES OF QUEER MOBILITY BETWEEN MAPUTO AND JOHANNESBURG (c. 1900–2020)

Caio Simões de Araújo

In mid-2019, I arrived in Maputo, Mozambique, as a grantee of the Governing Intimacies Project, based at the University of the Witwatersrand. Undertaken in collaboration with the GALA Queer Archive, my research involved the collection of life-history interviews with lesbian, gay, bisexual and transgender (LGBT) people who currently live in Maputo or who had previously lived in Lourenço Marques, as the city was known during the colonial period.[1] The project was intended to produce an archival collection of oral histories gathered in a context that – despite its dynamism – remains marginalized and underexplored in queer African scholarship. Between June 2019 and March 2020, my colleague Nelson Mugabe and I conducted eighteen in-depth life-history interviews, plus various shorter interviews with queer activists and artists working with Lambda, Mozambique's largest LGBT organization (based in Maputo, but with offices across the country). The interviews loosely followed a questionnaire with more than a hundred prompts, of which only five related specifically to migration.[2]

Yet, I was fascinated and intrigued by the frequency with which transnational mobility emerged in the oral histories. At times, mentions of border crossings appeared in the background, such as relatives or friends living abroad, mostly in South Africa but also in other locations, including the United Kingdom, Portugal and Germany. But practices and imaginaries of mobility, travel and nomadic living also figured prominently in people's narratives, in their modes of emplotment and self-making. For many interlocutors, experiences and processes of crossing multiple borders, of living abroad and returning 'home', were consequential to how they lived their lives and how they sought to shape or reorient relationships of intimacy and desire, both publicly and privately, both in and out of family structures and social constraints, both within and beyond normative parameters of gender and sexuality.

At the same time, the prominence of transnational mobility in the collected narratives was to be expected. After all, migration has been a regular historical force in Mozambique – as with other East African contexts – since at least the early modern period, propelled by Indian Ocean networks and, later, the slave trade and European colonization (Machado 2014; Alpers 2009; Isaacman and Isaacman 1975). From the late nineteenth century onwards, regional economic entanglements brought tens of thousands of Mozambicans to South African mines (First 1983; Katzenellenbogen 1982). Post independence, the civil war between Frelimo, the socialist ruling party, and Renamo, the main opposition, led to social strife and economic collapse. In the 1980s, thousands of Mozambicans fled to South Africa, escaping the conflict and looking for better socio-economic opportunities. It is estimated that the vast majority of Mozambican migrants in Johannesburg today arrived after 1980 (Vidal 2010). An amnesty in the 1990s allowed many undocumented Mozambicans to regularize their immigration status, while the 2000s brought a relaxation of migration controls and the introduction of an automatic thirty-day visa (Segatti 2009). Given this dense history of movement, it is hardly surprising that many of my interlocutors would have lived mobile lives, particularly along the so-called 'Maputo corridor' (Peberdy and Crush 2001).

Whether focused on the ever-present issue of labour migration or on more contemporary debates over cross-border mobility as a function of post-apartheid regionalization, scholarship on mobile lives between Johannesburg and Maputo has been – by and large – oblivious to queer historical subjectivities. In this chapter, I want to address this silence by engaging the literature from my own position as a queer scholar based in Johannesburg and carrying out research in Maputo. On the one hand, I want to make the obvious yet largely unacknowledged point that dissident sexualities and gender-nonconformity have been part of Mozambican life since at least the early twentieth century. This is not to suggest that these did not exist in previous periods, but merely that the twentieth century inaugurated the colonial investment in sexuality, which, consequentially, led to their inscription in the archive (Miguel 2021; Chipenembe 2018). In this perspective, the erasure of sexual dissidence(s) from the historical record is a function both of the archive, as a selective and politically oriented gatekeeper of historical 'stuff', and of historiography, as the practice of representing the imagined past. On the other hand, I want to point out that the territorialization of historical imagination within the limits of the nation-state – that is, as either 'South African history' or 'Mozambican history' – also contributes to queer erasures and marginalization. National histories tend to centre the citizen as their main protagonist (Aminzade 2013). In doing so, they work to exclude minoritized subjectivities that do not fit neatly into the dominant boundaries of citizenship and belonging, as is the case of sexual dissidents and gender-nonconforming folk. As Martin Manalansan (2014) suggests, a 'queer migrant archive' can potentially have a disorienting and productive effect, inviting us to depart from 'the planned coherent borders of the "archival"' (94) to focus instead on ephemeral arrangements, on the messy, non-linear relationships that entangle bodies, spaces and objects in queer migrant lives. In this chapter, I interrogate how queer subjectivities are displaced, marginalized, exiled or repatriated in certain historical narratives and archival formations.

Pink gold: Locating queer Mozambicans in Johannesburg's mines

Many of my interlocutors had at least one family member who had lived and worked in South Africa, including fathers who had worked in the Johannesburg mines. This is not surprising, given that this strand of male migration had been a defining feature of southern Mozambican social history for most of the twentieth century. I also knew that the 'mine compounds' housing African workers, from Mozambique and elsewhere, were notorious theatres for what colonial authorities called 'unnatural vice' – that is, various forms of same-sex relations, arrangements and desires (Epprecht 2001; Harries 1994; Moodie and Ndatshe 1994; Achmat 1993). Yet, when I asked one interlocutor if he had ever heard about such practices in relation to the mines, he was puzzled, telling me he had never thought of it. Considering the prominent place that migration to the Johannesburg mines has had in Mozambican national historiography, public memory and literary culture (Helgesson 2008), one must question why the queer dimensions of this history remain somewhat ignored in the country. As Francisco Miguel (2019) argues, the 'colonizing silence' existing around homoeroticism in Portuguese Africa – translated in the absence of archival traces of same-sex desire – may help us understand the persistent 'tradition' of silence among the peoples of southern Mozambique. While this point is persuasive, I am more interested in tracing the historiographic production of this silence.

In the postcolonial period, the writing of migrant labour histories was an integral component of what Carlos Fernandes (2013) describes as an intellectual project politically aligned with Frelimo's strategies of socialist transformation and national edification. Under the influence of Ruth First, the Centro de Estudos Africanos carried out a momentous study of the migrant miner. While the resulting publication discussed the impacts of regional labour systems 'on the social structures of the rural peasantry in Southern Mozambique' (Fernandes 2013: 150), it neglected the question of same-sex sexual practices or 'mine marriages' (Miguel 2019: 54). As Fernandes (2013) shows, in the Marxist tradition of writing history 'from below' that flourished in Mozambique in the 1980s, the migrant worker was, alongside the rural peasant, placed in a revolutionary history of African resistance to colonial rule. This heroic recasting of the working classes tended to be male-centric (Fernandes 2013). Even though research on women was already starting to emerge in the late 1980s, it was only in the context of democratization and feminist mobilizing in the 1990s that gender and women's studies gained space and institutionalized forms in Mozambique (Gasparetto 2020; Casimiro and Andrade 2009). At the same time, the HIV health crisis put sexuality on the political and academic agenda (Miguel 2020; Chipenembe 2018).

Across the border in South Africa, the late 1980s and early 1990s were marked by an amplification of political and historiographic interest in same-sex sexualities (Edwards and Epprecht 2020). In this period, historians started to look more closely and consistently at histories of same-sex desires, practices and experiences amongst black Africans in the region, a literature in which Mozambican migrant workers are featured quite prominently (Epprecht 2001; Harries 1994; Moodie and Ndatshe 1994; Achmat 1993; Moodie, Ndatshe and Sibuyi 1988). An earlier strand of this scholarship tended to tie same-sex sexual arrangements to conditions of racial (colonial) capitalist exploitation and rural-urban displacement. In this view, the strenuous and disciplinarian environment of the mine compound, which barred the presence of women, encouraged the recourse to same-sex sexual release. At the same time, 'mine marriages' – in which an older, more experienced miner would take a younger partner, often an apprentice, as his 'wife' – were seen as practices of socialization into the type of normative gender relations that migrants would find upon their return 'home' (Harries 1994; Moodie and Ndatshe 1994). A later approach criticizes this functionalist view for reifying a heteronormative perspective, as it implies that same-sex sexual practices were merely circumstantial, momentary anomalies ultimately leading to 'a "natural" heterosexual destiny' (Spurlin 2006: 44–5). Of course, the historical record is messier and more complicated. Migrant workers could cultivate configurations of reciprocity and desire that included 'strong feelings of attachment' (Epprecht 2004: 477) and that did not necessarily fit a normative pattern.

More recently, a volume edited by Iain Edwards and Marc Epprecht (2020) brings to the fore the voices of miners themselves, by compiling a series of excerpts and quotes gathered in the early twentieth century, within the context of an investigation into alleged practices of 'unnatural vices' in the mines. While surely constrained by the conditions of their production, these texts make for a rich repository of queer migrant lives and invite us to think about the critical potential of the archive as a site for queering the past. According to Edwards and Epprecht (2020), their volume's purpose is to 'gain insights directly from the men (and boys) involved in these relationships and hence to contribute towards an inclusive history of the making of modern South Africa' (2). Thus, it is critically positioned to contribute to current struggles for historical memory and minority rights in the country. While I sympathize with this politics, I also want to suggest that territorializing these texts within the limits of 'South African history' forecloses the possibility of their interpellation as a queer migrant archive. My argument here is that, in between an inclusive 'South African' history and a 'Mozambican' history from below, the queer migrant is stripped of its radical potentiality as a disorienting figure that rejects simple claims of origin and eludes the types of legibility associated with citizenship. Here, I suggest that a queer historiography needs to embrace the entanglements and messiness underlying these biographical routes, instead of subsuming them into histories of rainbow nations.

Settler queer: Gay white mobilities in the settler society

The mineral boom that drove thousands of rural Mozambicans to Johannesburg also bolstered the urbanization of Lourenço Marques. As the city grew around the port, an incipient service economy developed, set up to cater to a growing urban clientele, both European and African. Hotels and a variety of leisure establishments thrived in what Andrew MacDonald (2012) describes as a vibrant 'tavern economy' (171–6). During the first half of the twentieth century, Portuguese authorities were ambivalent about the rapid growth of bars and taverns, sometimes criticizing their presence (chiefly in reference to the inconvenient social 'side effects' of alcoholism, crime and prostitution) and sometimes admitting their social and economic utility (Zamparoni 1998).

By the 1950s, Lourenço Marques was developing rapidly. This process of urban change was prompted by renewed efforts by the Portuguese state to incentivize economic growth in its African territories, which was accompanied by substantial public investment in infrastructure and the simplification of emigration procedures to promote further white settlement (Jerónimo 2018; Castelo 2007). When armed struggle broke out in the 1960s, Portuguese troops joined the list of metropolitan arrivals. In the late colonial period, the urban fabric of Mozambique grew significantly, closely following the exponential increase in its white population.[3]

The growth of the middle class, both European and African, fuelled the expansion of a leisure economy servicing both local settlers and international visitors (Havstad 2019). In the 1960s and 1970s, tourism grew into a profitable economic activity, especially as white South Africans found in Mozambique's scenic landscape a promising destination (Morton 2015). In both Lourenço Marques and Beira – Mozambique's second-largest city – international tourism grew steadily, and visitors from South Africa and Southern Rhodesia (Zimbabwe) accounted for nearly 75 per cent of the total foreign clientele (Coelho 1973). In Lourenço Marques, the frontier taverns and bars of previous decades had been transformed into a vibrant 'pleasure economy'. Around the infamous Rua Araújo (Araújo Street), bars, discos, cabarets and restaurants invited a mixed clientele, including locals, tourists and sailors (Havstad 2019). This was also a theatre of sexual solicitation. As Allen and Barbara Isaacman (1984) argue, sex work 'flourished' in Mozambican cities, where tourists from South Africa and Southern Rhodesia joined a stable local clientele.

While undeniably valuable, this literature reproduces what Sarah Ahmed (2006) calls a 'straight orientation', one that places queerness 'out of sight'. This historiographic erasure is partially the product of a colonial archive built on an episteme of wilful ignorance: the Portuguese regime rarely prosecuted 'sodomy', preferring to turn a blind eye to the practice (Almeida 2010). The lack of punishment also means less instances of archival inscription. But the very nature of colonial queer life also resists *straight*forward assimilation into the language of the archive. As Estenban José Muñoz (1996) notes, queer acts tend to be ephemeral – they take place in spaces of secrecy, privacy or intimacy; they leave few traces and are mediated through coded sociabilities not easily translatable to mainstream society. In colonial Mozambique, the 'private party' was the chronotope of settler queerness: a selectively private space of open exploration of same-sex desires and dissident sexualities, to which entrance was allowed only if certain eligibility criteria were met. Guilherme de Melo (1981), an openly gay journalist at the time, describes the gay parties of Lourenço Marques in detail in his fictionalized memoir

A Sombra dos Dias. These spaces were, of course, raced, gendered and classed in particular ways, and included mostly white, middle-class and cisgender settlers.[4] This is not to say, however, that queer life could not happen in public. In his memoir, de Melo writes at length about the possibility of living 'out of the closet' in colonial Lourenço Marques.[5] Another insider to this 'coded world' is the writer Eduardo Pitta, who was born and lived most of his youth in Mozambique, before moving to Lisbon on the eve of independence. A connoisseur of the Lourenço Marques nightlife, Pitta remembers Rua Araújo as a cruising area, where it was possible to entice soldiers, sailors and passers-by into casual sexual encounters.[6]

Border crossing and white mobility are also part of this history. Queers on both sides of the border participated in the tourist trade between South Africa and Mozambique (even if the exact degree of this participation is impossible to ascertain). A point of contact between these 'gay worlds' was Gerry Wilmot. Canadian by birth, Wilmot was the programme director of the English-language section of Rádio Clube de Moçambique, a major Southern African radio station. Like de Melo, Wilmot was professionally and socially connected, a prominent gay man around whom others gravitated. He also hosted gay parties every weekend at his house in the village of Katembe, across the Maputo bay. As Pitta recalls, if Melo's gay parties were known for their soldiers, Wilmot's were famous for bringing South African men.[7] They were highly sexual gatherings: Pitta mentions that couples from South Africa would 'open' their relationships especially for the occasion,[8] indicating the construction of Mozambique as a place of sexual permissiveness in the South African tourist imagination. By the same token, queer Portuguese settlers also crossed the border, seeking ephemeral experiences of queer life in South Africa. Pitta recalls that it was in Durban that he went to a 'gay disco' for the first time.[9] He also had a white South African boyfriend for a while, which speaks to the possibility of emotional attachments across borders.[10] Lesbian women remain mostly 'out of sight' in these narratives of white gay mobility – just as women are marginalized in history more generally.[11] As Pitta told me, white lesbian women had their own networks and spaces to which gay men did not have access. Yet, there were points of contact, as private gatherings and downtown bars could bring together white gay men and lesbian women from both Mozambique and South Africa.[12]

Further research is needed if one is to make sense of these personal experiences of mobility. But it is not farfetched to speculate that they may point to the formation of a mobile queer culture amongst 'gay settlers' in Southern Africa, however ephemeral in its historicity or loosely defined in its form. In South Africa, these queer migrant histories are perhaps too minor, too elitist and too far removed from the core narratives of queer liberation and citizenship to have any resonance; in Mozambique, this past is – physically and metaphorically – in another country. In the aftermath of independence, many queer settlers, including de Melo and Pitta, left Mozambique along with the majority of its white population (Gupta 2019; Buettner 2016). To them, this was a moment of displacement, a 'return' to a 'home' they knew only in name.[13] While the reasons for this queer departure are complex, Pitta attributes his decision to a difficulty in imagining a queer future under Frelimo's socialist regime.[14] Surely, this rupture was not a complete process and, as Miguel (2019) points out, some queer whites, often of a younger generation, remained in the country as Mozambicans. Even then, Mozambique's post-independence historiography has ignored these narratives of same-sex desire within the settler population. They have been – along with the bodies of their perpetrators – uprooted and exiled from the national canon.

Homosexuality never dies: Queer mobilities under socialism and apartheid

Louiggi is a gay man of mixed background, born in Lourenço Marques to a 'very religious' Muslim family. He recalls having first gained some sense of his sexuality as a kid, when he and his cousin had their 'first sexual plays, even if we did not know they were sexual plays'. They fell in love, but were separated when Louiggi's family migrated to Portugal in 1978. When Louiggi returned to Maputo permanently in the 2000s, he could vividly remember his cousin's tears when they had bid farewell decades earlier.[15] Guto, a black gay man, told me a similar story. He also traced his awareness of his sexual orientation to childhood, when he used to play 'mom and dad' with an older cousin. They used to hug and cuddle – all 'child's play' – until their parents caught them and said 'this cannot be this way'. The year was 1973 or 1974, and the incident caused a 'mess at home'.[16] The critical difference is that Louggi had to leave the country, living abroad for decades before deciding to return 'home', whereas Guto got to stay, even if he lived on and off as a migrant in South Africa. My aim in sharing these two experiences is to allude to the multiplicity of social, political and personal situations facing queer Mozambicans in the aftermath of independence, specifically how these pushed individuals into diverse migrant itineraries. While decolonization and the exodus of white settlers disrupted the racialized patterns of mobility between Maputo and Johannesburg, connections remained. Guto puts this best when reflecting on gay life under Frelimo's socialist government: 'homosexuality never dies'.[17] This may be true, but it certainly goes through ups and downs.

Perhaps the first queer spaces to fall under the new regime were the cruising spots in downtown Maputo. As part of a Frelimo campaign to cleanse the 'depravities' of colonialism, the pleasure economy of Rua Araújo was subjected to a crackdown: bars, cabarets and discos were closed, and sex workers evicted.[18] As Benedito Machava (2018) demonstrates, Frelimo's political project was based on a combination of protestant puritanism and Maoist social revolution. The 'new man' emerging from the revolutionary process was expected to carry the values of self-discipline, moral purification and detachment from material indulgence (Machava 2018). The post-independence project was also oriented towards a particular imaginary of gender and sexuality, one that served to cement heteronormative masculinities (Katto 2020). Yet, as the official history goes, Frelimo never targeted homosexuals, partly because there were well-known gay men among the party's leadership.[19] But this ambivalence did not translate into support or acceptance.

As Miguel (2019) points out, the official party line was that homosexuality was a 'non-issue' (103). At any rate, independence drastically curbed both the South African tourist trade (Correia 1975) and the queer arrangements associated with it.

As the 1980s progressed, conditions in Mozambique deteriorated drastically. In a matter of years, the GDP was slashed almost in half, from US$2.1 billion in 1981 to US$1.2 billion in 1985 (Alden 2001). Chris Alden (2001) puts this down to several factors: the drop in revenue related to migrant mine labour,[20] which negatively affected the balance of payments and the availability of foreign currency; the collapse of the industrial sector, due to a lack of financing and skilled labour; the failure of state-run programmes for the collectivization of agriculture to increase productivity; the destruction of crops and displacement of thousands of people by a succession of natural calamities; and the global economic recession, which slashed the price of Mozambique's export commodities. Moreover, the South African apartheid government's support of Renamo, as part of its policy of regional destabilization, fuelled the armed conflict and provoked the forced displacement of hundreds of thousands, many of whom arrived in South Africa as refugees (Human Rights Watch 1998). It was in this context that Guto, too, decided to migrate, opting to live with a relative on the outskirts of Durban. More than anything, he was driven by the lived experience of economic collapse:

> [T]here was nothing here; the [shelves] were all empty. It didn't matter how much money you had, because there was nothing [to buy]. Like, for you to have a shirt, a pair of jeans, Adidas shoes, you had to go to South Africa. ... It was very difficult: there was apartheid so one could not [travel freely]. You know, I had to take a boat to get off there, and then I had to walk on foot for an entire day. It was very hard.[21]

But the mirage of prosperity soon vanished. After working in a grocery store for a few months, Guto returned to Mozambique, disillusioned: 'You had to work hard. It was almost as if you were illiterate [and unskilled]. You would have to take a construction job, whatever job you could find where they'd hire you, so I chose to come back home.' Guto's middle-class position afforded him the choice of return, which most other Mozambicans did not have. He relocated to South Africa a few years later, in 1990, to join a computer resale venture in Johannesburg. This time, his queer connections were consequential, particularly his friendships with a few Portuguese settlers who had migrated to South Africa after independence. With these relations, he ventured into the nightlife of Hillbrow, where he explored dark cruising alleys – places one could go 'for a quickie'.[22] Yet, he experienced an enduring sense of estrangement: 'I saw what I saw, but that was a country that wasn't mine.'[23]

Mobility was neither unidirectional nor linear. While the forms of economic migration described by Guto would have accounted for a substantial share of cross-border movement at the time, there were also people moving in the opposite direction, often for different reasons. Issa, for instance, landed in Maputo in the late 1970s, after having spent most of his life in Kliptown, a township on the edge of Soweto. He had lived with his grandparents (who were both factory workers) since he was two years old. Growing up in a predominantly coloured[24] and Muslim area, Issa remembers his childhood routine as one of 'school in the morning [and] mosque in the afternoon'. As a teenager, he gradually discovered a queer world revolving around hair salons, most of which were run by gay men or *travestis*, a term he used interchangeably with 'drag queen'.[25] He had a colourful youth: he recalls having 'more than one or two hundred' sexual encounters in his immediate area or in Soweto, where he would sneak to sleep with black men.

On the eve of Mozambican independence, Issa's grandmother decided to go 'to [her] country to watch the flag be raised'.[26] He followed her in 1979, after completing high school. Besides family reunification, Issa's migration was informed by his lived experience of South Africa's volatile political climate, especially following the Soweto uprising of 1976. He remembers rumours circulating about known 'fags' who had died in the midst of political violence: 'we would hear that so and so is gone, that someone else nearby had their house up in flames or had died inside their home, when a stray bullet went through the wall. That happened a lot.'[27] Upon arriving in Maputo, Issa quickly entered its queer world. One day, he was approached by a '*bicha*' ('fag'),[28] a sex worker offering their services, to which he replied: 'Sister, I'm like you.' This encounter led him to realize that 'I'm not the only one here', while also exposing him to a 'tight' network: 'when you meet one person, you get to meet them all.' These factors contributed to a smooth adjustment: 'I arrived normally, as if I was coming home.' Despite the moral puritanism of the Frelimo government, Maputo retained a sense of freedom, especially in comparison to the strict curfew observed in South Africa: 'Here [in Maputo]', Issa says, 'I felt greater freedom than there [in Johannesburg].'[29]

Proudly queer: LGBT migration in the democratic era

Both Guto and Issa continued to move around Southern Africa after the end of the armed conflict. In the 1990s, Issa lived in South Africa and Eswatini before returning to Maputo in 2004. In the 2000s, Guto lived in Pretoria, where he worked as a traditional healer, catering primarily to a South African clientele. Both Issa and Guto witnessed the fall of apartheid and South Africa's democratic transition. Throughout this period of immense political and social upheaval, they continued to cross the border in multiple directions. As a historian – fixated as we are on 'change' as a narrative trope – I was surprised when Issa told me he felt unaffected by the systemic shifts unravelling around him. In post-apartheid South Africa, he conjectured, 'all was the same: I did not see [any change]; you still need to fight to survive.'[30] Even the curfew, the aspect of apartheid governance he most detested, was still in place, dictated not by law but by the deteriorating state of urban safety: 'In Johannesburg, you have a cut-off time to be out. At around 17:00 or 18:00 hours, you are forced to go indoors.'[31] Guto also reported no changes in his circumstances. Everyday experiences of discrimination continued to leave him bitterly isolated in post-apartheid South Africa: 'I stayed in my own corner. Fuck them!'[32]

In Maputo, however, the experience of change was clear. The democratization of political and social structures following the peace process created a window of opportunity for both increased queer visibility and organizing. As Miguel (2019) shows, the private 'party scene' of the 1980s significantly expanded when a group of like-minded gay men, both black and white, began organizing parties at the Centro Hípico (the Equestrian Club), where one of them was a member.[33] These parties marked a historical shift: they were open to all and charged no admission fee, thereby allowing black working-class people access to Maputo's queer culture (Miguel 2019). The networks of queer sociability that existed in the previous decades, fractured as they were along racial, gender and class lines, came together in these events. As Danilo da Silva puts it, Centro Hípico became the 'great equalizer', especially as gender-nonconforming folk started to occupy the space.[34] Guto remembers the drag duo known as La Biba and La Santa,[35] who popularized drag performances in Mozambique:

> [T]hey were showing their faces, so people started to feel comfortable to go out on the street. So, this was when the revolution started. That was like a revolution. 'Wow! These people exist after all.' Even people who lived hiding, they finally opened themselves up.[36]

That the temporality of queer revolution diverged from the historical marker of independence is another reminder that queer histories tend to resist the territoriality and 'linear time' of the nation-state (Rao 2020). Of course, this is not to say that queer histories are always or necessarily 'outside' the nation, but merely that they can follow other, often overlapping cartographies, temporalities and trajectories. In Mozambique, for instance, the contemporary history of LGBT activism – which eventually led to the institutionalization of Lambda as an organization fighting for the rights of sexual and gender minorities in 2006 – is clearly tied to the process of liberalization and constitutional democratization in the 1990s, which included a neoliberal shift to international funding for local organizations, particularly those running HIV/AIDS programmes (Miguel 2020, 2019; Chipenembe 2018). But, at the same time, the movement's origins, imaginaries and unravellings are also routed through migrant itineraries. Miguel de Brito, a white Mozambican journalist, traces the origins of queer organizing in his country to the Johannesburg Lesbian and Gay Pride March, which some queer Mozambicans started to attend in the 1990s. In an interview with Miguel (2019), de Brito recalls:

> We started to go [to the pride march in Johannesburg]. Many of us went in 1999, [when] there were many celebrations in South Africa [in commemoration of the thirtieth anniversary of the Stonewall uprising]. … Thousands of people on the streets. Cops in uniform marching, too. … When we returned, that motivated a conversation: 'what can we do here in Mozambique?'

(162)

This nomadic itinerary of queer utopias – from New York to Johannesburg to Maputo – is surely not exceptional, but it does point to a broader circulation of queer affects, imaginings and languages of articulation under conditions of postcoloniality and neoliberal globalization. Rather than an 'event' – such as, for instance, gay pride – what is at stake here is an incomplete and ongoing process of conversation, engagement and, at times, resistance; what Rahul Rao (2020) describes as global frictions around queer politics.

As LGBT activism in Mozambique becomes increasingly transnational, we need to take seriously the mobility of activists themselves, including their experiences of departure, travel and return. When my interlocutors were asked about their 'activist travels' as representatives of Lambda, they provided insightful responses. Pepetsa, a trans activist, told me of a work trip she took to Cape Town, where she attended the 2019 Global Feminist LBQ Women's Conference. Soon afterwards, Pepetsa founded Transformar, Mozambique's first trans-specific organization.[37] Recalling the conference, Pepetsa said, 'it was … centred on women, only women. I did not see any gay men there. … I found myself there because I was talking woman to woman.'[38] Her words point to the 'disorienting effects' of mobility, which unsettle the borders between 'strange' and 'familiar' spaces, leading one to question how it is that certain bodies come to occupy certain spaces (Ahmed 2006). Perhaps Pepetsa's experience of a space where men were 'out of place' and 'out of sight' pushed her to imagine a political coalition beyond the leadership of gay men.[39]

The last two decades have seen a stark diversification and expansion of the queer scene in Mozambique. Lambda has become more representative, both in its geographic reach and in its constituency (gay men, once the protagonists of this history, now share the spotlight with lesbian, bisexual, trans and queer persons).[40] At the same time, the easing of travel restrictions between Mozambique and South Africa – most notably the introduction of an automatic thirty-day visa in 2005 – has allowed for a diversification of queer mobility patterns. Most of the younger interlocutors I spoke to have traversed the 'pink corridor' to Johannesburg and have done so for a great variety of reasons. Becky, a trans man born in 1988, first moved to Johannesburg to attend university and has since made frequent trips to and from the city. His is a story of queer entrepreneurship, travelling back and forth to Johannesburg to buy clothes to resell back at home. Pieces are chosen carefully so as to appeal to the local queer clientele.[41] If Becky's story attests to his keen (and queer) eye for business, it also goes to show that queer migrants – like everyone else – are devising new creative strategies of transnational mobility. A research agenda on queer migration along the Maputo-Johannesburg corridor will have to account for this radical diversity – for the thickness and messiness of this ethnographic terrain.

Conclusion

The questionnaire for my life-history interviews had only a few prompts related to migration. The purpose was to get a sense of my interlocutors' travel history and profile, and to find out whether experiences of mobility 'abroad' had reshaped their perception of queer issues and politics 'at home'. Interestingly, I seldom got to ask the questions in the order and manner designed. Migrant lives are too complicated for that. Often, by the time we reached that part of the questionnaire, my interlocutor and I had already spoken at length about their migration trajectories, with travel narratives emerging organically at various points in the interview. In other words, mobility is and was a messy affair – it could rarely be defined as a discrete experience, one that was well delimited in time and space. Rather, migrancy and mobility were fragmented experiences, infused in multiple aspects of one's biography. While some people tried to single out the 'migratory event' as an extraordinary occurrence – for example, a childhood spent in Johannesburg – others spoke of migrancy and mobility as processes, as ongoing realities and a fact of life, incrusted on their identities. As Issa told me: 'This is normal. I always travelled. I like travelling; it's in the blood. I don't stay in the same place for long. Three, four, five years – that's enough to bore me. Then I vanish.'[42]

This chapter has been an exploratory attempt to make sense of these mobile lives, and of the queer migrant archive they make. As my engagement with the existing literature has shown, histories of migration in and out of Mozambique have been male-centric and, by and large, oblivious to dissident sexualities – with the exception of research on the Johannesburg mines. Yet, as I argue, this alerts us to the dangers of territorializing queer mobilities within the boundaries of a national history, be it South African or Mozambican. Rather, the pink corridor connecting Johannesburg and Maputo cuts across porous borders and defies an easy understanding of grounded/fixed queer life. This context is home to mobilities of various kinds: black and white, colonial settlers and postcolonial citizens, social activists and queer entrepreneurs. The deep historicity of travel – its moments of departure, displacement and return – runs through the linear temporal markers of colonialism, independence, apartheid and the 'post-periods', and yet it is not subsumed by them. The various temporalities of queer migrant life push us to think of continuities and ruptures, of conjunctures and disjunctures, in a pace of their own, through the idiosyncrasies of the biographical register and the oral history archive. In this regard, queer migrant life histories challenge both the heteronormative orientation of nationalist historiography and the territoriality of the archive. By engaging with these oral narratives of queer mobility, of travel and displacement, of entanglement and dissonance, we may start to think about Southern African queer politics anew, moving beyond cemented views of South African exceptionalism and Mozambican marginality, while also destabilizing the assumption that movement flows in just one direction, from a periphery towards a centre. As this archive of queer mobility attests, bodies, object and ideas carve messier routes.

Acknowledgements

I am deeply thankful to GALA for facilitating this research and for providing institutional support, and to the Governing Intimacies project for funding several research trips to Maputo between 2019 and 2021.

Notes

1   In this paper, I maintain the terms used by my interlocutors and use the term 'LGBT' when referring to activism and institutions. I use 'queer' as an umbrella term and descriptive category to include the various identities and subjectivities that exist within the spectrum of genders and sexualities.

2   Most interviews were conducted in Maputo, except the interviews with Eduardo
     Pitta and São Almeida, who live in Lisbon. All interviews were conducted in
     Portuguese, and the excerpts included in this chapter have been translated by the
     author. Each interlocutor was asked to sign a release form, allowing the transcripts of
     their interviews to be deposited at the GALA Queer Archive and made available to
     researchers. They were given the option of using their real name or a pseudonym. The
     names used in this article reflect these decisions.
3   The white population in Mozambique, according to the official censuses, was 17,842
     in 1928; 23,131 in 1935; 27,438 in 1940; 31,221 in 1945; 48,213 in 1950; 65,798
     in 1955; 97,245 in 1960 and 162,967 in 1970. In 1970, around half of the white
     population (83,480) resided in the district of Lourenço Marques.
4   Interview with Eduardo Pitta, Lisbon, 2020.
5   The expression 'out of the closet' is not used by de Melo himself.
6   Interview with Eduardo Pitta, Lisbon, 2020.
7   Ibid.
8   Ibid.
9   Ibid.
10   A fictionalized version of Pitta's relationship with a South African is included in his
     book (Pitta 2019).
11   Interview with São Almeida, Lisbon, 2020.
12   Interview with Eduardo Pitta, Lisbon, 2020.
13   Pitta, for instance, was born in Mozambique and, prior to his migration to Portugal
     in 1975, had only been there as a tourist. The white population of Mozambique
     plummeted from 200,000 on the eve of independence to only 30,000 in 1972 (Alden
     2001).
14   Interview with Eduardo Pitta, Lisbon, 2020.
15   Interview with Louiggi Júnior, Maputo, 2019. Louiggi's family is of Indian origin on
     his mother's side, and of mixed Portuguese and Turkish origin on his father's side.
16   Interview with Guto, Maputo, 2019.
17   Ibid.
18   As part of a Maoist-inspired policy, Frelimo rounded up prostitutes, had them
     arrested and sent them to 're-education camps'. This has been recently narrated in the
     Mozambican film *Virgem Margarida*, by Licínio Azevedo.
19   This is the case of Gulamo Khan, whom Eduardo Pitta remembers as being 'nearly a
     trans person' (by which I think he meant extremely effeminate) and one of the only
     queers of colour to walk around in the same social circles as white gay men. Khan
     later rose to become Samora Machel's press secretary, dying in 1986, in the same
     plane crash that took lives of Machel and others.
20   On South Africa's decreasing dependence on Mozambican migrant labour, see Jonathan
     Crush, Alan Jeeves and David Yudelman (1991).
21   Interview with Guto, Maputo, 2019.
22   Ibid.
23   Ibid.
24   'Coloured' was a racial category imposed on mixed-race people during the apartheid
     period. The term continues to be used as a self-identification and is now widely
     considered to reference a specific ethnicity. Its general usage does not carry the
     pejorative meaning found in other countries.
25   That Issa used the Portuguese term '*travesti*' interchangeably with 'drag queen'
     suggests he was likely referring to female-presenting men, without necessarily
     alluding to non-normative gender identities. Of course, he is speaking of a period

in which the concepts of gender expression and gender identity were not available, and in which the boundaries between practices and identities were not clearly demarcated. His choice of words reflects this grey area. To this day, Mozambicans use the term *travesti* for different meanings. It historically originated to indicate practices of cross-dressing and a form of gender expression, but it was later taken on to refer to a non-normative gender identity, being at times used interchangeably with transgender. Still, the use of either term is not specific or unanimous, and to explore the politics of their deployment goes beyond the scope of this chapter.

26 Interview with Issa, Maputo, 2019. In Issa's account, his grandmother intended to return to Johannesburg after her 1975 visit to Maputo, but could not get her papers in order.

27 Ibid.

28 Ibid. The term '*bicha*' is often used to refer to an effeminate gay man.

29 Ibid.

30 Ibid.

31 Ibid.

32 Ibid. Guto used the Portuguese expression '*caguei pra eles*', which translates as 'I shit for them'. I do believe that the sense of disregard and dislike can be transmitted by 'fuck them' or 'I don't give a shit about them'.

33 Interview with Danilo da Silva, Maputo, 2019.

34 Ibid.

35 The duo is mentioned by nearly all of my interlocutors as queer pioneers in Mozambique. It was by watching their performances that many first realized what it meant to be queer. La Santa identifies as a trans woman and is still an activist in the LGBT movement.

36 Interview with Guto, Maputo, 2019.

37 Founded in early 2019 as the *Movimento Trans de Moçambique* (Mozambique Trans Movement), the group has been restructured as Transformar ('to transform'), a transgender organization.

38 Interview with Pepetsa, Maputo, 2019.

39 Indeed, Transformar has been operating within the physical and organizational space of Muleide, a women's rights organization based in Maputo.

40 Interview with Danilo da Silva, Maputo, 2019. It is interesting to note that after a decade under the leadership of da Silva, a gay man, Lambda opted, in 2020, for a dual leadership structure, with the executive directorship shared between a gay man and a lesbian woman, Roberto Nelson Paulo and Fauzia Naline Mangore, respectively.

41 Interview with Becky, Maputo, 2019.

42 Interview with Issa, Maputo, 2019.

References

Achmat, Z. (1993), 'Apostles of Civilised Vice: "Immoral Practices" and "Unnatural Vice" in South African Prisons and Compounds, 1890–1920', *Social Dynamics*, 19 (2): 92–110.

Ahmed, S. (2006), *Queer Phenomenology: Orientations, Objects, Others*, Durham: Duke University Press.

Alden, C. (2001), *Mozambique and the Construction of a New African State: From Negotiations to Nation Building*, Basingstoke: Palgrave MacMillan.

Almeida, S. J. (2010), *Homossexuais no Estado Novo*, Lisboa: Sextante Editora.

Alpers, E. A. (2009), *East Africa and the Indian Ocean*, Princeton: Markus Wiener Publishers.

Aminzade, R. (2013), *Race, Nation and Citizenship in Postcolonial Africa: The Case of Tanzania*, New York: Cambridge University Press.

Buettner, E. (2016), *Europe after Empire: Decolonization, Society, and Culture*, Cambridge: Cambridge University Press.

Casimiro, I. and X. Andrade (2009), 'Critical Feminism in Mozambique: Situated in the Context of Our Experience as Women, Academics, and Activists', in A. A. Ampofo and S. Arnfred (eds), *African Feminist Politics of Knowledge: Tensions, Challenges, Possibilities*, 137–56, Uppsala: Nordiska Afrikainstitutet.

Castelo, C. (2007), *Passagens para a África: o Povoamento de Angola e Moçambique com Naturais da Metrópole (1920–1974)*, Porto: Afrontamento.

Chipenembe, M. J. M. (2018), 'Sexual Rights Activism in Mozambique: A Qualitative Case Study of Civil Society Organisations and Experiences of Lesbians, Bisexual and Transgender Women', PhD dissertation, Vrije Universiteit Brussels and Universiteit Ghent, Brussels and Ghent.

Coelho, C. A. (1973), 'Elementos Estatísticos: Moçambique', *Finisterra*, 8 (15): 145–61.

Correia, J. M. (1975), 'Frelimo Fights for Tourists', *Rand Daily Mail*, 27 February: 2.

Crush, J., A. Jeeves and D. Yudelman (1991), *South Africa's Labour Empire: A History of Black Migrancy to the Gold Mines*, Boulder: Westview Press.

Edwards, I. and M. Epprecht (2020), *Working Class Homosexuality in South African History: Voices from the Archieve*, Pretoria: HSRC Press.

Epprecht, M. (2001), '"Unnatural Vice" in South Africa: The 1907 Commission of Enquiry', *The International Journal of African Historical Studies*, 34 (1): 121–40.

Epprecht, M. (2004), *Hungochani: The History of a Dissident Sexuality in Southern Africa*, Kingston: McGill-Queen's University Press.

Fernandes, C. (2013), 'History Writing and State Legitimisation in Postcolonial Mozambique: The Case of the History Workshop, Centre for African Studies, 1980–1986', *Kronos*, 39 (1): 131–57.

First, R. (1983), *Black Gold: The Mozambican Miner, Proletarian and Peasant*, Brighton: Harvester Press.

Gasparetto, V. F. (2020), 'O Campo de Estudos de Género em Moçambique/África', *Revista de Estudos Feministas*, 28 (1): 1–16.

Gupta, P. (2019), *Portuguese Decolonization in the Indian Ocean World: History and Anthropology*, London: Bloomsbury.

Harries, P. (1994), *Work, Culture and Identity: Migrant Laborers in Mozambique and South Africa, c. 1860–1910*, Portsmouth: Heinemann.

Havstad, L. (2019), '"To Live a Better Life": The Making of a Mozambican Middle Class', PhD dissertation, Boston University, Boston.

Helgesson, S. (2008), 'Johannesburg, Metropolist of Mozambique', in S. Nuttall and A. Mbembe (eds), *Johannesburg: The Elusive Metropolis*, 259–70, London: Duke University Press.

Human Rights Watch (1998), '*Prohibited Persons*': *Abuse of Undocumented Migrants, Asylum-Seekers, and Refugees in South Africa*, New York: Human Rights Watch.

Isaacman, A. and B. Isaacman (1975), 'The Prazeros as Transfrontiersmen: A Study in Social and Cultural Change', *The International Journal of African Historical Studies*, 8 (1): 1–39.

Isaacman, A. and B. Isaacman (1984), 'The Role of Women in the Liberation of Mozambique', *Ufahamu: A Journal of African Studies*, 13 (2/3): 128–85.

Jerónimo, M. B. (2018), 'Repressive Developmentalisms: Idioms, Repertoires, Trajectories in Late Colonialism', in A. Thompson and M. Thomas (eds), *The Oxford Handbook on the Ends of Empires*, 537–54, Oxford: Oxford University Press.

Katto, J. (2020), *Women's Lived Landscapes of War and Liberation in Mozambique: Bodily Memory and the Gendered Aesthetics of Belonging*, London: Routledge.

Katzenellenbogen, S. E. (1982), *South Africa and Southern Mozambique: Labour, Railways and Trade in the Making of a Relationship*, Manchester: Manchester University Press.

MacDonald, A. (2012), 'Colonial Trespassers in the Making of South Africa's International Borders 1900 to *c.* 1950', PhD dissertation, St. John's College, Cambridge.

Machado, P. (2014), *Oceans of Trade: South Asian Merchants, Africa and the Indian Ocean, c. 1750–1850*, Cambridge: Cambridge University Press.

Machava, B. (2018), 'The Morality of Revolution: Urban Cleanup Campaigns, Re-education Camps, and Citizenship in Socialist Mozambique (1974–1988)', PhD dissertation, University of Michigan, Ann Arbor.

Manalansan, M. M. (2014), 'The "Stuff" of Archives: Mess, Migration, and Queer Lives', *Radical History Review*, 120: 94–107.

Melo, G. (1981), *A Sombra dos Dias*, Lisbon: Bertrand and Círculo de Leitores.

Miguel, F. (2019), 'Maríyarapáxjis: Silêncio, Exoginia e Tolerância nos Processos de Institucionalização das Homossexualidades Masculinas no Sul de Moçambique', PhD dissertation, University of Brasilia, Brasilia.

Miguel, F. (2020), 'International Cooperation, Homosexuality and AIDS in Mozambique', *Contexto Internacional*, 42 (3): 647–64.

Miguel, F. (2021), 'Séculos de Silêncio: Contribuições de um Antropólogo para uma História da "Homossexualidade" no Sul de Moçambique (séc. XVI-XX)', *Revista Brasileira de História*, 41 (86): 111–34.

Moodie, T. D. and V. Ndatshe (1994), *Going for Gold: Men, Mines, and Migration*, Berkeley: University of California Press.

Moodie, T. D., V. Ndatshe and B. Sibuyi (1988), 'Migrancy and Male Sexuality on the South African Gold Mines', *Journal of Southern African Studies*, 14 (2): 228–56.

Morton, D. (2015), 'A Voortrekker Memorial in Revolutionary Maputo', *Journal of Southern African Studies*, 41 (2): 335–52.

Muñoz, E. J. (1996), 'Ephemera as Evidence: Introductory Notes to Queer Acts', *Women & Performance*, 8 (2): 5–16.

Peberdy, S. and J. Crush (2001), 'Invisible Trade, Invisible Travellers: The Maputo Corridor SDI and Informal Cross-border Trading', *South African Geographical Journal*, 83 (2): 115–23.

Pitta, E. (2019), *Persona*, Alfragide: Dom Quixote.

Rao, R. (2020), *Out of Time: The Queer Politics of Postcoloniality*, Oxford: Oxford University Press.

Segatti, A. W. K. (2009), 'Les Oubliés de la Croissance: Les Migrants Mozambicains dans l'Afrique du Sud de Mbeki (1999–2008)', *Lusotopie*, 16 (1): 67–84.

Spurlin, W. J. (2006), *Imperialism within the Margins: Queer Representation and the Politics of Culture in Southern Africa*, Basingstoke: Palgrave Macmillan.

Vidal, D. (2010), 'Living in, out of, and between Two Cities: Migrants from Maputo in Johannesburg', *Urban Forum*, 21 (1): 55–68.

Zamparoni, V. (1998), 'Entre Narros & Mulungos: Colonialismo e Paisagem Social em Lourenço Marques, *c.* 1890–1940', PhD dissertation, University of São Paulo, São Paulo.

Part II

BARRIERS TO PROTECTION: ETHICAL, PROCEDURAL AND
LEGAL CHALLENGES

Chapter 4

AN ETHICAL DILEMMA: WHEN RESEARCH BECOMES 'EXPERT TESTIMONY'

Agathe Menetrier

Since 2015, increasing numbers of young gay[1] Gambians have been seeking refuge in neighbouring Senegal. There, they tap into the underground gay network to learn how to get by in the big city, Dakar, and how to avoid homophobic attacks and police roundups. But Dakar is often regarded as a transit point, with most of the gay Gambians aiming to enter the international asylum system. Many have learnt that the United Nations High Commissioner for Refugees (UNHCR) resettles 'vulnerable LGBT refugees' to countries in the Global North. Such information is usually transmitted through informal networks – for example, those already resettled in Canada share their knowledge of the asylum system with acquaintances still in transit. Even with this circulation of information, one thing remains unclear to almost everyone: the criteria by which one is deemed a vulnerable LGBT refugee. While this aspect might remain opaque, the decision chain appears far more evident. The final decision, most agree, rests with *toubabs*[2] – white UNHCR officers from the Global North, rather than their Senegalese counterparts. It is the latter who conduct most refugee status determination (RSD) interviews, yet Gambian gay asylum seekers are most eager to narrate their flight stories to white UNHCR staff, convinced that this will help secure third-country resettlement.

From April 2017 to April 2018, I conducted an ethnographic study of the international asylum system as seen from Dakar, with a focus on the resettlement process for 'LGBT refugees'. Initially oblivious to the processes and power dynamics outlined above, I chose Dakar as a field site because I wanted to observe inter-organizational relationships. It seemed an obvious choice given that Dakar hosts the regional headquarters of most UN agencies, international organizations (IOs) and international non-governmental organizations (INGOs). It was while conducting participant observation at a Senegalese NGO that is an implementing partner for the UNHCR that I first met one of the gay Gambians seeking asylum. He brought me to the house he shared with other gay Gambian men and women (and occasionally with Senegalese counterparts) in a distant and poor suburb of Dakar. This house became my main research site, but I simultaneously developed ties with asylum agents working at the UNHCR, in order to gain insight into selection practices involving 'vulnerable LGBT refugees'. As a researcher of queer migration who is also a heterosexual cisgender woman *toubab* with access to Dakar's white 'expatriate'[3] networks, the gay Gambians identified me as a mediator, capable of both understanding their needs and deciphering the codes of the UNHCR. In this chapter, I show that accepting this mediator role confronted me with serious ethical questions. In acting as the 'expert' on gay asylum seekers' needs for the UN and INGOs, was I not capitalizing on assumptions of neutrality associated with white expatriates working in the Global South? Was I not perpetuating the myth of irrefutable 'proof' at play in the adjudication of asylum claims based on sexual orientation and/or gender identity (SOGI)? To guide my reflection on these ethical questions, I draw on the concept of the 'dual imperative' when conducting research with refugees, understood as the necessity to produce findings that are relevant to both scholars and humanitarian agencies (Jacobsen and Landau 2003). Building on Ulrike Krause's (2017) plea for an extended version of this concept and on Keith McNeal's (2019) critique of post-political injunctions weighing on researcher-experts, I argue for a *triple political imperative*, highlighting our responsibility to research participants who are themselves asylum seekers and refugees, notwithstanding the several ethical and moral quandaries that this reality might bear.

From witnessing to testifying

As part of her research into the French asylum system, Estelle d'Halluin (2006) writes about medical doctors who volunteer for Comede, a health and resource centre for asylum seekers. From the moment the clinic was established in 1979, the volunteer doctors were asked by both asylum seekers and administrative bodies to produce medical certificates attesting not only to asylum seekers' general health but also to marks on their bodies and whether these were consistent with acts of violence and torture. At first, the Comede doctors saw this new task, much like conference presentations and public reports, as a means to account for and denounce the violence experienced by those in their care.

In the 1990s, in order to win favour with the electorate, the French state dramatically decreased the number of claimants granted refugee status, abandoning its traditional role as a host country (Noiriel 1998). Debates on this issue focused on bureaucratic considerations, specifically how medical certificates and other documents could 'prove' past persecution and thereby distinguish between 'genuine' and 'bogus' claimants. With asylum seekers now increasingly bearing the burden of proof, they started – on the advice by lawyers and adjudicators – to pressure Comede doctors to provide medical certificates attesting to the veracity of their claims. What was once an occasional request for testimony morphed into an expertise service providing bodily 'proof' of persecution tailored to the state's asylum bureaucracy. This shift sparked concern among doctors regarding their role within Comede and within the broader asylum system. Miriam Ticktin (2011) refers to humanitarian immigration practices based on suffering and sickness as 'regimes of care', emphasizing that refugees are deemed worthy of compassion as vulnerable *objects* rather than being granted citizenship as rightful *subjects*.

The ethical debates around such practices resonate strongly with my own experiences. Both during and after my fieldwork, I found myself contemplating the extent to which my scholarly commitment to voicing the pitfalls of asylum systems, to updating country-of-origin information and to making conditions of persecution visible had actually turned into an 'expertise' on the suffering of LGBT West Africans.

The longer the gay Gambian asylum seekers waited for an interview with the UNHCR regional office, the more they feared an end to the resettlement programme. Torn between, on the one hand, the need to be discreet so as to avoid attracting the attention of homophobic vigilantes or the Senegalese authorities and, on the other, the desire to highlight their ongoing challenges, my research participants began looking for options other than refugee resettlement. Some reached out to friends already resettled in Canada, asking them to use their new contacts to help them emigrate. Others turned to the internet and social media. On Facebook, they joined groups for LGBT people (predominantly men) in Canada, the United States and the United Kingdom (chosen because English was the primary language of communication) and posted cries for help, describing their precarious situation in Dakar. Some of these attempts produced promising leads. For example, a middle-aged Canadian gay man who had befriended a gay Gambian resettled in Canada – the latter having transited through Dakar as part of his migration trajectory – was interested in organizing a crowd-funding campaign to support asylum seekers stuck in Dakar. Similarly, an older British gay man who had met one of my participants over Gay Romeo, a dating app, was willing to invite a young gay Gambian man to the United Kingdom in order for him to seek asylum there. However, before these men in the Global North would commit to concrete action, they demanded proof of the hardships described by the individuals they knew only virtually. The Gambians turned to me, the researcher, to testify to the suffering they had experienced. At the Gambians' insistence, I had phone conversations with these potential 'sponsors' in the Global North, exchanged emails and social media messages in which I presented myself as a researcher (often with a link to my institute's website), recounted what I knew of my research participants' situations and attached anonymized pictures illustrating their housing situations and/or the physical attacks they had endured. In most cases, my intervention had a positive impact, persuading potential sponsors to assist those they regarded as their new *protégés*. Even though my research participants celebrated such outcomes, I was not completely at ease with my new role. Who was I to attest to the hardship and suffering of gay Gambians in Senegal when I myself had only witnessed it for less than a year? Was it merely the fact that I was white – and therefore 'reliable' in the eyes of potential sponsors – that afforded me authority on the subject?

Virtual 'sponsors' in the Global North were not the only individuals to whom I was asked to provide testimony. The longer my fieldwork continued, the more I became an apparently trustworthy source of information for various aid organizations, including the UNHCR. I soon found myself being cast, inadvertently, as the 'expert' on LGBT asylum seekers, a role that initiated myriad ethical quandaries.

Becoming an expert

Which of my observations should I share, and which should I withhold? was a question with which I constantly wrestled. My difficulty in answering it became even more evident when, near the end of my fieldwork, I was unexpectedly invited to collaborate with the resettlement unit of the UNHCR regional office. To understand how this collaboration came about, it is necessary to go back a few months in time. In November 2017, after a violent attack on the house shared by the gay asylum seekers, UNHCR's Dakar office promised to help the occupants find a safer place to live. Nothing concrete followed, forcing the gay asylum seekers to find accommodation in another part of town through their own means. A couple of months later, at the end of February 2018, they were expelled from this apartment. Desperate for contact with UNHCR, but particularly hoping to attract the attention of *toubab* resettlement officers, they set up camp in front of the regional office.

Prior to moving to Dakar, I benefitted from a privileged contact within the UNHCR regional office. In April 2017, before my fieldwork commenced, Bastian, a white middle-aged German man working as senior staff in the resettlement unit, had provided helpful advice on moving to Dakar.[4] From the outset, I informed Bastian about my research on asylum issues. It was months, however, before I first met the gay Gambians. I decided that any information Bastian continued to share with me after I 'came out' about my fieldwork and reasons for being in Senegal could be considered data, except when expressly stated otherwise. Bastian showed little interest in my work and often implied that my knowledge would be better applied by working within UNHCR.[5]

Near the end of February 2018, Bastian invited me over to his house, where our conversation took on an unexpectedly frank tone. He recounted that, a couple of weeks earlier, he had been smoking a cigarette on the balcony of his office when he saw a group of Gambians camping out the front of the UNHCR building. He was quite surprised that there were so many gay asylum seekers still in Dakar. He was under the impression that the group resettled at the end of the previous year had been the last remaining gay Gambians in transit. It was my turn to be surprised, since employees of UNHCR Senegal had repeatedly told the Gambians that their demands for assistance and resettlement had been transmitted to the regional office (where Bastian worked). For the first time I shared with Bastian some of my observations regarding the gay Gambian asylum seekers left in Dakar, highlighting in particular their unsafe housing, their vulnerability to homophobic attacks and their inadequate access to healthcare and other services. Bastian was alarmed but not surprised that information about these 'cases' had not been passed on by his Senegalese colleagues, whom he considered not just 'incompetent' but also reluctant to assist LGBT claimants. These accusations of withholding information about the presence of gay Gambians aspiring to resettlement is quite telling of the mistrust between 'expatriate' staff[6] at the regional office and local staff[7] at the national office, a tension I explore in more detail elsewhere (Menetrier 2021).

At once convinced of the quality and utility of my research, Bastian asked me to put together a document listing all the gay asylum seekers in transit in Dakar, including details of their migration trajectories and the state of their asylum claims. I was torn: on the one hand, it was a unique opportunity to help my research participants move forward with their applications, which was exactly what they had always wanted; on the other hand, it meant embracing the role of 'expert' on behalf of the UNHCR, something I was not anticipating and about which I felt greatly conflicted. The proposition was hardly one of open collaboration, since Bastian insisted that he would have to keep the source of his information – me – secret (documents had to be sent to his private, rather than professional, email address). I was asked to deliver specific information on my research participants, corresponding to what the UNHCR had come to establish as identification data. This would allow the agency to flag individuals considered to be 'of concern' and therefore include them in official statistics. This was, in fact, Bastian's primary objective: creating ProGres entries for the gay Gambians, who at that point were unlisted in the UNHCR's database.[8] His objective cohered with the 'statistical ambition' (Glasman 2020: 5) of his employer and of UN agencies more broadly, as well as of many IOs. *Was this also my objective?* I wondered. It most certainly was not the outcome I had in mind when I began collecting stories from my research participants, but it was a way to make my knowledge on their situation legible to the UN. Caught between the expectations of my two sets of research participants – the gay Gambian asylum seekers and UNHCR staff – I was forced to reflect on my personal contribution to an asylum system that values 'expert evidence' over asylum seekers' personal testimonies.

Perpetuating the myth of proof

Like the Comede doctors, I was hesitant to take on the role of expert, a position that Bastian encouraged me to adopt. My apprehension was partly technical: how could I translate the complexity of the stories I had spent months trying to understand into a couple of bullet points destined to be converted into ProGres categories? But there was also a political dimension to my reluctance. By attesting to the persecution experienced by my research participants, I could indirectly undermine the principle of a 'well-founded fear of persecution' as set out in the Geneva Convention. According to the Convention, individuals who fear persecution in their country of origin – for example, because of their 'membership of a particular social group' – are entitled to seek protection elsewhere. Notably, there is no prerequisite for an individual to have already suffered violence. The double burden falling on those claiming SOGI-based asylum – that of 'proving' both their identity *and* related persecution – has been the subject of rich scholarly attention, particularly in the Global North (e.g. Murray 2018; Lee and Brotman 2011; Berg and Millbank 2009). Less has been written about Global South contexts, or the fact that the myth of proof is not the monopoly of asylum systems of the Global North (notable exceptions are Camminga 2019; Shakhsari 2014; Shuman and Hesford 2014). In fact, concerns around proof start forming early on in asylum seekers' trajectories, courtesy of interactions with various state and non-state actors. Surely, by certifying to the suffering of my research participants, I was perpetuating the deification of 'proof'. What about those who had fled the Gambia for fear of arrest by President Yahya Jammeh's secret service, individuals for whom I could not attest to their life histories or who may not carry physical marks of torture? Would they be disadvantaged when listed next to their acquaintances who had direct experiences of abuse? How should I retell and frame the complex narratives provided by my research participants to the UNHCR? It was certainly not my role to sanction my research participants' narration skills or to adjudicate the 'truth'.

There was a further ethical component to my unease. In my research, I strive to deconstruct the misconception that queer Africans are trapped on an intrinsically homophobic continent and that their only salvation is the 'queer-friendly' Global North. This is a trope widely circulated by politicians, humanitarians and journalists from the Global North, despite concerted efforts by scholars to challenge this narrative (e.g. Saleh 2020; Nyanzi 2016; Matebeni 2014). As with many researchers working on queer migration to the Global North, my work aims to challenge simplistic portrayals of queer asylum as a linear movement from 'uncivilized' countries of origin to emancipation in enlightened neo-liberal democracies (Murray 2018; Jenicek, Wong and Lee 2009). Rarer, and all the more necessary, is work focusing on queer migration within the African continent (Marnell, Oliveira and Khan 2021; Broqua et al. 2021; Camminga 2019; Bhagat 2018; Gouyon 2018). These studies not only dispel the myth that all queer Africans want to migrate to the Global North, but also highlight that the majority of displacements occur between African countries and cannot be easily distinguished from other types of migration. In the continuity of this literature, I documented during my fieldwork in Dakar the solidarity networks and complex livelihood strategies developed by gay asylum seekers between Gambia and Senegal.

When asked by Bastian to share the 'expertise' I had acquired, I knew I would have to be selective about the information I passed on. My research participants' efforts to tap into existing queer networks in Gambia, Senegal and other countries, their circulation of knowledge about asylum procedures (Menetrier 2019), their efforts to earn money through *mbaran*[9] or paid sex, and their mobility within West Africa were details that are crucial to my academic work but potentially risky to share with the UNHCR. Such information could be considered antithetical to the agency's resettlement selection criteria and therefore produce the opposite result to which my research participants were expecting. Representing my research participants in a favourable light for their resettlement cases implied portraying their mobility through the neo-colonial meta-narrative of progress (Giametta 2014) – the self-same narratives I strive to deconstruct in my research.

I discussed these concerns with my research participants. They were very much in favour of my sharing as much information as possible with the UNHCR, confident that I would do everything to avoid endangering their chances of resettlement. Thus, on their behalf, I decided to play the role of 'expert' that the UNHCR had invited me to take on. When compiling the list of profiles, I decided not to include information on individuals' reasons for migrating, focusing instead on their common hardships in Dakar. A couple of weeks after I sent the list to Bastian, my research participants received calls from the UNHCR inviting them to RSD interviews. The gay Gambians and their NGO contacts in Dakar had tried for months to attract the attention of the UNHCR, yet it was me – a white researcher from Europe – who made it happen.[10] And why? Because I had benefitted from the open ear of a prominent UNHCR decision-maker, over a glass of wine.

Certifying suffering

The first time I acted as an 'expert' for a Global North institution was not actually for the Gambian asylum seekers, but rather for three of their Senegalese friends. These three young gay men had been hosted by the Gambians since they were expelled from their family homes in the southern region of Casamance. Living in this shared accommodation, the Senegalese men quickly learnt that refugee status and resettlement – the primary aspiration of their Gambian friends – were not an option for them, given that they were Senegalese citizens in Senegal. Envious of the institutional recognition the Gambian asylum seekers enjoyed, and even more so of their chance to access international mobility, the young Casamançais were persuaded that an improvement of their own situation depended on the intervention of a large aid organization. Tapha, the most outspoken of the three friends, confided in me his hope of finding an organization 'like the Gambians' UN'.

An acquaintance of mine who had himself fled homophobic persecution in Senegal decades earlier and who now has refugee status in the United Kingdom advised me to put the three Senegalese men in contact with Rainbow Railroad (RR), an INGO based in Canada. According to the RR website, the organization is committed to 'helping LGBT people escape persecution and violence' by assisting them to travel to safe third countries (Rainbow Railroad 2019). When I Skyped with one of the RR programme coordinators, I learnt more about how cases are assessed and managed. Being a Canada-based organization, RR does not have antennas in all of the regions from which it 'help[s] LGBT people escape' (Rainbow Railroad 2019). Instead, RR staff work with a network of on-the-ground contacts who 'verify each case' and later 'provide pre-travel and logistical support'. When I discussed the hardships of the young Casamançais, the RR coordinator acknowledged that, though the organization's network in Senegal was limited, this case was one that could benefit from the INGO's assistance. I thus expected RR to start reaching out to Senegalese NGOs, perhaps those specializing in MSM[11] programming, in order to build a network of contacts. I was quite surprised, then, when they asked me to become their 'person of reference' (in RR's wording) and to testify to the authenticity of the Casamançais' experiences.

I had been the one who brought the case to RR's attention, and although I had been transparent about my ongoing involvement with the gay Gambians, RR considered me a suitable candidate for 'verifying' the cases under consideration. Though I was certainly equipped to deliver the types of materials RR viewed as 'proof', I do not think I acted in the neutral manner expected of an independent expert. I had digitized and archived identity documents of my research participants, as well as recording dates and injuries after various attacks. Unlike the Comede doctors, I did not produce certificates coded with medical jargon, but to some extent I produced 'certificates' of another kind. My documents were given legitimacy through the lexicon of LGBT/human rights (Altman 2001; Adam, Duyvendak and Krouwel 1999) and asylum categories (Glasman 2017). The documentation I produced was viewed as objective proof by asylum agents and actors like RR, who try to select the 'right' people to assist in verifying cases. In an age when asylum seekers' narratives of flight and suffering are systematically doubted, 'any evidence is welcome, but that which is produced by an agent assumed to be both neutral and expert has even more authority' (Fassin and d'Halluin 2005: 601). In other words, it is the expert's analysis that distinguishes between 'legitimate' and 'bogus' asylum seekers. Unlike the Comede doctors, I do not write under a practice letterhead, but my affiliation to both a research institute and an NGO that produces country-of-origin information[12] were regarded as adequate credentials. My assumed neutrality and expertise were, for my interlocutors at RR, very clearly read from my being a white European in West Africa. They took for granted that, like them, I was dedicated to the rights of LGBT people, but did not have a personal stake in the fate of the individuals for whom I was advocating.

Mediating between two groups of research participants

While undertaking her study on asylum in France, d'Halluin (2006) found that some of her interlocutors were eager to become regular confidants. For many, she was the only French citizen with whom they had regular contact, and they used the opportunity to learn the norms regulating their new society. They saw her as a mediator of French customs and society. As a European in Senegal, I could hardly play the same role for the gay Gambians participating in my research. Nevertheless, they saw me as a mediator of another type: between them and international aid workers. As a white person who had left Europe to reside in

Dakar, who spoke several UN languages, who understood the complexities of the international asylum system and who wanted to write a book about queer asylum, I was well placed to catch the ear of other *toubab*. My participants knew this – and they were right to think so.

When at home, European researchers might feel that their daily lives, wages and approaches are very different to these of aid workers. But this distance shrinks considerably once we are 'expatriated' in the Global South. Not only is our buying power much closer to that of aid workers than the average West African, but also our research participants are often the same as the aid workers' 'beneficiaries'.[13] It is quite telling that both researchers and aid workers refer to their stay in the Global South as 'being in the field'. Even without wishing to associate with aid workers from the Global North, I was invariably brought into contact with them once I started preparing for my move to Dakar. Be it through mutual friends who put me in touch with someone they knew in Dakar, or through Facebook groups dedicated to the sale of second-hand furniture, I was constantly reminded that I was considered an 'expat', just like aid workers from the Global North.

Upon arriving in Dakar, my first reaction was to reject the association with 'expat' aid workers, a link I feared would divert me from an 'authentic ethnography' (like many anthropology students, I still had a vague model of exotic fieldwork in a remote village). I soon realized that, apart from selling beautiful furniture when they left, aid workers, especially those working in the field of asylum, could become key voices in my research. Like Amélie Le Renard (2019), who joined 'expat' Facebook groups in Dubai, first to find a place to stay and later as a source of information and a way to access interview subjects, I made great use of social media such as LinkedIn and Facebook. Once I got to know a couple of expats working for UNHCR, I contacted their colleagues and former colleagues via LinkedIn or Facebook. I was able to easily obtain interviews or clarifications on specific subjects as soon as I mentioned that I had already talked to colleague A or B. Through my LinkedIn picture, my CV and my vocabulary, my interlocutors rapidly identified me as one of them – that is to say, someone whose passport matched their structural privileges.

As members of what Le Renard calls the 'pan-national category of Westerners' (2019: 13), my interlocutors in aid organizations associated me with a range of positive stereotypes. In Senegal, like many recently independent countries, the legacies of colonization have propagated the belief that expertise is a product of the Global North and, therefore, that anyone from the Global North is inherently competent (Le Renard 2019; Fechter and Walsh 2010). As a French researcher working on issues strongly associated with Western modernity, I was instantly regarded as capable, trustworthy and relatable. This is despite the fact that my aid worker contacts had known me for only a fraction of the time they had known local activists, many of whom have worked on LGBT asylum issues for decades (Armisen 2016). My perceived expertise in LGBT asylum meant that they readily asked me to translate my observations of the gay Gambians into information relevant to their organizations. In that sense, my institutional research participants, similar to my Gambian research participants, asked me to become a mediator between them and their 'beneficiaries'.

On both sides, my role as mediator was expected. It was understood as a form of reciprocity for the time and information that my interlocutors had contributed to my study. My Gambian research participants expected me to assist them materially, but also to advise them on the asylum procedure and, ideally, help them navigate various administrative hurdles. The written statements and pictures they shared with me had transformed me into a kind of repository, and I was expected to share this knowledge with individuals they could not access: *toubab* aid workers. Relying on Marcel Mauss' work on gift exchange (2002 [1954]), ethnographers have reflected on dynamics of reciprocity between themselves and their research participants, stressing the ambivalence of the latter's gift to 'voluntary' participate while obligating the researcher to reciprocate in one way or another. Stating that the researcher has to 'give back' to her participants in return for their time and information is too often presented as a financial equation, yet this downplays the complexity of finding a balance between observation and action, between research and engagement. Anthropologist Marion Fresia (2005) notes that the longer she stayed among groups of refugees in Senegal, and the more she was implicated and engaged in their politics, the more pressing and ambitious the expectations of reciprocity became, particularly in relation to resettlement and fundraising. I also noticed shifts the longer I stayed in Senegal. The more my research participants got to know me, the more they were able to appreciate the efforts I was making to assist them. This included my mediation efforts with aid workers, even when these did not yield immediate results. I did, however, receive some complaints that I was not doing as much as I could. The unspoken understanding was that any move to reduce the amount of assistance I was providing, or to refuse the role of mediator between them and expat aid workers, would be treasonous.

A triple political imperative

Scholars who reflect on the ethics of research on forced migration speak of a dual imperative, understood as the obligation to produce research that is 'both academically sound and policy relevant' (Jacobsen and Landau 2003: 185) in order to contribute to improving refugees' living conditions.[14] 'Policy relevant' is often conflated with 'expertise', such as when researchers are solicited as country experts in asylum adjudications. As mentioned earlier, the researcher-expert's authority is conditional on a certain level of objectivity – that is, not taking a stance in favour or disfavour of the claimant. As is clear from my fieldwork in Senegal, and as McNeal (2019) shows with his experiences in Trinidad and Tobago, the road to knowledge for researchers working with LGBT asylum seekers is paved with political decisions regarding our positioning vis-à-vis asylum seekers and aid organizations. It is this political aspect that I wish to emphasize here. Building on Krause's (2017) call for researchers to acknowledge the dual imperative of their work – that is, to value both their scholarly responsibilities *and* their duty towards the refugees and asylum seekers involved in their work – I argue that a third layer is also necessary. I call this a *triple political imperative*, in that migration researchers must acknowledge the political components intrinsic to their work, including recognizing that they can and sometimes must take a political stance while conducting fieldwork. It is more than disclosing findings at the conclusion of a project, or acting as a 'country expert' for asylum institutions. Rather, researchers must respond to the demands and expectations of participants during fieldwork. Often an asylum seeker will ask a researcher to advocate for their individual case – a request that puts the researcher in a difficult position, not wanting to favour some research participants over others. Yet such demands must be taken seriously. What actually is being asked of us is to use our role to mediate between research participants and humanitarian actors. As I have shown, a mediator role comes with great responsibility and serious ethical concerns, yet these should not be used as an excuse to avoid assistance, usually by retreating behind claims of 'objectivity' and 'neutrality'. When the demands for mediation from my humanitarian research participants threatened to collide with those of my asylum seeker research participants, I decided to act in the most favourable way for the least privileged group – that is, the gay Gambians, rather than the white UNHCR staff.

Mediation offers, in most cases, less visibility than denouncing the injustice of a situation to a wider non-academic audience. This is especially true when one studies a topic as emotionally charged as 'LGBT refugees'. In such cases, there is a strong temptation to keep research results private during fieldwork in order to turn them into impactful media articles upon returning to the Global North. Whether such exposure would be more beneficial to participants than mediation or other types of on-site assistance is a decision that must be reached collaboratively with the least privileged actors in any scholarly engagement. Researchers must beware of the white humanist's drive to make queer Africans 'come out' to an audience in the Global North (Giametta 2014). 'Coming out' as an act of emancipation and a supposedly necessary step towards equal rights was part of the activist repertoire deployed by LGBT movements in North America during the second half of the twentieth century, and since then it has undergone global diffusion (Chabot and Duyvendak 2002). Efforts by Global North states and organizations to mainstream the fight for LGBT rights in the Global South, especially since the 2000s, through HIV prevention programmes or by strengthening the LGBT 'community', have had mixed results (Broqua 2018). As Kira Kosnick puts it:

[T]he assumption of a queer solidarity that spreads from the West to non-Western locations and subjects usually carries with it a highly problematic teleological vision of white, male gayness as the most advanced stage of queer identity and life forms.

(2010: 126–7)

Global North states and organizations openly finance LGBT groups advocating for the decriminalization of homosexuality in African countries, prompting accusations of imperialism and interference. All too often, these 'humanitarian' initiatives assume that the desire of social and political recognition based on SOGI is the same in, say, Senegal as it is in, say, Canada. There is also a tendency to ignore the complex histories, nuances and contemporary realities in each location (Gallardo 2016; Currier and Cruz 2014; Ekine and Abbas 2013). In many African contexts, these types of initiatives have intensified popular resistance and, in some cases, led to stricter criminalization (M'Baye 2013; Awondo, Geschiere and Reid 2012; Nyong'o 2012).

'Critical loyalty', or the critique from within

We left the Comede doctors at their ethical dilemma: should they give in to the growing demand for medical certificates, or should they refuse to perpetuate the myth of irrefutable proof in asylum cases? In a heated discussion between several Comede doctors about the practice of issuing medical certificates, an interesting aspect was raised:

> Speaker 6: But you've got to evaluate the risk, if we fail [to convince the state to let go of these certificates altogether], that the requests from the institutions go to paid experts who will take advantage of it.
>
> (Fassin and d'Halluin 2005: 601)

Members of Comede and other organizations feared that rejecting the role of mediators would push the burden of proof onto asylum seekers themselves. In other words, the state's demand for proof would remain, regardless of the doctors' decision. The concern was that asylum seekers would then be forced to either display their suffering bodies in courts, unmediated, or accept court-appointed (paid) experts, for whom the wellbeing of asylum seekers would not be the priority. The dilemma I faced in being asked to mediate between the gay Gambians and the UNHCR, or between the Senegalese group and RR, felt similar.

To get a positive outcome from the UNHCR, I knew I would have to reproduce simplistic narratives about West African LGBT lives. On the other hand, if I rejected the role of 'expert', I risked being perceived by the asylum seekers as refusing to reciprocate their time and energy. This would also leave them in the position of having to seek other, potentially less scrupulous, mediators. In analysing the Comede doctors' decision to continue acting as mediators, despite their misgivings about the flawed system they were embroiled in, d'Halluin (2006) applies Albert Hirschman's concept of 'critical loyalty' (1995 [1970]). For d'Halluin, this form of loyalty is weighed against the cost of defecting from a system; it is taken up with full awareness, rather than being a product of blind devotion. It is, in a sense, being a critical voice within a given system, while continuing to take on the role of 'expert'.

However, the 'critique from within' approach is only possible as long as those acting as experts do not become professionally or financially dependent on the institutions they advise. It is a pitfall worth mentioning. Indeed, with increasing precarity in the global academy, many sociologists and anthropologists are being driven to collaborate with well-resourced institutions. Jérôme Valluy (2007) stresses the danger of 'ideological osmosis' between the UNHCR and researchers, with the latter needing the agency's financial support to pursue their scholarly activities. Giulia Scalettaris (2013) also highlights the tendency of researchers eager to contribute to alleviating refugees' struggles to, often inadvertently, adhere cognitively and morally to the mandate of the UN agency. Similarly, Fresia (2018) warns of institutions indirectly silencing critique through financial incentives, such as when the UNHCR supports scholars through paid consultancies or specialized journals. In the long run, these practices turn the UNHCR into the producer of its own critical evaluations.

Conclusion

The ethical dilemma announced in the title of this chapter is at the core of migration researchers' *raison d'être*, in that it is not limited to the field of queer asylum studies, even if it appears vividly here. Indeed, it is a question that all of us must reckon with: how, as researchers conducting fieldwork on forced migration, do we position ourselves vis-à-vis both our research participants who are refugees or asylum seekers *and* our research participants who are aid workers? How do we take demands formulated by the former seriously without losing sight of our own research interests? And how can we be taken seriously by institutional research participants without constricting ourselves to the role of the objective and neutral 'expert'?

In this chapter, I have reflected on my experience of embodying 'expertise' on behalf of gay Gambian asylum seekers for three separate yet interrelated constituencies: the UNHCR, for whom my expertise revolved around my capacity to provide data for the ProGres databank; private sponsors in the Global North, for whom my expertise meant providing 'proof' of suffering; and an INGO, for whom my expertise was supported by my presence 'in the field' and my affiliation with a research institute in the Global North. My modest solution to this ethical dilemma has been to recognize the political component of conducting fieldwork, thereby embracing the responsibilities that researchers like myself have towards our refugee participants. This does not mean advocating for them in all cases, but rather mediating between them and humanitarian actors, if this is what they want. Framing it as the triple political imperative – one that is conscious of researchers' responsibilities towards refugee communities, humanitarian actors and our scholarly peers – allows us to pursue a form of critical loyalty at the crossroad of research precision and policy relevance. Retrospectively, I would frame my position as a general adhesion to what Didier Fassin conceptualizes as 'public ethnography', referring to 'what is publicised and how such a process can be apprehended: it is simultaneously an ethnography made public and the ethnography of this publicisation' (2017: 4). In many ways, this echoes Michel Foucault's (2001 [1976]) idea of the 'specific intellectual'. As Laurent Dartigues (2014) explains, a specific intellectual interferes in particular sectors, becoming politicized when she deploys specialized knowledge or skills. She is, one might say, a 'modest' intellectual, one who does not seek to establish herself as a universal conscience. She refuses to transform her political positions into statements of truth. Furthermore, as Fassin contends, specific intellectuals 'recognise that, although they take full responsibility for their analyses and statements, they owe much of their understanding to the people they study and work with. They are both independent and indebted' (2017: 5). This is the role I strived to play; I wanted my fieldwork to be a site of exchange. This is something I hope to continue now that I am back in Europe and my Gambian research participants have, for the most part, been resettled in the Global North.

Notes

1   Whereas my Gambian and Senegalese research participants used diverse appellations to refer to their sexual orientation among themselves, they – women and men alike – used the English term 'gay' when presenting themselves to strangers. It is for this reason that I use this term here. 'LGBT' is used as international organizations' emic vocabulary. I use 'queer' when referring to non-heteronormativity.
2   In West Africa, *'toubab'* is used generally to refer to persons with white to lighter skins, or to Africans from the diaspora who are perceived to behave like white people. The origin of the term is debated. Some claim that the word was derived from the Arabic word *tabib* (doctor). Others think it comes from Wolof for 'transforming', referring to the white missionaries who converted local resources.
3   This term, along with its short form 'expat', is often used by white people living outside of their country of origin in an effort to dodge the idea of being a migrant. Being recognizable as an 'expat' is a form of white privilege that migrants from the Global North hold on to, even in destinations where they have little institutional privileges, as Amélie Le Renard (2019) has shown in the case of Dubai. In this chapter, I intentionally use the term as an emic appellation.
4   All names have been changed.
5   This is not untypical of the ambiguous relationships between researchers and UNHCR staff (see Fresia 2018).
6   Referred to as 'international staff' in UNHCR jargon.
7   Referred to as 'national staff' or 'local staff' in UNHCR jargon.
8   ProGres is the software used by the UNHCR to capture refugee data.
9   A Wolof term for an economically interested romantic relationship, similar to sugar daddies (see Fouquet 2011).
10 It is, of course, difficult to define the role that this mediation played in successful resettlements to the Global North. Some of the gay Gambians' cases were rejected by the UNHCR and they remain in Dakar.

11 Short for 'men who have sex with men', a term introduced by epidemiologists and public health programmes in the Global South since the emergence of HIV prevention campaigns.

12 I have volunteered for the NGO Asylos since 2014.

13 Florence Bouillon, Marion Frésia and Virginie Tallio (2005) offer an interesting perspective on the proximity of aid workers and researchers in 'sensitive fieldworks'.

14 This is in itself a contested imperative. Employees of humanitarian agencies are not always open to critique and, when they are, they do not necessarily have the means to interpret and adapt scientific results to their practical daily work. Beyond these practical limitations, which Krause (2017: 23–4) discusses, scholars have rightly pointed to the necessity for 'policy-irrelevant research' (Bakewell 2008).

References

Adam, B. D., J. W. Duyvendak and A. Krouwel (1999), *The Global Emergence of Gay and Lesbian Politics: National Imprints of a Worldwide Movement*, Philadelphia: Temple University Press.

Altman, D. (2001), *Global Sex*, Chicago and London: University of Chicago Press.

Armisen, M. (2016), *We Exist: Mapping LGBTQ Organizing in West Africa*, New York: Astraea Lesbian Foundation for Justice.

Awondo, P., P. Geschiere and G. Reid (2012), 'Homophobic Africa? Toward a More Nuanced View', *African Studies Review*, 55 (3): 145–68.

Bakewell, O. (2008), 'Research beyond the Categories: The Importance of Policy Irrelevant Research into Forced Migration', *Journal of Refugee Studies*, 21 (4): 432–53.

Berg, L. and J. Millbank (2009), 'Constructing the Personal Narratives of Lesbian, Gay and Bisexual Asylum Claimants', *Journal of Refugee Studies*, 22 (2): 195–223.

Bhagat, A. (2018), 'Forced (Queer) Migration and Everyday Violence: The Geographies of Life, Death, and Access in Cape Town', *Geoforum*, 89: 155–63.

Bouillon, F., M. Fresia and V. Tallio (2005), 'Introduction: Les terrains sensibles à l'aune de la réflexivité', in F. Bouillon, M. Fresia and V. Tallio (eds), *Terrains sensibles. Expériences actuelles de l'anthropologie*, 13–28, Paris: Centre d'études africaines, EHESS.

Broqua, C. (2018), 'La « communauté homosexuelle » comme peuple transnational', *L'Homme et la société*, 208 (3): 143–67.

Broqua, C., G. Laborde-Balen, A. Menetrier and D. Bangoura (2021), 'Queer Necropolitics of Asylum: Senegalese Refugees Facing HIV/AIDS in Mauritania', *Global Public Health*, 16 (5): 746–62.

Camminga, B (2019), *Transgender Refugees and the Imagined South Africa*, London: Palgrave.

Chabot, S. and J. W. Duyvendak (2002), 'Globalization and Transnational Diffusion between Social Movements: Reconceptualizing the Dissemination of the Gandhian Repertoire and the "Coming Out" Routine', *Theory and Society*, 31 (6): 697–740.

Currier, A. and J. M. Cruz (2014), 'Civil Society and Sexual Struggles in Africa', in E. Obadare (ed.), *The Handbook of Civil Society in Africa*, 337-60, New York: Springer.

Dartigues, L. (2014), 'Une généalogie de l'intellectuel spécifique', *Astérion. Philosophie, histoire des idées, pensée politique*. doi: 10.4000/asterion.2560.

Ekine, S. and H. Abbas (eds) (2013), *Queer African Reader*, Cape Town: Pambazuka Press.

Fassin, D. (2017), 'Introduction: When Ethnography Goes Public', in D. Fassin (ed.), *If Truth Be Told: The Politics of Public Ethnography*, 1–16, Durham: Duke University Press.

Fassin, D. and E. d'Halluin (2005), 'The Truth from the Body: Medical Certificates as Ultimate Evidence for Asylum Seekers', *American Anthropologist*, 107 (4): 597–608.

Fechter, A. M. and K. Walsh (2010), 'Examining "Expatriate" Continuities: Postcolonial Approaches to Mobile Professionals', *Journal of Ethnic and Migration Studies*, 36 (8): 1197–210.

Foucault, M. (2001), *Dits et écrits II, année 1976, n° 184*, Paris: Gallimard (Quarto).

Fouquet, T. (2011), 'Filles de la nuit, aventurières de la cité: Arts de la citadinité et désirs de l'Ailleurs à Dakar', PhD dissertation, EHESS, Paris.

Fresia, M. (2005), 'Entre mises en scène et non-dits: Comment interpréter la souffrance des autres', in F. Bouillon, M. Fresia and V. Tallio (eds), *Terrains sensibles. Expériences actuelles de l'anthropologie*, 31–54, Paris: Centre d'études africaines, EHESS.

Fresia, M. (2018), 'Enquêter au coeur de la bureaucratie transnationale de l'asile', in M. Fresia and P. Lavigne-Delville (eds), *Au coeur des mondes de l'aide internationale*, 41–74, Karthala: IRD et APAD.

Gallardo, L. (2016), 'Plaider la cause homosexuelle en Afrique: Engagements et enjeux de visibilité au sein d'un réseau franco-africain', *Critique internationale*, 70 (1): 71–86.

Giametta, C. (2014), '"Rescued" Subjects: The Question of Religiosity for Non-heteronormative Asylum Seekers in the UK', *Sexualities*, 17 (5/6): 583–99.

Glasman, J. (2017), 'Seeing Like a Refugee Agency: A Short History of UNHCR Classifications in Central Africa (1961–2015)', *Journal of Refugee Studies*, 30 (2): 337–62.

Glasman, J. (2020), *Humanitarianism and the Quantification of Human Needs: Minimal Humanity*, New York: Routledge.

Gouyon, M. (2018), 'La sincérité des sentiments et des mots. Les logiques essentialisantes d'une économie morale occidentale des homosexualités masculines au Maroc', *L'Année du Maghreb*, 18: 111–26.

d'Halluin, E. (2006), 'Entre expertise et témoignage: L'éthique humanitaire à l'épreuve des politiques migratoires', *Vacarme*, 34 (1): 112–17.

Hirschman, A. O. (1995), *Défection et prise de parole*, Paris: Fayard.

Jacobsen, K. and L. B. Landau (2003), 'The Dual Imperative in Refugee Research: Some Methodological and Ethical Considerations in Social Science Research on Forced Migration', *Disasters*, 27 (3): 185–206.

Jenicek, A., A. D. Wong and E. O. J. Lee (2009), 'Dangerous Shortcuts: Representations of Sexual Minority Refugees in the Post-9/11 Canadian Press', *Canadian Journal of Communication*, 34 (4): 635–58.

Kosnick, K. (2010), 'Diasporas and Sexuality', in K. Knott and S. McLoughlin (eds), *Diasporas: Concepts, Intersections, Identities*, 123–7, New York: Zed Books.

Krause, U. (2017), *Researching Forced Migration: Critical Reflections on Research Ethics during Fieldwork*, RSC Working Paper Series – 123, Oxford: Refugee Studies Centre.

Le Renard, A. (2019), *Le privilège occidental. Travail, intimité et hiérarchies postcoloniales à Dubaï*, Paris: Presses de SciencesPo.

Lee, E. O. J. and S. Brotman (2011), 'Identity, Refugeeness, Belonging: Experiences of Sexual Minority Refugees in Canada', *Canadian Review of Sociology*, 48 (3): 241–74.

Marnell, J., E. Oliveira and G. H. Khan (2021), '"It's about Being Safe and Free to Be Who You Are": Exploring the Lived Experiences of Queer Migrants, Refugees and Asylum Seekers in South Africa', *Sexualities*, 24 (1/2): 86–110.

Matebeni, Z. (2014), *Reclaiming Afrikan: Queer Perspectives on Sexual and Gender Identities*, Cape Town: Modjaji Books.

Mauss, M. (2002), *The Gift: The Form and Reason for Exchange in Archaic Societies*, London: Routledge.

M'Baye, B. (2013), 'The Origins of Senegalese Homophobia: Discourses on Homosexuals and Transgender People in Colonial and Postcolonial Senegal', *African Studies Review*, 56 (2): 109–28.

McNeal, K. E. (2019), 'Confessions of an Ambivalent Country Expert: Queer Refugeeism in the UK and the Political Economy of (Im)mobility in and out of Trinidad and Tobago', *Anthropological Theory*, 19 (1): 191–215.

Menetrier, A. (2019), 'Using Social Networking to Decipher Gender Stereotypes at Refugee Intake Points', *Hermès, La Revue*, 83 (1): 177–85.

Menetrier, A. (2021), 'Implementing and Interpreting Refugee Resettlement through a Veil of Secrecy: A Case of LGBT Resettlement from Africa', *Frontiers in Human Dynamics*, 3. doi: 10.3389/fhumd.2021.594214.

Murray, D. (2018), 'Learning to Be LGBT: Sexual Orientation Refugees and Linguistic Inequality', *Critical Multilingualism Studies*, 6 (1): 56–73.

Noiriel, G. (1998), *Réfugiés et sans-papiers: la République face au droit d'asile, XIXe–XXe siècle*, Hachette, Paris.

Nyanzi, S. (2016), 'When the State Produces Hate: Re-thinking the Global Queer Movement through Silence in the Gambia', in S. Bala and A. Tellis (eds), *The Global Trajectories of Queerness*, 179–93, London: Brill.

Nyong'o, T. (2012), 'Queer Africa and the Fantasy of Virtual Participation', *Women's Studies Quarterly*, 40 (1/2): 40–63.

Rainbow Railroad (2019), 'What We Do'. Available online: www.rainbowrailroad.org/whatwedo (accessed 15 January 2021).

Saleh, F. (2020), 'Queer/Humanitarian Visibility: The Emergence of the Figure of the Suffering Syrian Gay Refugee', *Middle East Critique*, 29 (1): 47–67.

Scalettaris, G. (2013), 'La fabrique du gouvernement international des réfugiés', PhD dissertation, EHESS, Paris.

Shakhsari, S. (2014), 'The Queer Time of Death: Temporality, Geopolitics, and Refugee Rights', *Sexualities*, 17 (8): 998–1015.

Shuman, A. and W. S. Hesford (2014), 'Getting Out: Political Asylum, Sexual Minorities, and Privileged Visibility', *Sexualities*, 17 (8): 1016–34.

Ticktin, M. I. (2011), *Casualties of Care: Immigration and the Politics of Humanitarianism in France*, Berkeley: University of California Press.

Valluy, J. (2007), 'Contribution à une sociologie politique du HCR: le cas des politiques européennes et du HCR au Maroc', *Recueil Alexandries, Collections Etudes*, 1. Available online: http://www.reseau-terra.eu/article571.html (accessed 12 January 2022).

Chapter 5

'SHEEP IN A PEN': HOW THE EXTERNALIZATION OF EU BORDERS IMPACTS THE LIVES OF GAY REFUGEES IN MOROCCO

Marien Gouyon

The United Nations High Commissioner for Refugees (UNHCR) has had a presence in Morocco since 1965. Its role was initially more symbolic than political (Valluy 2007), but this changed when the European Council endorsed the Hague Program in 2004 (European Council 2005). Billed as an effort to strengthen 'freedom, security and justice in the European Union', the Hague Program emphasized a need for 'integrated management of external borders'. European Union (EU) policy describes the externalization of borders as such:

> [A]ssisting third countries, in full partnership, using existing Community funds where appropriate, in their efforts to improve their capacity for migration management and refugee protection, prevent and combat illegal immigration, inform on legal channels for migration, resolve refugee situations by providing better access to durable solutions, build border-control capacity, enhance document security and tackle the problem of return.
>
> (European Council 2005: 5)

In other words, the EU attempts to control irregular migration flows by stemming movement at the borders of neighbouring states. One key site for achieving this goal is Morocco (Stock 2020).

Prior to the EU's adoption of the Hague Program, Morocco took a fairly lax approach to migration, concerned more with its own diaspora than with its status as a launching point for Europe (Lowe et al. 2020). The aforementioned shift in EU policy and the substantial economic incentives it brought for countries willing to assist in migration management heralded a new era for Morocco (den Hertog 2016). From that point on, the Moroccan state became increasingly focused on 'border controls and the prevention of irregular migration flows' (Lowe et al. 2020: 7). Indeed, the decade that followed was characterized by the enactment of security-focused legislation and regular violent crackdowns (Jacobs 2019).

In 2013, Morocco's migration policy shifted again courtesy of the new National Strategy for Immigration and Asylum (Grau et al. 2019; Royaume du Maroc 2013). A major change in the country's approach to asylum, the framework promised a 'humane and rights-based approach to migration management' (Lowe et al. 2020: 7). Focused not just on stemming the flow of movement but also on integrating migrants into Moroccan society, the 'policy had the potential to serve Europe's objective of reducing irregular onward migration to its borders, by providing opportunities and incentives for migrants to stay in Morocco' (Lowe et al. 2020: 8). The policy also allowed the UNHCR to grant asylum to a greater number of applicants as part of a wider effort to regularize migrants in the country (Lahlou 2018). Since then, the UNHCR has played a central role in managing migration flows by overseeing and implementing the EU's resettlement programme.

The growing influence of the UNHCR in Morocco has brought to light tensions in the handling of asylum claims based on sexual orientation. While Moroccan law now enshrines a rights-based approach to migration – although the on-the-ground reality is usually very different – it continues to punish sexual relations between people of the same sex through Article 489 of the Criminal Code. This is reinforced by Article 3, which prohibits organizations whose 'purpose or illegitimate objective contravenes laws or public morals' (Cairo Institute of Human Rights Studies 2018). The country's response to sexual and gender rights is at odds with international refugee law[1] and, at times, with the workings of the UNHCR, given that that latter nominally affords protection to lesbian, gay, bisexual, transgender, intersex and queer (LGBTIQ) people. This has fostered a fragile balancing act between the interests, policies and approaches of the UNHCR (and by extension the EU, as its second-largest funder) and those of the Moroccan state. This tension has become even more apparent as LGBTIQ people in Morocco are subjected to increasing levels of violence and repression (Hersh 2019). Examining this tension between local and international responses to LGBTIQ rights provides significant insights into how borders are represented, imagined, recomposed and transformed in different spaces and contexts.

Following Éric Fassin (2006), I seek to unpack how multiple borders work to protect the ideological foundation of 'sexual democracy'. This concept refers to both the legislative space guaranteeing rights for LGBTIQ persons in the Global North and the discursive space surrounding these issues. It represents an 'extension of the democratic domain, with the increasing politicisation of gender and sexuality issues, which is revealed and encouraged by the many current public controversies' (Fassin 2006: 123). In other words, the boundaries of sexual democracy are at once physical, discursive and symbolic: the first largely results from governmental control mechanisms, the second from debates in the public sphere and the third from evolving norms, moralities and social relations. The boundaries produced through such processes are amorphous, negotiated and shifted in line with local, regional and global trends. What remains constant is a loosely defined 'other' that threatens advances in sexual and gender rights. Asylum is a key domain in which these contestations play out; policy and procedural responses to LGBTIQ mobilities point to geopolitical tensions over the transmission, enactment, imposition and regulation of human rights.

In this chapter, I argue that LGBTIQ refugees and asylum seekers[2] in Morocco – specifically, in this context of this study, gay men – are exposed to, adopt and signify specific understandings of sexual and gender rights in the hope of being resettled. However, because of the externalization of the EU's borders, these individuals struggle to access the protections supposedly brought about by sexual democracy. The Moroccan state is now effectively a proxy for the EU, courtesy of its efforts to stop migration flows, often with the support of the UNHCR. Indeed, Morocco acts on behalf of the EU's and UNHCR's interests to ensure that migrants arriving in the country follow institutional norms and regulations as specified by these external organizations. As Jérôme Valluy (2007) states:

> In the European perspective of externalisation of asylum, organisations working and advocating for the right of asylum are given political and financial incentives to improve the reception conditions of sub-Saharan migrants in the Maghreb countries. This perspective is divided into two main areas of work, the main coordinator of which is UNHCR: (1) to develop in these countries, by diplomatic pressure and ideological training, the right of asylum in its restrictive conception linked to the Geneva Convention (2) to create, as in Europe, reception, waiting and social support centres for the rejection of exiles.
>
> (para. 59)[3]

Regulations and norms promoted by international actors such as the EU and the UNHCR are internalized and replicated by asylum seekers and those who manage them. This can be seen in the language, gestures and presentations adopted by hopeful applicants or in the practices and activities of civil society organizations. This reading aligns with Hastings Donnan and Thomas Wilson's (1999) concept of 'enacted borders', in which social norms and practices penetrate 'deeply into the territory of the state' (15). Yet, these international regulations and norms are still mediated through local values, beliefs and customs. In Morocco, this translates into LGBTIQ refugees being relegated to an in-between zone where they are simultaneously legal and illegal. They inhabit a perpetual state of limbo, torn between the norms of international actors and those of the society in which they are stuck.

The EU's approach to asylum based on sexual orientation has been critiqued in previous studies (Chossière 2020; Giametta 2017; Raboin 2017; Mai 2012). However, this literature is largely based on ethnographies carried out in France and the United Kingdom. It is also mainly concerned with how specific constructions of sexuality, gender and citizenship work to uphold sexual democracy within European states (Fassin 2006). As Calogero Giametta (2017) explains, discourses on asylum based on sexual orientation reproduce dominant stereotypes about sexual norms, prejudices and practices in the Global South, particularly in Muslim countries, and in doing so 'externaliz[e] the problems of sexism and homophobia outside the cultural and geographical frontiers of the EU' (17).

In response to the geographical and conceptual limitations of these studies, I examine how the externalization of the EU's borders in Morocco impacts the lives of gay Cameroonians seeking protection. My analysis shows that these individuals are forced to navigate local norms and regulations that often conflict with the principles of international refugee law. It also points to fractures within 'sexual democracy' when it is (forcibly) exported to contexts that criminalize same-sex relationships. I argue that contestations and incoherencies emerge not only through the externalization of physical borders but also through the dissemination of competing discourses about sex, gender and sexuality. As will be shown, gay refugees from sub-Saharan Africa experience particular forms of victimization in Morocco stemming from tensions between the operations of the UNHCR and the heteronormativity of their host country.

Externalization in action: Morocco's evolving approach to refugee management

Over the last two decades, the EU has put in considerable effort to 'strengthening' its border control mechanisms. As well as revising its visa protocols, the EU has encouraged neighbouring countries to standardize their migration policies in order to 'manage' movement into the suprastate. In 2005, for example, the EU launched its Global Approach to Migration Management, the objective of which was to combat and prevent irregular migration through international partnerships (among other aims). Morocco was one of the first countries targeted in this push to control migration flows, with the EU deploying a variety of bilateral instruments to promote external migration management (Zanker 2019). In 2013, Morocco signed one of the EU's so-called 'mobility partnerships'. These use a 'demand' and 'incentive' model to encourage the securitization of borders – in other words, visa facilitation for Moroccan nationals and access to EU funding are offered in return for the implementation of stricter migration controls (den Hertog 2016).

As noted, the EU's externalization of its border had a direct impact on Morocco's domestic policies, including the adoption of the National Strategy for Immigration and Asylum and the revival of the defunct Bureau des Réfugiés et des Apatrides (BRA). These changes also affected the UNHCR's operations, including temporarily handing over responsibility for registering refugees and for issuing residency permits to the Moroccan state. Although short lived – the UNHCR resumed these responsibilities after only a few weeks, once it became evident that the BRA did not have an effective system – the UNHCR has repeatedly expressed its commitment to supporting Morocco's efforts to formalize its national asylum framework and to take responsibility for refugee management within its borders.

What is particularly important in the context of this chapter is the UNHCR's endorsement (both implicit and explicit) of a local integration model, in which refugees and asylum seekers remain in Morocco rather than entering the EU.

Furthermore, the UNHCR's and EU's push to stabilize migrant populations in Africa is linked both practically and discursively to a programme of promoting 'humane' and 'rights-based' approach to migration on a global scale. This has close parallels with the notion of sexual democracy, in that both are built on the logic that human freedoms can be secured through legal reforms. The paradox created by Morocco's role as a guardian of Europe's borders while at the same time criminalizing LGBTIQ persons reveals the limitations of the EU's self-representation as a defender and promoter of global human rights. As Nicholas Hersh (2019) notes, 'local integration and voluntary repatriation are not durable solutions for LGBTI refugees in Morocco, so resettlement to another country is often their only chance of a life where they can freely and safely express their SOGIE' (300) – although such an outcome is almost impossible under the externalization of the EU's borders.

The exact number of LGBTIQ refugees in Morocco is unknown as there are no reliable statistics from either the UNHCR or the Moroccan state. According to UNHCR representative Jean-Paul Cavalieri – whom I interviewed for this study – 21 per cent of asylum claims submitted in Morocco in 2016 were on the basis of sexual orientation, compared to just 2 per cent in 2015. However, he was unable to disclose how many applications these percentages translate to, making it impossible to gauge the statistical significance of this increase. It is known that thirty-six individuals were awarded refugee status on the grounds of sexual orientation in 2018. Again, the percentage of applicants this represents, or whether any of these individuals received resettlement, remains unclear as this information was not disclosed. What is known is that refugee status and resettlement are rare for individuals coming from countries like Cameroon. While the criminalization of same-sex relations in Cameroon is recognized by the UNHCR, it is not enough to ensure a successful asylum application. This is because the UNHCR views most Cameroonians as economic migrants, even if they identify as LGBTIQ, as Cavalieri explains:

> It is true that many Cameroonians are people who have fled out of fear of persecution because of their sexual orientation. These people flee their country because of persecution from people around them and because the authorities are unable to protect them. The [same-sex sexual] act itself is penalised. Yet 90 per cent of Cameroonians who apply to UNHCR have their asylum applications rejected because most Cameroonians arriving in Morocco are economic migrants and not refugees.

Cavalieri's wording points to the pervasive belief that migrants can be divided into two categories: those who are 'deserving' of protection because they are 'legitimate' refugees and those who are 'undeserving' because they are trying to 'play the system' for economic gain. The negative impact of this belief on LGBTIQ asylum cases has been widely documented in other contexts (Akin 2018; Giametta 2017; Raboin 2017).

Methodology

The data presented here emerged from fieldwork carried out between July and August 2018 with twenty-one Cameroonians living in Rabat. All of my interlocutors identified as gay men, all came from lower- to middle-class families, and all had fled their homes out of fear that their sexual orientation would be discovered, particularly by their families. At the time of my fieldwork, only four interlocutors had been granted refugee status, while the rest either were busy preparing for status determination interviews or had already had their claims rejected. At the time of my research, my interlocutors had all been waiting in Morocco for more than a year. Given the uncertainty of their future, some were planning a sea crossing to Europe.

All of the men interviewed belong to the Association of Sub-Saharan Gays (ASGYS), a non-official collective of gay migrants living in Morocco. Members of the collective provide each other with emotional and financial support, which is particularly important considering the limited livelihood opportunities open to them. Members will often pool wages or resources (including support payments from UNHCR or civil society organizations) so as to benefit the larger collective.

My first encounter with ASGYS came through the gay networking app Grindr, which I hoped would provide access to sub-Saharan Africans living in Morocco. Initially, potential interlocutors tried to negotiate payment for interviews, a request I denied, and it was only after building a rapport with Gregoire[4] (see below) that I was able to 'access' the gay Cameroon community. Gregoire's interest in my work, combined with the trust that had begun to form between us, allowed me to build a snowball sample, with early interviewees encouraging others to take part.

My in-person fieldwork was only one step in gathering and analysing data. Communication with interlocutors continued via WhatsApp once I returned to France, allowing me to track developments in their cases and to build a more nuanced understanding of their lives. Almost all of my interlocutors asked to listen to their interview recordings so that they could provide additional comments. I also conducted follow-up telephonic interviews with some individuals in order to clarify key points.

It became evident early on that my interlocutors saw the project as a way to learn about and prepare for UNHCR interviews. Some saw our interviews as a practice run, leading them to present their life stories as they had rehearsed for refugee status adjudicators. Having multiple engagements allowed interlocutors to better understand the scope and purpose of my study, especially the fact that interviews with me would not directly influence the outcome of any resettlement assessments. Building this level of trust and understanding was not always easy given the limited time I was in Morocco. However, the more I engaged with my interlocutors, the more they began to open up about their experiences and to share their concerns, frustrations and hopes.

In addition to my engagements with the gay Cameroonians, I was able to interview an officer from the UNHCR branch office in Rabat. I had hoped this interview would shed light on how UNHCR views the paradoxical situation in which LGBTIQ asylum seekers in Morocco find themselves. However, as is often the case when dealing with intergovernmental agencies, it proved difficult to move the conversation beyond official rhetoric.

I was also able to interview a senior manager at an NGO that assists vulnerable communities, including LGBTIQ refugees. Civil society organizations are responsible for the vast majority of humanitarian assistance offered to displaced persons in Morocco. According to Inka Stock (2020), the predominance of NGO-led relief programmes is directly linked to the EU's policy of externalizing its borders. EU funding – often dispersed through the UNHCR and its partners – prioritizes a 'care and control' approach (Stock 2020: 13) that uses NGOs to fill gaps created by inadequate state services. Various financial incentives aimed at capacity-development and programmatic activities allow the EU to promote the narrative that Morocco can safely and accountably protect displaced persons within its borders. As well as assisting with asylum applications/interviews, the NGO I spoke to provides sub-Saharan Africans with employment assistance, language training (especially Arabic and English), housing information, medical support and psychosocial services. I have chosen not to name the organization here so as not to jeopardize its operation or beneficiaries.

A dangerous journey

Cameroonians and other sub-Saharan Africans hoping to access Europe via the western Mediterranean usually reach Morocco via a dangerous desert crossing (Malakooti and Fall 2020). Starting at the Gulf of Guinea, they follow the traditional route of trans-Saharan caravans through Arlit and Assamaka (Niger) and then onto Tamanrasset (Algeria), often with the assistance of Tuareg smugglers. They then move through Ghardaïa and Maghnia (Algeria) before crossing the border near Oujda (Morocco). Many try to access the heavily fortified Spanish enclaves of Melilla and Ceuta, and failing this may head towards Rabat or other metropolitan centres.

While this is the most well-known migration route to Morocco, it is not the only one. As many scholars point out, the journey from Africa to Europe can take myriad forms; strategies and routes are not a given for one and all (de Haas 2007). Rather, pathways are negotiated and transformed based on opportunities and challenges encountered along the way. Various political, social and economic factors within transit countries (e.g. armed conflict or disruption of smuggling networks) can shape migration trajectories, as can individual needs, resources and expectations. As an example, I spoke with a gay Cameroonian living in Dubai as part of later fieldwork. For him, the best strategy for accessing Europe was believed to be through the Middle East. In reaching this conclusion, he had weighed up the sheer physical strength required for overland migration roads in North Africa against the fact that he had established contacts in the United Arab Emirates. For many others, Morocco is the preferred launch pad for the EU, with the overland route described above (or a variation of it) the best option for gaining access.

Morocco's reputation as a desirable destination for potential LGBTIQ refugees is supported by informal knowledge exchange networks that circulate information about the UNHCR, specifically the potential for third-country resettlement. All of my interlocutors acknowledged hearing about this possibility during their migrations. Once in country, based on information they had received, they headed to Rabat to meet with other gay Cameroonians, who in turn introduced them to ASGYS and formal NGOs.

Although each of my interlocutors had a unique tale, their overall life experiences and migration trajectories were similar. They had each left Cameroon exclusively or in part because of their sexual orientation, with all but one using smugglers to facilitate clandestine border crossings. For this reason, I focus on just one account here to illustrate the complex and dangerous journeys undertaken by these men. When I met Gregoire, he was twenty-five years old. Back in Cameroon, he had worked in public administration. His parents were unaware that he was gay; only a select number of his friends knew about his sexuality. After the murder of his best friend by a homophobic relative, Gregoire decided to leave Cameroon. Fearful of having to explain his decision and potentially being detained by his parents, Gregoire resolved to leave in secret. He has since contacted his parents and explained that his migration was motivated by a desire to improve his socio-economic status in Europe. His parents remain unaware of the real reason for his departure. His social position and economic situation in Cameroon meant that he could not migrate to Europe via a tourist or student visa. Instead, he decided to 'burn the borders' – a common expression among migrants that is derived from the Arabic word '*hrague*'. According to geographer Chadia Arab, this expression can have various meanings, but is most often used to denote an illegal border crossing. To 'burn' in this sense is to transcend or transgress (Arab 2007: 87).

Gregoire was aware of the UNHCR's presence in Morocco at the time of his departure, but decided it was easiest to access the EU through Ceuta. He had saved some money to finance this long and treacherous journey. He knew there was a high risk of being robbed en route and so hid his money in the sole of his shoe. During the desert crossing, Gregoire was detained by bandits and forced to strip naked; while captive he was left without food or water and witnessed women being raped. He and other hostages were then sold in Algeria. Forcibly moved to a house and locked up, the group was told by their 'owner' that they could either buy their release or work off the debt. Thanks to the money in his shoe, which had still not been discovered, Gregoire was able to secure his freedom along with that of a man with whom he had become close. Without his precious savings, Gregoire could no longer continue with his original plan. He and his friend left for Algiers, where they attempted to earn enough money to move on. He was eventually able to cross the border near Oujda, a city in the northeast of Morocco. In comparison to Gregoire's earlier border crossings, the move from Algeria to Morocco was far less painful and difficult. This was in large part due to his romantic relationship with one of the smugglers, who helped facilitate his crossing. Once in Morocco,

Gregoire made his way to Rabat and initiated an asylum application with the UNHCR, based on information he had learnt while in transit.

When homophobia meets racism

The asylum process in Morocco is long and arduous, with claimants given little support while their applications are processed. When I met John, he was twenty-three years old. He had come to Rabat on a student visa, having been accepted for a tourism degree. Although he had not experienced direct homophobia in Cameroon, he had seen how violence was meted out against men like him, both by the state and by the broader community. Just like Gregoire, he felt an ever-present threat of danger. Before leaving Cameroon, John had not planned to stay in Morocco or travel to Europe, but his subsequent experiences pushed him to re-evaluate his future. By the time we met, John's goal was to reach Belgium or Germany, yet obtaining a work or study permit was not an option for him. Instead, he applied for asylum, but like many gay men he struggled to convince the UNHCR either of his sexual orientation or of a well-founded fear of persecution stemming from it. Despite the rejection, John is adamant that he cannot return home because, for him, living as a gay man in Cameroon is impossible. He believes that surviving homophobic violence in Cameroon is very much dependent on one's economic status and connection with the social and political elite. He told me that you have to 'have charisma and a family to be able to live without any problems'. He explained further that living as a gay man in Cameroon would mean 'a loss of speed in the race for hierarchy, the quest for power, and everything can fall on you'.

For now, John has chosen to remain in Morocco as an undocumented migrant, although this comes with its own challenges. In particular, he has experienced multiple instances of racism:

> I am waiting to get refugee status. But, in the meantime, Moroccans are racist towards me, even on dating applications. Some Moroccan gay [men] have told me that I am black so I am dirty and a slave. Daily life is not peaceful here. I do not even have my family or friends here, just [other gay] people I have met because we are in the same shit.

After completing his studies, John met a Swedish man working in Morocco. They began a romantic relationship and ended up living together, but were forced to separate when the latter took up a position in Geneva. When they were still together, the couple would host regular house parties to which they would invite John's friends, many of whom were from sub-Saharan Africa. In the complex where John and his partner stayed, parties were permitted as long as other residents were given advanced notice in writing. John says that he always complied with this requirement, but the concierge responsible for distributing the letters often refused to deliver them on John's behalf. He would tell John that he had no right to be in the residence, given that it was frequented by Western 'expats' and that he did not look like a Westerner. John told his partner about this exchange. His partner immediately went to speak to the concierge about John's right to live in the residence and to host parties, should he so desire. For John, the incident is an indication that 'you have to shout louder to be respected [in Morocco], especially if you are sub-Saharan [African]'.

John's reading of this situation may be true in a general sense, but the concierge's comments about 'being' and 'not being' a Westerner point to a particular dynamic that deserves close attention. John's partner had an influential international job and all of the prestige that accompanied it. Amélie Le Renard (2019) calls this 'occidental privilege' – a set of provisions that allow Western expatriates to exploit economic and social advantages while abroad. These facilitate a self-confidence that ensures the reproduction of status and entitlement. For Le Renard, occidental privilege is distributed according to the social positions occupied by Westerners. It constructs the mysteries of Westernness by instrumentalizing the relationships of gender, sexuality, class and race. This is evident in the case of John's partner and can perhaps also be observed in asylum regimes more broadly (see Agier 2018; Cantu Jr 2009; Luibheid 2002).

In this case, John's partner had an EU passport that provided him with almost effortless movement across borders. Even though he identifies as gay and engages in sex acts with other men, he is not required to confess these personal details to an international agency in order to access protection, but rather travels the world with little restriction. John's partner also had a certain level of economic security as indicated by his accommodation: he lived in a secure complex associated with largely white international workers. To echo the concierge's vocabulary, John's partner *looked* like a Westerner and was therefore able to claim his 'right' to respect and authority. In Morocco, Westerners often enjoy socio-economic positions that are unattainable to locals due to the unequal distribution of wealth in the country (Peraldi and Terrazzoni 2016; Khrouz and Lanza 2015). The respect the concierge eventually afforded John may have been a consequence of his being a 'loud' sub-Saharan African, but it was also likely a transference of occidental privilege courtesy of his white partner's intervention. Whatever the reason, it remains clear that men like John are forced to confront multiple forms of discrimination in Morocco, stemming not just from their sexual orientation but also from entrenched anti-black sentiments.

Solidarity efforts

As flagged above, gay sub-Saharan men living in Morocco have established informal collectives to assist in navigating and surviving daily life. However, the asylum application procedure can threaten these forms of solidarity. Those who have not been granted refugee status sometimes sideline those who have obtained it out of jealousy or frustration. This is the case with Gregoire:

When I learnt that I had the status, I went back to the neighbourhood and everyone said that I had slept with an agent to get it. Everyone was jealous of me because I was going to receive money from UNHCR and be resettled.

Gregoire was not alone in this experience, suggesting that the existential and legal limbo created by asylum adjudication procedures has significant social impacts that extend beyond the individual concerned. At the same time, divisions between gay migrants and local gay men can make it even more difficult to organize politically or respond to social challenges.

Gregoire is part of the ASGYS collective mentioned above. The group's members welcome new arrivals in Rabat, share information on the asylum procedure, and provide financial and material support to each other. Despite having strong internal solidarity, the group has little engagement with and support from the local LGBTIQ community. At the time of my fieldwork, the ASWAT Collective,[5] one of Morocco's most prominent LGBTIQ activist groups, did not have any ties with ASGYS. In fact, ASWAT members indicated that they were unaware of ASGYS or similar collectives, despite ASWAT's stated commitment to supporting LGBTIQ migrants living in Morocco.

Gregoire puts this lack of connection down to distrust, explaining that ASGYS members are wary of their local counterparts and vice versa. From the migrant side, reluctance stems from racist encounters, such as John's experiences on dating apps. To understand the other side, it is important to recognize the paradoxical situation that LGBTIQ Moroccans find themselves in. Unlike their sub-Saharan counterparts, gay Moroccans cannot apply for asylum in Morocco, even though the local UNHCR branch accepts and processes such claims (this exclusion stems from the 1951 Refugee Convention). The Moroccan state is oppressive to both groups through its legislation, yet Moroccans wishing to claim asylum have to leave their country to do so. Most head to the neighbouring Spanish enclaves, as these may be used as an entry point to Spain and thus the EU. Mohammed, a forty-year-old Moroccan whom I met in Rabat, made it clear that, for him, solidarity with asylum seekers, such as those in the ASGYS collective, was unthinkable. His attitude can be read as a manifestation of the externalization of borders: for Mohammed, solidarity cannot be built with those who are competing against him to obtain protection. This is especially true when those perceived as competitors are considered to have an advantage, in that they are at least able to lodge an asylum claim in Morocco.

Here the logics and operations of international protection mechanisms create a divide between people with comparable experiences and needs. Just like my Cameroonians interlocutors, LGBTIQ Moroccans remain stigmatized and criminalized, yet only the former are able to lodge asylum claims through UNHCR Rabat. This opportunity is denied to locals thanks to international refugee protocols and is exacerbated by the EU's failure to open up migration/asylum pathways for LGBTIQ persons stuck in repressive social contexts (Danisi 2018). In the case of Morocco, the divide between LGBTIQ locals and migrants is further entrenched by EU financial incentives, such as those offered to local and international NGOs. The EU's massive cash injection in Morocco means that 'vulnerable' migrant populations are able to receive social support that is denied to equally desperate locals. Indeed, it would seem that the presence of international agencies mandated to assist asylum seekers, and perhaps even the work of local organizations, forecloses the possibility of inter-community solidarity. In creating sites of support for non-nationals, the UNHCR and its institutional partners drive a wedge between individuals living in similar circumstances and enduring comparable struggles. This is most obvious in the fact that LGBTIQ Moroccans must go elsewhere before being eligible for assistance. Rather than heralding a new era for LGBTIQ rights in Morocco, the externalization of the EU's physical borders has solidified the legislative and discursive borders of sexual democracy, leaving both Moroccan and non-Moroccan LGBTIQ persons competing for access to basic rights.

Daily life while awaiting resettlement

LGBTIQ refugees in Morocco are technically protected by the UCHCR and therefore entitled to social assistance, but their everyday realities often tell a different story. In practice, they rarely receive immediate or appropriate forms of support, while also being subjected to various forms of violence and discrimination (Hersh 2019). This has certainly been the case for Romain. Only twenty-seven years of age when we met, Romain had already been confirmed as a refugee for eight years. The reasons why Romain was granted refugee status remain elusive, especially in light of the difficulties that other gay sub-Saharan applicants have encountered, and may simply be a result of the time in which his claim was lodged or the bureaucrat assessing it. What is of most interest here is the instability Romain continues to face even after a positive determination. For gay refugees like Romain, third-country resettlement seems increasingly unlikely. When it became clear to Romain that the process had stalled indefinitely, with no explanation from UNHCR and no indication of when – or even *if* – resettlement might one day transpire, he began planning to access Europe clandestinely. His goal was to 'burn the border' by first entering Spain and then making his way to France. When we met, he was just about to begin this journey. He had been in contact with people in Tangier who would help facilitate his sea voyage. Aware of the dangers the journey posed, yet also feeling like he had nothing left to lose, Romain took the difficult decision to risk his life. In his mind, having refugee status in a country that does not protect homosexuality was pointless; to stay in Morocco was to live without liberty or dignity. His planned leaving date was September 2019, but one month before then he learnt that the Moroccan authorities were – at the behest of the EU – more forcefully tracking and detaining sub-Saharan Africans attempting sea crossings. Concerned about punitive measures from the Moroccan state, Romain cancelled his plans. Interestingly, his change in circumstances prompted a shift in his perception of being stuck in Morocco. After years of doubts, he resigned himself to staying in Rabat and found a job through his gay migrant social networks. He started working in a restaurant as a cook, with the aim of learning how to run a restaurant:

> I am a manager in a small African restaurant in Rabat. ... I am still the same person except for the maturity that is growing in me. ... I cannot say that everything is rosy, but nevertheless I can manage situations better that I used to.

When I asked Romain if he believed he would eventually be resettled, he explained that he still hoped to one day make it to Canada. However, each time he checked with the UNHCR, he was told to wait. Even though he finds these dismissive responses distressing, he believes there is still hope, mainly because he knows of other gay men resettled to the EU. Yet these individuals were all resettled within two years. Romain felt that the length of his wait perhaps had something to do with 'the files and also on the category of people. ... It depends on the case. They believe that there are urgent cases and others that are less urgent.' In saying that he had no explanation for how urgency is determined or why some cases are prioritized. However, he does know that even if his resettlement slot comes through, he will have to face a whole new verification process by the team from the host country. This is perhaps why Romain refers to himself and others like him as 'sheep in a pen': despite being previously found to be a refugee due to persecution based on sexual orientation, Romain is stuck in a country that outlaws same-sex relations, his future determined by external forces and policy shifts.

Encounters with UNHCR

All of my interlocutors shared that their initial asylum interviews were conducted by Moroccan nationals employed by UNHCR – a practice confirmed by Cavalieri during our interview – and that cultural hurdles made it difficult for them to narrate their experiences or access support. Studies on asylum processes in France and England show that refugee status decisions are often shaped by a bureaucrat's personal beliefs and are therefore susceptible to bias (e.g. Bongiovanni 2018; Tissier-Raffin 2015). Why would it be different in Morocco? Laws prohibiting homosexuality influence local norms and values, and it is likely that these in turn shape how gay asylum claimants are perceived and treated. This is even more likely considering the limitations placed on organizations that might otherwise advocate for LGBTIQ migrant rights, as flagged in the introduction.

My interlocutors shared remarkably similar narratives about their engagements with UNHCR and so I will again use one illustrative example to show how the exportation of sexual democracy is complicated by geopolitical trends, institutional practices and cultural norms. Jean, who was twenty-five when we met, had left Cameroon five years prior due to homophobic persecution. Upon attending his asylum interview, he was shocked to discover that the simple facts of his life, such as being unable to acknowledge his sexuality to his family/community or to live openly with the man he loved, were insufficient grounds for protection. Instead, he was expected to detail all of the physical and psychological violence he had suffered across his lifetime. He was reluctant to do so because of the UNHCR representative handling his file:

> In Morocco, I am insulted in the street, even by [local] gays. Even when I need to take a taxi, the guy [driver] doesn't want to stop [and collect me]. So when I was assisted by a Moroccan woman [from UNHCR] and had to tell her my life story, I didn't trust her. In their country, you are not allowed to be gay, and they don't like black people, so why should she help me to get my status? No, it's not a situation that makes you feel comfortable.

In addition to having to navigate opaque procedural norms, gay asylum seekers like Jean are confronted with the additional stress of having to recount their experiences to bureaucrats whose personal views may reflect wider community prejudices. Even if this is a perception more than a reality, applicants can still feel intense anxiety about disclosing personal information. Jean emphasized that it was difficult for him to trust the UNHCR representative because he associated her with the racism and homophobia he had encountered in Morocco. Rather than provide an accurate account of his experiences, Jean narrated a version of his life that adhered to coded language/categories for securing asylum, based on advice that had been passed down by those with first-hand experience of the procedure:

> When you prepare to tell your life story, well, you don't really tell your life story. You say what others want to hear … You're the one who anticipates their reactions. In fact, you're the one who has to know what they think of you so that you don't go in a direction they don't like – you know?

Believing that one's asylum claim will be dealt with fairly and impartially is vital in an interview setting, but individuals like Jean are deeply apprehensive about being upfront with locals who may exhibit prejudice. The EU's and UNHCR's push for the Moroccan state to take over all responsibility for managing asylum claims, including those involving sexual orientation, may benefit their political interests, but it places LGBTIQ persons in an uncomfortable and potentially dangerous situation – certainly not the 'humane' and 'rights-based approach' touted in EU policies.

Conclusion

To be a gay refugee in Morocco is to inhabit a paradoxical state. It is to be criminalized and subjected to homophobic discrimination while under international protection for these very same reasons. Moreover, it is to straddle the metaphorical borders of sexual democracy, created and maintained through competing regulatory regimes. As noted, sexual democracy is an ideology that promotes a particular set of rights – based on Western values and norms – linked to sex, gender and sexuality. At its heart is an imagined division between states/

individuals that adhere to LGBTIQ rights (i.e. those deemed 'progressive' and 'civilized') and those that do not. These boundaries are made concrete when the institutions committed to defending this ideology play the role of border guards. The experiences described above reveal a new dimension in this ideological construction. The narratives show how the borders of sexual democracy are exported beyond national borders and sovereign states. The dissemination of sexual borders occurs through two simultaneous processes: first, in the name of human rights; second, as part of the externalization of the EU's borders. The paradox that emerges from the confluence of human rights and anti-migration policies generates opacity in asylum procedures. The ostensibly competing aims of human rights and anti-migration policies lead to arbitrary selection processes, varying levels of protection and indeterminate wait times. All the while, individuals like the gay Cameroonians featured in this chapter are relegated to a space between legality and illegality; they are simultaneously protected and unprotected. The presence of effectively parallel systems in Morocco – one enacted by the UNHCR, the EU and other international actors and the other emanating from local laws – leaves those on the ground vulnerable to discrimination and exploitation.

In the case of Morocco, tensions between physical and symbolic borders create opportunities for racism and homophobia to flourish, both within asylum systems and within daily life. While local UNHCR staff are only responsible for initial interviews and do not make final determinations on refugee status, their beliefs, values and actions can and do influence claimants' ability to access protection. In shaping a person's motivations and decisions, stereotypes participate in the displacement and regulation of borders, including the boundaries of sexual democracy.

The state – a construct that epitomizes the illusion of congruence between culture, identity, territory and nation – is a structure of power. Conflicts over territorial borders may serve as a convenient explanation for the displacement of many populations today, but this should not obscure the fact that everyone lives within or between boundaries, some of which are physical and some of which are symbolic. As shown here, the ideology of sexual democracy serves as a mechanism for the externalization of borders through the bodies of LGBTIQ persons. In examining the experiences of LGBTIQ refugees and asylum seekers in places like Morocco, it is possible to see how different economic, social, political and territorial borders intersect and operate.

Notes

1   Morocco has ratified both the 1951 Geneva Convention and the 1967 Protocol Relating to the Status of Refugees. In fact, it was the first Arab country to do so (GADEM 2014).
2   In this article, I distinguish between 'refugees' and 'asylum seekers' where appropriate. However, I occasionally use the term 'refugee' to refer to all LGBTIQ persons seeking protection. I do this in recognition of the barriers that prevent individuals from being formally recognized as refugees, despite often meeting the legislative criteria.

3   English translation provided by author.
4   All names are pseudonyms to protect the identity of participants.
5   ASWAT Collective uses Facebook as their main avenue of communication, see
     https://www.facebook.com/Collectif.Aswat/.

References

Agier, M. (2018), *L'étranger qui vient. Repenser l'hospitalité*, Paris: Seuil.

Akin, D. (2018), 'Discursive Construction of Genuine LGBT Refugees', *Lambda Nordica*, 23 (3/4): 21–46.

Arab, C. (2007), 'Le "hrague" ou comment les Marocains brûlent les frontières', *Hommes et Migrations*, 1266: 82–95.

Bongiovanni, A. (2018), 'Demande d'asile au motif de l'orientation sexuelle: la CJUE fait un tout petit pas … mais dans la bonne direction', *La Revue des droits de l'homme*. doi: 10.4000/revdh.4450.

Cairo Institute of Human Rights Studies (2018), *Freedom of Association in Morocco: Legal Loopholes and Security Practices*, Tunis: Cairo Institute of Human Rights Studies. Available online: https://cihrs.org/wp-content/uploads/2018/02/FreedomofAssociationinMorocco.pdf (accessed 5 June 2021).

Cantu Jr., L. (2009), *The Sexuality of Migration Border Crossings and Mexican Immigrant Men*, New York: New York University Press.

Chossière, F. (2020), 'Minorités sexuelles en exil: l'expérience minoritaire en ville à l'aune de marginalisations multiples', *Urbanités*, 13. Available online: https://www.revue-urbanites.fr/13-chossiere/ (accessed 17 April 2021).

Danisi, C. (2018), 'What "Safe Harbours" Are There for People Seeking International Protection on Sexual Orientation and Gender Identity Grounds? A Human Rights Reading of International Law of the Sea and Refugee Law', *GenIUS – Rivista di studi giuridici sull'orientamento sessuale e l'identità genere*, 2: 9–24.

de Haas, H. (2007), 'Turning the Tide? Why Development Will Not Stop Migration', *Development and Change*, 38 (5): 819–41.

den Hertog, L. (2016), 'Funding the EU–Morocco "Mobility Partnership": Of Implementation and Competences', *European Journal of Migration and Law*, 18: 275–301.

Donnan, H. and T. M. Wilson (1999), *Borders: Frontiers of Identity, Nation and State*, Oxford: Berg Publishers.

European Council (2005), 'The Hague Program: Strengthening Freedom, Security and Justice in the European Union', *Official Journal of the European Union*, 53: 1–14.

Fassin, É. (2006), 'La démocratie sexuelle et le conflit des civilisations', *Multitudes*, 26: 123–31.

Gadem (2014), 'Les textes d'application de la convention de Genève', *Le cadre relatif au statut des étrangers au Maroc*, 24 November. Available online: http://gadem-guide-juridique.info/asile/situation-refugies/les-textes-dapplication-de-la-convention-de-geneve/ (accessed 28 May 2021).

Giametta, C. (2017), *The Sexual Politics of Asylum: Sexual Orientation and Gender Identity in the UK Asylum System*, New York: Routledge.

Grau, E., C. Charras and E. Lucchi (2019), *UNHCR Country Portfolio Evaluation: Morocco (2016–2019)*, UNHCR Evaluation Service. Available online: https://www.unhcr.org/5e1f058d7.pdf (accessed 3 June 2021).

Hersh, N. (2019), 'Enhancing UNHCR Protection for LGBTI Asylum-Seekers and Refugees in Morocco: Reflection and Strategies', in A. Güler, M. Shevtsova and D. Venturi (eds), *LGBTI Asylum Seekers and Refugees from a Legal and Political Perspective: Persecution, Asylum and Integration*, 299–321, Cham: Springer.

Jacobs, A. (2019), 'Morocco's Migration Policy: Understanding the Contradiction between Policy and Reality', Moroccan Institute for Policy Analysis, 30 June. Available online: https://mipa.institute/6872 (accessed 4 June 2021).

Khrouz, N. and N. Lanza (2015), *Migrants au Maroc: Cosmopolitismes, présence d'étrangers et transformations sociales*, Rabat: Konrad-Adenauer-Stiftung.

Lahlou, M. (2018), 'Migration Dynamics in Play in Morocco: Trafficking and Political Relationships and Their Implications at the Regional Level', *MENARA Working Papers*, 28.

Le Renard, A. (2019), *Le privilège occidental. Travail, intimité et hiérarchies postcoloniales à Dubaï*, Paris: Presses de SciencesPo.

Lowe, C., N. Both, M. Foresti, A. Leach and K. Rist (2020), *What Drives Reform? A Political Economy Analysis of Migration Policy in Morocco*, London: Overseas Development Institute.

Luibheid, E. (2002), *Entry Denied: Controlling Sexuality at the Border*, Minneapolis: University of Minnesota Press.

Mai, N. (2012), 'The Fractal Queerness of Non-Heteronormative Migrants Working in the UK Sex Industry', *Sexualities*, 15 (5/6): 570–85.

Malakooti, A. and C. Fall (2020), *Migration Trends across the Mediterranean: Piecing Together the Shifting Dynamics*, Global Initiative against Transnational Organized Crime. Available online: https://globalinitiative.net/wp-content/uploads/2020/11/Migration-Trends-Across-the-Mediterranean-Piecing-Together-the-Shifting-Dynamics.pdf (accessed 4 June 2021).

Peraldi, M. and L. Terrazzoni (2016), 'Nouvelles migrations? Les Français dans les circulations migratoires européennes vers le Maroc', *Autrepart*, 77 (1): 69–86.

Raboin, T. (2017), *Discourses on LGBT Asylum in the UK: Constructing a Queer Haven*, Manchester: Manchester University.

Royaume du Maroc (2013), *Stratégie nationale d'immigration et d'asile*. Available online: https://marocainsdumonde.gov.ma/wp-content/uploads/2018/02/Strate%CC%81gie-Nationale-dimmigration-et-dAsile-ilovepdf-compressed.pdf (accessed 28 April 2021).

Stock, I. (2020), 'The Impact of Migration Policies on Civil Society Actors' Efforts to Improve Migrants' Access to Social and Economic Rights in Morocco', *The Journal of North African Studies*. doi: 10.1080/13629387.2020.1814751.

Tissier-Raffin, M. (2015), 'Crise européenne de l'asile: l'Europe n'est pas à la hauteur de ses ambitions', *La revue des droits de l'homme*. doi:10.4000/revdh.1519.

Valluy, J. (2007), 'Le HCR au Maroc: acteur de la politique européenne d'externalisation de l'asile', *L'Année du Maghreb*. doi: 10.4000/anneemaghreb.398.

Zanker, F. (2019), 'Managing or Restricting Movement? Diverging Approaches of African and European Migration Governance', *Comparative Migration Studies*, 7 (17). doi: 10.1186/s40878-019-0115-9.

Chapter 6

HOMOPHOBIA AS PUBLIC VIOLENCE: POLITICS, RELIGION, IDENTITY AND RIGHTS IN THE LIVES OF LESBIAN, GAY AND BISEXUAL ASYLUM SEEKERS FROM CAMEROON

Charlotte Walker-Said

For several decades, lesbian, gay and bisexual (LGB) Africans seeking asylum in the United States and the United Kingdom have been defined as possessing a particular identity trait. Scholars such as Laurie Berg and Jenni Millbank (2009) and Sean Rehaag (2009) have assiduously uncovered tensions inherent to LGB asylum claims and, in particular, the difficulties of self-identifying as a sexual minority in language and behaviour that is coherent to Global North constructions of LGB distinctiveness. Rampant procedural biases persist within these two asylum systems, with LGB applicants forced to articulate their identities and experiences in ways that are intelligible to culturally circumscribed notions of 'alternative' sexualities (Lee 2018; Murray 2015).

This chapter builds on previous investigations of how LGB asylum seekers struggle to fit within the parameters of admissibility used to assess sexuality-based protection claims. It also extends Millbank's (2009) deconstruction of the public-private divide in how reception countries envision vulnerability to persecution. In so doing, the chapter reassesses the criteria by which certain types of violence are deemed 'private'. It considers sexual acts and sexual identities as forms of politics, not simply as personality traits, or even as intrinsic features of the self that are relevant only to the private sphere. Religious and family authorities in Cameroon (as in many parts of Africa) view homosexuality as inherently seditious to communitarian bonds linked through heteronormative and patriarchal kinship relations, believing that LGB identities are inextricably linked with insurrectionary impulses that must be restrained and disciplined with violence.[1] In addition to criminalizing homosexuality, the Cameroonian state formally and informally partners with religious and/or family leaders to subject LGB individuals to persecution, strategically blurring political and social boundaries in the name of 'stability' and creating a totalizing atmosphere of repression for LGB people.

In troubling the public-private dichotomy through which homophobic persecution is typically understood, this chapter both challenges dominant asylum categories and presents an alternative framework for assessing refugee claims based on sexual orientation. To argue this position, I draw on fieldwork interviews conducted in 2014 and 2019 with members of the Justice and Peace Commission of the Archdiocese of Bamenda, the friars of the Maison Jésuite in Yaoundé, the Dioceses of Douala and Bafia and the Native Baptist Church.

Adjudicating forms of persecution against sexual minorities

The United States has a history of barring entry to 'foreign homosexuals' (Moore 1970). Scholars like Eithne Luibhéid (2002) have demonstrated how the US border continues to function as a place for contesting, constructing and renegotiating sexual identity. In the Refugee Act of 1980, the US Congress furthered implementation of the UN's 1967 Protocol Relating to the Status of Refugees and provided a permanent procedure for the admission and protection of refugees. Under US law, refugees are assessed according to the following definition:

> [A]ny person who is outside of any country of such person's nationality ... and who is unable or unwilling to return to, and is unable or unwilling to avail himself or herself of the protection of, that country because of persecution or a well-founded fear of persecution on account of race, religion, nationality, membership in a particular social group, or political opinion.
>
> (U.S. Immigration and Nationality Act 1965)

Since 1965, sexual minorities seeking asylum in the United States have had to argue for their right to protection as a result of their 'membership in a particular social group'. However, many have been rejected for not making a strong enough case that their sexual orientation makes them a 'member' of a 'particular social group'. This is usually because of subjective assessments regarding their credibility (e.g. their apparent inability to convince a judge they are 'genuinely' homosexual) or because of purported inconsistencies in their professions of a homosexual orientation, such as their having married someone of the opposite sex (Topel 2017; Flores 2015; Magardie 2003).

The current iteration of the Refugee Act of 1980 provides vague provisions for the protection of LGB persons and grants considerable latitude to individual judges to determine the merit of individual claims. These already opaque pathways to protection have been further eroded in recent years. This includes efforts to restrict the scope of consideration under existing provisions – such as former president Donald Trump and attorney general Jefferson Sessions' attempt to overhaul the definition of a 'particular social group' (Department of Justice 2020) – and certain courts' compliance with these narrower interpretations. Such actions portend an uncertain future for LGB asylum in the United States.

Many human rights scholars, including this author, have analysed the precedential American asylum decision known as *Matter of A-R-C-G-* et al.,

Respondents 26 I&N Dec. 338 (BIA 2014), which allowed foreign women to seek refuge in the United States as a result of domestic violence in their home countries, as well as the decision four years later to overturn that ruling, known as *Matter of A-B-*, Respondent 27 I&N Dec. 316 (AG 2018) (Lee 2020; Walker-Said 2020; Musalo 2014). Attorney general Sessions argued in *Matter of A-B-* that victims of domestic violence suffered a form of 'private violence' that was legally and materially distinct from 'persecution'.[2] In sharply differentiating between 'private actors' and 'state actors', Sessions placed domestic and family-based violence outside of the political sphere, diminishing the capacity of the asylum system to protect those most vulnerable to violence, torture and death by relatives, spouses and close community members (Leask 2017; Fluri 2011; Shively 2011).[3] Although American appellate courts have effectively abrogated Sessions' decision in *Matter of A-B-*, victims of sexuality- and gender-based violence continue to face additional hurdles in substantiating claims of 'persecution' (Hoffman 2021).

In the United Kingdom, controversies over sexual minorities' eligibility for refugee protection also involve legal interpretations, but generally focus more on applicants' ability to 'control' or mitigate exposure to persecution. Under Article 1(A) of the UN's 1951 Refugee Convention – to which the United Kingdom's national laws are subject – applicants can claim asylum on the basis of their sexual orientation if they can establish 'a well-founded fear of being persecuted'. The language in UK law appears to provide greater prospect for LGB claims in comparison to US asylum law, as the former does not stipulate that a person must have a well-founded fear of future persecution only on account of a protected ground (U.S. Immigration and Nationality Act 1965). In the past, the United Kingdom's First Tier and Upper Tribunals (Immigration and Asylum Chamber) have demanded that applicants for asylum must prove they *cannot reasonably be expected to avoid persecution* by denying the characteristics for which they fear persecution (Millbank 2009). Even in the seminal decision *HJ (Iran) and HT (Cameroon) v Secretary of State for the Home Department* (2010), in which the UK Supreme Court ruled that LGB asylum seekers cannot be expected to be discreet about their sexuality in order to avoid persecution, the court noted that the 1951 Convention deals with state-sponsored or state-condoned harm and therefore does not extend to '[f]amily or social disapproval in which the state has no part' (see also Gray and McDowall 2013; Gray 2010). Overall, the *HJ (Iran) and HT (Cameroon)* ruling offered the prospect of promoting fairer treatment for LGB asylum seekers, but there has been little real progress in standardizing recognition of LGB refugee claims (Heimer 2020).

Both the UK Tribunals and the US Supreme Court demonstrate a problematic bias against all gender- and sexuality-based asylum claims relative to political asylum claims, as those seeking protection for political activities are not expected to conceal their political opinions or deny their involvement in activism, nor are they believed to be *merely* facing 'family or social disapproval'. Political asylees' threats are presumed to emanate from the state, which is acting against a universally recognized human right to political opinion, not a more recent assertion of the freedom to express one's intrinsic identity characteristics. As in similar procedures in the United States, LGB asylum applicants in the United Kingdom must work to demonstrate their 'membership' to a recognizable and targeted community that is experiencing (or has previously experienced) death, torture or imprisonment, with an arguably higher burden of evidence than for those seeking political asylum (Raboin 2016).

Feminist legal theorist Trish Luker (2015) identifies the evolution of refugee law during the late 1990s, when courts in the Global North began recognizing gender-based harms, shifting the narrative of refugee law away from its focus on harm in the 'public domain' (i.e. men escaping violence perpetrated by the state) to recognizing women escaping harm perpetrated by non-state agents, such as intimate partners or family members. Luker (2015) also confirms that sexuality-based asylum claims began to be heard at the same time as those relating to gender-based persecution, and discusses how these were subject to problematic interpretations of harm that questioned whether common forms of homophobic violence are 'public' enough to constitute state-based persecution. Yet, as Millbank (2009) found when reviewing asylum decisions from Canada and Australia, sexuality-based claims are often deemed 'too private', with applicants presumed to have the 'option' of avoiding state violence.

Case law on religious-based asylum holds that the forced concealment of one's religious views itself constitutes persecution. Thus, applicants claiming a well-founded fear of persecution on account of their religion cannot be expected to simply conceal their beliefs to avoid persecution (Smith 2012).[4] Likewise, it is arguable that the concealment of one's sexuality is either impossible or abhorrent enough to constitute persecution and is therefore not a reasonable measure by which to assess the threat sexuality poses in the public or private spheres. Similarly, religious- and political-based asylum claims are typically established as 'state-based' persecution in that they are assumed to involve government action and 'public' forms of harm (Weis 2020; *Matter of A-B-* 2018). Even in asylum cases featuring countries that directly criminalize same-sex relations, often with harsh penalties, refugee determination procedures resist sexual minorities making political-based claims and instead categorize the persecution against them as based on 'membership in a particular social group'. This erroneously suggests that the violence they face is purely 'domestic' – in other words, that it is always possible to distinguish between violence by state actors, such as enforcement agents, and non-state actors, such as spouses, elders, kin, parents and community members (Shiff 2020; Bookey 2013).[5] In my own experience observing asylum processes involving LGB claimants, I have noticed that courts require evidence that laws criminalizing homosexuality are *regularly enforced* – as opposed to being legislative façades or performative decrees designed to appease religious conservatives – in order to be convinced that persecution does not principally emanate from the private sphere.

However, asylum claims based on homophobic persecution cannot be segregated from the realm of politics, the public sphere or the actions of government. This is certainly true in relation to Cameroon, but is equally relevant to LGB cases from a great number of African countries, irrespective of whether they formally criminalize LGB expressions, behaviours and/or identities. It also offers possibilities for assessing other 'gender-based' asylum claims as political, as the state in question is ultimately expected to control the means of violence and uphold the rule of law. In many African countries, claims of sexuality- and gender-based victimization typically present a political challenge to the government.[6]

LGB asylum seekers from Africa: A Cameroonian case study

In Cameroon, as in a number of countries on the African continent, criminal codes prohibit same-sex sexual activity or the 'promotion' of such activity. Its domestic laws do not enshrine protection from harm or persecution based on gender and sexuality, and law enforcement agencies regularly participate in violence against sexual minorities (Nzouankeu 2016; Eloundou 2014; Human Rights Watch 2013).

The assessment frameworks outlined in US and UK refugee law suggest that many Cameroonian LGB asylum seekers would qualify for protection, yet admissibility criteria are not applied consistently. Moreover, the centrality of 'credibility' when adjudicating an asylum claim hinders many Cameroonian LGB applicants, as these individuals face particular hurdles in making their sexuality legible to Global North bureaucracies. Put another way, applicants struggle to 'prove' not just their sexual identity but also its indisputability to their asylum claim.

The credibility hurdle can often be higher for LGB asylum seekers than for other categories of asylum seekers. This is because applicants' accommodations of heteronormative expectations are frequently interpreted as counterevidence of their stated identity. By contrast, accommodations of political repression by political asylum seekers are not necessarily viewed as contradicting their political opinions. The totalizing repression of non-heterosexual persons in Cameroon, and the ruthlessness with which non-heteronormative behaviours, identities and expressions are policed and punished, forces many LGB Cameroonians to engage in behaviours that US and UK administrators perceive as atypical for LGB persons. These include heterosexual marriage (either within monogamous or polygamous formations), the building of families and lineages, sexual relationships with opposite-sex partners, childbearing out of wedlock, participation in conservative religious denominations and other seemingly incongruous lifestyle 'choices'. Cameroon's penal code, supported by popular anti-LGB rhetoric, vigilante enforcement of heteronormativity and the endemic nature of family violence, domestic abuse and discrimination within one's intimate community – fully endorsed by customary law, policing practices and cultural leaders – pushes LGB persons to disguise their orientations and practices (Awondo, Geschiere and Reid 2012). However, many LGB Cameroonians argue in their asylum claims that this forced discretion is itself persecution, noting that revealing their authentic sexual identities (or having them revealed) opens them up to violence from both the state and broader society. While few LGB asylum seekers articulate political claims – or claims concerning the politics of rejecting or resisting laws governing sexuality – it is arguable that homosexuality is a political act within the Cameroonian context. Such actions undermine the authority of the government and weaken the state's ability to regulate morality, while also strengthening the power and status of sexual minorities and countering dominant ideologies about homosexuality.

It is essential that Cameroon's anti-LGB persecution be understood in its multiple dimensions, *not only* so that members of this particular social group are recognized as victims of state-based persecution emanating from the political elite and supported through grassroots cooperation, *but also* so that assessments of credibility appropriately discern the varied behaviours and practices of LGB individuals.

Homosexuals as 'enemies of the state'

Article 347a of Cameroon's penal code criminalizes sexual contact between members of the same sex, with penalties ranging from fines to imprisonment. Additionally, Article 83 of Law No. 2010/21 relating to Cybersecurity and Cybercrime outlaws 'sexual propositions to another person of the same sex' by electronic communications (Humanity First Cameroon et al. 2017). Legal sanctions can also be taken against citizens who are perceived as 'promoting homosexuality' through acts such as gender-nonconformity, advocating liberalism or criticizing cultural and political norms (Human Rights Watch 2021; Stewart 2018).

Cameroon's anti-gay legislation is not simply a form of window dressing that signals the state's protection of traditional family life. The past decade has seen a steady increase in harassment, threats, arrests and assaults targeting sexual and gender minorities by both civilians and state representatives. At least twenty-eight Cameroonians were prosecuted for same-sex conduct between 2010 and 2013 (Freedom House 2014; Human Rights Watch 2013). Human rights workers estimate that several dozen more were prosecuted between 2012 and 2017, although official statistics are hard to find (Stewart 2017). In 2017, dozens of men were arrested on suspicion of homosexuality after a raid on a nightclub (Williams 2016) and the following year police arrested suspected homosexuals, including employees and patrons of gay-friendly clubs and restaurants (Ford 2018). Another spike in police action was recorded in February 2021, when Colibri, a Bafoussam-based organization providing HIV prevention and treatment services, was raided and thirteen people were arrested (Human Rights Watch 2021). Three months later, in May 2021, two transgender women were sentenced to five years in prison after being found guilty of 'attempting homosexuality' and outraging public decency (Ghoshal 2021).

Media articles condemning sexual and gender diversity, and which either explicitly or implicitly encourage forms of violence against LGB persons, are common in Cameroon (Pharel 2017). In July 2020, Pierre Mila Assouté, a former activist in the ruling Cameroon People's Democratic Movement (CPDM) party and current promoter of the Rassemblement Démocratique pour la Modernité du

Cameroun (RDMC) party, publicly denounced Gabon's parliamentary decision to revise the penal code to decriminalize homosexuality,[7] stating:

> We must not legalise homosexuality in Cameroon. Once we start talking about decriminalising perversion we begin changing the nature of sexual orientation ... some among you justify this abomination which amounts to allowing the abuse of one's body. This cause has been imposed on us by exogenous cultural forces and accepting homosexuality is not considered a precondition of economic cooperation and development aid. To pretend to help Africa in exchange for her soul is blackmail and an oppressive new form of cultural alienation.
>
> (Liliane 2020)

Strongly worded condemnations such as these are often cited by LGB asylum seekers as evidence that 'homosexuals' in Cameroon constitute a 'particular social group'. Applicants argue that statements like Assouté's prove that 'homosexuals' are both 'defined with particularity' and 'socially distinct within the society in question', as per the American Board of Immigration Appeals' formulation of the 'particular social group' category in *Matter of Acosta* 19 I&N Dec.[8]

Religious leaders strongly support the state's persecution of LGB individuals and amplify political criticism of LGB rights by providing religious grounds for criminalizing homosexuality (Marnell 2021; Walker-Said 2018). For example, in 2016 the Catholic Archbishop of Yaoundé, Tonyè Bakot, described homosexuals as 'corrupters of society' and blamed them for 'threatening procreation' (Nzouankeu 2016). The new archbishop of Douala, Monsignor Samuel Kleda, and his colleague, Cameroonian Cardinal Christian Tumi, have called for 'war against homosexuality' and emphatically denounce homosexuality as evil (Shine 2016). The 'war' envisioned by many Catholic leaders must take place not simply at the level of the state, but also within the family and household.[9] Catholic and Protestant religious leaders have urged 'zero tolerance' for homosexuality and have stated that homosexual acts are an 'abominable thing that goes against nature [and] risks becoming a social outbreak' (Shine 2016). Religious rhetoric parallels political rhetoric on the dangers of accepting LGB individuals, positioning any form of tolerance as an immediate and serious risk to society and governance.

The prevalence and virulence of homophobia in Cameroonian political discourse provide support for the claim that identifying as LGB or engaging in homosexual relations is, in fact, a form of political opinion. Certainly, LGB expressions and activities undermine the authority of the state to police personal morality and sexuality. But, more importantly, homophobic political rhetoric demonstrates that the state conceptualizes homosexuality politically, transforming the 'homosexual' into an internal enemy and non-citizen. Put another way, homosexuality is regarded as a seditious crime threatening the stability and operations of the state. Politicians from across the African continent frequently portray sexual and gender rights activism as the influence of Western homosexual identity and commingle heterosexuality with political inclusion (Nyanzi 2013; Msibi 2011). State leaders repeatedly and explicitly make sexuality a question of citizenship, thereby rendering sexual minorities who seek protection political refugees (Alimi 2015; Tamale 2014). Although Cameroonian LGB asylum seekers in the United States and the United Kingdom almost unanimously claim asylum on the basis of persecution due to membership of a social group, rather than on the basis of their political opinion, it remains salient that homosexuality is seen as a cultural and national betrayal in Cameroon, with government representatives repeatedly and consistently designating homosexuals enemies of the state.

Family violence as public harm: The public-private fiction

Cameroon does not recognize domestic violence as a specific crime; its national criminal code is silent on family and domestic violence, leaving victims to rely on general laws against assault (Women's International League for Peace and Freedom Cameroon 2019; Immigration and Refugee Board of Canada 2016). There is likewise no reference in the penal code to violence against children, youth or younger kin, or against family members. These omissions might appear to stem from a lack of consideration for the rights and needs of vulnerable individuals, but they are in fact the product of a different regulatory system. The lack of civil law or government oversight implies that family and lineage heads, customary authorities and community patriarchs are responsible for managing the domestic sphere, which in turn provides the foundation for a disciplined and well-regulated state.

Police solidarity with state mandates to punish homosexuality functions as a strategy to uphold both the law and the customary authority of family leaders and community elders. Homophobia in Cameroon cannot be understood without reference to domestic violence and domestic regulation. Yet, at the same time, this cannot be conceived as purely 'private' violence. The public-private divide is a fiction in a state that constructs the legal system in ways that buttress the authority of non-state agents to impose violence and deny individuals their human rights. From this vantage point, it is arguable that mob violence is an extension of family violence. Mob justice or 'street justice' is extremely common in Cameroon's cities and towns (Orock 2014). Many local communities commit acts of violence against LGB persons, and the police either do not protect the victims or participate in persecuting them, such as by extorting them for money or by arresting and torturing them.

As Rogers Orock (2014) notes, 'The widespread sense of anxiety over various forms of violent crime and state failure to guarantee protection for citizens generates a quest for alternative practices of safety-making' (1). By discursively framing sexual minorities as 'hazards' to the future of the nation – in both a spiritual and a procreative sense – political authorities are able to legitimize violence towards LGB persons, presenting it as a justifiable defence against an imminent social threat. As mentioned above, religious discourse both foments and mirrors this impulse. Speaking at the 2009 special Synod of Bishops for Africa, then archbishop

Robert Sarah said, 'Africa must protect itself from the contamination' of Western ideas about family life and sexuality (Wooden 2013).

The Cameroonian state both actively and passively contributes to family and mob violence through the enforcement of anti-homosexuality laws (Mbonteh 2017). The practice of mob justice is so widespread that, in February 2017, the Cameroonian Supreme Court felt compelled to remind citizens to bring all actions before the courts rather than resort to violence (Mbonteh 2017). While some jurists decry the widespread phenomenon of vigilante justice, Cameroon's legal framework and political discourse concerning LGB persons empower communities to collaborate in the 'defence' or 'protection' of the state and the citizenry. The police in Cameroon do not interfere in violence that occurs within the domestic or family sphere, or in some instances even in the local community. Rather than demonstrate that there is a strong 'private sphere' that is outside of government control, the collaboration between law enforcement and family/ community leaders who wield violence against their members validates that 'private violence' is indeed state violence, as the state passively *and* actively allows persecution to occur. In Cameroon, 'private actors' – as former attorney general Sessions termed family leaders, cultural guardians and others who mete out violence against marginalized persons – are not so much disconnected from the state as much as they are subsidiaries of state power.

As an example, following the October 2014 arrest of seven men in Cameroon on charges related to homosexuality, local human rights observers discovered that the arrests were made after neighbours involved in 'community policing' claimed a certain house was a haven for 'effeminate men' and demanded the arrest of its residents (Freedom House 2014). Activists fighting for sexual and gender rights in Cameroon also face grave danger, including being vulnerable to burglaries, arson attacks, arbitrary arrests and even violent deaths (Hirsch 2013).

Kinship relations as domains of state discipline and control

In Cameroon, the enforcement of behaviours at the family level is considered essential to political order (Walker-Said 2020; Nyamnjoh 2015; Chem-Langhee 1983). Moreover, state enforcement agencies uphold local authorities in their management of the social order. Family gossip and public opprobrium can very quickly escalate into mob attacks, ritual violence and even death at the hands of relatives and/or neighbours (Corey-Boulet 2013). The police in Cameroon rely on witnesses – often family members and local residents – for evidence on which to make arrests and then follow up using torture and ill-treatment (Human Rights Watch 2013).

Although same-sex activities are criminalized under Cameroonian law, sexual minorities are most frequently and typically harassed, assaulted, tortured or killed by members of their own families and intimate communities (Walker-Said 2020). Research also presents convincing evidence that stringent legal codes that criminalize homosexuality passively authorize the use of violence against sexual minorities by both law enforcement and regular civilians, creating a coordinated disciplinary regime that bolsters the legitimacy of a government that otherwise has very little grassroots support (Ngwa Nfobin 2014; Awondo 2010, 2011). Fear of homophobic violence from close kin motivates LGB Cameroonians to adopt behaviours that outwardly signal conformity to social norms, such as initiating sexual relationships with opposite-sex partners, entering into heterosexual marriages (whether monogamous or polygamous), producing children and participating in or leading religious groups. In some instances, asylum seekers' families cooperate in constructing a heteronormative façade – or forcibly impose such a façade – in order to avoid social opprobrium and violence.[10] This frequently results in arranged or forced marriages, a problem that is endemic in Cameroon (Free Speech Radio News 2015; International Women's Health Coalition 2015; Immigration and Refugee Board of Canada 2013). LGB persons' short- or long-term commitments to these enterprises can, as noted, jeopardize their asylum applications, undermining not only the credibility of their claim but also their contention that the private sphere is a deeply threatening space for them. When asked to adjudicate such cases, asylum evaluators often struggle to comprehend the pressure and risk-facing applicants: *How dangerous can such pious and traditionalist communities be?* Answering this question is particularly challenging given that LGB asylum seekers struggle to document persecution when it is imposed by non-state actors in the realm of social and family contacts (Akin 2018), which is closed to the kind of scrutiny, reporting and documentation that typically occurs with public acts of persecution by state agents (e.g. arrests, executions, violence against demonstrators, politically motivated prosecutions of government opponents).

Some family leaders with LGB relatives note that being part of a pious and traditionalist community forces an obligation to publicly perform outrage and discipline or to expel their non-normative kin – even if they, themselves, are not personally compelled to respond with violence. In one interview, a mother explained that the severe stigma she would face as the mother of a gay child impelled her to demonstrate her humiliation and anger and to refute her association with her son so that she and other family members would not face community scorn.[11]

The household has been confirmed as an important category of historical production in Africa and is also recognized as not simply a 'private' domain, but rather an active mechanism for building communities, constituting belonging and establishing boundaries of inclusion and exclusion (Nolte 2017; Burrill 2015; Jean-Baptiste 2014). Emily Osborn (2011) argues that household-making and statecraft are one and the same in West Africa. Current political trends demonstrate this vividly. Cheikh Ibrahima Niang, Ellen Foley and Ndack Diop (2020) show that the emergence of democratic governance in Senegal has seen religious, political and cultural leaders embrace anti-homosexual platforms as a way to signal their moral legitimacy, using the rhetoric of family values to make arguments about what kind of citizens should be protected and recognized. In Burkina Faso, homophobic speech for political gain often invokes 'the house' as a space to be protected from criminal sexuality (Bardou 2019; Niang et al. 2004).

In Cameroon, violence against sexual and gender minorities is legitimized by officialdom and state law, but the government also supports and condones homophobic violence by kin because it depends on the family as an agency of state stability. Reciprocally, religious and family authorities support the state in shaping the boundaries of recognized citizenship. Many family, community and religious leaders whom I have interviewed expressed a fear that LGBT activists conflate censurable activities with human rights, thereby reducing the possibility of the state's embrace of human rights for Cameroonian society broadly.[12] Religious leaders condemn African societies as *undeserving* of rights or democratic participation if they 'produce' homosexuals.[13] Cardinal Robert Sarah alludes to the rejection of homosexuality as part of good governance in his speeches: 'There is no peace, no justice, no stability in society without family ... without a father and without a mother' (Wooden 2013). One pastor I spoke with concurred: 'Civil rights are also a responsibility.'[14] He explained that people must demonstrate that they are capable of obeying laws and decency in order to be considered citizens with rights. In short, family, community and religious leaders restrict the political agency of LGB persons, usually through violence, in an attempt to preserve the right to (limited) political agency for 'ordinary' citizens.

The various homophobic aggressions charted above suggest that violence against sexual and gender minorities is thoroughly a state-making process, as is the imposition of gendered and sexualized categories of family, household and national belonging. These aggressions also show that conflicts and tensions over sexual and gender identity within families have endogenous energy. Families and households are not simply passive agents in this process. They extend their cooperation for homophobic violence and even make an axiological case for their participation in moulding incorruptible members of society. In Cameroon, the regulation of heteronormativity emerges simultaneously 'from above' (i.e. the state) and 'from below' (i.e. the family and local authorities), making it impossible to neatly distinguish between 'public' and 'private' forms of persecution. This has serious ramifications for LGB Cameroonians driven to seek refuge in the Global North via traditional asylum pathways.

Everything is politics: Grounds for LGB asylum

Cameroonian society's violence towards LGB persons is inextricably linked to its ongoing struggle for economic justice and political coherence. Persecution can embed itself within liberal movements if it is perceived as a form of discipline over rebellious and antagonistic forces that inhibit progress. LGB asylum seekers make claims that they are persecuted on the basis of their sexuality (an 'immutable characteristic' that they are unable to change or hide) and their 'membership in a particular social group'. But it is also arguable that LGB Cameroonians are political dissidents. Politically motivated homophobia has mobilized regressive forces such as cultural guardians and religious leaders to repress rights-based activism and emphasize duty-based responsibilities to fulfil obligations to communities and the bonds that tie them. For the state, the happy result is the maintenance of civil order through the strengthening of long-established social hierarchies. Family leaders and other local authorities also turn towards established sexual and gender norms as stabilizing forces, using violence against LGB persons to demonstrate their resistance to civil disorder and therefore their deservingness for political rights. Comprehending the *politicization* of sexuality – both for the state that makes normative sexual and gender roles attendant with full citizenship and for the individual who defies attempts to disable their empowerment – is critical if existing protection mechanisms are to meet the needs of LGB asylum seekers.

US and UK administrators/judges have a moral and legal duty to understand the complex dynamics of homophobia so that they can more accurately and fairly evaluate sexuality-based asylum claims involving Cameroonians (and Africans more broadly). Recognizing persecution by non-state actors as legitimate grounds for refugee protection will not only bring about more compassionate treatment of LGB asylum seekers but will also ensure that status determinations comply with domestic and international legal obligations. In the case of Cameroon, violence against LGB persons is a form of political repression, with the state encouraging, sponsoring and excusing homophobic attacks through both official and unofficial actions. By tying homophobia to good governance, national security and moral citizenship, the Cameroonian state is able to position LGB citizens as an internal threat to social and political stability. The comparative limitations of the US and the UK asylum systems may be addressed through the introduction of alternative frameworks for assessing cases involving sexuality. Any such framework must not perpetuate the false distinction between public and private forms of violence. Continuing to reduce sexual- and gender-based persecution to a domestic matter undermines LGB Africans' ability to access refugee protection and the rights associated with it.

Notes

1 Interview with Msgr Athanase Bala, Maison de Retraite, Congrégation du Saint Esprit, Chevilly, Paris, 4 September 2015; interview with Père Benoit Andoa, Eglise Saint Gabriel De Bonamikano, Bonaberi, Douala, 19 March 2019; interview John the Baptist Zamcho Anyeh, S. J., Maison Jesuite, Mvolyé, Cameroon, 25 May 2014.

2 Sessions' decision vacated a Board of Immigration Appeals (BIA) decision of 6 December 2016 in *Matter of A-B-*, as well as overruled the decision in the *Matter of A-R-C-G-*, upon which the BIA had relied to decide *A-B-*. The US Court of Appeals for the Sixth Circuit and the First and Ninth Circuits rejected Sessions' view that the particular social group relied upon in *A-B-* was legally unsound (Chase 2021).

3 This article refers to 'family-based violence' rather than 'domestic violence' as sexual and gender minorities typically suffer from more than spousal abuse – for example, they remain susceptible to violence from a range of family, lineage and community members.

4   The Seventh Circuit decision *Muhur v. Ashcroft* stands for the proposition that an
     applicant may prove that she has a well-founded fear of persecution if the only way
     to avoid persecution would be to conceal her religious beliefs (see *Muhur v. Ashcroft*,
     355 F. 3d958, 960 (7th Cir. 2004)), holding that the ability of the asylum applicant to
     conceal his or her religion does not defeat the claim of religious persecution.
5   Blaine Bookey (2013) notes that a wide range of gender-based violence is coded
     as 'domestic violence' in asylum databases and procedures, including child abuse,
     forced marriage, sale into human trafficking and other forms of violence far afield of
     intimate partner violence.
6   Here, I use the term 'gender-based' to include gender and sexuality, as well as
     orientation and identity claims. As *Matter of A-B-* is often considered applicable
     to asylum claims rooted in sexuality and gender identity (although it specifically
     discussed women fleeing domestic violence), 'gender-based asylum' in this usage is
     inclusive of a number of categories of sexual and gender minorities.
7   An important caveat to this development is worth mentioning: Gabon abruptly
     criminalized homosexuality in 2019 (it was not part of the penal code beforehand)
     and *then* reversed course with decriminalizing only a year later (see Savage 2019).
8   For more on how the BIA built on the *Acosta* definition in a series of cases, see
     'Immigration Law. Asylum. Ninth Circuit Holds That Persecuted Homosexual
     Mexican Man with a Female Sexual Identity Qualifies for Asylum under Particular
     Social Group Standard. Hernandez-Montiel v. INS, 225 F.3d 1084 (9th Cir. 2000)'
     (2001).
9   Interview with Msgr Athanase Bala, Maison de Retraite, Congrégation du Saint
     Esprit, Chevilly, Paris, 4 September 2015.
10   Interview records, Mvolyé and Yaoundé, Cameroon, 12–13 May 2014 (see Eliwo
     2012; Johnson-Hanks 2003).
11   Interview with Monique Onomo, Mvolyé and Yaoundé, Cameroon, 12–13 May 2014.
12   Interview with Msgr Athanase Bala, Maison de Retraite, Congrégation du Saint
     Esprit, Chevilly, Paris, 4 September 2015; interview with Samuel Mzeanj (Papa
     Sam) and Otto Biba, Bastos, Yaoundé, 2 September 2007; interview with Révérend
     Ogwandi, Native Baptist Church, Buea, 4 September 2007.
13   Interview with Msgr Athanase Bala, Maison de Retraite, Congrégation du Saint
     Esprit, Chevilly, Paris, 4 September 2015; interview with Soeur Suzanna, Bonadibong,
     Douala, 19 March 2019.
14   Interview with Pasteur Alexandre Ntone, Eglise Evangélique, Paroisse de Besseke,
     Douala, 19 March 2019.

References

Akin, D. (2018), 'Discursive Construction of Genuine LGBT Refugees', *Lambda Nordica*,
    23 (3/4): 21–46.
Alimi, B. (2015), 'If You Say Being Gay Is Not African, You Don't Know Your History',
    The Guardian, 9 September. Available online: http://www.theguardian.com/
    commentisfree/2015/sep/09/being-gay-african-history-homosexuality-christianity
    (accessed 12 December 2018).
Awondo, P. (2010), 'The Politicisation of Sexuality and Rise of Homosexual Movements in
    Post-Colonial Cameroon', *Review of African Political Economy*, 37 (125): 315–28.

Awondo, P. (2011), 'Identifications homosexuelles, construction identitaire et tensions postcoloniales entre le Cameroun et la France', *L'Espace politique*. doi: 10.4000/espacepolitique.1818.

Awondo, P., P. Geschiere and G. Reid (2012), 'Homophobic Africa? Toward a More Nuanced View', *African Studies Review*, 55 (3): 145–68.

Bardou, F. (2019), 'On est loin d'envisager une gay pride au Burkina Faso', *Libération*, 5 April. Available online: https://www.liberation.fr/planete/2019/04/05/on-est-loin-d-envisager-une-gay-pride-au-burkina-faso_1714521 (accessed 5 April 2019).

Berg, L. and J. Millbank (2009), 'Constructing the Personal Narratives of Lesbian, Gay and Bisexual Asylum Claimants', *Journal of Refugee Studies*, 22 (2): 196–223.

Bookey, B. (2013), 'Domestic Violence as a Basis for Asylum: An Analysis of 206 Case Outcomes in the United States from 1994 to 2012', *Hastings Women's Law Journal*, 24 (1): 107–48.

Burrill, E. S. (2015), *States of Marriage: Gender, Justice, and Rights in Colonial Mali*, Athens: Ohio University Press.

Chase, J. S. (2021), 'Hon. Jeffrey S. Chase on Matter of A-B-: A Parting Shot at Women', *LexisNexis Immigration Law*, 19 January. Available online: https://www.lexisnexis.com/legalnewsroom/immigration/b/insidenews/posts/hon-jeffrey-s-chase-on-matter-of-a-b--a-parting-shot-at-women (accessed 30 March 2021).

Chem-Langhee, B. (1983), 'The Origin of the Southern Cameroons House of Chiefs', *The International Journal of African Historical Studies*, 16 (4): 653–73.

Corey-Boulet, R. (2013), 'Cameroon Officials Torture Gay Suspects, Says Human Rights Watch', *South Florida Gay News*, 21 March. Available online: https://southfloridagaynews.com/World/cameroon-officials-torture-gay-suspects-says-human-rights-watch-report.html (accessed 25 July 2015).

Desmond, V. (2020), 'LGBT+ Community in Gabon Fears Backlash after Vote to Legalise Gay Sex', *Reuters*, 24 June. Available online: https://www.reuters.com/article/us-gabon-lgbt-lawmaking-trfn-idUSKBN23V2XE (accessed 7 December 2020).

Eliwo, A. (2012), 'Déterminants socio-culturels de la mortalité des enfants en Afrique noire, Hypothèses et recherche d'explication au Cameroun, au Kenya et au Sénégal', PhD dissertation, Institut de Dernographie, Université Catholique de Louvain, Belgium.

Eloundou, J. C. (2014), 'Stigma and Discrimination of LGBT in Cameroon', *European Forum of Lesbian, Gay, Bisexual and Transgender Christian Groups*, 11 October. Available online: https://www.lgbtchristians.eu/resources/stigma-and-discrimination-of-lgbt-in-cameroon/ (accessed 8 March 2018).

Flores, A. (2015), 'Double Jeopardy in a New World: Challenges Facing Homosexual Immigrants', *Harvard International Review*, 36 (4): 22–3.

Fluri, J. L. (2011), 'Bodies, Bombs and Barricades: Geographies of Conflict and Civilian (in)Security in Afghanistan', *Transactions of the Institute of British Geographers*, 36 (2): 280–96.

Ford, Z. (2018), 'Cameroon Police Arrest 25 Men for Homosexuality Because "Cameroon Has Laws to Enforce"', *ThinkProgress*, 15 May. Available online: https://thinkprogress.org/cameroon-homosexuality-arrests-c9d63ac22855/ (accessed 12 June 2018).

Free Speech Radio News (2015), 'Young Girls in Cameroon Face Forced Marriage at High Rates', *Free Speech Radio News*, 9 April. Available online: http://fsrn.org/2015/04/young-girls-in-cameroon-face-forced-marriage-at-high-rates/ (accessed 23 April 2017).

Freedom House (2014), 'Cameroon Criminalises LGBTI Community after Arrests for "Homosexuality"', Freedom House, 3 October. Available online: https://freedomhouse. org/article/cameroon-criminalizes-lgbti-community-after-arrests-homosexuality (accessed 3 June 2020).

Ghoshal, N. (2021), 'In Cameroon Transgender Women Given Five-Years in Prison', Human Rights Watch, 12 May. Available online: https://www.hrw.org/ news/2021/05/12/cameroon-transgender-women-given-five-years-prison (accessed 17 May 2021).

Gray, A. and A. McDowall (2013), 'LGBT Refugee Protection in the UK: From Discretion to Belief?', *Forced Migration Review*, 42 (22): 22–5.

Gray, L. M. (2010), *Failing the Grade: Home Office Initial Decision on Lesbian and Gay Claims for Asylum*, London: UKLGIG.

Heimer, R. (2020), 'Homonationalist/Orientalist Negotiations: The UK Approach to Queer Asylum Claims', *Sexuality & Culture*, 24: 174–96.

Hirsch, A. (2013), 'Cameroon Gay Rights Activist Found Tortured and Killed', *The Guardian*, 18 July. Available online: http://www.theguardian.com/world/2013/jul/18/ cameroon-gay-rights-activist-killed (accessed 30 April 2021).

HJ (Iran) and HT (Cameroon) v. Secretary of State for the Home Department, (2010) UKSC. 31, United Kingdom: Supreme Court, 7 July 2010.

Hoffman, G. (2021), 'The "Complete Helplessness" of Matter of A-B- and One More Last Ditch Effort to Torpedo Asylum, by Geoffrey A. Hoffman', *Yale Journal on Regulation: Notice and Comment*, 19 January. Available online: https://www.yalejreg.com/nc/the-complete-helplessness-of-matter-of-a-b-and-one-more-last-ditch-effort-to-torpedo-asylum-by-geoffrey-a-hoffman/ (accessed 30 March 2021).

Human Rights Watch (2010), 'Criminalisation des identités', 4 November. Available online: https://www.hrw.org/fr/report/2010/11/04/ criminalisation-des-identites/atteintes-aux-droits-humains-au-cameroun-fondees-sur (accessed 7 February 2021).

Human Rights Watch (2013), 'Cameroon: Rights Abuses in "Homosexuality" Prosecutions, Record Arrests for Same-Sex Intimacy; Rule of Law Violations', 21 March. Available online: https://www.hrw.org/ news/2013/03/21/cameroon-rights-abuses-homosexuality-prosecutions (accessed 25 June 2020).

Human Rights Watch (2021), 'Cameroon: Wave of Arrests, Abuse against LGBT People', 14 April. Available online: https://www.hrw.org/ news/2021/04/14/cameroon-wave-arrests-abuse-against-lgbt-people (accessed 30 April 2021).

Humanity First Cameroon et al. (2017), 'The Violations of the Rights of Lesbian, Gay, Bisexual, and Transgender (LGBT) Individuals in Cameroon: To Be Submitted for Consideration at the 121th Session of the Human Rights Committee', October. Available online: http://tbinternet.ohchr.org/Treaties/CCPR/Shared%20 Documents/CMR/INT_CCPR_CSS_CMR_29079_E.pdf (accessed 26 February 2021).

Immigration and Refugee Board of Canada (2013), 'Cameroon: Prevalence of Forced Marriage in Southern Cameroon, Particularly in the Southwest Region, Including State Protection Available; Forced Marriage as Practiced by Chiefs, and Whether the Girls or Women That Are Forced to Marry Chiefs Must Be Virgins and Childless', *Refworld*, 10 April. Available online: http://www.refworld.org/docid/5193855a2bdb.html (accessed 23 September 2015).

Immigration and Refugee Board of Canada (2016), 'Cameroon: Domestic Violence, Including Legislation; Protection Provided by the State and Support Services Available to Victims (2014–2016)', *Refworld*, 21 April. Available online: https://www.refworld.org/docid/5729a55e4.html (accessed 6 November 2018).

'Immigration Law. Asylum. Ninth Circuit Holds That Persecuted Homosexual Mexican Man with a Female Sexual Identity Qualifies for Asylum under Particular Social Group Standard. Hernandez-Montiel v. INS, 225 F.3d 1084 (9th Cir. 2000)' (2001), *Harvard Law Review*, 114 (8): 2569–75.

International Women's Health Coalition (2015), *Child, Early, and Forced Marriage in Cameroon: Research Findings*, New York: International Women's Health Coalition.

Jean-Baptiste, R. (2014), *Conjugal Rights: Marriage, Sexuality, and Urban Life in Colonial Libreville, Gabon*, Athens: Ohio University Press.

Johnson-Hanks, J. (2003), 'Education, Ethnicity, and Reproductive Practice in Cameroon', *Population*, 58 (2): 153–79.

Leask, A. (2017), 'Family Violence: New Holistic Approach Announced', *New Zealand Herald*, 7 June. Available online: https://www.nzherald.co.nz/nz/news/article.cfm?c_id=1&objectid=11871182 (accessed 12 May 2019).

Lee, E. O. J. (2018), 'Tracing the Coloniality of Queer and Trans Migrations: Resituating Heterocisnormative Violence in the Global South and Encounters with Migrant Visa Ineligibility to Canada', *Refuge*, 34 (1): 60–74.

Lee, L. (2020), 'Sanctuary, Safe Harbour and Asylum, but Is It Available for Domestic Violence Victims? The Analysis of Domestic Violence Asylum Seekers in the United States and Internationally', *San Diego International Law Journal*, 21 (2): 495–532.

Liliane, N. (2020), 'Pierre Milla Assouté: 'Il ne faut pas légaliser l'homosexualité au Cameroun', *Agence Cameroun Presse*, 2 July. Available online: https://agencecamerounpresse.com/tribune-libre/pierre-milla-assout%C3%A9-%E2%80%9Cil-ne-faut-pas-l%C3%A9galiser-l-homosexualit%C3%A9-au-cameroun%E2%80%9D.html (accessed 2 February 2021).

Luibhéid, E. (2002), *Entry Denied: Controlling Sexuality at the Border*, Minneapolis: University of Minnesota Press.

Luker, T. (2015), 'Performance Anxieties: Interpellation of the Refugee Subject in Law', *Canadian Journal of Law and Society*, 30 (1): 91–107.

Magardie, S. (2003), '"Is the Applicant Really Gay?" Legal Responses to Asylum Claims Based on Persecution because of Sexual Orientation', *Agenda*, 55: 81–7.

Marnell, J. (2021), *Seeking Sanctuary: Stories of Sexuality, Faith and Migration*, Johannesburg: Wits University Press.

Matter of A-B-, 27 I. & N. Dec. 316, 321 (Att'y Gen. 2018)- abrogated by *Grace v. Whitaker*, 344 F. Supp. 3d 96 (D.D.C. 2018).

Mbonteh, R. (2017), 'Cameroon: Supreme Court Denounces Mob Justice', *Cameroon Tribune (Yaoundé)*, 23 February. Available online: https://allafrica.com/stories/201702240122.html (accessed 4 April 2020).

Millbank, J. (2009), 'From Discretion to Disbelief: Recent Trends in Refugee Determinations on the Basis of Sexual Orientation in Australia and the United Kingdom', *The International Journal of Human Rights*, 13 (2/3): 391–414.

Moore, J. E. (1970), 'Mental Illness Exclusions in United States Immigration Procedure', *Case Western Reserve Journal of International Law*, 3 (1): 71–87.

Msibi, T. (2011), 'The Lies We Have Been Told: On (Homo)Sexuality in Africa', *Africa Today*, 58 (1): 54–77.

Murray, D. (2015), *Real Queer?: Sexual Orientation and Gender Identity Refugees in the Canadian Refugee Apparatus*, New York: Rowman & Littlefield.

Musalo, K. (2014), 'Personal Violence, Public Matter: Evolving Standards in Gender-Based Asylum Law', *Harvard International Review*, 36 (2): 45–8.

Ngwa Nfobin, E. H. (2014), 'Homosexuality in Cameroon', *International Journal on Minority and Group Rights*, 21 (1): 72–130.

Niang, C. I., E. Foley and N. Diop (2020), 'Colonial Legacies, Electoral Politics, and the Production of (Anti) Homosexuality in Senegal', in L. Boyd and E. Burrill (eds), *Legislating Gender and Sexuality in Africa: Human Rights, Society, and the State*, 150–70, Madison: University of Wisconsin Press.

Niang, C. I., A. Moreau, C. Bop, C. Compaoré and M. Diagne (2004), *Targeting Vulnerable Groups in National HIV/AIDS Programs: The Case of Men Who Have Sex with Men in Senegal, Burkina Faso, the Gambia*, Washington, DC: The World Bank.

Nolte, I. (2017), 'New Histories of Marriage and Politics in Africa', *Gender & History*, 29 (3): 742–8.

Nyamnjoh, F. B. (2015), *Modernising Traditions and Traditionalising Modernity in Africa: Chieftaincy and the Game of Legitimacy in Cameroon and Botswana*, Cameroon: Langaa RPCIG.

Nyanzi, S. (2013), 'Rhetorical Analysis of President Jammeh's Threats to Behead Homosexuals in the Gambia', in S. N. Nyeck and M. Epprecht (eds), *Sexual Diversity in Africa: Politics, Theory, and Citizenship*, 67–88, Montreal: McGill-Queen's University Press.

Nzouankeu, A. M. (2016), 'Gay Rights Groups Brave Abuse, Violence to Fight HIV in Cameroon', *Reuters*, 27 December. Available online: https://www.reuters.com/article/us-cameroon-lgbt/gay-rights-groups-brave-abuse-violence-to-fight-hiv-in-cameroon-idUSKBN14G0AC (accessed 8 November 2017).

Orock, R. (2014), 'Crime, In/Security and Mob Justice: The Micropolitics of Sovereignty in Cameroon', *Social Dynamics*, 40 (2): 408–28.

Osborn, E. (2011), *Our New Husbands Are Here: Households, Gender, and Politics in a West African State from the Slave Trade to Colonial Rule*, Athens: Ohio University Press.

Pharel, C. (2017), 'Cameroun: Un homme soupçonné d'homosexualité lynché à mort', *CL2P News*, 22 June. Available online: http://www.cl2p.org/cameroun-un-homme-soupconne-dhomosexualite-lynche-a-mort/ (accessed 6 November 2018).

Raboin, T. (2016), *Discourses on LGBT Asylum in the UK: Constructing a Queer Haven*, Manchester: Manchester University Press.

Rehaag, S. (2009), 'Bisexuals Need Not Apply: A Comparative Appraisal of Refugee Law and Policy in Canada, the United States, and Australia', *The International Journal of Human Rights*, 13 (2/3): 415–36.

Savage, R. (2019), 'Gabon Bans Gay Sex as Global Pace of Reform Falters', *Reuters*, 13 December. Available online: https://www.reuters.com/article/us-global-lgbt-crime-trfn-idUSKBN1YH1FN http://www.cl2p.org/cameroun-un-homme-soupconne-dhomosexualite-lynche-a-mort/ (accessed 13 December 2019).

Shiff, T. (2020), 'Revisiting Immutability: Competing Frameworks for Adjudicating Asylum Claims Based on Membership in a Particular Social Group', *University of Michigan Journal of Law Reform*, 53 (3): 567–96.

Shine, B. (2016), 'LGBT Advocates to Cameroon's Bishops: Retract Demand of "Zero Tolerance" for Homosexuality', *New Ways Ministry*, 16 February. Available online: https://newwaysministryblog.wordpress.com/2016/02/16/cameroons-bishops-demand-zero-tolerance-of-homosexuality/ (accessed 16 February 2016).

Shively, K. (2011), 'When Domestic Violence Is Not "Intimate Partner Violence": Cases from Turkey and Elsewhere', *Practicing Anthropology*, 33 (3): 13–16.

Smith, P. J. (2012), 'Suffering in Silence: Asylum Law and the Concealment of Political Opinion as a Form of Persecution Note Opinion as a Form of Persecution', *Connecticut Law Review*, 44 (3): 1021–56.

Stewart, C. (2017), 'Under Siege, LGBT Rights Centre Closes in Cameroon', *Erasing 76 Crimes*, 26 July. Available online: https://76crimes.com/2017/07/26/under-siege-lgbt-rights-center-closes-in-cameroon/ (accessed 12 December 2018).

Stewart, C. (2018), 'In Cameroon, Life Is Hell because I Support My Gay Brother', *Erasing 76 Crimes*, 6 June. Available from: https://76crimes.com/2018/06/06/in-cameroon-life-is-hell-because-i-support-my-gay-brother/ (accessed 8 January 2019).

Tamale, S. (2014), 'OPINION: Homosexuality Is Not Un-African', *Al Jazeera*, 26 April. Availbale online: http://america.aljazeera.com/opinions/2014/4/homosexuality-africa museveniugandanigeriaethiopia.html (accessed 8 January 2019).

Topel, K. D. (2017), '"So, What Should I Ask Him to Prove that He's Gay?": How Sincerity, and Not Stereotype, Should Dictate the Outcome of an LGB Asylum Claim in the United States', *Iowa Law Review*, 102 (5): 2357–84.

U.S. Department of Justice (2014), Matter of A-R-C-G-et al., Respondents, 26 I&N Dec. 388 (BIA 2014).

U.S. Department of Justice (2018), Matter of A-B-, Respondent, 27 I&N Dec. 316 (A.G.2018).

U.S. Department of Justice (2020), Procedures for Asylum and Withholding of Removal; Credible Fear and Reasonable Fear Review; RIN 1615-AC42 / 1125-AA94 / EOIR Docket No. 18-0002/ A.G. Order No. 4714-2020.

U.S. Immigration and Nationality Act (1965), INA 101(a)(42), 8 U.S.C. 1101(a)(42).

U.S. Refugee Act (1980), PL 96-212, 94 Stat. 102 (1980).

Walker-Said, C. (2018), *Faith, Power & Family: Christianity and Social Change in French Cameroon*, Oxford: James Currey.

Walker-Said, C. (2020), 'Family Violence in the Refugee Claims of Asylum Seekers from West Africa', in L. Boyd and E. Burrill (eds), *Legislating Gender and Sexuality in Africa: Human Rights, Society, and the State*, 125–49, Madison: Wisconsin University Press.

Weis, A. (2020), 'Fleeing for Their Lives: Domestic Violence Asylum and Matter of A-B', *California Law Review*, 108 (4): 1319–55.

Williams, J. (2016), 'Police Raid Gay Bar, Arrest Every Person Inside', *Pink News*, 10 October. Available online:https://www.pinknews.co.uk/2016/10/10/police-raid-gay-bar-arrest-every-person-inside/ (accessed 19 May 2019).

Women's International League for Peace and Freedom Cameroon (2019), *Women's Economic, Social and Cultural Rights in Cameroon: Parallel Report to the UN Committee on Economic, Social, and Cultural Rights*, Cameroon: WILPF International.

Wooden, C. (2013), 'Cardinal Sarah Known as Defender of Rights, Promoter of Charity', *The Catholic Sun*, 22 February. Available online: https://www.catholicsun.org/2013/02/22/cardinal-sarah-known-as-defender-of-rights-promoter-of-charity/ (accessed 9 March 2012).

Part III

THE DIGITAL AND THE TRANSNATIONAL

Chapter 7

'WHERE IS HOME?' NEGOTIATING COMM(UNITY) AND UN/BELONGING AMONG QUEER AFRICAN MIGRANTS ON FACEBOOK

Godfried Asante

The creation of safe spaces remains an important area of discussion for those whose bodies are marked as 'other' and subject to both state-sanctioned violence and normalized forms of exclusions. For lesbian, gay, bisexual and transgender (LGBT) individuals, access to safe spaces can provide the relative security to explore and enact their identities, create networks and form political alliances (Cooper 2010; Oswin 2008). However, queer safe spaces tend to be theorized as in opposition to, and as transgressions of, the white heterosexual space. This definition of queer safe space creates a binary stabilizing heterosexual space and LGBT space as distinct spaces (Oswin 2008). Moreover, the discursive framing of queer safe space as opposition to white heterosexual space assumes that queer safe spaces are outside the matrices of social hierarchies and power in both online and offline spaces. Counter to such claims, this study shows how power relations circulate and influence the construction of queer safe spaces through an examination of a queer African migrant virtual community.

While virtual communities construct imaginations of home, safety, belonging and togetherness to help LGBT individuals construct their identities and create alliances, these communities are not outside regimes of normalization, both offline and online (Duggan 2002; Skeggs 1999). Virtual communities, in particular, have been constructed as relatively 'safe' for LGBT people desiring safety from heteropatriarchal spaces infused with oppression and violence. For instance, research on virtual communities shows that such spaces provide anonymity, privacy and confidentiality, allowing LGBT people to temporarily create an 'imagined safety' (Cooper and Dzara 2010) outside the white heterosexual space. While such studies have opened the door for further analysis of the internet as a relatively safe space for LGBT people, I show how power relations in the offline

This chapter previously appeared in *Borderlands* (no longer available) and is republished here with permission. Minor editing has been done to align with the house style and UK publishing conventions.

spills into constructions of an online queer community, complicating notions of queer safe spaces as 'safe' for all LGBT individuals.

This study relates to my experience as a queer African migrant in the United States. Understanding my black and queer identities in relation to racialized structures and institutions in the United States made me yearn for a community comprising African/African-American queers. Therefore, I joined two closed Facebook groups and also began to meet with other same-gender-loving migrants from continental Africa. Subsequently, we formed a physical community outside the virtual community and met once a year at an annual New Year's Eve party. During conversations at these parties, it became evident that we had multiple framings of the closed Facebook groups as spaces where inclusivity was encouraged. While the closed Facebook groups were created as spaces where queer African migrants could unite and form a community around their 'shared gayness' (Massad 2002) and Africannnes, social hierarchies in relation to nationality, class and language saturated the space.

Scholarly material on queer African migrants, as well as on how queer African migrants create safe spaces through virtual communities, is rare. This is despite there being scholarly materials focusing on queer Africans in continental Africa (Ekine and Abbas 2013; Tamale 2011; Epprecht 2008; Hoad 2007), queer blogging in Indian digital diasporas (Mitra and Gajjala 2008) and post-colonial queer scholars who examine queer diasporas from Asia (Puar 2007; Gopinath 2005). Therefore, this study builds on research on queer space (e.g. Hartal 2017; Oswin 2008; Valentine 2007) and queer African diasporic identity and belonging (Adjepong 2019; Otu 2016; Asante 2015). In the following section, I explore the concept of home, especially what it means in the construction of queer African migrant communities. Next, I explain the literature on queer safe spaces and how it materializes online. Then, I explore the methods used in this study. Finally, I explicate the analysis and conclusions.

Where is home? (Queer) African migrants and the desire for queer safe spaces

Since the 1990s, the United States, in particular, has seen a significant increase in immigrants from the continent of Africa. Africans from Anglophone and Francophone countries, including those from various religious backgrounds (e.g. Muslim, Christian and Traditionalist) and ethnic backgrounds (e.g. Akan, Zulu and Igbo), have migrated to the United States. Changes in immigration laws, beginning with the Hart-Cellar Act of 1965, the Immigration Reform and Control Act of 1986 and the Immigration Act of 1990, have opened the door for more immigrants, mainly from Africa, to migrate to the United States voluntarily. The increase in African migrants has complicated what it means to be black in the United States (Adjepong 2018; Asante, Sekimoto and Brown 2016). LGBT African migrants have also questioned conceptions of diasporic home and identity in their African immigrant communities.

The structural dynamics of safety become reflected in the imageries of home. Multiple and fluid meanings of home shift across a number of discourses: from private to public spheres, between the nation as an 'imagined community' and mythic spaces of belonging. 'Home' can mean 'where one usually lives', says Sara Ahmed (2000), 'or it can mean where one's family lives, or it can mean one's native country' (86). In defining 'home', I side with Avtar Brah (1996) that it is a 'mythic place of desire and the lived experience of a locality, which evokes tensions inscribing a homing desire while simultaneously critiquing discourses of fixed origins' (188). The longing for a queer African migrant community is a 'homing desire' due to the symbolic representation of Africa as a space of return for black diasporic subjects in the West. Queer African migrants' attachment to Africa, even though their relationship to the continent could evoke memories of violence and pain, is partially due to forms of exclusion based on race and class that they experience in the West (Asante 2015). In this way, home manifests itself as desire based on separation and its potential antagonism; the split between the wish to return and the impossibility of its satisfaction shapes queer African migrants desire for a queer safe space.

Most post-colonial critics have focused on the disaffection suffered by African migrants in the United States and Europe, while others have dwelled extensively on queer issues, without a critical deliberation of how experiences based on migration, race and sexuality intertwine. While being unable to fully integrate into the white Western LGBT community, queer African migrants also suffer discrimination within African migrant communities due to the extension of hetero-nationalist cultural practices. Marc Epprecht (2008) argues that there is a clear privileging of a modern heteronormative African citizen that situates non-heteronormative practices into the margins of society. Within such a framing, any queer identity would be considered outside the mainstream. In this material context, queer African migrants feel such restrictions re-imposed by their immigrant community members. Consequently, creating an online queer community mitigates the intersectional oppressive structures influencing the queer African migrant identity. This means re-creating a community on the margins of their already ostracized identities as black, queer and immigrant.

Constructing and (re)negotiating queer safe spaces online

In the mid-1990s, research by David Bell (1995), Jon Binnie (1997) and Gill Valentine (1996) revamped arguments that situated queer theory within geographical studies focusing on sexuality. A central part of their argument is that spaces in and of themselves are not authentically straight and do not have pre-existing sexual categories. Rather, Binnie (1997) notes, spaces are produced and (hetero)sexualized through forms of spatial control. (Hetero)sexualized spaces are made possible through diverse mechanisms that restrict queer bodies to and in specific spaces. Subsequently, these social processes reconfigure queer desires, relationality and embodiment in/into such spaces.

Feminist geographers, in particular, have called for the shifting of studies on queer space to focus on the 'mutual constitution of gendered identities and spaces' (Bondi and Rose 2003: 234). Gilly Hartal (2017) asserts that most current debates on safe spaces are influenced by this body of knowledge. She contends that current work by feminist geographers has opened the door for the examination of the 'mutual construction of LGBT subjectivities and their experiences in space, specifically, queer space' (Hartal 2017: 3). Catherine Jean Nash's (2006) study of the development of Toronto's gay village shows how multiple subjectivities shape queer space:

> [It is] a location deeply scarred by myriad battles fought over the social, political and cultural meanings attributed to the existence of individuals interested in same-sex relationships ... The implications arising from the apparent relationship between certain homosexual identities and particular places is far more complicated than merely a battle over the ability to visibly inhabit and appropriate identifiable territories or neighbourhoods.
>
> (Nash 2006: 2)[1]

In short, Toronto's gay village is a space where contestations of the homosexual identity become visible.

In contrast to heterosexual space, LGBT spaces are constructed and represented as safe, tolerant and inviting, while in actuality such spaces reproduce power relations based on heteronormative constitutions of identity (Oswin 2008). Nash (2006) contends that queer spaces are actually unfixed and contested, and also serve as a disciplinary space. Christine Quinan (2016) asserts that queer spaces often go unexplained and unquestioned, which is applied as a broader concept in multiple settings, such as gay bars, LGBT community centres and virtual queer communities. Unquestioning the discourses that frame queer safe spaces leaves room for dominant narratives of race, language, nationality and class to overshadow less dominant voices.

Catherine Fox and Tracy Ore (2010) argue that omitting intersectionality from the analysis of safe spaces leads to reliance on a particular identity around which safe spaces are constructed. Barbara Stengal and Lisa Weems (2010) note that power relations constrain and enable certain ways of speaking and acting, as it is connected to the classroom or home. Therefore, applying intersectionality as an analytical lens shows how certain subject positions are imagined to inhabit the discursive boundaries of 'safe space'. Given the material context shaping what safe spaces mean in the offline, what does it mean to construct a safe space online? Do the negotiations of power relations and the hegemonic relations of power suddenly disappear online?

While there are increasing studies on LGBT identity and online media, these mostly gear towards a celebratory form of identity expression (see Pullen and Cooper 2010). Few studies problematize tensions that arise from class, language and gender performativity differences, or any other issues related to the socio-cultural and economically situated identity formations, in how new media shapes identity formations and senses of belonging (Gajjala 2003). Socio-cultural aspects of online activity and discursive formations online in relation to subjectivities that emerge online, and in relation to such issues as voice and voicelessness, still remain outside the scope of academic inquiry. This research complicates discussions of virtual communities as safe spaces where LGBT identities are celebrated and emancipated.

Facebook provides the interface for LGBT subjects to create, negotiate and construct their identities in virtual spaces due to users' ability to create online profiles. These profiles represent who users are, as the assumption is that users are creating and presenting their 'real' selves through what they post on their Facebook walls and accentuate in their profiles. Facebook also allows users to create an online community by only admitting members they trust and sometimes know face-to-face. Currently, there are many closed Facebook groups where participants can have access to and the opportunity to express their intimate desires and interests. For instance, Margaret Cooper (2007) discovered that rural lesbians who are married to men were now able to go online and seek out communities where they could gain information and support from others in similar situations. Steffen Dalsgaard (2008) writes that Facebook allows people to display themselves not just as self-made individuals but also as individuals. In one way, having a profile on Facebook permits users to be individualistic in the chance of being unique. Facebook allows for people to 'develop their identity' (Buhrmester and Prager 1995) through the process of revealing their thoughts and feelings to their peers or their imagined community.

In order to speculate on the cultural meanings that emerge from participating in closed Facebook groups, it is essential to carve out complex notions of culture and technology. I argue that culture is a site of contested meanings (Moon 2010). This argument underscores the dynamic nature of culture, suggesting that it is made up of heterogeneous meanings and of values that are contested and negotiated. In this sense, people's existence within culture is made up of a variety of practices that constitute the 'everydayness', with online social networks forming part of living in that culture (Rybas 2012).

Online identities have often been studied with emphasis on difference, particularly gender, sexuality and race. Gender identity is often studied in relation to sex and sexuality as well as race (Kolko, Nakamura and Rodman 2000). This kind of research argues that race matters both offline and online because we are already shaped by racial and cultural values, and we bring that knowledge to online spaces when we log on. Given the knowledge that queer safe spaces are entrenched in hegemonic relations of power, such re-workings of power spill into online safe spaces. In virtual communities, doing identity differently could have consequences. Valentine (2007) contends that 'when identities are done differently in particular temporal moments they rub up against, and so expose, these dominant spatial orderings that define who is in place/out of place, who belongs and who does not' (19). In this study, I situate race, class, gender and sexuality in the transnational to highlight how hierarchies of nationality, language, class, sexuality and other markers of difference are highlighted in discourses of queer safe spaces.

Method

In this study, I participated in and analysed two closed Facebook groups, which I refer to as AB and ACST, and which had a combined total of approximately 200 members. Both are closed Facebook groups for same-gender-loving African men. They differ from hook-up sites such as Grindr, Tinder and Planet Romeo, among others. These groups do not have a political presence outside of social media and only function as a networking platform for same-gender-loving African migrants. There are two reasons why I choose to analyse these groups. First, they are a representation of how queers appropriate a mainstream site such as Facebook. This shows the resilience of queers of colour, in particular, to construct their marginalized identities in and against majoritarian spaces (Muñoz 1999). Second, these groups provide the opportunity to study the offline and online interactions of members, while also pointing out the strategic voices that are given credence and those that are silenced.

There is an ethical dimension to this study. Access to the groups is granted to same-gender-loving African men on the basis of being known to existing members and the use of 'real' Facebook accounts. This means that members' faces and real names are visible to those in the groups. Therefore, I sought permission from the group administrators and members to conduct research in AB and ACST. To protect confidentiality, I have disguised the names of the groups and members. However, posts from members are quoted verbatim. The anonymity of members was central to my study because sometimes journalists from conservative African newspapers lurk in such groups to eventually publish the names of members. Since I am publically known to most of the members, and also attend parties organized by some of the members, my presence in the group was not unusual. Thus, I have become a trusted co-participant and observer within these two groups.

AB was the first group to emerge in 2013. ACST emerged later after a conflict between members of the original group. The two groups consist of same-gender-loving men from continental Africa who have migrated to Canada, the United States and the United Kingdom as international students or permanent residents. Some of the members are also located in different parts of Africa. The first group, AB, was started by a US-based member who wanted to create a platform for queer African migrants to get to know each other and also be able to enact their 'authentic' and 'true' selves in a private setting.

The internet is an open context for social interactions, where practices, meanings and identities are intermingled on a local and global scale (Atay 2015). Social interactions in virtual environments present a challenge for social researchers and open up a new field for qualitative research. The internet provides an interesting platform to study the making and un-making of identities and communities.

Danah Boyd (2008) cautions digital ethnographers to acknowledge the internet as a context in their work and also to let it go. She posits that, ultimately, it is about the cultures being studied and not the technology. Therefore, I supplant my ethnographic work with interviews that I translate as conversations with members of these groups. Ethnographic interviews were conducted with twelve members of the closed Facebook groups, either through Skype or in person. Since members live in different parts of the world, Skype offered the most cost-effective way to reach some of the people who wanted to participate in the research.

To analyse my data, I read through the interview transcriptions, posts and comments to get a holistic picture. In so doing, I analysed the content of the posts to see what is generally being talked about and to identify micro-level speech acts. During this stage, I noted statements describing queer African identities. I looked for implicit and explicit avowals and ascriptions about queer African migrant identity. Next, I noted how other members were positioned in relation to the norms of heteronormativity, Africanness and sexual freedom. For instance, some members wrote that they did not want the group to be represented as 'LGBT African Americans'. I then conducted inductive coding to uncover forms of identity negotiation. After doing both inductive and deductive coding, I looked for similarities in comments and claims, and organized them into preliminary categories and themes. When satisfied with a theme, I looked at how thematic categories emerged in context to one another. Two themes became salient, and they are explicated below.

Negotiating 'home' and belonging(s) in the offline and online

There have been rich debates on the liberating potential of the internet. These have primarily focused on how the internet has broken down physical barriers that obstruct the construction of certain identities in physical space. Nina Wakeford (2002) writes that the LGBT community was among the first to adopt cyber technologies because it provided space for anyone to be what they wanted. So, the internet has always been a place to seek networks, relationships and potential sex partners. For the queer African migrants in this study, the internet offers a way to temporarily satisfy the (im)possibility of their 'homing desire'. In other words, the internet allows them to construct an identity where they can be both African and queer.

David Eng (1997) argues that despite 'frequent and trenchant queer dismissals of home and its discontents, it would be a mistake to underestimate enduring queer affiliations to this concept' (32). For the queer African migrants in this study, there is a simultaneous avowal and disavowal of belonging to an 'imagined Africa' and a global queer community in the West. Nonetheless, the construction of a queer African migrant identity is worked and reworked within the dynamics of an imagined home and its extension online. It is never fixed, but rather redefined and reconfigured in specific contexts. In this case, the internet provides a relatively safe space for queer African migrants to negotiate their multiple identities within the contours of being a queer black/African immigrant in the West.

Interview discourse from participants in this study suggests that queer African migrants encounter racism and homophobia within the context of their otherness as an immigrant. For instance, in a conversation with John from Liberia, he mentioned that he hardly associates with other African migrants because they are more likely to be religious and not welcoming of his queerness. Hence, most of his friends are white Americans, as he believes 'they [white people] are more likely to understand his sexual orientation'. Kwame from Ghana also stated, 'I stopped going to the Ghanaian church because they are all gossips, they want to know if you are gay and then bring it up in church sermon.' When I asked Kwame where he attends church now, he mentioned another church with 'a lot of white people'. The comments from John and Kwame position white bodies as more liberal and accepting of their sexual orientation. This problematic assumption could be the result of what Jasbir Puar (2007) critiques as homonationalism – a merging of nationalism and global LGBT politics that positions the West as friendlier to queers than, typically, Muslim countries. In this intersectional complexity, a sense of belonging is not about one's national or racial background but is instead directed at white bodies, which have been continually represented as progressive towards LGBT human rights politics, in contrast with 'backward' brown bodies (Eng 2010).

However, another participant mentioned that he would rather stick to the 'ignorance' of African migrants because 'Americans' do not understand him and his sexual identity. James from Nigeria said the following when I asked why he joined the online Facebook group: 'Sometimes I get tired talking to Americans. I have to explain everything. So, I will rather stick to my people [African migrants]. They are ignorant, but I can deal with them. They understand me to a point, or I can talk to African Americans.' James' statement sheds light on the politics of belonging. He explains his association with other African migrants who might be homophobic as better than experiencing social exclusions based on race. James', John's and Kwame's statements show that queer migrants' sense of belonging is rather fluid and complex. These statements juxtapose earlier communication research on identity and identity negotiation, which emphasizes the will of immigrants to assimilate or adapt as a form of learning and growth (Kim 2001). The complex negotiation of multiple selves – African, queer and immigrant – cannot be reduced to the binary of assimilation or resistance. This reading aligns with Shinsuki Eguchi and Godfried Asante's (2016) argument that 'intercultural negotiations of identity and practices of belonging are never a simple process of life learning and growth; they are on-going complex and paradoxical dialectics of life struggle in historical and ideological spaces' (187). Thus, the desire to join an online queer community can be a way to negotiate the self, to give the queer African migrant identity a form of coherence that is not achievable offline.

The articulation of the internet as the space to envision a coherent queer African identity was expressed by a member. During a conversation at a yearly party organized by the AB administrators, I asked Tangy, an Ivorian migrant to the

United States, why he joined the online group, to which he offered the following response:

> Sometimes, I want to talk to my African people about my [queer] life, but it seems they want to know everything except that part of my life. For instance, I wanted to take my African friend to a pride parade last year, but he did not want to go with me. He said 'Africans don't do these kinds of stuff.' I mean ... where can I be myself without losing one part of me? So, that's why I go online; I can say anything I want.

Tangy's statement shows how online spaces provide the relative safety for him to negotiate his queer African migrant identity. In his study of online behaviours of queer youth, Jonathan Alexander (2004) finds that users write online in complex and provocative ways that exceed the limits of just coming out. Similarly, the internet allows members of these groups to negotiate seemingly polar identities and belongings as black, queer and African migrant, just as Tangy described.

Some members did not want to go online to express themselves, but rather wanted a space to speak about whiteness and racialized sexual desire. Kokovi is from Togo, and when asked about why he regularly visits the closed Facebook group, he said the following:

> Somehow I am always attractive to old white men. They are always coming for me at clubs. Every time I am at a bar or club, they talk to me and ask me questions about Africa. In fact, some of them are so dumb, and I am so tired of answering questions about where I am from. At least online, I know I will not be asked any stupid questions about Africa. Also, it is always difficult to have a relationship with them. They just want to taste Africans but not looking for real relationships with us.

Angel, from Burkina Faso, dated an older white man for seven years. He mentioned the following when I asked why he regularly visits the closed Facebook group:

> Angel: I know them [white gay men] very well. I have lived with one for a while. I know his friends were jealous of me and all that. I am sure that contributed to our break-up.
> Researcher: Why did you break up?
> Angel: He said I am too feminine for him. He wanted a real man. I was like ... I am the same person from seven years ago. I am sure he wants another African ... fresh meat.

Angel's and Tangy's statements are symptomatic of black experiences of being desired in a racialized society. As bell hooks (1992) notes, 'from the standpoint of white supremacist capitalist patriarchy, the hope is that desires for the "primitive" or fantasies about the Other can be continually exploited and that such exploitation will occur in a manner that reinscribes and maintains the *status quo*' (367). Racialized desires for queer African migrants, particularly by older white men, to borrow from hooks, are a form of commodification, which constitutes an alternative playground where older white men affirm their power-over intimate relations with the other. For queer African migrants navigating the racialized desires of white supremacy, the internet provides an assumed de-racialized space where 'real' relationships can be pursued. Thus, members use the closed Facebook groups to seek relationships interpreted as 'genuine' and free from the gaze and desires of white supremacist capitalist heteropatriarchy.

Some of the posts and comments in the two closed Facebook groups pointed to a *queering* of 'coming out'. There are several posts showing pictures of members with their boyfriends, attending gay events and pride parades. Since I am friends with Tangy on Facebook, I noticed he does not post anything regarding his boyfriend on his main Facebook page. I asked Tangy why this is the case. He explained that he wanted to keep his sexual life away from the scrutiny of family and friends who have access to his profile. The fragmented spaces of Facebook provide for the presentation of different selves to public and private audiences. Code-switching and dis/identifications with communal meanings of gender and sexuality are not new to racialized queer bodies who have had to constantly negotiate their intersectional identities at the margins of racialized, gendered and sexual normalities (McCune 2014; Cohen 1997). Thus, members of the closed Facebook groups do not 'come out' of the closet per se when they visit these online spaces. Rather, they collapse the binary between the closet and coming out. The internet provides the space where a particular kind of queer African migrant subjectivity can be imagined and enacted without involving 'coming out' to family and friends.

Negotiating comm(unity) and identity online: Class and language struggles

As detailed in the previous theme, group members explained that going online to network and form relationships with other queer African migrants helped them construct a sense of coherence in their multiple identities as black, African, queer and immigrant in the West. With 'home' as an organizing principle, members of the closed Facebook groups transcended regional, national and ethnic boundaries to construct a sense of belonging around their queer African migrant identity online. The dis/embodied performativity of cyberspace provided a temporary safe space where queer African migrant identity can be re-configured.

However, meaning-making in cyberspace intersects with offline communities and global formations shaped through transnational flows of capital and media. This means offline social hierarchies based on class, sexuality and language also intersect with the creation of virtual communities. Writing about cyberqueer communities in India, Rahul Mitra (2010) contends that the construction and representation of digital queer communities involve 'critical silences' and strategic negotiations where particular queer identities and voices are valorized, and others are left out. While the internet provides a safe space for queer African migrants to construct and represent their identities, it is evident that class and language hierarchies intersected with these processes. Members of AB who were perceived to be 'over-expressing' or 'loud' (which is linked to being less classy and uneducated) about their sexuality were scrutinized and sometimes removed from the group. This theme shows that while diasporic home is an organizing principle for the negotiation of a queer safe space online, the construction and representation of such spaces are not free from social hierarchies existing in face-to-face communities.

In this theme, I specifically examine discourses of inclusion and exclusion that emerged from a conflict in AB. I recount this event to consider the politics of visibility and invisibility that mark it. This conflict led to the creation of another closed Facebook group: ACST. The 'break-up' was initiated by a member who felt his posts and engagements were being controlled and over-regulated by the administrators. In March 2014, the administrators of AB began to express concerns over what members can and cannot post. The issue of what to post and what conversations were allowed showed the merging of offline and online discourses of ethnicity, civility and professionalism, which are used to silence queers of colour in mainstream offline conversations about social inequalities and oppression (Jones and Calafell 2012).

In a statement by an administrator of AB to the group during the conflict, he asserted that he does not want group members to post nude photos or highly sexual content because, according to him, 'it offends other members'. In a conversation after the conflict, he opined that he is aware of other black closed Facebook groups that have been reduced to 'posts' about nude men and conversation about sex. He stated, 'we are Africans, not African Americans, so members of this group should have conversations beyond sex.' I asked him what he meant and he explained that other closed Facebook groups with predominantly African-American members do not engage in conversations beyond sex so if queer Africans want to establish their space it should be more professional. His statement shows how tensions around race, class and ethnicity between African Americans and African migrants (Langmia and Durham 2007) are re-activated in discussions of online queer safe spaces. Referring to 'professionalism' also points to issues of class hierarchy.

In his research about queer cyber communities in India, Rohit Dasgupta (2017) explains that class is linked intrinsically to sexual identity. He explained that identities such as 'hijra and kothi are seen as non-metropolitan subaltern sexual identities as opposed to the neoliberal modern urban and socially mobile gay identity' (78). In his research on queer subjectivities in Ghana, Asante (2017) also found that masculine gender conformity was considered desirable and associated with class. In the context of Ghana, queer men who are feminine and also open about their sexuality were characterized as less classy and thus deserving of social stigma and violence. These two studies point to how class hierarchy shapes queer communities. In the context of this study, class hierarchy is linked to sexual openness. Those who shared more information about their sexuality through posts depicting nude men or who shared stories about gay sex were portrayed as lacking class.

Consequently, an inter-group conflict emerged about the restrictions being imposed on members. Responding to one of the administrators of AB, Johnson commented: 'I cannot talk to many people about who I like or what I like, I feel I can share my feelings [desires] here but again, I am not allowed to do that. Where should I go now?' Johnson is worried that as well as being restricted to enact his sexual identity offline, he now has to conform to another set of rules and regulations online. The conflict presented a conundrum to queer African migrants' construction of the closed Facebook group as an inclusive queer safe space.

Stuart Hall (2002) writes that identification – the process of building the self – is always strategic and positional in relation to others because institutional and historical sites allow or limit specific discursive formations and practices, and invite specific enunciative strategies. Although most of the members explained how they found a sense of 'home' and belonging in AB and ACST, where they can safely share information and have 'real' conversations, it became evident that class tensions shaped how members framed AB as a queer safe space. For instance, Ike, from Sierra Leone, said the following during a conversation:

> Some of these young people think they can control what I want to say and write. I like to post things I can't share on my page ... like sexy men's bodies, but the administrators say I cannot post this because it offends other people. I mean c'mon, this is a group for gay men not some businessmen on a trip. So, I left the group and joined another group where I can post what I like.

Kojo is from Ghana and lives in Boston with his partner. During our conversation, I asked him why he left AB and joined ACST:

> I was so tired of the drama; this Liberian boy wants to tell us what to do and what to post. In fact, I was disappointed in this decision to delete some people because he did not like their post[s]. Some of us did not go to Ivy League schools, but we are confident in ourselves. Just leave us to post what we want.

Digital spaces like Facebook contribute to negotiating issues critical for constructing queer safe spaces. However, power, authority, knowledge and representation spill over into digital sites. For instance, the statement from Kojo shows how offline tensions can spill into the formation of online queer safe spaces. Kojo is from Ghana, which has a large population of Liberians who relocated to Ghana due to the Second Liberian Civil War (1999–2003). This ignited nationalistic rivalries between some Ghanaians and Liberians due to representations of Liberian refugees as criminals. Given this context, Kojo's reference to 'this Liberian boy' points to the administrator's social positioning in relation to him. Even though their queer identity unified the two men in virtual space, their offline social hierarchies in relation to nationality emerged in discussions of inclusion and exclusion.

Another discourse linked to class that emerged during the conflict is 'educated' versus 'uneducated'. In one of the comments replying to the post by the administrator, Albert from Cameroon said the following: 'Why are we making a fuss about this issue like we are uneducated people? I mean ... just don't post anything about sex here. You can use other platforms for that. Let's just get over this and move on.' Above, Kojo from Ghana stated that not all members are educated or have college degrees from Ivy League schools, indicating how educational status is linked to class. Even though Facebook has constantly been in flux, adding more features and lines in menus to capture the complexity of individual identities, users are forced to choose identity markers that erase their intersecting identities in order to meet perceived audience expectations. As Natalia Rybas (2012) eloquently states, participating in the online network creates and erases difference at the interface. Albert's comment above – 'let's just get over this and move on' – signifies the multiple erasures that members who do not meet the expectations of the neoliberal modern, urban and socially mobile gay identity have to endure in order to participate in this imagined 'unity'. While checking to see which members' comments were receiving more attention, I realized that members from English-speaking African countries received the most feedback. I also witnessed one member mocking the grammatical errors of a member from Togo trying to enter the conversation with an unfamiliar language. The exclusions and simultaneous mocking of the Francophone and Lusophone members echo Radhika Gajjala's (2003) argument that there is an accepted norm that the internet is a white, English-speaking space. The persistence of English as the un/official queer language of the internet means that access to these sites is limited to particular queer subjects.

Although not directly stated as the only means of communication, English remains the predominant language used in both AB and ACST. The unquestioned acceptance of English makes French- and Portuguese-speaking members practically voiceless. In November 2016, a member of the newly formed group, ACST, posted a news story written in French about gay bashings in Senegal. While other French speakers responded to the post, the members from English-speaking African countries jokingly typed in fake French words. During a conversation with Idris from Burkina Faso, I asked him what he thought about this experience: 'Actually, I do not care, it seems everyone assumes we should all type in English. But we do not mock them when they type in English. They assume it's just normal to type in English.' Idris' comment suggests that even though most of the Francophone members in AB left to join ACST because the administrators stated that English is the official language in AB, exclusions based on language persist in ACST.

Conclusions and implications

This study points to the conceptual, representational and material limitations of queer safe space, as it is produced online. Connecting safe spaces to the process of building a queer African migrant community in the West, I have shown that queer communities as they exist online and offline carry meanings that are, problematically, not shared by all members in the group. While virtual communities that act as safe spaces such as AB and ACST can provide the needed space for queer African migrants to reconfigure their African identities outside the scrutiny of their migrant communities and families, these virtual communities also reproduce power relations that recreate social hierarchies and exclusions. Thus, the study shows the importance of interrogating queer safe spaces through intersectionality to complicate abstract calculations of domination and resistance (Oswin 2008).

The first theme explored how queer African migrants negotiate their intersectional identities as black/African, queer and immigrant in the West. Some of the members mentioned that joining the virtual community provided a sense of coherency to the queer African migrant identity. Hence, the internet provides the interface for queer African migrants to speak back to issues of racism in the white US queer community and homophobia in the African migrant community, without jeopardizing their relationships with them. As indicated by Cathy Cohen (1997), raced and class labels act of vehicles of resistance that queers of colour strategically deploy to dis/identify with interlocking oppressive systems.

The second theme examined the processes of building a queer community and the intricacies of building a coherent identity without considering the specific lens of intersectionality. Using the conflict that emerged in AB as a context, I unravelled how meaning-making in cyberspace intersects with offline social structures and global formations shaped through transnational flows of capital and media. This research makes visible the duality of queer communities as spaces for exploration, identity construction and visibility *and* as spaces where forms of normalization and social boundaries are drawn.

The findings from this research imply that queer safe spaces are not outside the matrices of social hierarchies and power. Furthermore, academic inquiry that examines safe spaces based on identities obscures particularities since identities cannot but work within the confines of power and normativity. Natalie Oswin (2008) notes that the task of queer theorists 'is to embrace the critique of identity to its fullest extent by abandoning the search for an inherently radical queer subject and turning attention to the advancement of a critical approach to the workings of sexual normativities and non-normativities' (96). In other words, identities that normalize particular ways of community participation should be the subject of queer critique. It became evident in this study that notions of what it means to be 'African' were points of contention. Without examination of how Africanness has been constructed through colonialism and whiteness, the members of AB and ACST could not envision a radically queer African subjectivity. Rather, these closed Facebook groups became a reflection of the social hierarchies that engulf queer safe spaces. This shows the necessity to continually critique how sexual normativity and power relations shape queer safe spaces. Gloria Anzaldua (1987) pushes scholars to envision alternative spaces where bridges are constructed, rather than those that offer the illusion of safety. She asserts:

There are no safe spaces. To step across the threshold is to be stripped of the illusion of safety because it moves us into unfamiliar territory and does not grant safe passage. To bridge is to attempt community and for that we must risk being open to personal, political and spiritual intimacy, to risk being wounded.

(3)

I share Hartal's (2017) concerns that there will always be conflict in the processes of creating queer safe spaces because of its reliance on identity politics and liberal discourses. However, I add that queer activists and theorists should resist the illusion of safety that queer safe spaces suggest and endeavour to destabilize intersecting cultural normativities that engulf them.

Note

1   This quote has been corrected from the *Borderlands* version in order to match the original source.

References

Adjepong, A. (2018), 'Afropolitan Projects: African Immigrant Identities and Solidarities in the United States', *Ethnic and Racial Studies*, 41 (2): 248–66.

Adjepong, A. (2019), 'Invading Ethnography: A Queer of Color Reflexive Practice', *Ethnography*, 20 (1): 27–46.

Ahmed, S. (2000), *Strange Encounters: Embodied Others in Post-Coloniality*, New York: Psychology Press.

Alexander, J. (2004), *In Their Own Words: LGBT Youth Writing the World Wide Web*, New York: GLAAD.

Anzaldua (1987), *Borderlands/La Frontera: The New Mestiza*, San Francisco: Aunt Lute Books.

Asante, G. A. (2015), '(De)stabilizing the Normative: Using Critical Autoethnography as Intersectional Praxis to (Re)conceptualise Identity Performances of Black Queer Immigrants', *Kaleidoscope*, 14 (1): 83–8.

Asante, G. A. (2017), '"Reproducing the Ghanaian/African Queer Subject": Ideological Tensions and Queer Subjectivities in Postcolonial Ghana', PhD dissertation, University of New Mexico, Albuquerque.

Asante, G. A., S. Sekimoto and C. Brown (2016), 'Becoming "Black": Exploring the Racialised Identity of African Immigrants in the United States', *Howard Journal of Communication*, 27 (4): 367–84.

Atay, A. (2015), *Globalization's Impact on Cultural Identity Formation: Queer Diasporic Males in Cyberspace*, New York: Lexington Books.

Bell, D. (1995), 'Pleasure and Danger: The Paradoxical Spaces of Sexual Citizenship', *Political Geography*, 14 (2): 139–53.

Binnie, J. (1997), 'Coming Out of Geography: Towards a Queer Epistemology?', *Environment and Planning D: Society and Space*, 15 (2): 223–37.

Bondi, L. and D. Rose (2003), 'Constructing Gender, Constructing the Urban: A Review of Anglo-American Feminist Urban Geography', *Gender, Place & Culture*, 10 (3): 229–45.

Boyd, D. (2008), 'Can Social Network Sites Enable Political Action', *International Journal of Media and Cultural Politics*, 4 (2): 241–4.

Brah, A. (1996), *Cartographies of Diaspora: Contesting Identities*, Abingdon: Psychology Press.

Buhrmester, D. and K. Prager (1995), 'Patterns and Functions of Self-Disclosure during Childhood and Adolescence', in K. J. Rotenberg (ed.), *Disclosure Processes in Children and Adolescents*, 10–56, Cambridge: Cambridge University Press.

Cohen, C. J. (1997), 'Punks, Bulldaggers, and Welfare Queens: The Real Radical Potential of Queer Politics?', *GLQ*, 3 (4): 437–65.

Cooper, M. (2010), 'Lesbians Who Are Married to Men: Identity, Collective Stories and the Internet Online Community', in C. Pullen and M. Cooper (eds), *LGBT Identity and Online New Media*, 75–86, London: Routledge.

Cooper, M. and K. Dzara (2010), 'The Facebook Revolution: LGBT Identity and Activism', in C. Pullen and M. Cooper (eds), *LGBT Identity and Online New Media*, 100–12, London: Routledge.

Dalsgaard, S. (2008), 'Facework on Facebook: The Presentation of Self in Virtual Life and Its Role in the US Elections', *Anthropology Today*, 24 (6): 8–12.

Dasgupta, R. K. (2017), *Digital Queer Cultures in India: Politics, Intimacies and Belonging*, Abingdon: Routledge.

Duggan, L. (2002), 'The New Homonormativity: The Sexual Politics of Neoliberalism', in R. Castronovo and D. D. Nelson (eds), *Materializing Democracy: Toward a Revitalized Cultural Politics*, 175–94, Durham and London: Duke University Press.

Eguchi, S. and G. Asante (2016), 'Disidentifications Revisited: Queer(y)ing Intercultural Communication Theory', *Communication Theory*, 26 (2): 171–89.

Ekine, S. and H. Abbas (eds) (2013), *Queer African Reader*, Oxford: Pamzuka Press.

Eng, D. L. (1997), 'Out Here and Over There: Queerness and Diaspora in Asian American Studies', *Social Text*, 52/53: 31–52.

Eng, D. L. (2010), *The Feeling of Kinship: Queer Liberalism and the Racialization of Intimacy*, Durham and London: Duke University Press.

Epprecht, M. (2008), *Heterosexual Africa? The History of an Idea from the Age of Exploration to the Age of AIDS*, Athens: Ohio University Press.

Fox, C. O. and T. E. Ore (2010), '(Un) Covering Normalised Gender and Race Subjectivities in LGBT "Safe Spaces"', *Feminist Studies*, 36 (3): 629–49.

Gajjala, R. (2003), 'South Asian Digital Diasporas and Cyberfeminist Webs: Negotiating Globalisation, Nation, Gender and Information Technology Design', *Contemporary South Asia*, 12 (1): 41–56.

Gopinath, G. (2005), *Impossible Desires: Queer Diasporas and South Asian Public Cultures*, Durham and London: Duke University Press.

Hall, S. (2002), 'Political Belonging in a World of Multiple Identities', in S. Vertovec and R. Cohen (eds), *Conceiving Cosmopolitanism: Theory, Context, and Practice*, 25–31, Oxford: Oxford University Press.

Hartal, G. (2017), 'Fragile Subjectivities: Constructing Queer Safe Spaces', *Social & Cultural Geography*, 19 (8): 1053–72.

Hoad, N. (2007), *African Intimacies: Race, Homosexuality, and Globalisation*, Minneapolis: University of Minnesota Press.

hooks, b. (1992), *Black Looks: Race and Representation*, Boston: South End Press.

Jones, R. G. and B. M. Calafell (2012), 'Contesting Neoliberalism through Critical Pedagogy, Intersectional Reflexivity, and Personal Narrative: Queer Tales of Academia', *Journal of Homosexuality*, 59 (7): 957–81.

Kim, Y. Y. (2001), *Becoming Intercultural: An Integrative Theory of Communication and Cross-Cultural Adaptation*, London: Sage Publications.

Kolko, B., L. Nakamura and G. Rodman (2000), 'Race in Cyberspace: An Introduction', in B. Kolko, L. Nakamura and G. Rodman (eds), *Race in Cyberspace*, 1–13, New York: Routledge.

Langmia, K. and E. Durham (2007), 'Bridging the Gap: African and African American Communication in Historically Black Colleges and Universities', *Journal of Black Studies*, 37 (6): 805–26.

Massad, J. A. (2002), 'Re-Orienting Desire: The Gay International and the Arab World', *Public Culture*, 14 (2): 361–85.

McCune, J. Q. (2014), *Sexual Discretion: Black Masculinity and the Politics of Passing*, Chicago: University of Chicago Press.

Mitra, R. (2010), 'Resisting the Spectacle of Pride: Queer Indian Bloggers as Interpretive Communities', *Journal of Broadcasting & Electronic Media*, 54 (1): 163–78.

Mitra, R. and R. Gajjala (2008), 'Queer Blogging in Indian Digital Diasporas: A Dialogic Encounter', *Journal of Communication Inquiry*, 32 (4): 400–23.

Moon, D. G. (2010), 'Critical Reflections on Culture and Critical Intercultural Communication', in T. K. Nakayama and R. T. Halualani (eds), *The Handbook of Critical Intercultural Communication*, 34–52, Chichester: Wiley-Blackwell.

Muñoz, J. E. (1999), *Disidentifications: Queers of Color and the Performance of Politics*, Minneapolis: University of Minnesota Press.

Nash, C. J. (2006), 'Toronto's Gay Village (1969–1982): Plotting the Politics of Gay Identity', *The Canadian Geographer*, 50 (1): 1–16.

Oswin, N. (2008), 'Critical Geographies and the Uses of Sexuality: Deconstructing Queer Space', *Progress in Human Geography*, 32 (1): 89–103.

Otu, K. E. (2016), 'Saints and Sinners: African Holocaust, "Clandestine Countermemories" and LGBT Visibility Politics in Postcolonial Africa', in C. Ukpokolo (ed.), *Being and Becoming: Gender, Culture and Shifting Identity in Sub-Saharan Africa*, 195–216, Denver: Spears Media Press.

Puar, J. K. (2007), *Terrorist Assemblages: Homonationalism in Queer Times*, Durham and London: Duke University Press.

Quinan, C. (2016), 'Safe Space', in N. M. Rodrigues, W. J. Martino, J. C. Ingrey and E. Brockenbrough (eds), *Critical Concepts in Queer Studies and Education*, 361–8, New York: Palgrave.

Rybas, N. (2012), 'Producing the Self at the Digital Interface', in P. H. Cheong, J. N. Martin and L. P. Macfadyen (eds), *New Media and Intercultural Communication: Identity, Community, and Politics*, 93–107, New York: Peter Lang.

Skeggs, B. (1999), 'Matter out of Place: Visibility and Sexualities in Leisure Spaces', *Leisure Studies*, 18 (3): 213–32.

Stengel, B. S. and L. Weems (2010), 'Questioning Safe Space: An Introduction', *Studies in Philosophy and Education*, 29 (6): 505–7.

Tamale, S. (ed.) (2011), *African Sexualities: A Reader*, Cape Town: Pambazuka.

Valentine, G. (1996), '(Re)negotiating the "Heterosexual Street": Lesbian Productions of Space', in N. Duncan (ed.), *BodySpace: Destabilising Geographies of Gender and Sexuality*, 146–55, New York: Routledge.

Valentine, G. (2007), 'Theorizing and Researching Intersectionality: A Challenge for Feminist Geography', *The Professional Geographer*, 59 (1): 10–21.

Wakeford, N. (2002), 'New Technologies and "Cyber-Queer" Research', in D. Richardson and S. Seidman (eds), *Handbook of Lesbian and Gay Studies*, 115–44, London: Sage Publications.

Chapter 8

WHAT IS PRIVATE ABOUT 'PRIVATE PARTS'? ON NAVIGATING THE VIOLENCE OF THE DIGITAL AFRICAN TRANS REFUGEE ARCHIVE

B Camminga

Dearth and the digital

In 2004, two seemingly unconnected events took place in very different parts of the world. First, the initial iteration of Miss International Queen – what would quickly become the world's largest beauty pageant for transgender women – had its inaugural show in Thailand (Martínez 2017). Second, a transgender woman named Miss Sahhara left Nigeria for London, believing that if she did not escape her country of birth, her next suicide attempt would be her final one (Miss Sahhara 2018). Fast forward seven years and that very same woman was making history, proudly announcing herself to the Miss International Queen audience: 'I am contestant number 2 and I am representing the giant of Africa: NIGERIA' (Keeling 2012). This moment was significant not just for the pageant – it had never before had an entrant from the African continent, let alone crowned a black woman – but also for the entrant herself, in that she declared to the world that she is both transgender *and* Nigerian. An immediate strong contender, Miss Sahhara used the pageant as a platform to establish herself as the 'first transgender Nigerian' (Anon 2016). Although Miss Sahhara has gone on to win several pageant crowns, including Miss Super Sireyna Worldwide in the Philippines in 2014, it was her 2011 debut that brought her into the purview of the country she had left seven years earlier (Mordi 2019). Nigerian media articles from that time constitute a particular archive, increasingly focused as they are on transgender people who have sought asylum in the Global North. Intentionally shocking headlines such as 'Meet Four Known Nigerian Transgenders [*sic*] (PHOTOS)' (Expressng Reporters 2015), usually accompanied by images of Miss Sahhara and others, have become a regular feature in Nigeria's tabloids. In the archive created by these articles, fragments of Miss Sahhara's life appear filtered through a deeply misogynistic, sexist, homophobic and transphobic lens.

In the wake of the Miss International Queen pageant, Miss Sahhara became a household name in Nigeria, courtesy of digital stories that could be rapidly shared. The year after her crowing saw a staggering number of articles published, coupled with regular harassment from Nigerian bloggers and journalists. There is presently a sense of denial across the African continent regarding the existence of transgender people. I have argued elsewhere that 'transgender' is still a relatively new concept on the African continent, although the lived experiences that the term attempts to describe are very much not (Camminga 2019). As Victor Mukasa, a trans man from Uganda, explains, gender-nonconforming people on the African continent are 'automatically' branded homosexuals by most communities (Mukasa and Balzer 2009: 124). As a refugee living outside of the continent, Miss Sahhara recognized her potential to be a role model and began to cultivate a distinctive online presence via several social media platforms. However, with very few – if any – rights in her home country, stemming from both her status as a refugee and her self-identification as a transgender person, and exacerbated by the Nigerian state's denial of her existence, Miss Sahhara's online presence became easy fodder for the tabloid press. Online 'news' outlets frequently re-appropriate and manipulate Miss Sahhara's posts with scant regard for their intended meaning. Libellous headlines are commonplace, and most articles openly misgender her. Perhaps the most disturbing practice is the use of photographs that, in a sense, 'catfish' readers. Often a webpage will lead with a string of Miss Sahhara's modelling and beauty pageant photos. The images are presented in such a way as to be enticing and titillating, inviting the reader to enter into a relationship of desire with her. However, the final photo, once the viewer has scrolled through anywhere between five and twenty images, will be of a man or boy – usually a different person entirely – with the words 'But she was a man!' emblazoned across the top. The ultimate aim is to imply duplicitousness on the part of Miss Sahhara, while also arousing revulsion and disgust in the reader. These misgendering practices are very often accompanied by Miss Sahhara's deadname, information about her parents and wild suggestions about her sexual behaviours and intimate relationships.

The proliferation of these articles has created a significant online archive, perhaps the first of its kind, of visible African transgender existence. I use 'archive' here in an expansive sense, to signal an 'overarching protean category' that holds 'a diversity of information' precipitated by various technologies (Waterton 2010: 646). I understand the documents of this archive, its digital contents, as 'active, generative substances with histories, as documents with their own itineraries' (Stoler 2009: 2). This diversity of information, marked as it is by the particularity of its digital production, holds and presents divergent experiences and perceptions, allowing for movement between global and local at great speed.

The primary appeal of the archive is that it shows, paradoxically, that Miss Sahhara is that which the Nigerian state denies existing. Indeed, its digital nature means that it brings firmly into the public realm – seemingly unintentionally – a transgender woman who is also Nigerian (Camminga 2020). But to look to this archive presents particular ethical concerns and challenges. Research, particularly from the Global North, on the role of the internet and digital media in the lives of trans people, and on the emergence of online trans archiving, tends to foreground and celebrate the democratic potential of cyberspace (Rawson 2014b). The internet allows for transgender history and people, especially those inhabiting hostile socio-political environments, to come into visibility – often, but not always, on their own terms (see Vartabedian 2019; Mhiripiri and Moyo 2016). Miss Sahhara's experience raises the question of the current and future role of digital media in the lives of transgender refugees.

In this chapter, I consider the ethical challenges of engaging with the digital archive of a diasporic subject. In my work with Miss Sahhara's archive, I have found myself facing a scholarly crisis that stems from three interweaving dynamics: first, this archive is freely available to anyone with an internet connection; second, the subject (Miss Sahhara) is written about in ways that are both violent and traumatic; third, because the subject is both a refugee and transgender – an identity widely perceived as illegal in Nigeria[1] – she has no recourse to hold the tabloid press to account. Jacques Derrida (1995) reminds us that although the archive can be a site of domination, it is also a space from which we might promote social justice. However, achieving the latter requires a particular ethical sensibility and responsibility. It demands something of me as a researcher. At its most basic level, this means not colluding with oppressive power structures. As Maria Martinez (2014) notes, 'the crux of the problem is that of exposing historical violence and power without reproducing their forms' (173). As a researcher with access to an unmediated digital archive, I must ask serious questions about my obligations and responsibilities, not just to the disciplinary conventions underpinning my academic practice but also to the individuals and communities with whom I work. These responsibilities extend in multiple directions, encompassing not only the archived past and the researched present but also the (imagined) future. Is there a way to navigate archives that are inextricably linked to the violent logics of domination without reinstating those logics in a far more salacious way? In responding to this ethical quandary, I focus here on three interrelated concerns: (dead)naming, the politics of citation and archival violence.

The African trans archive

Michel Foucault (1972) notes that archives are both configurations of power and documents of exclusion. In his view, the archive is a system of statements establishing what has been said, but also what *cannot* be said. Much of this pivots on power, intentionality and the meaning of representation. As Joan Schwartz and Terry Cook (2002) point out, users of archives – including archivists themselves – who refuse to engage in debates about power and its impacts are, in fact, making 'a strong choice in favour of the status quo, with all its implications for buttressing mainstream power' (19). When Africa is considered or written about in relation to sexuality, sexual orientation, or gender identity and expression, the terms most commonly used are 'unAfrican', 'abomination', 'penal code', 'Western import' and 'sin'. Words that rarely appear are 'joy', 'survival', 'liberation', 'pleasure', 'intimacy' or 'celebration'. One of the ways in which scholars and activists have attempted to push back against these negative connotations is by looking to the colonial archive and highlighting how homosexuality and gender-nonconformity existed (and were accepted) prior to colonization (Morgan and Wieringa 2005; Epprecht 2004; Amadiume 1987).

In 2015, a few years after Miss Sahhara's emergence on the world stage, Liesl Theron and Tshepo Ricki Kgositau published 'The Emergence of a Grassroots African Trans Archive' in *Transgender Studies Quarterly*. Focused largely on English-speaking sub-Saharan Africa, the archive as presented by Theron and Kgositau is one of physical official documents. Neither Miss Sahhara nor the emergence of a broader digital archive is mentioned. To be fair, there are many activists and individuals who are not mentioned. The archive presented is brief and heavily weighted towards South Africa. It is, in many ways, restrictive, unimaginative, a vacuum. What is available within it is marred by 'the confusion between gender identity and sexual orientation, [meaning that] the documentation around trans lives, trans bodies, trans persons, and gender-nonconforming people has been inaccurate' (Theron and Kgositau 2015: 580). To this end, Dipesh Chakrabarty (1998) notes that archives and histories have an investment in a certain kind of rationality, 'a particular understanding of the "real" means that history's, the discipline's, exclusions are ultimately epistemological' (16). This is especially true for trans identities and experiences, which are not only forcibly excluded from the archive but also systemically erased from communities and whole countries. Such identities are framed as not *really* African in order for them to be denied, ignored or shunned (Camminga 2017; Marnell 2014).

In his work on the haunting of the trans archive, AJ Lewis (2014) argues that the vacuum we encounter in relation to trans existence is an active epistemological exclusion that relies on perceptions of madness. Through the framing of madness, trans people are 'subjected to and subjectivised by an unknowable power … [and] are eventually silenced by the foreclosure of their narrative authority' (Lewis 2014: 27). If we take Miss Sahhara's digital archive as it currently stands, her voice – though present in her own media productions – is far from dominant. Indeed, it is easily lost within the absurd tabloid materials that constitute the bulk of this digital archive. In addition to sensationalizing Miss Sahhara's life, these articles consistently denigrate and deny both her existence and identity. This is achieved by framing her as mentally unwell. The image presented in the archive, freely available to anyone with the correct search terms, is a set of exaggerated and overly simplified traits, most of which are linked to her physicality.

Stuart Hall (1997) argues that stereotyping rests on a strategy of 'splitting' – dividing the normal from the abnormal in an effort to maintain the symbolic order. This 'tends to occur where there are gross inequalities of power' (258). This way of structuring the archive is not new, particularly for trans women of colour. In looking at the major figures in transgender history in the United States, Lewis (2014) notes an alarming trend, with trans women of colour consistently branded as 'eccentric' or 'kooky' personalities, in ways that stubbornly overpower 'their political work, even in activist histories' (22). As Chakrabarty (1998) notes, the narratives of those considered – or, in this case, framed – as mad are relegated to 'not history' (16).

Derrida (1995) explains that the structure of the archive is such that it determines the structure of what is archivable. In a sense, then, we might be able to think of this archive, Miss Sahhara's digital archive, as inherently structured around crisis. It is a crisis of absence – more specifically, the absence of transgender voices on and from the African continent. Concomitantly, as digital technologies provide 'new mechanisms for archiving, such technologies will simultaneously change the production and interpretation of history' (Rawson 2013: 7). In this instance, Miss Sahhara's self-produced digital content, such as her blogs or Facebook and Instagram posts, is mined and re-appropriated, arguably overpowering her own activist intentions. Due to her geopolitical positioning as a trans refugee, she is unable to intercede in any meaningful way because she holds no rights in Nigeria. Questions about the ethics of accessing and using this archive, given the dominance of transphobia within it, are therefore critical. Ethical use of archives is not a new challenge. This is something Nicholas Matte (2015) reflects on in relation to archives containing pornographic materials that fetishize trans people for commercial exploitation. Such materials could be considered transphobic, but they are none the less part of trans history. One way in which physical archives have managed this has been to ensure archivists 'interpretively contextualize and critically mediate [such materials] for researchers in ways that avoid simply reproducing the power dynamics at play in their production and consumption' (Matte 2015: 598).

Digital documents represent a unique challenge for archives, archivists and researchers. Margaret Hedstrom (2002) notes that debates over digital media focus on how online information can be captured and transferred. What receives little attention is how we might contextualize and use this digital information once it is captured. Often there is no archivist to act as mediator, leaving decisions about ethical practices in the hands of the researcher. The challenge of digital technologies, specifically the immense power wielded by researchers engaging with online media, remains 'largely absent from the traditional archival perspective' (Schwartz and Cook 2002: 5). The relationship between researcher and archive, and the issues of power it raises, sits at the interstices of the digital and the diasporic. Researchers too often overlook the power they wield – the power to name, validate and even spotlight certain events, individuals, identities or movements. In some senses, to return to Chakrabarty (2000), researchers are left with the power to designate what *is* history. Keguro Macharia (2015) implores researchers, when approaching archives such as these, to think through the present as a political position, 'within which livability is produced and bodies are enfleshed. What types of enfleshments do we want to make possible?' (144). Perhaps the most critical question for transgender people is how we name those enfleshments.

What's in a name?

In transgender studies, you cannot consider the archive without turning to the work of KJ Rawson (2014a). In the first edition of *Transgender Studies Quarterly*, Rawson broaches the question of naming within the archive:

And what of the history that is hoped to be forgotten? Transgender people who transition their gender presentation may feel betrayed by the archive's stubborn and insistent refusal to forget. Thus, while archiving transgender materials is important for community and personal identity formation, political advocacy, and historical memory, it should be treated as a powerful mechanism of memory and identity with far-reaching impacts.

(26)

In Miss Sahhara's digital archive, the majority of headlines begin by deadnaming her. A 'deadname' is the name a trans person was assigned at birth but which they no longer use. Deadnaming serves as a means to undermine a trans person's gender identity by 'outing' what is perceived to be their 'real' selves. It suggests that the person in question is someone other than the person they present to be. Or, at the very least, that their current presentation is false and deceptive. In an article entitled 'Deadnaming a Trans Person Is Violence – So Why Does the Media Do It Anyway?', Sam Riedel (2017) argues that deadnaming violates a deeply personal boundary by perpetuating 'the single most harmful misconception about trans people all over the world: that our true gender identities – who we are at our core – are the ones we were assigned at birth' (para. 6). In so doing, the perpetrator suggests that any violence that trans people experience stems from their fraudulence and is therefore deserved. Studies show that being deadnamed is stigmatizing, abusive and often causes severe mental distress (Vance 2018; Dunne et al. 2017). As many trans people will attest, hearing or seeing one's deadname can induce a visceral sense of terror. It is often a considerable negative emotional trigger (Gratton 2016). Riedal (2017) uses the experience of Caitlyn Jenner to illustrate his point: 'When mainstream news reports constantly reference deadnames like Caitlyn Jenner's, they propagate the idea that transphobia is just a difference of opinion – that when sites like *Breitbart* stubbornly deadname and misgender her, it's simply a political disagreement' (para. 22).

The general expectation of trans people is that our chosen names will be respected, yet our approach when working with trans archives is, somewhat surprisingly, the opposite. In thinking through the ethical conundrums of this digital diasporic archive, I realized that I know the deadnames of several key figures in trans history from the Global North. I began to wonder how is it that I know the deadname of Christine Jorgenson and Lili Elbe. This raised another question: how, as researchers, academics and archivists, do we determine what happens with names, chosen or dead? Do we reveal them? And, if so, for what reason? It seems that, within transgender studies, the standard practice is to openly state deadnames, particularly in reference to individuals who have passed on. This is visible in the work of key figures in the discipline, including in scholarship by Joanne Meyerowitz (2006) and Sandy Stone (2006) – and they are not the only two.

In discussing the ethics of this issue with colleagues, some pointed out that both the Pope and Mother Theresa have deadnames. In Australia, it is considered best practice, once an Aboriginal person has passed, to use a substitute name or 'bereavement name' usually provided by families so as not to recall or disturb the spirit of the deceased (Korff 2019; The Australian Institute of Aboriginal and Torres Strait Islander Studies 2015).[2] Monarchs, too, often adopt a regnal name upon ascending the throne. Yet society seems content to accept and respect such processes of self-naming. As a Twitter user quoted in an article on trans citation stated:

> Literally no other group of people has a mass of assholes insisting on using a name they no longer want to be used. The only purpose of intentional deadnaming is harassment, no matter how 'good faith' you think it is.
>
> (Quoted in Coman 2018)

As a trans person, I, too, experience the use of my deadname as deeply destabilizing and violent. Less so in instances where it is used without nefarious intent, but still deeply stigmatizing and unsettling. Given this, how could I do the same to Miss Sahhara when drawing on this archive? What of her deadname? If I quote from or promote this archive, am I inadvertently moving into the realm of harassment? In referencing the digital and the potential for violence in relation to diasporic lives, Adi Kuntsman (2009) notes that 'language, and violent language in particular, is not only a constitutive field; it is a field of struggle and contestation. This contestation becomes particularly clear when words travel across time and space; as happens in migration' (24). It is not simply the fact that Miss Sahhara is a black trans woman from Nigeria that is important here. She is also a refugee creating a digital archive that is being consistently ransacked and written over. This rewriting is, in part, being facilitated by her absence from Nigeria and distinct lack of rights. In approaching Miss Sahhara's archive, I take up Saidiya Hartman's (2008) challenge in 'Venus in Two Acts', where, with awe-inspiring brilliance, she wrestles with the limits of the unspeakable and the unknown in the archive of Atlantic Slavery, and its perpetual violence. Hartman asks, 'is it possible to reiterate her name and to tell a story about *degraded matter* and dishonoured life that doesn't delight and titillate, but instead ventures toward another mode of writing?' (6–7).

There are ways in which archivists are able to protect names in physical repositories, but this is not the case with publicly accessible online materials. Without an archivist acting as our compass, the responsibility falls squarely on the researcher. My approach when using this digital archive has been to redact the deadname from all headlines and articles, as per the following examples:

Meet Nigeria's 1st Transgender [MISGENDERING], [DEADNAMING] … Miss Sahhara (Anon 2012)[3]

[DEADNAMING] to Rep Nigeria in Transgender Beauty Pageant as Sahhara Benson (Anon 2014b)

Miss SaHHara, [DEADNAMING], Pictures: [MISGENDERING] Living in UK as a Woman in UK Drops Pics (Anon 2014a)

I recognize that this approach takes some citational licence. As Martinez (2014) warns, there is a fine line between subverting and reproducing: 'fragments of lives are all that archives offer, if that. The connections of record-keeping practices, power, and history, or traps set up by the "long arm" of the archive, can be tenacious, deceitful, and wily indeed' (174). By inserting the verb 'deadnaming', rather than simply redacting with the noun 'deadname', I intend to indicate who is responsible for this violence. My goal is to place it as an action being undertaken, something active and ongoing. This is certainly not enough, but it is a way to start circumventing the obvious violence of this archive. To use these headlines without redaction would be to validate what Sahhara herself calls the 'trashy behaviour' of the tabloid press (Miss Sahhara 2019).

Citation and production

From the street to the Internet, particularly on blogs, Facebook and Twitter, vitriolic tweets and venomous Facebook post are being thrown at Miss Sahhara, so strong-worded that, as a matter of fact, she seems to be the most hated indigene of the moment.

(Lee 2017)

If I struggle with deadnaming in this archive, how do I even begin to point to it? Gesturing to it via any search term, even glancing in its direction, is enough to provide its digital location – that is, its URL. How do I do this knowing that the contents go far beyond deadnaming? Indeed, these materials include discussions of genitals, images of random men passed off as 'pre-transition images' and suggestions about various kinds of sexual 'indecency', all intended to elicit feelings of disgust and revulsion in the viewer.

Drawing from African feminist thinking, I believe it is crucial that we consider the role that intellectuals, researchers and the academy have in validating dominant forms of power through writing, or simply through being allowed in via the front entrance of the academy – a threshold usually closely off to those being written about, which in this instance is transgender refugees. Danai Mupotsa (2010) refers to this as a key element of 'African feminist intellectual ethics' (15–16). Following this, Neo Musangi (2018) urges us not to re-inscribe our variously condemned statuses, to not use our power in the service of an archive that would do more harm than good. For Musangi (2018), writing on being gender-nonconforming and from the African continent requires one to become undisciplined. One must resist the temptation to do what is easy – that is, to use the archive without question, without hesitation, without problem. In a similar way to Mupotsa and Musangi, Kate Eichorn (2013) is deeply concerned about the politics of knowledge production:

The archive is where academic and activist work frequently converge. Indeed, the creation of archives has become integral to how knowledges are produced and legitimised and how feminist activists, artists, and scholars make their voices audible. Rather than a destination for knowledges already produced or a place to recover histories and ideas placed under erasure, the making of archives is frequently where knowledge production begins.

(3)

These positions prove there are precedents for ethical ways of engaging with an archive, digital or not. In a footnote in *Figurations of Violence and Belonging: Queerness, Migranthood and Nationalism in Cyberspace and Beyond*, Kuntsman (2009: 13) explains that she does not provide URLs for the discussion threads to which she refers in an effort to protect participants. If deadnames are redacted, as in the examples above, then it makes sense to also redact URLs, since the address of a digital article often includes its title. For instance:

Anon (2012), 'Meet Nigeria's 1st Transgender [MISGENDERING], [DEADNAMING] ... Miss Sahhara', 27 May, NaijaGists. Available online: [WEBSITE REDACTED] (accessed 23 September 2016).

Of course, this opens up other issues and concerns, including the ability to fact-check the claims of researchers. This is, after all, the function a citation is meant to facilitate. In thinking through this and other ethical constraints, I realized that perhaps one of the reasons we, as archivists, academics and researchers, are so willing to deadname is because the person being named is usually dead. For many researchers, this is a critical element of the archives they work with. In my case, however, Miss Sahhara is very much alive. Thus I have a unique opportunity to ask her directly how she wants me to handle her archive. There are many things I wanted her guidance on. What is strictly off limits? How might I mitigate the violence and trauma that has already been experienced? How do I do justice to her legacy?

In discussing queer migrations and migrants in relation to archives, Martin Manalansan (2014) explains that ethical responsibility means holding an 'openness to the future' (103) and recognizing the limitations and exclusionary impulses of state and other institutional archives that seek to 'officialize' historical knowledge, tethering analyses of the past to dominant groups/perspectives and failing to engage with views from below. In a sense, then, I am testing not just the limits of the archive but also the limits of academic writing. Like others, I view the archival process as an exercise of power: 'despite changes in the nature of records, the uses for those records, and the need to preserve them, archives ... have been about power – about maintaining power, about the power of the present to control what is, and will be, known about the past, about the power of remembering over forgetting' (Schwartz and Cook 2002: 3). If creating, engaging with and writing about the archive are about power, then are there ways that I, as a researcher, can afford Miss Sahhara some level of control? Machaira (2015) reminds us that there is much 'routine despair' concerning the fact that academic 'writing cannot intervene in real-world situations, especially in moments of crisis' (141) – but what if, in some small way, it could?

Miss Sahhara and I: An interlude

'And use without consent of the used is abuse'

(Lorde 1984: 58)

*

We sit on the recently refurbished seating of Crooked Billet in Clapton Pond, Miss Sahhara in a red dress that matches my red velvet jacket. We are perhaps a bit more than the Saturday afternoon pub crowd has bargained for. Miss Sahhara confesses that she has had a string of terrible dates and plans to attend a club night in the next borough, a space known to be particularly welcoming to trans women. She also confesses that she hasn't yet read the paper I emailed. It is the first in a series I am writing on trans people in the African diaspora using digital tools to project a message of trans identity back at the African continent. Our conversation is typical of two trans people from Africa: the situations we often find ourselves in; the latest court cases; progresses and setbacks in rights; and jokes about idiotic leaders. The sometimes subtle – but often not so subtle – divide between us is my whiteness, my passport and my recognized citizenship, however precarious, as a transgender person in South Africa, my home.

Over the course of our conversation, Miss Sahhara tells me three significant things about her archive. First, the deadname used in the Nigerian media is not correct. To this end, she would not only like it redacted, but also for its inaccuracy to be clearly flagged when the redactions are explained. She does find its usage deeply upsetting, and experiences it as a kind of ongoing violence. Second, she is aware of the necessity of the archive and my struggles over citation. Third, she points out that although her experiences of misrepresentation are predominantly linked to Nigerian digital media, and that as a transgender woman and refugee she has very limited, if any, ways to hold these content producers to account, there have also been incidents in the UK. Her point is that this is not an 'African problem', nor should questions of ethics and usage only be relevant to those working with archives of trans people in or from the Global South. Being mistreated, deadnamed and/or misgendered is not something done only by and in African states, even if it may be more regular and gratuitous in such contexts. In 2012, Miss Sahhara featured in a documentary produced by Sky Living called LadyBoy *(Keelin, 2012). At the time of filming, the production company told her that the show did not have a name. This means that its broadcast title,* LadyBoy, *was never cleared with her. As a trans woman and refugee living in the UK, she felt at the time that she had very few means through which to hold the producers accountable, without risking her own precarious legal situation. She considers this name to be a slur and a denigration of who she is.*

*

I want to return to Macharia's suggestion that researchers cannot intervene in the real world. I had assumed that the challenges I was encountering with Miss Sahhara's archive were somehow outside of her own struggles, but in reality they were problems with which she was grappling. This realization helped me reorient my ethics and approach. Can I – and indeed other researchers – draw on this archive without re-enacting the violence that marked its formation? How do I approach citations, considering that a deadname redacted from the main text will likely appear again within a URL? If those framed as 'mad' or 'abnormal' are blocked from writing history, then what is it that they do? What if they could leave a map? A letter to the archive. A will of sorts, one that sets the historical record straight, or at least provides some of the necessary interventions. This is by no means a panacea to all of the ethical quandaries presented here, but perhaps it is one way to bridge the past, the present and the future. A means to rectify the archive as it stands. A course correction. A guide. One that highlights the fallacies and erasures. In Miss Sahhara's case, this means an opportunity for her not just to reject practices such as deadnaming and gratuitous language (i.e. *Ladyboy*) but also to clearly articulate her wishes and instructions. Not simply a guide to her personal archive, but rather a compass for those of us working with any difficult trans archives, especially those of people who are marginalized and silenced, both physically and geographically.

I am not saying this is the answer to the silences and absence of the African trans archive. But in environments where the voices of people like Yoweri Museveni, David Bahati and Robert Mugabe ring far louder than those of activists and community members, and where practices of visibility are consistently delegitimized as 'deranged', 'sick' or 'possessed', such an approach has significant and useful applications. What we need, I propose, is a manifesto to the future archive. In my discussion with Miss Sahhara, it was decided that my power lay not only in redacting but also in amplifying the demands of those at the centre of the archive. Miss Sahhara has provided some guidance notes for those who wish to work with this archive. Her words, printed below, offer an entry point for ethical engagement with digital archives of all trans people, but particularly trans women of colour who are also refugees:

To those who may access or use this archive in future,

I wish to make the following clear as a trans woman from Nigeria living in the diaspora. I have always been female. I did not have any epiphany of self-discovery after living in one gender all my life. My body has never been wrong. I am a woman. Whoever uses this archive in future, I request that they redact all names other than 'Miss Sahhara'. Though none of these other names are mine, their use is intended to do violence and to treat my gender as somehow false. Redacting these names also affects how these websites are referenced, since removing them from the headline means removing them from the URL. I request that this is also done, as has been done in this article. Lastly, as a woman, my pronouns are she/her. As with deadnaming, the use of any other pronouns is an effort to degrade me. I would like my pronouns treated in the same way as my deadname.

With thanks – Miss Sahhara 2019

Conclusion: The object of the archive

Once, after listening to a paper by a white cisgender woman at a massive sociology conference, I commented that there is a space between the words 'trans' and 'woman'. There is no such thing as a 'transwoman', in the sense of an entirely new species of hominids that has been discovered. Rather, 'trans' is an adjective used to further specify the noun 'woman'. The presenter responded that she had indeed seen this, but had chosen to keep it as 'transwoman'. Chosen. This brings us back to Audrey Lorde's (1984) warning: the power to choose how to represent other people, whether to make them one thing or another, and then to legitimize and reproduce such decisions in spaces, academic or otherwise, must not be taken lightly. Indeed, it is a power of the highest order. It can, as this instance illuminates, mean treating people as human beings or something other – with the latter having deadly consequences for trans women of colour.[4] In coming to Miss Sahhara's archive, I wanted to do more than recount and reconstitute its violence. It was important to me that I did not validate that violence in the guise of objective scholarship, parading it in various academic spaces and treating trans women as though they are simply things to be studied, as I have seen researchers do time and time again. Hartman (2008) notes how refusal can 'raise important questions regarding what it means to think historically about matters still contested in the present and about life eradicated by the protocols of intellectual disciplines' (9– 10). I have taken up this challenge by refusing to deadname, both in my main text and in my citations, no matter how much this is branded as a failure to meet the minimum standards of 'academic rigour'.

In 'Venus in Two Acts', Hartman acknowledges that her essay duplicates or mimics the violence of the archive she wishes to speak from. This is, in part, because dealing with slavery is dealing with the dead. Unlike Hartman, I can grasp Miss Sahhara's life in its free state, or as close to free as a black trans woman from Nigeria living as a refugee in the United Kingdom can get in this world. I am not faced with Hartman's impossibilities. Rather, I am faced with a living, extending, mutating and, at times, vicious archive. One that does not require any particular research skills to access. Indeed, this archive's ease of access is one of its defining features. The digital, as it engages with identity – in this case, a particular diasporic identity – provides researchers and academics with an opportunity to expand 'the important work of … what counts as history and what constitutes an archive' (Rawson 2013: 11). I am also *choosing* an archive. I am calling this an archive and labelling it as such. The way it is constituted matters. As Schwartz and Cook (2002) note, the ideal of 'objectivity and neutrality' is an 'archival myth' (18), particularly when we move away from mainstream culture and records. Refusing to acknowledge this, they suggest, especially with regard to the proliferation of electronic records – 'where active intervention by archivists in the creation process of records, rather than passive receipt of records created long before and later discarded, is the only hope that today's history will be able to be written tomorrow' (Schwartz and Cook 2002: 18) – would only hobble the research process. With regards to ethics and the digital, Schwarts and Cook (2002) emphasize the urgent need for new scholarly practices:

> Archives then are not some pristine storehouse of historical documentation that have piled up, but a reflection of and often justification for the society that creates them. With the increasing complexity of society, its means of communication, and its information requirements, not only have record-keeping practices changed among those who create records, but archives as institutions of collective memory have changed as well. Yet perception of those changes has lagged behind, with significant consequences for all who seek to understand the past.
>
> (12)

Given Miss Sahhara's place in history as the first out Nigerian trans woman, I will not be the last to come to her archive. It is my hope, though, that whoever does arrive at it also arrives at this chapter. Perhaps that is the best I can offer for now. In a sense, I am presenting a warning to you, my future reader. When you find us, trans people, but especially trans women of colour, within archives that present us in violent, traumatic or dehumanizing ways, I implore you to weigh up the ethics of how such information can and should be use. Would it be okay, for example, to publicize such things were the person alive? Does revealing such details truly lend value to one's academic pursuits? James Baldwin's (1985) imperative to 'bring out your dead' (39) – an injunction against denial, complicity and erasure – rings true here. Does death make treating someone as more of an object than a subject easier or more acceptable? Are you exercising a power to choose at someone else's expense? And what of the impacts for those left living, or even yet to be?

Acknowledgements

This work was supported by the National Research Foundation of South Africa (Grant Number 129848).

Notes

1   At present, no African state explicitly outlaws or criminalizes trans people *as trans people*. There are, however, other ways in which trans people are harassed or criminalized. These include antiquated penal codes that outlaw same-sex sexual relations. These are often used to target trans people as the most visible members of the LGBT community.

2   I would like to thank my co-editor John Marnell for this particular point and the reviewer of this chapter who noted the common misconception that the taboo against using these names is eternal. Rather, 'as time passes and mourners become reconciled to their loss, the person's name and image are permitted to resurface. How long this takes

varies considerably' (Thomas 2013). This perhaps adds even greater nuance to the idea that we might be able to respect names and naming practices across a lifetime.

3   At the request of Miss Sahhara, it is noted here that though a deadname does appear in the original of these articles, it is not correct. In fact, all deadnames suggested thus far by the tabloid media have been incorrect.

4   This reality is evidenced in the recent murder of two trans women in the United States, bringing the 2019 death toll to at least twenty-six. As Gina Martinez and Tara Law (2019) note, there is 'an epidemic of violence against the transgender community, an epidemic which disproportionately affects trans women of color'.

References

Amadiume, I. (1987), *Male Daughter, Female Husbands: Gender and Sex in an African Society*, London: Zed Books.

Anon. (2012), 'Meet Nigeria's 1st Transgender [MISGENDERING], [DEADNAMING] Now a Woman, Miss Sahhara', *NaijaGists*, 27 May. Available online: [WEBSITE REDACTED] (accessed 23 September 2016).

Anon. (2014a), 'Miss Sahhara, [DEADNAMING] Pictures: Nigerian [MISGENDERING] Living as a Woman in UK Drops New Pics', *NaijaGists*, 13 February. Available online: [WEBSITE REDACTED] (accessed 23 September 2016).

Anon. (2014b), '[DEADNAMING] to Rep Nigeria in Transgender Beauty Pageant as Sahhara Benson', *NaijaGists*, 11 July. Available online: [WEBSITE REDACTED] (accessed 23 September 2016).

Anon. (2016), 'The Story of Nigeria's First Transgender Woman', 11 June, *Africa.com*. Available online: https://web.archive.org/web/20160611060244/http://www.africa.com/story-nigerias-first-transgender-woman/ (accessed 13 October 2019).

The Australian Institute of Aboriginal and Torres Strait Islander Studies (2015), *Guidelines for the Ethical Publishing of Aboriginal and Torres Strait Islander Authors and Research from those Communities*. Available online: https://aiatsis.gov.au/sites/default/files/docs/asp/ethical-publishing-guidelines.pdf (accessed 5 June 2020).

Baldwin, J. (1985), *The Evidence of Things Not Seen*, New York: Henry Holt.

Bowker, G. C. (2008), *Memory Practices in the Sciences*, Cambridge: The MIT Press.

Camminga, B (2017), 'Am I Cait? Am I Abba? From MultiChoice to No Choice – Representations of Transgender in Nigeria', *Global Humanities: Gender and Public Opinion*, 5: 61–76.

Camminga, B (2019), *Transgender Refugees and the Imagined South Africa: Bodies over Borders and Borders over Bodies*, New York: Palgrave Macmillan.

Camminga, B (2020), 'Digital Borders, Diasporic Flows and the Nigerian Transgender Beauty Queen Who Would Not Be Denied', *Gender Questions*, 8 (1): 1–14.

Chakrabarty, D. (1998), 'Minority Histories, Subaltern Pasts', *Postcolonial Studies*, 1 (1): 15–29.

Chakrabarty, D. (2000), *Provincializing Europe: Postcolonial Thought and Historical Difference*, Princeton: Princeton University Press.

Coman, J. (2018), 'Trans Citation Practices – A Quick-and-Dirty Guideline', *Medium*, 28 November. Available online: https://medium.com/@MxComan/trans-citation-practices-a-quick-and-dirty-guideline-9f4168117115 (accessed 21 June 2019).

Derrida, J. (1995), 'Archive Fever: A Freudian Impression', *Diacritics*, 25 (2): 9–63.

Dunne, M. J., L. A. Raynor, E. K. Cottrell and W. J. A. Pinnock (2017), 'Interviews with Patients and Providers on Transgender and Gender Nonconforming Health Data Collection in the Electronic Health Record', *Transgender Health*, 2 (1): 1–7.

Eichhorn, K. (2013), *The Archival Turn in Feminism: Outrage in Order*, Philadelphia: Temple University Press.

Epprecht, M. (2004), *Hungochani: The History of a Dissident Sexuality in Southern Africa*, Montreal: McGill-Queen's University Press.

Expressng Reporter (2015), 'Meet Four Known Nigerian Transgenders (PHOTOS)', Expressng, 4 July. Available online: [WEBSITE REDACTED] (accessed 23 September 2016).

Foucault, M. (1972), *The Archaeology of Knowledge and the Discourse on Language*, New York: Pantheon.

Gratton, C. (2016), 'Resisting the Gender Binary: The Use of (ING) in the Construction of Non-binary Transgender Identities', *University of Pennsylvania Working Papers in Linguistics*, 22 (2): 51–60.

Hall, S. (1997), 'The Spectacle of the "Other"', in S. Hall (ed.), *Representation: Cultural Representations and Signifying Practices*, 223–90, London: Sage Publications.

Hartman, S. (2008), 'Venus in Two Acts', *Small Axe*, 26 (June): 1–14.

Hedstrom, M. (2002), 'Archives, Memory, and Interfaces with the Past', *Archival Science*, 2 (1/2): 21–43.

Keeling, T. (2012), *Ladyboy S01E02*. Available online: https://www.youtube.com/watch?v=uP38g4BDknc (accessed 19 May 2019).

Korff, J. (2019), 'Sorry Business: Mourning an Aboriginal Death', *Creative Spirits*. Available online: https://www.creativespirits.info/aboriginalculture/people/mourning-an-aboriginal-death (accessed 5 June 2020).

Kuntsman, A. (2009), *Figurations of Violence and Belonging: Queerness, Migranthood and Nationalism in Cyberspace and Beyond*, Oxford: Peter Lang.

Lee, K. (2017), 'Untold Story of Miss Sahara, the Nigerian Man from Idoma Transformed to a Woman (Photos+Video) – Gistmania', *Naijapals*, 4 September. Available online: [WEBSITE REDACTED] (accessed 14 May 2019).

Lewis, A. J. (2014), '"I Am 64 and Paul McCartney Doesn't Care": The Haunting of the Transgender Archive and the Challenges of Queer History', *Radical History Review*, 120: 13–34.

Lorde, A. (1984), *Sister Outsider*, New York: Ten Speed Press.

Macharia, K. (2015), 'Archive and Method in Queer African Studies', *Agenda*, 29 (1): 140–6.

Manalansan, M. F. (2014), 'The "Stuff" of Archives: Mess, Migration, and Queer Lives', *Radical History Review*, 120: 94–107.

Marnell, J. (2014), 'Imagined Worlds', *Overland*, 216: 12–18.

Martinez, G. and T. Law (2019), 'Two Recent Murders of Black Trans Women in Texas Reveal a Nationwide Crisis, Advocates Say', *Time*, 12 June. Available online: https://time.com/5601227/two-black-trans-women-murders-in-dallas-anti-trans-violence/ (accessed 18 September 2019).

Martínez, J. (2017), 'Beyond Diversity Ventriloquism: How *Mujer T* Is Transing Inclusion in Bogotá', *Hypatia*, 32 (3): 679–95.

Martinez, M. E. (2014), 'Archives, Bodies, and Imagination: The Case of Juana Aguilar and Queer Approaches to History, Sexuality, and Politics', *Radical History Review*, 120: 159–82.

Matte, N. (2015), 'Highlighting Trans Archival Materials without a Minority/Identity Framework at the University of Toronto's Sexual Representation Collection', *Transgender Studies Quarterly*, 2 (4): 596–606.

Meyerowitz, J. (2006), 'Transforming Sex: Christine Jorgensen in the Postwar U.S.', *OAH Magazine of History*, 20 (2): 16–20.

Mhiripiri, N. A. and S. B. Moyo (2016), 'A Resilient Unwanted Civil Society: The Gays and Lesbians of Zimbabwe Use of Facebook as Alternative Public Sphere in a Dominant Homophobic Society', in B. Mutsvairo (ed.), *Digital Activism in the Social*

Media Era: Critical Reflections on Emerging Trends in Sub-Saharan Africa, 249–69, London: Palgrave Macmillan.

Miss Sahhara (2018), 'Miss SaHHara', in C. Craggs (ed.), *To My Trans Sisters*, 43–50, London: Jessica Kingsley Publishers.

Miss Sahhara (2019), interview with Miss Sahhara, Crooked Billard, London: Hackney.

Mordi, M. (2019), 'Trans Women Speak on Western Influence and Being Transgender in Nigeria', *The Guardian Nigeria News – Nigeria and World News*, 27 March. Available online: https://guardian.ng/features/gender-politics/trans-women-speak-on-western-influence-and-being-transgender-in-nigeria/ (accessed 14 May 2019).

Morgan, R. and S. Wieringa (2005), *Tommy Boys, Lesbian Men and Ancestral Wives: Female Same-sex Practices in Africa*, Johannesburg: Jacana Media.

Mukasa, V. and C. Balzer (2009), '"People Have Realized the Need for an African Trans Movement": Interview with Victor Mukasa, African Trans Activist Representing IGLHRC (International Gay and Lesbian Human Rights Commission) and TITs Uganda (Transgenders Intersex Transsexuals Uganda)', *Liminalis*, 3: 122–7.

Mupotsa, D. (2010), 'If I Could Write This in Fire/ African Feminist Ethics for Research in Africa', *Postamble*, 6 (1): 1–18.

Musangi, N. S. (2018), 'Homing with My Mother / How Women in My Family Married Women', *Meridians*, 17 (2): 401–14.

Rawson, K. J. (2013), 'Transcript of Rhetorical History 2.0: Toward a Digital Transgender Archive', *Enclutration*, 28 May. Available online: http://enculturation.net/system/files/RawsonRhetHistScript.pdf (accessed 20 June 2019).

Rawson, K. J. (2014a), 'Archive', *Transgender Studies Quarterly*, 1 (1/2): 24–6.

Rawson, K. J. (2014b), 'Transgender Worldmaking in Cyberspace: Historical Activism on the Internet', *QED: A Journal in GLBTQ Worldmaking*, 1 (2): 38–60.

Riedel, S. (2017), 'Deadnaming a Trans Person Is Violence – So Why Does the Media Do It Anyway?', *HuffPost*, 17 March. Available online: https://www.huffpost.com/entry/deadnaming-a-trans-person-is-violenceso-why-does_b_58cc58cce4b0e0d348b3434b (accessed 21 June 2019).

Schwartz, J. M. and T. Cook (2002), 'Archives, Records, and Power: The Making of Modern Memory', *Archival Science*, 2 (1/2): 1–19.

Stoler, A. (2009), *Along the Archival Grain: Epistemic Anxieties and Colonial Common Sense*, Princeton: Princeton University Press.

Stone, S. (2006), 'The "Empire" Strikes Back: A Posttranssexual Manifesto', in S. Stryker and S. Whittle (eds), *The Transgender Studies Reader*, 221–35, New York: Routledge.

Theron, L. and T. R. Kgositau (2015), 'The Emergence of a Grassroots African Trans Archive', *Transgender Studies Quarterly*, 2 (4): 578–83.

Thomas, M. (2013), '"Because it's Your Country": Bringing Back the Bones to West Arnhem Land', *Australian Book Review*, April. Available online: https://www.australianbookreview.com.au/abr-online/archive/2013/98-april-2013-no-350/1400-because-it-s-your-country (accessed 18 November 2020).

Vance, S. R. (2018), 'The Importance of Getting the Name Right for Transgender and Other Gender Expansive Youth', *Journal of Adolescent Health*, 63 (4): 379–80.

Vartabedian, J. (2019), 'Bodies and Desires on the Internet: An Approach to Trans Women Sex Workers' Websites', *Sexualities*, 22 (1/2): 224–43.

Waterton, C. (2010), 'Experimenting with the Archive: STS-Ers as Analysts and Co-Constructors of Databases and Other Archival Forms', *Science, Technology, & Human Value*, 35 (5): 645–76.

Chapter 9

TIES THAT MATTER: QUEER WAYS OF SURVIVING A TRANSIT COUNTRY

Gonca Şahin

Since the 1980s, Turkey has functioned as a key transit point for people seeking entry into Western Europe and North America, hosting large numbers of asylum seekers and migrants from Asia, Africa and the Middle East (İçduygu and Yükseker 2012). Although Turkey is a signatory of the 1951 Geneva Convention, the country limits its application by only granting refugee status to citizens of European Council member states (Şimşek 2018). Until recently, nationals of non-European countries have had to register their asylum claims with both the United Nations High Commissioner for Refugees (UNHCR) and the Turkish Ministry of the Interior. If protection claims are approved by the UNHCR, non-European refugees become eligible for resettlement (Shakhsari 2014).[1] While cases are pending, claimants are allowed to temporarily remain in Turkey. Queer refugees[2] are among those who use Turkey as a transit country, either hoping to obtain formal resettlement in a third country or planning to take their chances at accessing Europe via a sea or land crossing.

In blocking potential (non-European) refugees from long-term residence or social integration, Turkey's asylum regime cements the country's position as a transit point. The state's approach produces a kind of liminality for those seeking international protection, including queer refugees. Liminality is often used in migration literature to refer to the 'in-betweenness' of the asylum experience, which for most is characterized by 'waiting, suspense and uncertainty' (O'Reilly 2012: 831). For the vast majority of refugees in Turkey, being in-between means having to find a way to survive economically (Kara and Çalık 2016). Most are unable to access decent employment and so become dependent on the formation and mobilization of social networks. These are usually in-country or transnational networks based on ethnicity or nationality. Indeed, the social capital[3] that comes with transnational networks plays a key role in shaping migration patterns and trajectories.

Queer migration is often understood as 'a form of starting over that involves exchanging one set of social networks for another' (Fortier 2001: 410). In other words, it is presumed to involve an enduring fracture between a person's country/community of origin and their country/community of reception. For this reason, studies of transnationalism largely ignore the experiences of queer refugees, assuming that relationships based on ethnicity or nationality are simply not possible. And, in many cases, this is true: given the basis for their protection claims, queer refugees rarely have access to social networks in the same way as their non-queer counterparts. Yet, queer refugees in transit do form social connections. Indeed, while queer refugees are regularly ostracized by both family networks and country-of-origin communities, they often use queer social ties as a security net (Gorman-Murray 2009). Queer networks not only offer physical and emotional support, but also become 'de facto families' (Plummer 1992: 109).

The findings presented in this chapter emerge from in-depth interviews and informal conversations held in Turkey between 2016 and 2019. I conducted semi-structured interviews with ten participants, aged between twenty-four and thirty-four. However, I confine my analysis here to the experiences of Ahmad – a 27-year-old gay man from North Africa who was diagnosed with a life-threatening illness while in Turkey – and five Iranian refugees: Aida, a lesbian woman; Mariam, a transgender woman; Sajjad, a gay man; Hamid, a gay man; and Shayan, a gay man.[4] My interview with Ahmad was unplanned. When we met, Ahmad was very ill and lying in bed. He urged me to conduct an interview, emphasizing that he feels better after recounting his story. Ahmad was my only interlocutor from North Africa. Queer refugees in Turkey predominantly come from Iran, Iraq and Syria. Given the size of these queer refugee communities, it is possible to reference a person's country of origin without revealing their identity (as I do for my Iranian interviewees). In the case of Ahmad, I refer only to his region of origin. This is because there are very few queer refugees from his home country in Turkey.

At the time of my fieldwork, all six interviewees were temporarily residing in Turkey while awaiting third-country resettlement. All had been recognized as refugees under international law and were registered with both the Turkish authorities and the UNHCR. Turkish law obliges all refugees and asylum seekers to reside in one of sixty-two satellite cities, as assigned by the Directorate General of Migration Management (DGMM). They are required to 'sign in' to the authorities of their allocated satellite city at regular intervals (this can range from every day to once a week, depending on local regulations). A person's asylum application/status is withdrawn if they breach their reporting duties three times in a row. An allocated satellite city can only be changed in specific circumstances, such as to be reunited with family, to access education or to seek medical care (Directorate General of Migration Management 2020). All of my interviewees were registered in a small city near Istanbul. This city is increasingly recognized as a home to queer refugees from different nationalities and so I have chosen, as a precautionary measure, not to reveal its name.

In this chapter, I unpack how support networks are formed and sustained by queer refugees, as well as the types of social relationships that precipitate them. Based on my reading of Ahmad's experiences, I argue that queer community ties need to be recognized in instances when individuals cannot easily tap into ethnic or national networks. For those who come to Turkey from geographical regions with limited home–host country ties, alternative relationship formations are critical. In exploring these alternative relationships, I consider different types of social connections – including those in the digital sphere – that queer refugees forge and sustain, not only in Turkey but also in their countries of origin and in the countries where they hope to be resettled.

By reading Ahmad's experiences alongside those of my Iranian interviewees, I hope to draw attention to under-researched dynamics in migrant social networks, particularly in countries that are not regular transit points for queer African refugees. I believe that comparing Ahmad's story with those of queer refugees from other geographical regions can expand our understanding of queer survival tactics. Contrasting these sets of experiences provides critical insights into the agency of individual queer Africans on the move, even in the most precarious and liminal of circumstances.

Refugee transnationalism and queer migration

Transnationalism can be understood as 'a process by which migrants, through their daily activities and social, economic, and political relations, create social fields that cross national boundaries' (Basch, Schiller and Blanc 1994: 27). They are 'simultaneous multi-stranded social relations that link together their societies of origin and settlement' (Schiller, Basch and Blanc 1995: 48). Such linkages encompass not only people but also objects and ideas. Facilitated by the technologies of transportation and communication, transnational ties embed migrants in more than one society.

Studies on transnationalism largely focus on voluntary immigrants, with scholars working under the assumption that refugees either cut ties with their home countries or have little to no remittances to offer. However, recent research suggests that this may not be entirely true. For example, Dogus Şimşek (2018) finds that transnational activities and networks are vital for Syrian refugees in Turkey. In addition to aiding basic survival, transnational networks facilitate a certain level of integration, which is especially important considering the insecure legal status of this population. Similarly, research with Eritrean and Bosnian refugees in Europe points to various economic, social, political and cultural activities that connect individuals with their home countries (Al-Ali, Black and Koser 2001).

More recently, an emergent field of research is beginning to link transnationalism to what is often referred to as 'sexual migration' or 'queer migration' (Manalansan 2006). For example, Aryan Karimi (2020) looks at transnational connections in the lives of Iranian queer refugees in Canada, finding that these individuals engage in transnational activities at multiple levels, including with friends still awaiting resettlement in Turkey (transit country), friends and families in Iran (county of origin) and the wider queer Iranian diaspora (reception countries). The emergence of digital technology has opened up new possibilities for transnational connection (Lennes 2021; Szulc 2020; Shield 2019). In tracking how queer refugees from the Middle East navigate their way through Turkey to Germany, Yener Bayramoğlu and Margreth Lünenborg (2018) show that messaging platforms and dating applications offer possibilities for developing new coping strategies and for fostering a sense of belonging at different stage of the migration experience.

Recent years have seen a growing interest in queer migration in the Turkish context, with a particular focus on the UNHCR's resettlement programme and how notions of 'authenticity', 'deservingness' and 'legitimacy' are constructed in relation to queer refugees (Koçak 2020; Sari 2020). Aydan Greatrick (2019) notes the 'coaching' role that queer NGOs play to build the 'credibility' of queer refugees in accordance with Global North discourses around sexual and gender identities. Zeynep Kivilcim (2017) notes the paradox at heart of the UNHCR's resettlement scheme: on the one hand, queer refugees in Turkey must hide their sexual orientation and/or gender identity to successfully navigate and survive the everyday discrimination they face, yet they must also visibly perform their sexual and/or gender identity in accordance with Western categories so as to be eligible for protection. Fadi Saleh (2020) builds on this analysis by noting the 'queer/humanitarian media visibility paradigm' that characterizes most Western representations of Syrian queer refugees. These tend to reduce the lives of queer refugees to experiences of oppression and suffering. Despite this growing body of scholarship on queer (im)mobilities in Turkey, there has been little research on queer refugees' use of transnational connections to negotiate the precarious life circumstances they face while awaiting resettlement.

This chapter sits at the intersection of transnational studies, queer migration studies and digital media studies. In bridging these fields, I seek to achieve three objectives: first, to extend the concept of refugee transnationalism to incorporate the experiences of queer refugees; second, to demonstrate the importance of sexuality and/or gender for transnational migration; third, to highlight the role of digital transnational networks for queer refugees. Existing literature suggests that sexuality and/or gender can be a direct or indirect cause of transnational movement, but this is not the only relationship between sexuality/gender and migration. Indeed, transnational migration might precipitate queer practices, identities and subjectivities (Manalansan 2006). Building on this observation, the present study demonstrates that queer networks can actually enable transnationalism.

Sustaining connections with home

By definition, being a refugee involves leaving one's country of origin with no prospect of return, unless the circumstances precipitating one's forced departure change. But it is not just a country that refugees give up – they also lose the ability to maintain all sorts of formal in-person relationships. Yet, queer refugees in Turkey sustain multiple connections with their countries of origin – relations that encompass the social, economic and cultural fields – often facilitated by communication technologies, given that cross-border mobility is not a possibility for those stuck in transit. Nadje Al-Ali, Richard Black and Khalid Koser (2001) note that an individual's desires and capacities determine the level of this engagement. Given that queer refugees experience social isolation and other forms of persecution in their countries of origin, as well as being frequently ostracized by ethnic/national communities while in transit, their desire for connection is often constrained. Networks are usually confined to a limited number of people due to safety concerns and previous experiences of psychological/emotional hurt. In the sections below, I recount how queer Iranians forge networks of support in Turkey, before comparing these strategies with Ahmad's experience as a queer North African who lacks a sizeable country-of-origin network.

Almost half of the interviewees for this study reported receiving money from families in their countries of origin. In the absence of regular paid work in Turkey, this financial support acts as their primary source of income, although the size and frequency of payments depend on each family's socio-economic position. Furthermore, as the waiting periods for resettlement are extended (Kara and Çalık 2016), financial support from families becomes less sustainable, putting pressure on refugees to find alternative sources of income.

But transnational networks are not just economic. Almost all of the interviewees stated that they regularly communicate with people back home. These are usually relatives who tolerate their queer identities, predominantly mothers and siblings, as well as (mostly queer) friends. The internet was the primary instrument of communication, though some interviewees reported in-person visits with relatives who are also in Turkey. For Aida, contact with Iran is limited to key people:

> I have connection with my sister and sometimes my friends on Instagram. That is it. No more connection. And I don't actually want to have any connection [with other people] because I don't feel like going back.

Contact with queer friends back home was seen as an important source of emotional support, both for those who had departed and for those who were left behind. It also allows for the exchange of knowledge about asylum procedures. These exchanges can help prospective asylum seekers weigh up the costs and benefits of migrating. For instance, when talking with her queer friends back in Iran, Aida emphasizes that seeking asylum in Turkey carries risks. Not only do prospective refugees give up everything they have invested in their lives to date, but they also waste time, energy and resources while awaiting resettlement:

> [M]any of my friends asked me [about coming to Turkey]. I told them … if you have money, if you can, if you don't have partner, if you are not in danger, then try to go to another country directly. Go to Europe. Don't come to Turkey because being a refugee is not a good thing. You will not be happy [here]; you will not be successful. You are just in the middle. … You don't know what you should do, how long you will stay here – five years, two years, forever?

In such transnational exchanges, potential asylum seekers can access information that is not normally available, including a more realistic representation of what it means to be a queer refugee in transit. Aida's reflections confirm findings in other studies. Research on gay Iranian men resettled in Canada suggests that digital media is used to sustain connections with key relatives and friends back in Iran and Turkey (Karimi 2020). These digital transnational networks are used to provide emotional and material support and to circulate knowledge on the asylum process.

My Iranian interviewees not only stay in touch with people back home, but also actively maintain elements of their culture. For example, Iranian national holidays are often used to facilitate social gatherings and cultural practices:

> We have very nice customs. ... For instance, there is Nature's Day [*Sizdah Beda*]. No matter where we are living in the world, all the Iranians celebrate it. We go to nature to regenerate our connection with the nature, to rejuvenate ourselves. People gather in a place and stay awake together till the morning to greet a new beginning. We, as the Iranian LGBTI refugees, sustain these cultural events here in Turkey.
>
> (Shayan)

As mentioned above, transnational connections involve not only the movement of people but also 'the movement of ideas and objects' (Basch, Schiller and Blanc 1994: 28). For Sajjad, whose mother visits him in Turkey, access to certain foods helps him sustain cultural linkages:

> My mother does really amazing pickles, like sour cherry pickles. And also she makes jam with honey. ... [Her food] is one of a kind, unique. ... It is just the whole idea of bringing a little bit of home. ... It brings memories.

For Shayan and Sajjad, the movement of artefacts and ideas – as well as the emotions associated with them – provides an important connection to Iran.

Forging connections within Turkey

Social relations within Turkey were considered vital for day-to-day survival. My Iranian interviewees mentioned three key types of connection: queer ethnic/national networks, institutional networks and digital social networks. These types of support were always considered preferable to potentially dangerous encounters with (non-queer) ethnic/national communities.

Aida shared a negative experience involving her partner, in which an Iranian man repeatedly harassed her at her workplace. Aida's partner's experience resonates with those of my other Iranian interviewees, who actively avoid their compatriots out of fear of violence and discrimination. For some, the decision to dissociate themselves from ethnic/national communities stems from a lack of belonging and attachment. In the quote below, Sajjad describes the emotional rupture he feels:

> Whenever someone asks me where I am from, I say I am Persian, not Iranian. ... Belonging to a certain community is like being them, thinking like them,

talking like them. I speak Farsi, but I am not like other Iranians. ... I have never felt that I am part of that community. ... I was always the gay one, the not-man-enough one.

Ahmad, however, faces a different challenge, given that he lacks any form of ethnic/national community network.[5] Aware that Ahmad shares a language with many people in Turkey, I asked him if he finds support from other Arabic-speaking people. In his response, Ahmad expressed a number of concerns about harnessing language networks, some of which were based on direct personal experience and others due to rumours and stereotypes:

I was no good with the Arabs. With Syrian and Iraqi people, I did not have any communication because I was scared ... I was trying to avoid the Arab people because I had heard so many bad things here. They have a bad reputation, and I had a very bad experience with a Syrian guy. ... Even when seeing people for fun, when I want to meet someone, when I find out he is Arab, I don't want to meet him. ... I am an Arab person, too, but I don't like the Arab people. ... They could set traps.

Overall, the data shows that non-queer ethnic/national/linguistic networks offer less value in terms of survival and support. As the quotes above testify, interviewees prefer to avoid non-queer people from their countries of origin, mainly out of concern that they would encounter the same prejudices and insecurities that they are trying to escape. This suggests that ethnic/national/linguistic networks do not offer the same benefits for queer refugees as they do for other persons on the move. However, this observation does not disprove the value of ethnic networks theory; rather, it shows that ethnic/national/linguistic networks are not immune to internal power relations and dominant social norms, particularly along the patriarchal and heteronormative axes. Yet, as will be shown in the next section, country-of-origin networks can still prove useful for marginalized persons.

Queering ethnic networks

Recent studies demonstrate that the Iranian queer refugee population has not only expanded globally, but also accumulated valuable experience in managing support networks, even producing its own social structure (Karimi 2020). For my interviewees, the flow of information between Iran and Turkey about asylum procedures was a key part of their journey:

While I was in Iran, I had a friend who one day told me: 'I have a plan. I have friends in Turkey. They fled this way and they saved themselves from Iran. You are in a bad situation. So I am. I will flee. When I get there, I will share all the information with you.' I learnt everything this way ... I decided to come to

Turkey. ... When I arrived here, I went to my friend's house. He was introduced to me by my other friend who had come [to Turkey] way before and then been resettled to Canada. If he wasn't here, I wouldn't have come to Turkey. He made circumstances here safe and secure for me. This was the first door I knocked on [in Turkey] and I still continue to live here. .... He not only opened his house to me but also helped me access the asylum procedures.

(Mariam)

The flow of information through queer networks shapes decision-making and facilitates access to asylum systems. Friends and acquaintances introduce the idea, often via online channels, that international protection might be a way out of persecution and then contribute their own understandings and experiences of what it means to seek asylum. This can even include practical advice on how to file an asylum claim, as well as material and social support once a person arrives in country. Thus, the flow of knowledge and resources through queer networks can be seen as enabling migration, in that it decreases the costs and risks involved.

Queer networks continue to play a key role for people once they arrive in Turkey. The Iranian queer community uses online platforms to stay connected across Turkey's provincial borders (remembering that refugees and asylum seekers are assigned to specific locations). These digital networks also provide critical access points for new arrivals, not only allowing them to connect with people who have had similar life experiences, but also allowing them to acquire and share knowledge: 'In Turkey, there are WhatsApp groups in different cities. ... These groups involve from 300 to 500 people. If we get any information on anything, we share in the group' (Shayan). These online networks allow group members to raise issues and seek support:

Sometimes we find ourselves so desperate with our financial problems. If you have a job, you give twenty liras, fifty liras, whatever you can, and we unite all the money and make it to 600–700 liras. When someone has a problem – for instance, renting a place or covering medical expenses – we lend him/her this money. When he/she gets a job, he/she pays back. We have nobody here other than us.

(Hamid)

When someone is raped and does not know what to do, which actions to take, if she/he writes to this group on the incident, the person will be informed on the steps to be taken. ... Even if nothing can be done, she/he will be supported psychologically. Secondly, people in need can be referred to service providers. ... Of course, it is not always possible to find a solution ... but we still work hard to help our friends because we are a family. We should never forget this.

(Shayan)

The quotes above show that Iranian queer refugees have developed some degree of material and symbolic support, both within and outside of Turkey's borders, leading to acts of solidarity and reciprocity. This helps Iranian queer refugees in different stages of their migration journeys, from helping people decide whether or not to migrate through to helping them settle and adapt to life in Turkey. This suggests that smaller identity-based ethnic/national networks – such as those centred on sexuality and/or gender – offer significant value when general ethnic/national networks are unavailable or potentially dangerous.

However, there are individuals like Ahmad who find themselves completely alone, neither part of a larger ethnic/national community nor a smaller queer ethnic/national network. As will be shown below, Ahmad was forced to develop alternative strategies to cope with loneliness and disconnection, including using online media to create new ties.

Navigating a new society through online media

As noted, research is beginning to map the value of digital networks for queer refugees, with studies pointing to messaging platforms and dating apps as sites in which coping strategies and social belonging are forged (Szulc 2020; Shield 2019; Bayramoğlu and Lünenborg 2018). The fact that digital interactions do not require physical proximity makes them particularly useful for those in unfamiliar environments and/or those concerned about safety and security (Lewis 2014). Kostia Lennes' (2021) analysis of Mexican gay men's use of dating apps in the United States draws attention to the vital role that smartphones play in queer migration trajectories. He argues that Mexican gay men creatively use dating apps to facilitate integration and forge connections. Apps enable them to form key networks, composed of friends, lovers and partners, within new and potentially hostile social settings.

In the absence of ethnic/national networks, Ahmad also turned to social media. Geosocial dating apps like Grindr allowed him to connect with other gay men and begin building social linkages. In turn, these connections helped him understand and navigate his new social reality:

> I arrived to the airport. I was very happy, even though I was in a complete[ly] foreign country. I didn't know where I was and I didn't know where I was going. I had no idea about Turkey. A friend of mine had told me: 'Go to Taksim.' I just remembered that name and went to Taksim. I started to make some new friends via the internet. I noticed also Grindr does not work in Turkey. It was forbidden by the government. … I was sending messages to people, but they were not delivering. They were sending messages, but I was not able to answer. And then one guy told me: 'Please download VPN application so you will be able to use Grindr.' Then I was able to talk to all the boys. It was like I was in paradise. I have

met many, many boys. ... Then I made some friends. ... They took me to the clubs and showed me area.

Ahmad's experience aligns with those of Mexican migrants in the United States, where dating apps like Grindr function as an instrument of 'entering this new system' (Lennes 2021: 4) and 'offering the first introduction to gay culture' (11).

Ahmad also used social media as a support mechanism, using it to find solutions to different challenges. For instance, on arrival in his satellite city, where he had to formally register as a refugee, he used social media to find temporary accommodation:

> When I arrived there, I had to be very careful about my budget, my money ... I was not able to find very cheap hotel. ... I decided to search [on dating apps] to see if I could find someone to host me because I arrived a little bit late. ... I found some Iranian people. They were refugees. He told me: 'Hi, are you looking for someone?' I said, 'I am searching for someone to host me because I just arrived here. I am so tired.' ... He said, 'Okay, I am gonna talk to my friends. You can come to us.' Then he talked to his friends and they all agreed I could come and spend the night there. I was feeling very happy because they opened their house for me ... They cooked tea for me and some cakes ... They told me their stories. They said they are refugees from Iran. That is the first time I felt myself as refugee. They started to tell me to go to migration office, going for signature and ask permission to go to Istanbul. So, I started to know what refugee means. I kind of got scared, but I told myself: 'Oh God, I am not the only one. There are so many people who are just like me.' That made me feel good.

In addition to using social media for support, Ahmad used it to deal with feelings of loneliness and isolation. Dating applications allow for a variety of social interactions and were used by Ahmad to form both platonic and romantic relationships. In the quote below, he recalls a very positive encounter:

> I met this Turkish guy. It was magical. I felt something so strong. He was very different from the others. He invited me for dinner. We had a very cute conversation. I completely fell in love with him. He opened his house to me. He completely trusted to me.

Digital technology took on an even bigger role in Ahmad's life once he became immobile due to his illness. Social media became his gateway to the outside world; he used it to deal with his isolation and fears. He described making two friends on dating apps who visited him on several occasions, making him feel less trapped. Ahmad also began using Instagram to communicate and work through his emotions:

> I felt bored because most of the time I was sitting at home. I could not move. I was in bed all the time. Using Instagram made me feel better. ... I was using my

old pictures [from before his illness]. I used these old pictures to show people that I was still doing things, that my life did not stop there.

At different stages of his migration journey, Ahmad used social media to negotiate his new social reality and to foster a sense of connection. Digital networks proved especially important because he lacked an in-person ethnic/national community. By harnessing online communication, Ahmad was able to forge transnational queer networks, linking up with both local queer persons and queer refugees from other countries. His use of social media aligns with findings from other studies, in that it offered a vehicle for connection and belonging. Indeed, virtual queer spaces have the potential to introduce people to safe physical spaces. The circulation of knowledge through digital networks helped Ahmad understand 'where safe queer spaces can be found' (Bayramoğlu and Lünenborg 2018: 1022). Dating apps helped him 'fill a lack of sociability in the host country' and build 'a new framework of relationships in a new place, far from family members, peers and other relatives' (Lennes 2021: 13).

Global connections

All of my interviewees indicated having contact with people in the Global North. These transnational networks took two forms: first, queer friends or acquaintances who had been resettled; second, English-speaking queer persons, mostly European, whom interviewees had met on dating apps and sustained relationships with via social media. The first type was more prominent among Iranian queer refugees, who remained in contact with people they had met either back home or while in transit. Those who had already been resettled continued to offer both emotional and economic support, as evidenced in the quotes below:

> My friend who helped me to come to Turkey had been resettled from Turkey to the USA. We are talking, but since there is a twelve-hour time difference, we are not able to talk regularly. I have another friend in Canada who had been resettled there. She is a very close friend of mine. We talk every now and then. … I tell her about my problems here; she tells me about her problems there. She says she is alone there and wants me to be there too … She always tells me that whenever I need money, she will send it to me.
>
> (Mariam)

> My ex-partner was resettled to Australia. There were occasions when he sent me some money from Australia … Having friends in Turkey or outside Turkey helps a lot. Because when you need help, when your family cannot be there for you, friends can be there for you. … It is your friendship network that you can fall back on. It is like a net, a safety net, when things are getting hard, not only financially but also psychologically.
>
> (Sajjad)

These quotes align with established conceptions of migrant networks (Massey et al. 1993), indicating that Iranian queer refugees have formed a transnational community that connects individuals at different stages of migration, including those in the country of origin, those in transit countries and those in resettlement countries. Early gay Iranian refugees actively contributed to the formation of transnational networks by building connections with people at different stages of the asylum process, writing blogs in Farsi about their experiences in Turkey and other transit countries, and sharing honest accounts of resettlement in the Global North via online channels (Karimi 2020). These networks are based not only on shared ethnic/national origins but also on common experiences of sexual- and gender-based oppression (Massey et al. 1993). As Karimi (2020) notes:

> There is now a chain of connections built around sexual identities and belonging ... between gay Iranian men who have sought asylum and have been resettled, those awaiting the results of their cases in Turkey, and those gay men who remain in Iran and are considering seeking asylum as an option should their situation there worsen.
>
> (78)

The quotes presented above, when read in conjunction with Karimi's findings, suggest that resettlement to a third country – popularly understood as the end of the migration journey – does not mean people leave behind or exit transnational networks. Instead, emotional support continues to flow in all directions, including to those in the Global North, even if financial support tends to flow in just one direction.

The experiences of my Iranian interviewees contrast significantly with those of Ahmad, who depends more heavily on the second type of transnational network – that is, queer persons removed from his ethnic/national/linguistic community. For Ahmad, dating apps facilitate contact with queer persons in the Global North. These interactions have sometimes morphed into stable, long-term friendships that continue to provide much-needed support. It was through one of these friendships that Ahmad was able to learn the basics of the Turkish asylum system:

> I had a friend from Belgium. He is a gay. He works there in an NGO on LGBTI issues. He helped me a lot. He explained to me all the procedures and how to apply as a refugee. He told me I can find help [in Turkey] and stay there securely.

Another online connection became an invaluable economic and emotional support, particularly during his first months in Turkey:

> I had a gay friend from Germany. He kind of saved my life basically. He supported me financially, even though we do not know each other. When I came here, in the first days, he sent me money. I met him on [Gay] Romeo. He was sending me about 100 Euro per month, just as a help. We became kind of good friends. ... I become so emotional [when talking] about this because when he sent the money

that first time, I did not believe it is because he believed in me. He believed I am a good person. I was kind of shocked because even your family does not help you. I have uncles in France. Actually they did not help at all, and I found help in a complete stranger [whom] I have never met in my life. ... I found humanity. People still care and still want to help, even though they don't know you. They want to help you from the bottom of their heart. I was very happy. I had hope again.

Ahmad's interactions with another European friend show how digital support systems can be mutually beneficial. In recounting this experience, Ahmad emphasized that emotional and knowledge exchange happened in both directions:

I had a friend from Poland. He was a very nice guy. We were chatting on Facebook. It was really nice to know someone from another country and to speak about how people are living in other countries. I first connected with him on [Gay] Romeo. He was telling me all about his life. I was so attached to him. I was talking to him all the time: I was telling him everything about my life, and he was telling his life. He had HIV and was in a very bad health situation. ... I was really feeling something for him. We were just talking on Facebook. Sometimes on video calls. We got so attached over time. He actually wanted to come to my country and meet me, and bring me to his country. He wanted [us] to have a life together and [to] marry me.

Ahmad's limited access to networks of support, both in his country of origin and in Turkey, means that transnational digital connections have come to play a larger role in his migration journey and his life more generally. By chatting with online friends, Ahmad was able to gain knowledge about asylum systems, build strong friendships and access financial support. His experience demonstrates the enormous potential of social media to help queer refugees whose migration routes might come with a lack of ethnic/national/linguistic networks or familial support. Lacking these connections often exacerbates a person's economic disadvantage and social isolation, potentially placing them at greater risk of violence and exploitation. Ahmad's reliance on digital networks as a means of forging connection, as opposed to simply facilitating communication, shows how vital online technology is for individual queer refugees, especially those with little in-country support.

Conclusion

While transnationalism has received significant critical attention in recent years, there continues to be little attention afforded to transnationalism in the lives of queer refugees, particularly those enduring protracted forms of transit. As shown above, queer refugees in Turkey engage in a range of transnational relationships that encompass their countries of origin, country of transit and countries of potential resettlement. However, for some individuals, more traditional forms of transnationalism may be lacking or inaccessible. Ahmad's experience foregrounds the importance of recognizing new forms of transnationalism, especially for those who cannot easily turn to ethnic/national/linguistic communities, queer or otherwise. Instead, these individuals may exploit networks that disrupt the linear axis of home–host country.

In this chapter, I have shown that the formation and mobilization of transnational networks is an important element of queer ways of surviving in Turkey. However, the transnational strategies used can differ based on a person's background, nationality, ethnicity or language. In comparing the experiences of queer refugees from Iran with those of a queer refugee from North Africa, it is possible to see different transnational strategies in action. To survive their time in Turkey, queer refugees from Iran have developed an expansive support network that connects them not only with each other but also with those who have been resettled and with those back home. Lacking a similar network, Ahmad uses online platforms and dating apps to penetrate local and international queer networks. He uses these to secure both material and emotional support, while also forging a sense of belonging. Drawing on Ahmad's experience, I argue that alternative transnational relationships/connections, including those formed online, may be critical for queer refugees from geographical regions with fewer in-country community members and limited home–host country ties. While it is impossible to generalize from this particular study, its findings open up important lines of inquiry when considering queer African refugees in transit or living in countries with limited support networks.

Crucially, Ahmad's story serves as a reminder that queer African refugees can be overlooked in academic literature when they are not part of visible migrant networks. This means that their particular struggles over community, inclusion, connection and access to support may not be adequately considered. Documenting the experiences of queer African refugees in countries not commonly associated with queer African mobilities – especially as part of comparative analyses – is vital if we are to better theorize (digital) transnationalism and queer ways of surviving, be it in Turkey or any other location.

Notes

1   On 10 September 2018 the UNHCR ceased managing refugee status determinations and the Directorate General of Migration Management declared itself, with the support of the UNHCR, the single authority responsible for processing asylum claims in Turkey. However, the UNHCR still identifies the most vulnerable refugees for resettlement processing (UNHCR 2018).

2   I use 'queer' as an umbrella term for persons who identify as gay, lesbian, bisexual and transgender. It captures how certain bodies and identities transgress hegemonic forms of sexuality and gender. Rather than perpetuating the idea that subjectivities are fixed, homogenous and stable, 'queer' points to subversion of the heterosexual/

homosexual binary and underlines diversity and fluidity. However, when referring to specific individuals, I use their preferred identity categories. I also use the term 'refugees' when referring to my interviewees as a group. This highlights their shared experiences of forced displacement, regardless of their legal status before the Turkish authorities. I choose to rely on the definition specified in the Geneva Convention.

3   I draw on Pierre Bourdieu's (1986) definition of social capital as 'the aggregate of the actual or potential resources which are linked to possession of a durable network of more or less institutionalised relationships of mutual acquaintance and recognition – or in other words, to membership in a group – which provides each of its members with the backing of the collectively owned capital, a "credential" which entitles them to credit, in the various senses of the word' (247).

4   For ethical reasons, all identifying data has been removed. I use aliases for all interviewees.

5   Mert Koçak (2020) notes, in passing, a similar issue with regard to the experiences of a trans woman from Zimbabwe seeking asylum in Turkey and the impacts of this lack of in-country community for queer African refugees in Turkey.

References

Al-Ali, N., R. Black and K. K. Koser (2001), 'Refugees and Transnationalism: The Experience of Bosnians and Eritreans in Europe', *Journal of Ethnic and Migration Studies*, 27 (4): 615–34.

Basch, L., N. G. Schiller and C. S. Blanc (1994), *Nations Unbound: Transnational Projects, Postcolonial Predicaments, and Deterritorialized Nation-States*, London: Gordon and Breach Publishers.

Bayramoğlu, Y. and M. Lünenborg (2018), 'Queer Migration and Digital Affects: Refugees Navigating from the Middle East via Turkey to Germany', *Sexuality and Culture*, 22 (4): 1019–36.

Bourdieu, P. (1986), 'The Forms of Capital', in J. G. Richardson (ed.), *Handbook of Theory and Research for the Sociology of Education*, 241–58, New York: Greenwood.

Brun, C. and A. Fábos (2015), 'Making Homes in Limbo? A Conceptual Framework', *Refuge: Canada's Journal on Refugees*, 31 (1): 5–17.

Directorate General of Migration Management (2020), 'Law on Foreigners and International Protection'. Available online: https://en.goc.gov.tr/lfip (accessed 13 September 2020).

Fortier, A.-M. (2001), '"Coming Home": Queer Migrations and Multiple Evocations of Home', *European Journal of Cultural Studies*, 4 (4): 405–24.

Gorman-Murray, A. (2009), 'Intimate Mobilities: Emotional Embodiment and Queer Migration', *Social & Cultural Geography*, 10 (4): 441–60.

Greatrick, A. (2019), '"Coaching" Queer: Hospitality and the Categorical Imperative of LGBTQ Asylum Seeking in Lebanon and Turkey', *Migration and Society*, 2 (1): 98–106.

İçduygu, A. and D. Yükseker (2012), 'Rethinking Transit Migration in Turkey: Reality and Re-presentation in the Creation of a Migratory Phenomenon', *Population, Space and Place*, 18 (4): 441–56.

Kara, H. and D. Çalık (2016), *Waiting to Be 'Safe and Sound': Turkey as LGBTI Refugees' Way Station*, Ankara: Kaos GL.

Karimi, A. (2020), 'Refugees' Transnational Practices: Gay Iranian Men Navigating Refugee Status and Cross-border Ties in Canada', *Social Currents*, 7 (1): 71–86.

Kivilcim, Z. (2017), 'Lesbian, Gay, Bisexual and Transsexual (LGBT) Syrian Refugees in Turkey', in J. Freedman, Z. Kivilcim and N. Ö. Baklacıoğlu (eds), *A Gendered Approach to the Syrian Refugee Crisis*, 26–41, New York: Routledge.

Koçak, M. (2020), 'Who Is "Queerer" and Deserves Resettlement? Queer Asylum Seekers and Their Deservingness of Refugee Status in Turkey', *Middle East Critique*, 29 (1): 29–46.

Lennes, K. (2021), 'Queer (Post-)Migration Experiences: Mexican Men's Use of Gay Dating Apps in the USA', *Sexualities*, 24 (8): 1003–18.

Lewis, N. M. (2014), 'Moving "Out," Moving On: Gay Men's Migrations through the Life Course', *Annals of the Association of American Geographers*, 104 (2): 225–33.

Manalansan, M. F. (2006), 'Queer Intersections: Sexuality and Gender in Migration Studies', *The International Migration Review*, 40 (1): 224–49.

Massey, D. S., J. Arango, G. Hugo, A. Kouaouci, A. Pellegrino and J. E. Taylor (1993), 'Theories of International Migration: A Review and Appraisal', *Population and Development Review*, 19 (3): 431–66.

O'Reilly, K. (2012), *International Migration and Social Theory*, Houndmills: Palgrave Macmillan.

Plummer, K. (1992), *Modern Homosexualities: Fragments of Lesbian and Gay Experience*, London: Routledge.

Saleh, F. (2020), 'Queer/Humanitarian Visibility: The Emergence of the Figure of the Suffering Syrian Gay Refugee', *Middle East Critique*, 29 (1): 47–67.

Sari, E. (2020), 'Lesbian Refugees in Transit: The Making of Authenticity and Legitimacy in Turkey', *Journal of Lesbian Studies*, 24 (2): 140–58.

Schiller, G. N., L. Basch and C. S. Blanc (1995), 'From Immigrant to Transmigrant: Theorizing Transnational Migration', *Anthropological Quarterly*, 68 (1): 48–63.

Shakhsari, S. (2014), 'The Queer Time of Death: Temporality, Geopolitics, and Refugee Rights', *Sexualities*, 17 (8): 998–1015.

Shield, A. (2019), *Immigrants on Grindr: Race, Sexuality and Belonging Online*, Cham: Palgrave Macmillan.

Şimşek, D. (2018), 'Transnational Activities of Syrian Refugees in Turkey: Hindering or Supporting Integration', *International Migration*, 57 (2): 268–82.

Szulc, L. (2020) 'Queer Migrants and Digital Culture', in K. Smets, K. Leurs, M. Georgiou, S. Witteborn and R. Gajjala (eds), *SAGE Handbook of Media and Migration*, 220–32, London: Sage Publications.

UNHCR (2018), 'Registration and RSD with UNHCR'. Available online: https://help.unhcr.org/turkey/information-for-non-syrians/registration-rsd-with-unhcr/ (accessed 7 September 2020).

Part IV

BORDERING IN ACTION: IDENTITY, BELONGING AND WELLBEING

Chapter 10

'KINDNESS IS A DISTANT AND ELUSIVE REALITY': CHARTING THE IMPACTS OF DISCRIMINATION ON THE MENTAL AND SEXUAL WELLBEING OF LGBT REFUGEE YOUTH IN KENYA

Emmanuel Munyarukumbuzi, Margaret Jjuuko and James Maingi Gathatwa

Lesbian, gay, bisexual and transgender (LGBT) people often experience discrimination and trauma from a young age (Hopkinson et al. 2017). In many contexts, they endure emotional, sexual and physical violence, including harassment, beatings, rape, extortion and social exclusion. LGBT people may also struggle to find housing or employment, or be denied access to healthcare, justice and other social services. Some are forcibly excluded from families, communities and/or religious institutions on the basis of being disgraceful (Murray and Viljoen 2007). While societal attitudes and legal systems are shifting in many parts of the world, the vast majority of African countries continue to outlaw consensual same-sex relations under colonial-era penal codes (Jjuuko and Tabengwa 2018). Even in African countries that protect sexual and gender minorities, or at the very least do not explicitly criminalize them, LGBT people remain vulnerable. Fergus Kerrigan (2013) notes that in South Africa – which has numerous legal protections against homo/transphobic discrimination – 'lesbians and transgender people are particularly at risk of rape and other violence' (124). In East Africa, the region of interest for this chapter, LGBT people are regular targets of state-sanctioned violence, often justified on religious or cultural grounds (Johnson and Falcetta 2021; Kaoma 2018).

Consequently, to be an LGBT person in Africa is, to varying degrees, to live in uncertain circumstances and to experience various stressors that undermine one's physical and emotional health. For the purposes of this chapter, we understand health as 'a state of complete physical, mental and social wellbeing and not merely the absence of disease or infirmity' (World Health Organisation 1948: 1). Negative health and wellbeing impacts stemming from homo/transphobia are by no means unique to Africa. However, there are nuances on the African continent that deserve close attention. One is the emergence of a new generation of LGBT people – those we might classify as LGBT youth – who constitute a visible migratory demographic and who face particular forms of persecution. This is especially true in East Africa, where increasingly restrictive socio-legal environments have precipitated a sharp rise in LGBT youth on the move. Many head to Kenya, where the visibility of the United Nations High Commissioner for Refugees (UNHCR) inspires hope for eventual third-country resettlement (Camminga 2020a).

LGBT youth are an understudied demographic within the broader category of refugees. This is certainly the case in Africa, where LGBT migration has only recently emerged as an area of study. Research to date has concentrated on the difficulties LGBT Africans face when engaging with dehumanizing asylum bureaucracies, especially barriers to 'proving' eligibility for protection (Marnell 2021). Very little attention has been afforded to the health and wellbeing of LGBT refugees, many of whom have histories of trauma and violence. This chapter responds to this gap by centring the everyday experiences of LGBT refugee youth living in Nairobi. These individuals continue to face regular homo/transphobia, often perpetrated by those mandated to provide care and support, leading to poor health and wellbeing outcomes.

This overall finding accords with broader research charting the negative impacts of homo/transphobia on the African continent, including significant health inequalities:

> Pervasive poor understanding of the gender- and sexuality-related circumstances of LGBT persons continues to expose them to multiple dangers, poor health outcomes, elevated levels of exclusion from critical social, economic and political processes, and violations that not only often go largely unchallenged and unprosecuted, but have major sexual and reproductive health (SRH) implications.
>
> (Izugbara et al. 2020)

Kerrigan (2013) also notes the immense socio-cultural pressures that LGBT Africans face, including the expectation that they will marry and maintain a conventional family life. Failing to do so can result in intimidation, exclusion or violence, placing individuals under considerable emotional strain. A desire for social acceptance and approval has been linked to self-destructive tendencies, especially among young people (Zahn et al. 2016). Finally, in addition to a shortage of specialized mental and sexual health services, LGBT persons may be reluctant to access support due to safety and/or privacy concerns (Mkhize and Maharaj 2021).

This chapter contributes to this emerging field of study by providing insights from a demographic that has thus far received little scholarly attention. It draws on empirical data from focus-group discussions (FGDs) with LGBT refugees between the ages of twenty and thirty-five,[1] as well as in-depth interviews with two sets of key informants. Our analysis shows that entrenched homo/transphobia hinders access to services, resulting in negative physical, psychological and socio-economic outcomes. In Kenya, as in many African contexts, the failure to provide inclusive and affirming services is legitimized by social perceptions, religious discourses and the existing political order (Harper et al. 2021).

LGBT mobilities in East Africa

East Africa, as defined by the East African Community, comprises six nations: Burundi, Kenya, Rwanda, South Sudan, Tanzania and Uganda. In recent years, the region has seen significant tensions over sexual and gender rights. These have been shaped by a number of local and international forces, such as the growing influence of US-based evangelical churches and the strategic use of homo/transphobic rhetoric by political and cultural leaders (Marnell 2021). Uganda is perhaps the best-known example of this trend. In February 2014, President Yoweri Museveni signed into law the Anti-Homosexuality Act (AHA) – popularly known as the 'Kill the Gays' Bill – which not only intensified penalties for sexual acts between persons of the same sex but also introduced new prohibitions against 'promoting' or 'abetting' homosexuality. The legislation was later nullified by the courts, but the moral panic on which it was predicated continues to shape societal attitudes. Anti-LGBT sentiments continue to be regularly expressed in parliament, often framed as concerns over young Ugandans being recruited into a 'gay lifestyle' (Johnson and Falcetta 2021). In neighbouring Tanzania, government ministers have deployed similarly inflammatory rhetoric, calling for LGBT people to be identified, tracked down and arrested (Kirby 2018). This state-led crackdown forced LGBT communities into hiding, driving people away from vital health and social services (Human Rights Watch 2020). While there have been fewer high-profile debates over sexual and gender rights in the rest of the region, this should not be mistaken as a culture of permissiveness or acceptance. Rwanda has largely remained silent on LGBT issues, and like many former Francophone colonies does not expressly criminalize same-sex sexual activities, yet anti-LGBT stigma remains widespread (ILGA World 2019). In 2010, Burundi outlawed 'indecency contrary to Burundian morals', mandating a punishment of up to two years' imprisonment (ILGA World 2019). The South Sudanese penal code also contains provisions against 'gross indecency', with same-sex relations punishable by up fourteen years' imprisonment (ILGA World 2019). There is currently very little data on LGBT experiences in these countries, making it difficult to gauge the full extent of homo/transphobia.

The Kenyan state is similar to its neighbours in that it criminalizes same-sex relations, but it remains distinct in one key respect: for the last decade it has hosted a growing community of LGBT refugees. This is in large part due to the resettlement programme run out of Kenya by the UNHCR (Kremin 2017). The UNHCR's operations place LGBT refugees in Kenya in a unique and somewhat murky legal position: while they are technically criminalized under Kenyan law, they have protection under international law, courtesy of the recognition afforded to them by the UNHCR. According to Denis Nzioka, founder of the Gay and Lesbian Coalition of Kenya, this has led to divergent responses from the state: 'despite the lack of a clear government policy with regard to the LGBT community in Kenya, humanitarian organisations such as the UNHCR working primarily in this space have been left to thrive' (quoted in Wesangula 2017).

LGBT Ugandans began moving into Kenya from as early as 2005, but it was only after the AHA was adopted in 2014 that they started moving en masse, with almost 400 people fleeting between January 2014 and February 2015 (Zomorodi 2016). Yet, while the AHA played a significant role in the displacement of LGBT Ugandans, it was not the only push factor. Multiple forms of homo/transphobic persecution, including police brutality, media intimidation, family rejections and employment discrimination, were documented in Uganda well before the law was introduced (Oloka-Onyango 2015). Still, the surge in LGBT migration triggered by the AHA marks it out as a turning point.

The influx of LGBT persons into Kenya around 2014 put pressure on international humanitarian agencies, leading the UNHCR to prioritize the unexpected new caseload and expedite third-country resettlement for LGBT Ugandans (Zomorodi 2016). At first, LGBT persons seeking resettlement had two options: staying either in Kakuma Refugee Camp or in Nairobi. Those who chose the latter were provided with housing and a monthly stipend through a UNHCR partner. This changed in 2017, when more stringent vetting of LGBT refugees was introduced due to concerns that non-LGBT claimants were taking advantage of 'preferential treatment' (Wesangula 2017). As a result, LGBT asylum seekers were no longer automatically categorized as vulnerable and were instead assessed on a case-by-case basis. This move coincided with a larger shift in migration governance in Kenya, ostensibly motivated by fears of terrorist attacks by the Al-Shabaab militant group (Pincock 2021). Asylum processing centres in Nairobi were closed and all refugee applicants, including LGBT persons, were relocated to Kakuma. While this policy change had serious impacts on LGBT refugees, it was not necessarily targeted at them, instead being part of a broader crackdown by the state. Regardless, LGBT refugees hoping for quick resettlement found themselves facing serious threats to their wellbeing, including discrimination from camp staff, harassment from the Kenyan state and physical attacks from other refugees (Bhalla 2018). Following a sharp rise in homo/transphobic incidents within Kakuma, the UNHCR began relocating some LGBT refugees to safe houses on the outskirts of Nairobi. This brought some level of safety and security, but also created its own challenges, as the findings of this study attest. Those who were left behind were encamped in a special section of the main camp, a response that fuelled animosity from other Kakuma residents (Camminga 2020b).

Many of the obstacles faced by LGBT refugees in Kenya are similar to those experienced by their counterparts in other contexts. International research shows that LGBT persons encounter discrimination from the moment they enter asylum systems, with numerous studies tracking the procedural hurdles that block them from accessing protection (e.g. Güler et al. 2019). Recent years have also seen a decrease in third-country resettlements for all refugees, a trend that places LGBT refugees at particular risk due to their susceptibility to violence, discrimination and exploitation (Pincock 2021). This last point is particularly relevant to the current discussion, in that LGBT refugees are likely to find themselves in hostile social conditions for a long time, if not indefinitely.

Although they are nominally protected by the UNHCR, LGBT refugees in Kenya continue to occupy a precarious social position (Nanima 2017). Anecdotal and empirical evidence suggests that they are vulnerable to arbitrary imprisonment, sexual violence, physical attacks, harassment, humiliation, unemployment and poverty (Fitzsimons 2020; Taylor 2019). News reports document LGBT refugees in Kenya suffering from broken limbs, injured eyes, stab wounds and other physical injuries. In extreme circumstances, LGBT refugees have been driven to suicide (Bhalla 2018; Mustanski et al. 2016). Overall, this leads to an erosion of trust in systems ostensibly designed to protect; LGBT refugees themselves have pointed to serious failings within protection systems in Kenya (Camminga 2020a). A lack of finance-generating opportunities has also driven many LGBT refugees to sex work (Hodal 2020; Wesangula 2017), potentially placing them at increased risk of HIV and other health complications (Nyanzi 2013).

The conditions outlined above are in many ways a product of entrenched prejudices within Kenyan society. However, it would be wrong to portray Kenya as a wholly hostile context. Recent years have seen concerted efforts by Kenyan LGBT activists to confront homo/transphobia, including a highly publicized litigation campaign to overturn the country's sodomy laws (van Klinken 2019). At the same time, HIV organizations have worked hard to address the health needs of LGBT persons, particularly men who have sex with men, under the guise of 'key population' interventions (Sanders 2015). While this advocacy and programmatic work is yet to produce widespread attitudinal shifts, its presence signals push back against restrictive policies and the initiating of conversations around diversity.

Mental and sexual health issues facing LGBT people

Globally, the social, cultural and economic disadvantages faced by LGBT people are well documented. Of particular concern for this chapter are the negative health outcomes that can result from inadequate or discriminatory service provision (Albuquerque 2016). In Africa, empirical evidence on health inequalities related to sexual orientation or gender identity is drawn mostly from Southern Africa, although an increasing number of studies look towards East Africa and parts of West Africa. Research from South Africa shows that legal prohibitions and social taboos leave many LGBT people, including refugees, with limited access to health information or services (Alessi et al. 2020; Luvuno 2019; Müller et al. 2018). Similarly, studies in Malawi and Zimbabwe have shown that health professionals frequently mistreat and humiliate LGBT persons (Kaliza, 2017; Evans et al. 2016). One study reports that LGBT persons seeking medical support are blamed for their poor health because of 'bad behaviour' (Hunt et al. 2017: 4). There is also evidence of health workers refusing medical care to LGBT persons on the basis of religious and cultural beliefs (Mprah 2016). In many contexts, access to healthcare becomes contingent on conforming to societal norms or, if one cannot convincingly conform, on avoiding disclosure at all costs (Mkhize and Maharaj 2021). This can discourage LGBT people from seeking treatment.

As well as facing institutional stigma and discrimination, LGBT Africans are frequent targets for physical, sexual and emotional violence, perpetrated by both state and non-state actors. This has been well documented in South Africa (Zahn et al. 2016) and is increasingly recognized in other parts of the continent, including East Africa (Müller et al. 2021; Millo 2013). When combined with limited access to health, justice and social services, this susceptibility to violence is a recipe for disaster, especially in relation to HIV risk and complex trauma. These factors result in LGBT Africans experiencing significantly increased morbidity and mortality (Evans et al. 2016).

Although each identity category represented by the LGBT acronym has its own specific health issues, research shows that, as a group, LGBT people face disproportionately high mental health challenges in comparison to their non-LGBT peers. The discrepancy has been attributed to the general stigmatization that LGBT people experience (Moagi et al. 2021). Accessing mental health support is challenging for several reasons, not least of which is the threat of having to disclose one's sexual orientation or gender identity to potentially prejudicial staff (Harper et al. 2021).

In sub-Saharan Africa, where the provision of psychosocial support is often minimal, traditional healers and faith leaders often step in to provide care (Esan et al. 2018). Research has also shown that African communities have alternative ways of perceiving and dealing with trauma, often grounded in indigenous spiritual practices (Mutambara and Sodi 2018). These non-medical interventions have a strong focus on collective healing and have been advocated by some as more useful in African social contexts (Motsi and Masango 2012). However, in cases where local customary practices cannot provide solutions, access to Western healthcare is crucial. This is particularly important in cases where community models may cast certain individuals – for example, those who are gender-nonconforming – as possessed and unworthy of support.

It must be noted that the existence of services does not necessarily translate to equitable access. Recent studies contain disturbing accounts of minority groups facing discrimination when trying to navigate health systems. Research suggests that LGBT people face everything from harassment by healthcare providers through to being publicly outed and turned away (Hunt et al. 2017). Such barriers are likely intensified for individuals who face both homo/transphobia and xenophobia, such as LGBT refugees. International research shows that limited access to LGBT-specific resources, often coupled with discriminatory service provision, produces a culture of fear and misinformation that can endanger the wellbeing of LGBT refugees (Hopkinson et al. 2017). Similar findings have also been captured in relation to South Africa (Alessi et al. 2020).

A shortage of specialized sexual and psychological health services in many African contexts creates an additional barrier for heavily marginalized communities, including LGBT refugees. Given the multiple forms of marginalization and violence that LGBT refugees are likely to have experienced, there is a strong chance they will suffer from complex mental health issues, such as post-traumatic stress disorders (PTSD). Ariel Shidlo and Joanne Ahola (2013) note that PTSD for LGBT refugees can result in 'self-destructive behaviour, amnesia, intense shame, difficulties with intimacy, experiencing bodily pains in response to psychological distress, and despair about finding loving relationships' (9).

Aware of the context outlined above, we sought to understand the impacts of alienation, victimization and stigmatization on LGBT refugee youth living in Nairobi, particularly in relation to their sexual and mental health needs. In tracking barriers to services, and in exposing the physical, psychological and material impacts of discrimination, this study suggests that improved service provision is urgently needed for this population group.

Methodology

This chapter draws on two FGDs and four key informant interviews with LGBT refugee youth. The majority of participants were gay men from Uganda; the other countries represented were Burundi, DR Congo, Ethiopia, Somalia and South Sudan. All participants had lived in Kenya for multiple years, including time spent in Kakuma.

Participants for the FGDs were recruited through snowballing sampling (Heckathorn 2011). LGBT refugee youth tend to be discreet about their identities due to the threat of victimization. Given this reality, we relied on trusted contacts to recommend suitable individuals. Key informants were recruited through purposive sampling and were not part of the FGDs.

To supplement our data, we conducted a further five interviews with representatives of community-based organizations (CBOs). The CBOs selected for the study are tasked with supporting LGBT refugees in Kenya.

To comply with ethical standards, we used an anonymized coding system to protect participants' identities. Quotes from FGDs are identified as either FGD1 or FGD2. LGBT refugee youth who were interviewed are referred to as KIR1, KIR2, etc. and key informants from CBOs are referred to as KIA1, KIA2, etc. Given the intensely hostile context in which this study was conducted, we have omitted specific demographic information about each individual.

Findings and discussion

Mental and sexual health issues

International research shows that LGBT refugees experience a number of stressors that carry significant health risks (Hopkinson et al. 2017; Mustanski et al. 2016). Shidlo and Ahola (2013) demonstrate a clear link between accumulated stress and mental health struggles, finding that 'many [LGBT refugees] suffer from significant mental health consequences as a result of a lifetime of cumulative trauma' (9). They note that LGBT refugees often spend years battling feelings of fear, shame and guilt. Many also experience internalized homophobia, which can be exacerbated by a lack of affirming support structures. Data from this study corroborate these findings, as the following quote attests: 'The most prevalent mental health issues include trauma, stress and inability to engage in quality-of-life improving activities. These then usher in feelings of inadequacy' (KIR1). A similar point was made in the focus groups:

> It just makes you feel you are worthless … You come [to Kenya] hoping to get a better life, then you are subjected to the same things you ran away from: you are alone, hungry and always stressed. A friend of mine has ulcers … Some people cry every day, and you have heard that some [LGBT refugees] commit suicide.
>
> (FGD2)

Reflecting on their experiences of providing care, the CBO representatives referenced the severe mental health challenges they had observed:

> [These] include stress, depression and psychosis. People become unapproachable; they loathe themselves and other people around them. We have also seen cases of psychosis. There was a case where one person was undressing themselves in public.
>
> (KIA1)

Self-loathing stemming from internalized homo/transphobia emerged as a common theme. Impacts of this can include self-isolation, feelings of inadequacy, acute distress and suicide ideation. The deep emotional pain carried by LGBT refugee youth is evident in the quote below:

> Self-hate is natural to us. We have consistently been abused and openly despised. I would abandon me if I had an option. [Life] is painfully unbearable. … Kindness is a distant and elusive reality.
>
> (FGD2)

Overall, the LGBT refugee youth in this study did not feel integrated into the wider community, resulting in feelings of alienation and worthlessness:

> Everywhere you go people treat you like a bad person, someone with no value. People on the street harass you [and] many service providers insult you before attending to you. It gets to you. … You sometimes think they are right and wonder if you have any value in this world.
>
> (KIR3)

For many, this sense of isolation is exacerbated by their categorization as an LGBT refugee. Participants explained that refugees receive mandate letters proving their legal status. These official documents disclose the basis for the holder's refugee claim – in this case, the person's sexual orientation and/or gender identity. Refugees are expected to present their letter to administrators and service providers when seeking access to basic needs, such as food and medication. Because of the social stigma and legal prohibitions linked to LGBT identities in Kenya, many local workers hold prejudicial beliefs that carry through to their work. This can evoke fear among LGBT youth, leading them to avoid public clinics: 'Homophobia makes us fear getting services there' (KIR1). At its most extreme, homo/transphobia among service providers can result in physical or sexual violence (Fitzsimons 2020). According to the FGDs, some LGBT refugee youth have even died when seeking access to care. The sense of danger this generates among LGBT refugee youth leads them to avoid places deemed risky or dangerous. Their reluctance to attend healthcare services can mean that serious conditions go untreated.

As well as highlighting mistreatment by service providers, participants pointed to the negative health impacts that emerge from feeling stuck and useless. Participants emphasized that they are not without talents and that their forced inactivity takes a significant toll on their wellbeing. Waiting for resettlement means putting one's life on hold, and many informants reported anxiety over not being able to make long-term plans: 'Idleness is killing people. Some of us come with a lot of skills. When we get [to Kenya], we get stuck' (FGD1). For KIR1, being trapped in Kenya is a form of not-being, in that the normal trajectory of one's life becomes suspended. He saw resettlement as the only way in which he could move forward, both literally and figuratively: 'If UNHCR advocates [for us to be resettled], more third-party countries will give us more slots. Being resettled – people live a whole new life. It is like being born again.'

Limited livelihood options were also identified as a major concern. Participants' ongoing struggle with poverty, including the boredom and hopeless that accompanies it, was seen as a threat to their health and wellbeing. Many turn to sex work to survive, potentially increasing the risk for negative outcomes, including sexual violence, exposure to STDs or substance abuse. These dangers could be exacerbated by the young age of many LGBT refugees in Kenya. Research suggests that young people are more impulsive and susceptible to peer pressure, which can lead to self-destructive behaviours (Zahn et al. 2016).

With regard to sexual health, the FGDs emphasized concerns about HIV and treatable STDs, such as anal warts and syphilis. This was supported by the CBO representatives, many of whom expressed frustration at the lack of prevention measures and support services:

> Three LGBT [refugees] died in 2016 due to complications related to HIV. There was a lot of stigma, even though the medicine was there. [They] did not have access to the medicine or any other supplements because they didn't know about its existence.
>
> (KIA2)

As is clear from this quote, limited service provision directly impacts the health of LGBT refugee youth; in extreme cases, it can result in death. The failure to provide appropriate care can be partly explained by inadequate sensitization training for service providers, but it is also likely a product of Kenya's socio-legal context. The criminalization of same-sex relations creates a culture of animosity towards LGBT people and their health needs. Some Kenyan health workers are not only hostile towards LGBT individuals, but also actively report those suspected of being LGBT to the authorities (Shangani et al. 2018). Based on the data collected for this study, LGBT refugee youth seem to receive similar treatment to their local counterparts, although there are additional hurdles stemming from their status as 'foreigners'. For example, participants in FGD2 indicated that an inability to speak a local language creates a significant barrier when trying to access care.

Mental and sexual health resources available to LGBT refugee youth

A repeated theme in the data was the notion of 'choice' – or, more accurately, healthcare workers' perception that LGBT persons make the *wrong* life choices and therefore do not deserve care:

> When you go to some clinics and you are a gay or bisexual refugee, it is common for them to ask you: 'Why are you gay? Why do you do this?' Why do you sleep with men [when] there are many women out there?'
>
> (KIR1)

The assumed wrongness of people's choices stems from a belief that being LGBT is contrary to 'real' African values and traditions, a view reinforced by the illegality of same-sex relations in countries like Kenya (Ibrahim 2015). Such attitudes remain pervasive, despite efforts by local activists to confront religious or cultural objections to LGBT rights (van Klinken 2019).

In both the FGDs and key informant interviews, participants spoke of regular mistreatment on religious and/cultural grounds. As well as being referred to as sinners, some informants were told by healthcare workers that extending care to LGBT persons would attract punishment from God, a narrative that has been reported elsewhere on the continent (Kaliza 2017):

> I once went to one of these hospitals. One doctor told his colleague in Kiswahili that these people are sinners, you know, treating them attracts curses on you. ... I think he did not think I could understand his language.
>
> (KIR1)

CBO workers shared similar perspectives, noting that religious-based homo/transphobia undermines service provision:

> Some healthcare providers are not friendly to gay people. They sometimes ask questions such as 'Why are you doing that? Why are you even gay? You know you are sinning?' That kind of behaviour traumatises people.
>
> (KIA2)

The CBO informants described the denial of service on religious or cultural grounds as pointless. By not providing affirmative and inclusive support, Kenyan healthcare workers are not 'fixing the LGBT problem' (KIA4) but merely driving the issue underground, further exposing LGBT refugee youth to inhumane conditions and increasing their susceptibility to physical disease and emotional distress. It must be noted that the impacts of religious-based homo/transphobia extend beyond healthcare settings. Participants reported police brutality justified on the grounds of 'wrong choices' – that is, not living according to Christian values – though this finding is not discussed in detail here due to the focus of the chapter.

Both LGBT refugee youth and the CBO informants felt that misconceptions constitute a major impediment to support. As KIR1 puts it, 'healthcare people should treat LGBT people like other people', regardless of their personal beliefs. A number of informants were aware of services and resources, but felt that these were inaccessible due to the lack of staff training on LGBT issues. Ignorance, often combined with an unwillingness to behave professionally, means that LGBT refugee youth are frequently treated with derision.

In terms of mental health services, it was noted that limited support is available: 'Some CBOs offer psychosocial support sessions ... These sessions are monthly and are carried out in safe houses' (KIA4). Such services are offered by civil society groups, rather than the Kenyan state or international agencies such as UNHCR. While not wanting to diminish the efforts of these groups, it is important to stress that these are not specialized services; not all facilitators have the skills or resources to deal with complex trauma. Moreover, the infrequency of these services and the fact they are offered in group settings may not allow individuals to receive an appropriate level of care.

One area in which informants did demonstrate clear knowledge of service provision was in relation to safe-sex materials, specifically the distribution of condoms and lubricants. Information about these services is spread through the UNHCR and interpersonal networks:

> I was informed by a fellow refugee when he overheard my concerns about lack of condoms and lubricants. He directed me to a clinic that is LGBT friendly. I have [since] referred a hundred of my fellow refugees.
>
> (KIR3)

However, as noted above, the existence of services does not always mean easy access. Participants explained that their limited financial resources impeded their access to these services. LGBT refugee youth tend to live on the outskirts of Nairobi, far from healthcare providers, and most do not have the financial means to afford transport:

> The money I have mostly goes to food ... clinics and centres that accommodate us are located far, and transport costs cripple us. No one should ever live like this – [having to choose] whether to eat or receive healthcare.
>
> (FGD2)

Even if one is able to make such a journey, there is still a high probability of discrimination, both when in transit and at the clinic. This can make LGBT refugee youth apprehensive about seeking help:

> There is not enough counselling. People do not feel it is their right to go and pick [up] drugs. Sometimes the medication is there, but we do not have the means to get to the clinic to get the medication.
>
> (KIR2)

This finding aligns with reports of harassment, beatings and other forms of abuse when LGBT people travel to or from clinics (Taylor 2019; Ibrahim 2015).

Coping mechanisms

LGBT refugee youth employ various strategies for dealing with stress and anxiety. Self-isolating in order to remain safe was mentioned repeatedly:

> When you are alone, you no longer have to keep explaining yourself and justifying your value to persons who intend on demeaning and making fun of you. I don't understand why people imagine being gay is a choice. If it was, who would choose to be abused, hated, despised and degraded?
>
> (KIR3)

Yet isolation brings its own difficulties, in that it can aggravate rather than alleviate mental health issues, leading to long-term impacts. For this reason, the FGDs and key informants flagged the importance of having peer-support networks:

> There are fellowship groups where we meet every Friday and pray. We talk about other things as well ... Other LGBT organisations have camps that we attend for two to three days. All this is helpful.
>
> (KIR1)

As this quote suggests, LGBT refugee youth appreciate moments of connection, as these can foster a sense of belonging and worth. It also suggests that spiritual engagement can provide a level of release for those who are socially isolated.

Coping mechanisms are not necessarily positive, with drug and alcohol use emerging as a strong theme across the FGDs and interviews. Some of the drugs commonly consumed include weed and *khat* (known in Nairobi as *miraa* or *muguka*). Substance abuse as a consequence of trauma, shame, fear and guilt amongst LGBT populations has been widely documented, including among LGBT communities in Kenya (Doshi et al. 2020; Müller and Daskilewicz 2018; McKay 2011). In this study, participants offered multiple explanations for the use of drugs and alcohol, including financial precarity and limited social outlets. FGD1 also noted that psychoactive substances can make difficult circumstances tolerable, such as when they are driven to engage in sex work.

Other coping mechanisms include living together in high-walled compounds or houses. Shared accommodation provides LGBT refugee youth with more room and improved security. It can also provide opportunities for social connection: 'People ... held small parties at some houses, created some entertainment, so that people may relax. It became like a family' (KIR4). Not all LGBT refugee youth live in shared houses, but those who do not visit often, sometimes for extended periods, to escape the daily stressors of economic hardship and community discrimination. Whatever their living situation, LGBT refugee youth highlighted social activities as a key outlet for stress, noting that being around people with similar life experiences provides comfort and encouragement.

Formal interventions, such as support groups and prayer sessions, were regarded by some as a lifeline, in that they create opportunities for LGBT refugee youth to connect, share and confront issues:

> The support groups are unique ... they offer a safe space where one can open up, become vulnerable without having to answer the judgmental questions posed by ignorant and inconsiderate officials who don't understand how a gay man can be African and continue 'practising sin'.
>
> (KIR3)

Perhaps surprisingly, some of these psychosocial services are provided by the National Church Consortium of Kenya. While these programmes might offer spiritual nourishment, they are not always as affirming as people would like. Participants in FGD1 shared their appreciation for these efforts, even when they are accompanied by religious and moral judgments: 'even though they criticise us, they [still] have those services.' While there might be room for the healing and prayer sessions to improve, there is clear evidence of their value.

Strategies for improving health outcomes

By far, the most popular recommendation was for a more streamlined resettlement process, a finding that was not unexpected given the context. This was followed by recommendations aimed at making healthcare services more accessible, both in a physical sense (e.g. affordable transport options) and in an emotional sense (i.e. addressing insensitivity towards LGBT people). Participants emphasized the need for better dissemination of information about health services, including how these might be reached. Ideally, a network of service providers would be established and be given sensitization training. Expanding existing services to meet the unique needs of LGBT refugee youth was regarded as a sensible and achievable strategy for improved health outcomes. Participants also suggested sensitization training for CBOs, to be run parallel with education campaigns for frontline health workers. In particular, participants emphasized that organizations providing services to refugees should be trained on LGBT issues, while organizations targeting LGBT people should learn more about refugee needs. Beyond this, we suggest that non-medical community-based therapies may prove useful, given their efficacy in some African contexts (Motsi and Masango 2012). A comprehensive mental healthcare response for LGBT refugee youth could include more storytelling nights, sporting activities, prayer meetings and social events in safe houses, run in tandem with psychological interventions (especially for those dealing with trauma, isolation and internalized homo/transphobia). It must be emphasized that this recommendation draws directly on inputs from the FGDs and key informant interviews, and is suggested here in light of existing research on non-medical community-based therapies.

Participants also shared a desire to become self-sufficient through income-generating activities, arguing that this would assist in easing financial stress and help them cope with boredom and feelings of inadequacy. LGBT refugee youth have a clear desire to stay busy, as this would help keep their minds off their previous ordeals and present realities. Proposed income-generating activities included handicrafts and tailoring. Participants in the FGDs mentioned partnerships between NGOs and the UNHCR as a possible way to make this happen.

LGBT refugee youth also expressed a desire for safe spaces where they can gather regularly to update each other on what is going on in their lives and to discover each other's talents. Many suggested this would go a long way in fostering a positive self-identity among those struggling with shame, fear and guilt. These spaces would provide an opportunity for LGBT refugee youth to present themselves as something other than *just* LGBT refugees.

Finally, LGBT refugee youth recommended better monitoring of financial support by introducing a biometric cash-transfer scheme, as those most in need often miss out on resources channelled through CBOs. In particular, concerns were raised about potential stockpiling of donor resources: 'We sometimes hear that some people get money and organise a small event, take a few pictures for reporting, and then keep the biggest chunk of the money for themselves' (KIR3). Participants also recommended that the UNHCR resumes direct financial support to LGBT refugees in Nairobi. Currently, only the 'neediest' or most 'vulnerable' receive direct funding, yet the criteria for vulnerability remain opaque. Participants expressed frustration over this point, noting that resettled LGBT refugees seem to be deemed vulnerable and in need of financial assistance, whereas those still waiting in Kenya have no rights and are left to fend for themselves. Confusion over how financial support is distributed and accounted for fuels anger and mistrust among LGBT refugee youth and has the potential to exacerbate physical, sexual and mental health issues.

Conclusion

This chapter has revealed the salient health needs of LGBT refugee youth in Nairobi. In particular, it has explored the hurdles they face when seeking sexual and mental health support. The data shows that LGBT refugee youth lack the information and resources needed to safely access facilities, placing them at risk of negative health outcomes. While a small number of support services are operational, these are not always appropriate for this population. Other impediments include homo/transphobic behaviours of healthcare providers and the long distances to and from service locations, which can expose people to violence and deplete their limited finances. This combination of limited access and negative experiences intensifies the already precarious physical and mental state of LGBT refugee youth, resulting in self-loathing, isolation and depression.

In addition to identifying obstacles to health and wellbeing, this chapter has highlighted efforts by LGBT refugee youth to cope, such as seeking out the company of like-minded peers and using alcohol and substances, with the latter potentially leading to negative outcomes. Small social gatherings and CBO-led psychosocial and/or prayer sessions serve as crucial sites of affirmation for some individuals. However, while these interventions may provide relief, they are inadequate for addressing the significant health and wellbeing needs of this group.

Critically, there is a need for further research on the health needs of LGBT refugees in African contexts. This is particularly acute in states with limited protection mechanisms. Documenting the experiences of transgender people and lesbian woman is urgently needed, given that these groups rarely have access to appropriate and affirming services. Sourcing additional empirical data will not only expose limitations in healthcare provision for LGBT refugees – including LGBT refugee youth – but also draw attention to less studied aspects of LGBT mobilities.

Note

1   This is based on participants' disclosed ages. There are reports of LGBT refugees in Kenya changing their age so as not to appear a minor.

References

Albuquerque, G. et al. (2016), 'Access to Health Services by Lesbian, Gay, Bisexual, and Transgender Persons: Systematic Literature Review', *BMC International Health and Human Rights*, 16 (2). doi: 10.1186/s12914-015-0072-9.

Alessi, E. et al. (2020), '"Those Tablets, They Are Finding an Empty Stomach": A Qualitative Investigation of HIV Risk among Sexual and Gender Minority Migrants in Cape Town, South Africa', *Ethnicity & Health*. doi:10.1080/13557858.2020.1817342.

Baptiste, N. (2014), 'It's Not Just Uganda: Behind the Christian Right's Onslaught in Africa', *Foreign Policy in Focus*, 2 April. Available online: https://fpif.org/just-uganda-behind-christian-rights-onslaught-africa/ (accessed 1 October 2019).

Bhalla, N. (2018), 'U.N. Moves LGBT+ Refugees to Safe Houses after Kenya Camp Attacks', *Reuters*, 13 December. Available online: https://www.reuters.com/article/kenya-lgbt-refugees/un-moves-lgbt-refugees-to-safe-houses-after-kenya-camp-attacks-idUSL3N1YH3GX (accessed 25 March 2020).

Camminga, B (2020a), 'Encamped within a Camp: Transgender Refugees and Kakuma Refugee Camp (Kenya)', in J. Bjarnesen and S. Turner (eds), *Invisibility in African Displacements: From Structural Marginalization to Strategies of Avoidance*, 36–52, London: Zed Books.

Camminga, B (2020b), '"Go Fund Me": LGBTI Asylum Seekers in Kakuma Refugee Camp, Kenya', in C. Jacobson, M. Karlsen and S. Khosravi (eds), *Waitinghood: Unpacking the Temporalities of Waiting and Irregular Migration*, 131–48, London: Routledge.

Doshi, M. et al. (2020), 'Beyond Biomedical and Comorbidity Approaches: Exploring Associations between Affinity Group Membership, Health and Health Seeking Behaviour among MSM/MSW in Nairobi, Kenya', *Global Public Health*, 15 (7): 968–84.

Esan, O. et al. (2018), 'A Survey of Traditional and Faith Healers Providing Mental Health Care in Three Sub-Saharan African Countries', *Social Psychiatry and Psychiatric Epidemiology*, 54 (3): 395–403.

Evans, M. G. B., A. Cloete, N. Zungu and L. C. Simbayi (2016), 'HIV Risk among Men Who Have Sex with Men, Women Who Have Sex with Women, Lesbian, Gay, Bisexual and Transgender Populations in South Africa: A Mini-review', *Open AIDS Journal*, 10: 49–64.

Fitzsimons, T. (2020), 'Gay Refugees in Kenya Report Repeated Attacks from Locals', *NBC News*, 10 January. Available online: https://www.nbcnews.com/feature/nbc-out/gay-refugees-kenya-report-repeated-attacks-locals-n1113456 (accessed 25 March 2020).

Güler, A., M. Shevtsova and D. Venturi (eds) (2019), *LGBTI Asylum Seekers and Refugees from a Legal and Political Perspective: Persecution, Asylum and Integration*, Cham: Springer.

Harper, G. et al. (2021), 'Mental Health Challenges and Needs among Sexual and Gender Minority People in Western Kenya', *International Journal of Environmental Research and Public Health*, 18 (3). doi: 10.3390/ijerph18031311.

Heckathorn, D. (2011), 'Comment: Snowball versus Respondent-Driven Sampling', *Sociological Methodology*, 41 (1): 355–66.

Hodal, K. (2020), '"A Step away from Hell": The Young Male Refugees Selling Sex to Survive', *Guardian*, 21 February. Available online: https://www.theguardian.com/global-development/2020/feb/21/a-step-away-from-hell-the-young-male-refugees-selling-sex-to-survive-berlin-tiergarten (accessed 27 March 2020).

Hopkinson, R. A. et al. (2017), 'Persecution Experiences and Mental Health of LGBT Asylum Seekers', *Journal of Homosexuality*, 64 (12): 1650–66.

Human Rights Watch (2020), '*If We Don't Get Services, We Will Die': Tanzania's Anti-LGBT Crackdown and the Right to Health*, New York: Human Rights Watch.

Hunt, J., K. Bristowe, S. Chidyamatare and R. Harding (2017), '"They Will be Afraid to Touch You": LGBTI People and Sex Workers' Experiences of Accessing Healthcare in Zimbabwe: An In-depth Qualitative Study', *BMJ Global Health*, 2 (2). doi: 10.1136/bmjgh-2016-000168.

Ibrahim, A. (2015), 'LGBT Rights in Africa and the Discursive Role of International Human Rights Law', *African Human Rights Law Journal*, 15 (2): 263–81.

ILGA World (2019), *State-Sponsored Homophobia 2019: Global Legislation Overview Update*, Geneva: ILGA.

Izugbara, C. et al. (2020), 'Regional Legal and Policy Instruments for Addressing LGBT Exclusion in Africa', *Sexual and Reproductive Health Matters*, 28 (1). doi: 10.1080/26410397.2019.1698905.

Jjuuko, A. and M. Tabengwa (2018), 'Expanded Criminalisation of Consensual Same-sex Relations in Africa: Contextualising Recent Developments', in N. Nicol et al. (eds), *Envisioning Global LGBT Human Rights: (Neo)colonialism, Neoliberalism, Resistance and Hope*, 63–96, London: Institute of Commonwealth Studies.

Johnson, P. J. and S. Falcetta (2021), 'Beyond the Anti-Homosexuality Act: Homosexuality and the Parliament of Uganda', *Parliamentary Affairs*, 74 (1): 52–78.

Kaliza, M. (2017), 'Malawi's LGBT Battle for Health Care', *Deutsche Welle*, 26 January. Available online: https://p.dw.com/p/2WQL1 (accessed 25 September 2019).

Kaoma, K. (2018), *Christianity, Globalization, and Protective Homophobia: Democratic Contestation of Sexuality in Sub-Saharan Africa*, London: Palgrave.

Kerrigan, F. (2013), *Getting to Rights: The Human Rights of Lesbian, Gay, Bisexual, Transgender and Intersex People in Africa*, Copenhagen: Danish Institute for Human Rights.

Kirby, J. (2018), 'Tanzania's Anti-gay Crackdown Is Sending People into Hiding', *Vox*, 9 November. Available online: https://www.vox.com/2018/11/5/18057112/tanzania-anti-gay-crackdown-makonda-lgbt-arrest-dar-es-salaam (accessed 6 June 2020).

Kremin, M. (2017), 'To Be Out and In: Influencing Factors in the Recognition of SOGI-based Asylum Claims in South Africa and Kenya', MA dissertation, Columbia University, New York.

Luvuno, Z. et al. (2019), Evidence of Interventions for Improving Healthcare Access for Lesbian, Gay, Bisexual and Transgender People in South Africa: A Scoping Review', *Afr J Prim Health Care Fam Med*, 11 (1). doi: 10.4102/phcfm.v11i1.1367.

Marnell, J. (2021), *Seeking Sanctuary: Stories of Sexuality, Faith and Migration*, Johannesburg: Wits University Press.

McKay, B. (2011), 'Lesbian, Gay, Bisexual and Transgender Health Issues, Disparities and Information Resources', *Medical Reference Services Quarterly*, 30 (4): 393–401.

Millo, Y. (2013), *Invisible in the City: Protection Gaps Facing Sexual Minority Refugees and Asylum Seekers in Urban Ecuador, Ghana, Israel, and Kenya*, New York: HIAS.

Mkhize, S. and R. Maharaj (2021), 'Meeting the Sexual Health Needs of LGBT Youth: Perceptions and Experiences of University Students in KwaZulu-Natal, South Africa', *Journal of Social Service Research*, 47 (1): 56–72.

Moagi, M. M. et al. (2021), 'Mental Health Challenges of Lesbian, Gay, Bisexual and Transgender People: An Integrated Literature Review', *Health SA Gesondheid*. doi: 10.4102/hsag.v26i0.1487.

Motsi, R. G. and M. J. Masango (2012), 'Redefining Trauma in an African Context: A Challenge to Pastoral Care', *HTS Theological Studies*, 68 (1): 1–8.

Mprah, A. (2016), 'Sexual and Reproductive Health Needs of LGBT', *African Journal of Reproductive Health*, 20 (1): 16–20.

Müller, A. and K. Daskilewicz (2018), 'Mental Health among Lesbian, Gay, Bisexual, Transgender and Intersex People in East and Southern Africa', *European Journal of Public Health*, 28 (4): 270–1.

Müller, A., S. Spencer, T. Meer and K. Daskilewicz (2018), 'The No-go Zone: A Qualitative Study of Access to Sexual and Reproductive Health Services for Sexual and Gender Minority Adolescents in Southern Africa', *Reproductive Health*, 15 (12). doi: 10.1186/s12978-018-0462-2.

Müller, A. et al. (2021), 'Experience of and Factors Associated with Violence against Sexual and Gender Minorities in Nine African Countries: A Cross-sectional Study', *BMC Public Health*, 21 (1). doi: 10.1186/s12889-021-10314-w.

Murray, R. and F. Viljoen (2007), 'Towards Non-discrimination on the Basis of Sexual Orientation: The Normative Basis and Procedural Possibilities before African Commission on Human and Peoples' Rights and the African Union', *Human Rights Quarterly*, 29 (1): 86–111.

Mustanski, B., R. Andrews and J. Puckett (2016), 'The Effects of Cumulative Victimization on Mental Health among Lesbian, Gay, Bisexual, and Transgender Adolescents and Young Adults', *American Journal of Public Health*, 106 (3): 527–33.

Mutambara, J. and T. Sodi (2018), 'Exploring the Role of Spirituality in Coping with War Trauma among War Veterans in Zimbabwe', *SAGE Open*, 8 (1). doi: 10.1177/2158244017750433.

Nanima, R. D. (2017), 'An Evaluation of Kenya's Parallel Legal Regime on Refugees, and the Courts' Guarantee of Their Rights', *Law, Democracy & Development*, 21 (1): 42–67.

Nyanzi, S. (2013), 'Homosexuality, Sex Work, and HIV/AIDS in Displacement and Post-conflict Settings: The Case of Refugees in Uganda', *International Peacekeeping*, 20 (4): 450–68.

Oloka-Onyango, J. (2015), 'Debating Love, Human Rights and Identity Politics in East Africa: The Case of Uganda and Kenya', *African Human Rights Law Journal*, 15: 28–57.

Pincock, K. (2021), 'UNHCR and LGBTI Refugees in Kenya: The Limits of "Protection"', *Disasters*, 45 (4): 844–64.

Sanders, E. et al. (2015), 'Kenyan MSM: No Longer a Hidden Population', *AIDS*, 25 (3). doi: 10.1097/QAD.0000000000000928.

Shangani, S., V. Naanyu, D. Operario and B. Genberg (2018), 'Stigma and Healthcare-Seeking Practices of Men Who Have Sex with Men in Western Kenya: A Mixed-Methods Approach for Scale Validation', *AIDS Patient Care and STDs*, 32 (11): 477–86.

Shidlo, A. and J. Ahola (2013), 'Mental Health Challenges of LGBT Forced Migrants', *Forced Migration Review*, 42: 9–11.

Taylor, J. (2019), 'Imprisoned LGBTQ Kenyan Refugees Report Physical and Sexual Abuse from Guards and Prisoners', *NewNowNext*, 21 March. Accessed online: http://www.newnownext.com/lgbt-kenyan-refugees-abuse-prison/03/2019/ (accessed on 1 October 2019).

van Klinken, A. (2019), *Kenyan, Christian, Queer: Religion, LGBT Activism, and Arts of Resistance in Africa*, Pennsylvania: Penn State University Press.

Wesangula, D. (2017), 'On the Run from Persecution: How Kenya Became a Haven for LGBT Refugees', *Guardian*, 23 February. Available online: https://www.theguardian.com/global-development-professionals-network/2017/feb/23/on-the-run-from-persecution-how-kenya-became-a-haven-for-lgbt-refugees (accessed 27 March 2020).

World Health Organisation (1948), *Constitution of the World Health Organization*. Available online: http://apps.who.int/gb/bd/PDF/bd47/EN/constitution-en.pdf?ua=1 (accessed 25 June 2020).

Zahn, R. et al. (2016), 'Human Rights Violations among Men Who Have Sex with Men in Southern Africa: Comparisons between Legal Contexts', *PLoS ONE*, 11 (1). doi: 10.1371/journal.pone.0147156.

Zomorodi, G. (2016), 'Responding to LGBT Forced Migration in East Africa', *Forced Migration Review*, 52: 91–3.

Chapter 11

DIFFERENTIAL MOVEMENTS: LESBIAN MIGRANT WOMEN'S ENCOUNTERS WITH, AND NEGOTIATIONS OF, SOUTH AFRICA'S BORDER REGIME

Verena Hucke

'It's not easy living in South Africa as an LGBTI, especially if you are black.'
(Tamayi, lesbian migrant)[1]

In both academic literature and policy responses, the migrating subject is overwhelmingly constructed as heterosexual, cisgender and male. Despite emerging recognition that migration processes are not only gendered but also heavily shaped by sexuality – as Eithne Luibhéid (2004) notes, 'sexuality more generally also structures every aspect of immigrant experiences' (227) – only a few studies systematically include gender and sexuality in their analyses (e.g. Luibhéid 2008; Manalansan 2006). The little research that currently exists shows that cisgender migrant women's bodies are heavily exposed to normativization and exclusion within border regimes (Luibhéid 2002). This is intensified for migrants who identify as lesbian and who often experience a double marginalization stemming from their gender *and* their sexuality. Scholars of queer migration have begun to highlight the ways in which sexuality and gender shape experiences of migration, yet the bulk of research focuses on cisgender gay men (e.g. Carrillo et al. 2014; Eboko and Awondo 2013; Manalansan 2003). Alternatively, they rely on the LGBT acronym (meaning 'lesbian, gay, bisexual and transgender') or use 'queer' as an umbrella term, thus obfuscating the ways in which cisgender gay men are the primary subjects of research (e.g. Hübner 2016; Zomorodi 2016; Fobear 2015).

In light of this trend, it would seem that lesbians suffer the fate of being part of the acronym without quite being present.[2] While there are exceptions (e.g. Alvarez 2020; Liinason 2020; Luibhéid 2020; Lewis 2013), research in both the Global North and the Global South largely disregards the experiences of cisgender lesbian women who migrate. In the South African context, researchers respond to the silencing of lesbian voices in various ways: in many cases, lesbian experiences are subsumed under the LGBT acronym and largely disregarded (e.g. Bhagat 2018; Beetar 2016), while other researchers include the voices and experiences of lesbian women alongside those of gay and transgender migrants (e.g. Marnell, Oliveira and Khan 2021; Dill et al. 2016). This chapter takes these observations as its starting point and adds to the expanding field of research on sexualities[3] and migrations by shifting focus to lesbian migrant experiences in a key Global South location.

In this chapter, I argue that lesbian migrant[4] women in South Africa make visible social conflicts around mobility, rights and social participation by actively reconfiguring multiple borders. This is most obvious in how lesbian migrant women navigate the disconnect between their de jure rights and how these are recognized and applied in practice (de facto). This produces visible inconsistencies between the Rainbow Nation narrative promoted by the South African state and the everyday lived realities of lesbian migrant women who could potentially apply for asylum on the basis of sexuality.[5] Drawing on narrative interviews conducted in Johannesburg in 2019, this chapter shows how these women navigate borders at multiple scales and in complex ways. It first outlines the asylum process in South Africa and interrogates the narrative of the Rainbow Nation before examining how bordering processes are experienced and negotiated by these women.

The theoretical perspective outlined here brings the experiences of lesbian migrant women to the fore, highlighting how they negotiate the disjuncture between the rights enshrined in the South African constitution and the heteronormative logic underpinning social relationships and state practices. At the same time, the chapter opens up space for individual agency to be recognized by documenting the ways in which lesbian migrant women negotiate South Africa's migration and border regime. A regime perspective recognizes that discourses, practices and politics relating to migration and borders can be configured in different ways and are therefore open to contestation (Pott, Rass and Wolff 2018). A border regime is a set of practices and structures related to migration, such as discourses, politics and different actors, whose positionalities are dynamic and flexible, rather than fixed (Schwenken 2018; Karakayalı and Tsianos 2007). For the purposes of this chapter, I limit my analysis of the challenges and negotiations linked to South Africa's border regime to two social arenas: labour rights and faith practices.

The structure of asylum

The implementation of the South African Refugees Amendment Act on 1 January 2020 was accompanied by extensive critique from civil society (e.g. Nyoka 2020; Shivji 2020). Rather than address the myriad challenges that have been documented since the introduction of the original Refugees Act in 1998,[6] the Amendment drastically limits the rights of refugees and asylum seekers, reinforcing their vulnerability and precarity (Scalabrini Centre 2020). The Amendment – introduced alongside a restructuring of the Department of Home Affairs (DHA), the entity tasked with implementing the Refugees Act – is suggestive of growing efforts by the state to reduce specific migration flows and strengthen the country's borders (Carciotto 2020; Mathers and Landau 2007). This move continues a trend – first noted a decade ago – of transforming 'the protective nature of the refugee system … into one of control' (Amit 2011: 458). The government's actions point to a re-configuration of South Africa's border regime, in which the country's territorial and socio-cultural boundaries are increasingly presented as under imminent threat and therefore in need of safeguarding. In rebranding international migration as a security issue, South Africa has firmly aligned itself with Global North responses to migration 'management' (Mthembu-Salter et al. 2014).

Despite South Africa's long-standing efforts to curb migration, the country continues to be a major destination for those fleeing homophobia and transphobia (Palmary 2016; Oliveira, Meyers and Vearey 2016). This is, in large part, due to being the only country on the continent that offers constitutional protection against discrimination based on sexuality and/or gender, with the latter encompassing both gender identity and expression. According to the South African Refugees Act, read in conjunction with the South African constitution, LGBT persons who flee their countries of origin because of homophobic or transphobic persecution can qualify for refugee status. However, the South African state's efforts to strictly control human mobility, coupled with negative perceptions of and general scepticism towards migrants at the government and societal levels, are reflected in the operations of the country's asylum system (McKnight 2008).

Upon reaching a port of entry for South Africa, a prospective asylum seeker must indicate their intention to apply for protection, after which they will be granted a non-renewable transit permit. This gives the holder five days to lodge a formal claim at the nearest Refugee Reception Office (RRO).[7] To complete this process, the person is required to present their transit permit, proof of identification from their country of origin and any travel documents. In the initial eligibility interview, conducted by a Refugee Reception Officer, the person's biographical data, photograph and fingerprints are captured, as well as their reason for applying for asylum. After the interview, a temporary Section 22 Permit is issued – usually with a validity period of six months – which allows the applicant to stay in South Africa until a final adjudication is reached.[8] According to DHA regulations, the merits of an asylum claim should be assessed through a second interview with a Refugee Status Determination Officer (RSDO), who has the power to grant refuge, reject the application or refer it to the Standing Committee for Refugee Affairs. In practice, applicants wait many years, sometimes decades, for an RSDO interview, forcing them to survive on temporary permits that must be renewed every three or so months (Camminga 2019). These bureaucratic delays leave applicants in a state of limbo, either forced to expose themselves repeatedly to interrogation by DHA officials or to live without papers. Research suggests that the eventuality of being granted asylum is highly improbable for most applicants (Marnell, Oliveira and Khan 2021; Dill et al. 2016). Reasons for this range from 'corruption to inaccessibility of the system to appallingly poor decision-making by the Refugee Status Determination Officers' (Palmary 2016: 16).

Beyond the Rainbow Nation

The narrative of the Rainbow Nation, in which South Africa is not only regarded as a supposed safe haven for LGBT persons but also actively markets itself – especially in international tourism – as the 'gay capital of Africa' (Camminga and Matebeni 2019; Davids and Matebeni 2017), continues to shape how the country is perceived. As B Camminga (2019) notes:

> [South Africa] is widely considered the most multicultural and egalitarian state on the continent, especially given the growing antagonisms across the continent regarding human rights, issues of sexuality, gender identity/expression and sexual orientation, the legacy of colonial era penal codes, and a rise in a particular kind of unrelenting heteronormativity.
>
> (10)

The country's high rate of xenophobic violence stands in stark contrast to its self-representation as the Rainbow Nation. Various governance failures have led to deep social tensions around a perceived influx of migrants to the country. Such concerns erupt periodically into widespread violence, especially in Gauteng province, which includes the metropolises of Johannesburg and Pretoria. In September 2019, an outbreak of violence caused the death of at least twelve people and left many more injured (Mlilo 2019). Notably, this violence is not directed at all migrants equally, but rather at those perceived to be a 'problem' (Landau 2019). Public discourse concerning such violence centres on the term 'xenophobia' or 'Afrophobia', as attacks most often target black migrants from elsewhere on the African continent (Dadoo 2019). However, there is a danger in reducing this violence to a migration issue, as to do so masks the underlying reasons and conditions that drive such tensions in the first place. As Loren Landau notes, xenophobic violence is better understood as a societal and governmental issue, arising from massive social inequality and the inability of the ruling African National Congress party 'to truly take on the responsibility of governing a deeply divided, angry country' (2019). Xenophobic violence is, he argues, a manifestation of local struggles around land, work and political influence, rather than a straightforward 'migration problem'.

Despite its progressive laws and Rainbow Nation image, South Africa remains a largely hostile environment for LGBT persons. Non-heterosexual desires are widely regarded as 'un-African' and sinful, leading to violent punishments for those seen to transgress sexual and gender norms (Gunkel 2010; Gontek 2009). 'Un-African' also reads as foreign, which points to the complex entanglement of homophobia/transphobia and xenophobia in the reading of lesbian migrant bodies, as well as to Christian missionarism and European colonialism. The combination of homophobia/transphobia with xenophobia creates 'a complex set of legal and political structures that render them [LGBT migrants] hyper-visible and invisible at different moments and with different consequences' (Palmary 2016: 21). Due to entrenched misconceptions at both a societal and an institutional level, LGBT asylum claimants are expected to narrate their experiences and perform their sexuality and/or gender in ways that align with popular stereotypes. Yet this hyper-visibility can be dangerous, often exposing LGBT claimants to danger while queuing at an RRO or accessing other services (Camminga 2017). This means that LGBT claimants end up in a paradoxical situation: they need to be hyper-visible to be believed but must simultaneously avoid being noticed to stay safe.

Bordering processes

'In South Africa, I am allowed to be *who I am* and *do what I want* – like my sexual preference, right. But, at the same time, it is not favouring for foreigners.'

(Amahle, lesbian migrant, emphasis in original)

When reflecting on their lives, many of the interviewees stressed that they feel a certain level of freedom. Amahle, a self-identified lesbian woman in her late twenties, lives in the metropolitan area of Johannesburg. She was born in a Southern African country[9] and followed her mother to South Africa as a young adult. She points to the possibilities her migration has offered her, specifically the chance to be herself and do what she wants. Her comments draw on the Rainbow Nation narrative, as materialized through the constitutional protection against homophobia and related laws, including the possibility of applying for asylum based on homophobic persecution. Sexuality in this sense refers not only to a certain kind of desire, identity or practice, but also to social structures, norms and discourses: 'The bare biological facts of sexuality do not speak for themselves; they must be expressed socially. Sex feels individual, or at least private, but those feelings always incorporate the roles, definitions, symbols and meanings of the worlds in which they are constructed' (Ross and Rapp 1981: 51). Amahle's statement suggests that sexuality is also a category of power and social organization (Tamale 2011a), as it has the potential to place individuals at the centre or the periphery (Hark 2005), depending on the state in which they live and the geographical area they inhabit within that state (Marnell, Oliveira and Khan 2021). Thus, for Amahle, her sexuality relates her in a specific way to opportunities, rights and protection. As a lesbian woman in South Africa, she experiences a certain level of freedom, yet at the same time her status as a foreigner brings problems. As will be shown below, the intersection of these two identities adds a unique level of complexity to the experiences of lesbian migrant woman.

In order to consider these complexities of experience and relate them to the variety of actors, interests and institutions that give shape to them, I draw on the concept of the border regime. As flagged above, this refers to discourses, practices and structures that shape responses to migration. The very notion of a border regime is intended 'to generate answers to the questions and problems that are raised by the dynamic elements and processes related to migration' (Karakayalı and Tsianos 2007: 13 – own translation). A closely linked concept is the 'autonomy of migration' (e.g. Mezzadra 2010; Bojadžijev and Karakayalı 2007; Moulier-Boutang 1992), which focuses on processes of negotiation and possible resistance by people on the move. In such a reading, migrants are understood as active agents in the configuration of a border regime, rather than as passive objects controlled by the politics of the states and/or supranational areas they may enter, leave or transit through. Recognizing migrants as political actors means that social conflicts around migration, rights and social participation need to be brought into focus (Schwenken 2018), while also foregrounding the border regime 'as an effect of a multiplicity of agents and practices' (Hess and Kasparek 2017: 59). This echoes Étienne Balibar's point about the impossibility of defining borders:

> [T]o mark out a border is, precisely, to define a territory, to delimit it, and so to register the identity of that territory, or confer one upon it. Conversely, however, to define or identify in general is nothing other than to trace a border, to assign boundaries or borders ... The theorist who attempts to define what a border is is in danger of going round in circles, as the very representation of the border is the precondition for any definition.
>
> (2002: 76)

Amahle's experiences offer a powerful example of bordering in action. When reflecting on her desire for decent work conditions, Amahle describes her struggle to access legal documentation. She entered South Africa on a study visa,[10] but due to unfortunate circumstances is no longer in possession of her passport. The embassy for her country of origin has refused to issue a new one, claiming that they do not have the materials needed: '[They say] there is no papers to print the passport.' Her multiple attempts to formalize her stay in South Africa have failed:

> Honestly, I gave up because going over, over and over again trying to get papers and you get rejected or you get told that 'I know a guy that you can pay'. I have done it before. ... But you cannot get paperwork and you cannot get a proper job ... and for me, judging from my [academic] results, I should be working, like having a proper job, a better job, and most of us [migrants] end up working in restaurants or jobs that do not allow you to have paperwork. Like, people obviously fear work, a job that does not care for the people [employees]. People [employers] that obviously want to use you and then like 'Yeah, we can pay peanuts and that is fine' because they know you are not going to complain at the end of the day. ... Where are you going to complain?

There is a clear link between the actions of her country of origin – the refusal to issue a new passport – and Amahle's situation in South Africa. Struggles with the former result in struggles with the latter, and vice versa. That this is a form of bordering is even more evident when read in light of the recent Refugees Amendment Act, under which seeking consular services of any kind can potentially result in the revocation of a permit (Freedom House 2020). Such policies create continuing precarity. Amahle's lack of papers mean that, despite her good academic performance, she is forced to undertake informal, poorly paid jobs in which employers exploit her inability to exercise her labour rights.

> Then you get police officers. [They], like, take advantage of the fact that you do not have paperwork. They stop you along the way: 'Passport! ID!' 'I do not have my passport.' 'Okay, give us 150 [rands] and then you can go.' At the same time, we are also trying to work for that money that they want, and they take it away. ... It is a stumbling block. ... I was arrested once for my [lack of] paperwork. ... I think it was 2015, if not 2014, and my mom had to pay 500 bucks for me ... to be let go from the holding cell. That takes the whole week [to be released] and the holding cells are not holding cells for foreigners. One gets a holding cell for everyone. So, we go [in] there as thieves ... [even if] you have never done a crime in your whole life.

In addition to employers, police officers play a key role in the border regime. Both Amahle and her mother are forced to pay bribes so that they are not arrested, or to secure their release if they are detained. Those without papers, including Amahle, are subjected to overexploitation, in that they must negotiate bordering techniques in multiple social fields. Without minimizing the brutality of this overexploitation, it is worth noting that moments of negotiation are present, such as using cash payments to avoid criminal prosecution. This shows that the border regime is 'a space of conflict and contestation between the various actors trying to govern the border and the movements of migration' (Hess and Kasparek 2017: 60). Bordering materializes around the absence or presence of papers, as Raphael Dou'a, LGBTI Migrant Refugee Coordinator at Access Chapter 2 (a local NGO), explained in an interview:

> Everything is interconnected through papers. Because if you do not have papers, you cannot sign [a lease]. You cannot have a decent house, ... if you want to live like in a decent area where you feel totally safe you cannot, because they are going to ask you [for papers].

At first, Amahle applied for a study permit and not for asylum, because she did not feel safe enough to speak about her sexuality: 'It was during the time when ... I was just applying for a study permit. So, I was not in a comfortable *space* to talk about anything else' (emphasis in original). This points to the contradictory discourses that Amahle has to navigate. On the one hand, sexual diversity is embraced under the Rainbow Nation, but on the other it is widely regarded as sinful and unnatural. Yet this is more than a matter of personal feelings or whether one feels comfortable disclosing one's identity. Dou'a believes that South Africa's asylum system discriminates against LGBT applicants on a structural level:

> For them [DHA] to actually recognise the fact that you are in South Africa ... because your life was in danger because of your sexual orientation or gender expression. That's the main problem leading to all the abuse, because what they

are going to tell you is that maybe you do not look lesbian ... or they are also going to tell you to bring proof of your sexuality. ... But *how* even do you prove your sexuality? ... And then everyone that is actually applying on the basis of that is systematically rejected.

(emphasis in original)

The experiences of Amahle and others point to complex bordering processes in which sexuality as both a category of power and a form of social organization is used to re/produce and maintain borders (Hucke 2021). Interlinked bordering techniques serve as a way to regulate the ability of certain bodies, sexualities and genders to enter the territory, either by rejecting them outright or by relegating them to a limbo state.

Differential movements

Borders are characterized by 'their polysemic character – that is to say, the fact that borders never exist in the same way for individuals belonging to different social groups' (Balibar 2002: 78–9). Lesbian migrant women experience intersecting forms of discrimination and oppression – for example, when trying to access safe housing or decent working conditions, or when searching for acceptance in religious spaces. Individuals like Amahle, who need to navigate bordering processes while questioning the hetero-patriarchal order through their very existence, might be considered inhabitants of what Gloria Anzaldúa calls the borderland. This is defined as 'a vague and undetermined place created by the emotional residue of an unnatural boundary. It is in a constant state of transition. The prohibited and forbidden are its inhabitants' (2012 [1987]: 3). As a lesbian migrant woman, Amahle straddles multiple borders – or, in Anzaldúa's terminology, unnatural boundaries. As a woman born outside of South Africa who does not possess documentation, Amahle finds herself in a precarious state, frequently exposed to exploitation. The inhabitants of the borderland develop agency through their capacity to navigate complex and contradictory social conditions (Kron 2010). These 'differential movements' (Sandoval 1998) are not necessarily related to territorial borders, but negotiations and movements 'through, over, and within any dominant system of ... race, gender, sex, class, or national meanings' (Sandoval 1998: 360). The notion of differential movements points to the ways that border regimes are extended to sexual and gender boundaries and to processes that naturalize both heteronormativity *and* state sovereignty (Salter 2011). Referring to the asylum application process, Dou'a points to the violent interrogations of LGBT persons who apply for asylum with the DHA:

And they will actually ask you so many questions: Are you with a woman or are you with a man? Are you playing the man's role? Are you playing the woman's role? They are going to ask you so many embarrassing questions. ... They [DHA] do not believe that they [LGBT migrants] are actually in danger in their countries [of origin] for being gay. Even with the presence of these laws that are getting people out of their countries, because [of] how laws are dangerous, but they do not believe them. They say 'No, your country is a democratic country. Your country is a free country, so your country can provide you protection.'

This quote highlights the relationship between sovereignty and sexual/gender boundaries, in that the borders of the heterosexual matrix must also be constantly regulated so as to maintain the illusion of coherency and stability (Reddy, Monro and Matebeni 2018; Tamale 2011a; Butler 1990). By questioning who plays the 'man' in a lesbian relationship, DHA officials engage in a form of policing, demanding that lesbian relationships be conceptualized and read within a heteronormative framework.

Tamayi, a self-identified lesbian woman who also comes from a Southern African country, lives in the metropolitan area of Johannesburg. Now in her late twenties, she followed her mother to South Africa as a young child. Like Amahle, Tamayi has struggled to formalize her stay, but was successful in gaining documentation through informal channels. Speaking about the xenophobic attacks that took place in Gauteng province in September 2019, Tamayi shares her view on how violence and hate can be overcome. By framing her response in terms of unity, Tamayi echoes discourses of the Rainbow Nation, but quickly points out that this concept is far from a lived reality:

I feel like we just need to be together and be united, stick together, stop discriminating [against] one another. Just live in peace and harmony. I mean, this is a *free* world. God created this world. So, I do not think ... anybody has any right or whatsoever to chase anyone away. I feel like we all deserve a chance and an opportunity. So, I feel like we must be united, but South Africa is *not* united. It is *not* a Rainbow Nation. Yes, they may paint it like it is a Rainbow Nation, [that] people live in peace and harmony. That is a lie. A complete lie, you know. There is no such thing.

(emphasis in original)

Tamayi elaborates her desire to live free from discrimination and oppression, but simultaneously questions how realistic the Rainbow Nation concept is. In referencing this hegemonic narrative, Tamayi points to the persistence of the 'imagined South Africa' (Camminga 2019) and the fact that, despite its progressive laws, the country remains a hostile environment for LGBT persons. Tamayi further mentions her belief in a higher power that created the world, thus offering a religious justification for her right to stay in South Africa and to live in peace and harmony. In particular, she refers to the Christian principle of loving one's neighbour. This can also be interpreted as insisting on rights associated with citizenship. Tamayi and others who are migrating to the country '*act* as citizens and insist that they *are* already citizens' (Mezzadra 2011: 12, emphasis in original). Speaking about her childhood, Tamayi further elaborates on her religious beliefs:

I was brought up Christian. I am still Christian. ... I am very religious, and most of the LGBTI community living in South Africa are religious as well, although they do not agree with certain things [scriptural interpretations] ... that forbid [the] LGBTI community. But that does not take it away from them. They still go to church. ... We have had several cases where the pastors would, like, chase the LGBTI members from the church and say 'I know that you are an LGBTI member so leave. Go away! Get out of my church!' ... We have had cases like that but still it does not change the fact that we are religious and that we also believe in God and we are not sinners, you know. We are not sinners. We just love the same gender and that does not make us sinners. We do not kill. We do not do anything bad. We do not steal. ... I mean they should just let us live our lives. I mean, we do nothing bad. We just love each other and that is all, you know.

In this excerpt, Tamayi positions herself as a proud Christian. She frames her belief with a broader claim that most of the LGBT community in South Africa are religious and attend church, even when there are various contestations and barriers, such as pastors who denounce particular sexual and/or gender practices. Tamayi explicitly refuses to be cast out as a sinner. Her strong assertion of faith allows her to transgress the subject position foreseen for her in discourses linking homosexuality to sin. Instead, she posits a counterargument about 'real' sinners – that is, people who do 'bad' things, such as killing or stealing, rather than those who do 'good' things, like loving. Significantly, Tamayi distances herself from attempts to control her body and beliefs. She refuses to be excluded and demands the right to stay and be recognized, not simply as a lesbian woman, but also as a lesbian *migrant* woman. The pastor, as a representative of the local church, reproduces the 'unnatural boundaries' of heteronormativity, a practice that harks back to missionarism and colonialism. Religion is a site of power, whether for reinforcing or challenging authority. When Tamayi articulates her beliefs *within* Christian traditions and claims those traditions as her own, religion becomes a site of power not only 'for oppression and exclusion but also for empowerment and agency' (van Klinken 2019: 15).

Amahle experiences similar encounters in church, where non-heterosexual desires are framed as a sin:

Because you are told, as a Christian, Sodom and Gomorra happened because there were lesbians and gays. ... I go to churches; I pray ... I am a Christian, but then most of the time, I end up not going to church because I end up wondering what are they going to preach about. Because what if, on that day, they are going to speak about Sodom and Gomorra? ... I go back home with all those thoughts going on in my head and I am like, 'Okay, I know for a fact I am going to die one day, but I do not know where I am going to go.' As a *Christian*, I know there is *hell* and I know there is *heaven* and somebody has already told me that I am going to hell. ... I am like, 'I have been to hell anyway ... I am *not* that person, just ... because the church said [I am].'

(emphasis in original)

Amahle applies a different strategy when facing exclusion at church, choosing to separate herself rather than demand the right to stay. She rejects the association of her sexuality with sin and questions the power of the church to define who is and is not going to hell. It is possible to observe her efforts to exert control over her destiny, albeit in a very different way to Tamayi.

The exclusion of LGBT people from the social arena of religion is reflected in the asylum system (Marnell 2021). Dou'a elaborates on the impossibilities of being gay and Christian within South Africa's bureaucratic asylum system:

> First of all, what we should understand that the South African constitution ... says that no one is allowed to be discriminated ... on the basis of his race, his religious beliefs or sexual orientation and gender expression. But that is not what is happening at Home Affairs because they will tell you that you cannot say that you are a Christian and then you are gay. That does not match. ... One of our clients went there and was told that. They gave him a very discriminative response, very discriminative answer. They told him that ... he cannot say that he is from a Christian country and that he is gay. It is impossible for him to be gay and Christian.

This points not only to the overlap between these different social arenas, but also to the interdependence of discourses on homosexuality, Christianity, nationhood and the asylum system. This echoes Luibhéid's (2002) argument that '[s]exual regulation at the border articulates sexual regulation within' (xxi). In other words, sexualities and genders that are socially and politically privileged within the state – or, in this case, within the micro-politics in daily life – are also privileged by the border regime. Despite the narrative of the Rainbow Nation, the sexual and gendered borders within South African society materialize in the rejection of asylum claims and hence limit the rights of those living in the country.

Conclusion

In this chapter I have applied a border regime perspective to analyse the experiences of lesbian migrant women in South Africa, exposing social conflicts around migration, rights and social participation. In particular, I have argued that migrants must be seen as key actors within border regimes. As the data above suggests, migrants are active participants in the configuration of border regimes, rather than passive objects.

The empirical examples introduced show that different actors, such as DHA officials, police officers, employers and preachers, are involved in the production of borders, be it through acts of bribery, arrest, exploitation or moral condemnation. The attempt to govern both sexual/gender borders and territorial borders is reflected in the disjuncture between, on the one hand, the rights outlined in

South Africa's constitution and the Rainbow Nation narrative and, on the other, the precarity within the lives of lesbian migrant women. Thus, the border spreads 'from the territorial borders at the edge of the states into a multiplicity of locations' (Yuval-Davis, Wemyss and Cassidy 2019: 1).

Being a lesbian migrant in South Africa involves conflicts in different parts of life. In the cases discussed here, contestations around faith and religion are enmeshed with claims to citizenship, recognition, safety and security. In demanding space within a religious community – not only as a migrant, but also as a lesbian woman – Tamayi refuses subject positions foreseen for her in dominant discourses, particularly those that meld religious conservatism to xenophobia and homophobia. Exclusionary practices within churches affect not only LGBT migrants but also all LGBT persons living in South Africa.[11] In such a situation, a border regime perspective can tell us something important about the operations and functions of migration systems. This is evident in Dou'a's quotes above, which show how DHA officials reject intersectional positionalities and use sexuality/ gender as grounds for rejecting protection claims. Tamayi and Amahle navigate the complex and sometimes contradictory social conditions they find themselves in and thus challenge the heteronormative and national borders that are produced and drawn symbolically, structurally and in everyday practices. Both interviewees reject exclusionary practices, both in church and in society more generally. They navigate homophobic and xenophobic discourses and exclusionary politics through differential movements, which are configured as a demand for citizenship rights – the right to stay in church and the right to stay in the country.

Acknowledgements

I would like to thank all of the interviewees for generously sharing their time, stories and experiences. I would also like to thank the editors and the reviewers for their feedback, the Diversity Lab for their comments on an earlier version of this chapter and Sophia Pianowski for proofreading.

Funding

The field research was funded by the University of Kassel, the Kasseler International Graduate Centre for Social Sciences, and by the Sulzmann-Foundation through a scholarship awarded to Dr Elisabeth Grohs.

Notes

1　All names are pseudonyms.
2　Which is, in a different way, also the case for transgender migrants.

3   'Reference to sexuality in the plural does not simply point to the diverse forms of orientation, identity or status. It is a political call to conceptualise sexuality outside the normative social orders and frameworks that view it through binary oppositions and simplistic labels. In other words, thinking in terms of multiple sexualities is crucial to disperse the essentialism embedded in so much sexuality research' (Tamale 2011b: 11).

4   Despite having exposed themselves repeatedly to the South African asylum system, the interviewees referred to themselves as 'migrant' or 'foreigner', rather than as 'refugee' or 'asylum seeker'. Therefore, I use the term migrant as an umbrella term for (forced) migrants, refugees and asylum seekers. For a critique on the distinction between migrating people in different (state-defined) categories, see Heaven Crawley and Dimitris Skleparis (2018).

5   Several of the interviewees did not move to South Africa solely because of their sexuality, but because of family ties, educational opportunities and employment prospects. This is why I borrow the notion of the 'potentiality of asylum' from Camminga whose 'use of asylum spread to those that could potentially apply for asylum but for various reasons had chosen not to' (2019: 274).

6   These challenges include, among others, an overwhelmed asylum system, resource limitations, a lack of information for applicants, a lack of quality of interpreters, corruption, misapplication of legal concepts and serious flaws in the status determination process (Amit 2011).

7   An overview of the asylum application process can be found on the DHA website: www.dha.gov.za/index.php/immigration-services/refugee-status-asylum (accessed 1 September 2020). For details of how the new Amendment may limit a person's ability to apply for asylum (e.g. because they did not enter through a port of entry or because they were not granted a transit visa), see Scalabrini Centre (2020).

8   Before the introduction of the Amendment, a temporary asylum permit would nominally grant the holder automatic work and study rights. While this right has now been revoked, it is yet to be widely enforced by the state.

9   To preserve anonymity, interviewee's country-of-origin information and exact ages will be omitted.

10 Anecdotal evidence suggests that this is a common method of entering South Africa for LGBT people who fear/wish to avoid the stresses of the asylum system (Marnell 2021; Camminga 2019).

11 It is important to note that there are also inclusionary practices within the social arena of religion, such as the LGBT Ministry at Holy Trinity Catholic Church in Johannesburg (Marnell 2021).

References

Alvarez, E. F. (2020), 'Finding Sequins in the Rubble: The Journeys of Two Latina Migrant Lesbians in Los Angeles', *Journal of Lesbian Studies*, 24 (2): 77–93.

Amit, R. (2011), 'No Refuge: Flawed Status Determination and the Failures of South Africa's Refugee System to Provide Protection', *International Journal of Refugee Law*, 23 (3): 458–88.

Anzaldúa, G. (2012 [1987]), *Borderlands/La Frontera: The New Mestiza*, San Francisco: Aunt Lute Books.

Balibar, É. (2002), *Politics and the Other Scene*, London: Verso.

Beetar, M. (2016), 'Intersectional (Un)Belongings: Lived Experiences of Xenophobia and Homophobia', *Agenda*, 30 (1): 96–103.

Bhagat, A. (2018), 'Forced (Queer) Migration and Everyday Violence: The Geographies of Life, Death, and Access in Cape Town', *Geoforum*, 89: 155–63.

Bojadžijev, M. and S. Karakayalı (2007), 'Autonomie der Migration: 10 Thesen zu einer Methode', in Transit Migration Forschungsgruppe (eds), *Turbulente Ränder: Neue Perspektiven auf Migration an den Grenzen Europas*, 203–9, Bielefeld: transcript.

Butler, J. (1990), *Gender Trouble: Feminism and the Subversion of Identity*, New York: Routledge.

Camminga, B (2017), 'Categories and Queues: The Structural Realities of Gender and the South African Asylum System', *Transgender Studies Quarterly*, 4 (1): 61–77.

Camminga, B (2019), *Transgender Refugees and the Imagined South Africa: Bodies over Borders and Borders over Bodies*, London: Palgrave Macmillan.

Camminga, B and Z. Matebeni (eds) (2019), *Beyond the Mountain: Queer Life in 'Africa's Gay Capital'*, Johannesburg: Unisa Press.

Carciotto, S. (2020), 'Making Asylum Seekers More Vulnerable in South Africa: The Negative Effects of Hostile Asylum Policies on Livelihoods', *International Migration*. doi: 10.1111/imig.12788.

Carrillo, H., J. Fontdevila, R. A. Lewis and N. A. Naples (2014), 'Border Crossings and Shifting Sexualities among Mexican Gay Immigrant Men: Beyond Monolithic Conceptions', *Sexualities*, 17 (8): 919–38.

Crawley, H. and D. Skleparis (2018), 'Refugees, Migrants, Neither, Both: Categorical Fetishism and the Politics of Bounding in Europe's "Migration Crisis"', *Journal of Ethnic and Migration Studies*, 44 (1): 48–64.

Dadoo, S. (2019), 'South Africa: Xenophobia Is in Fact Afrophobia, Call It What It Is', *The Elephant*, 11 September. Available online: www.theelephant.info/op-eds/2019/09/11/south-africa-xenophobia-is-in-fact-afrophobia-call-it-what-it-is (accessed 1 September 2020).

Davids, N. and Z. Matebeni (2017), 'Queer Politics and Intersectionality in South Africa', *Safundi*, 18 (2): 161–7.

Dill, L. J., J. Vearey, E. Oliveira and G. M. Castillo (2016), '"Son of the Soil … Daughters of the Land": Poetry Writing as a Strategy of Citizen-Making for Lesbian, Gay, and Bisexual Migrants and Asylum Seekers in Johannesburg', *Agenda*, 30 (1): 85–95.

Eboko, F. and P. Awondo (2013), 'Homo-mobilités, du Cameroun vers la France', *Africultures*, 96 (6): 188–203.

Fobear, K. (2015), '"I Thought We Had No Rights": Challenges in Listening, Storytelling, and Representation of LGBT Refugees', *Studies in Social Justice*, 9 (1): 102–17.

Freedom House (2020), 'South Africa: Authorities Must Improve Treatment of Refugees and Asylum Seekers', press release, 14 January. Available online: www.freedomhouse.org/article/south-africa-authorities-must-improve-treatment-refugees-and-asylum-seekers (accessed 1 September 2020).

Gontek, I. (2009), 'Sexual Violence against Lesbian Women in South Africa', *Outliers – A Collection of Essays and Creative Writing on Sexuality in Africa*, 2: 36–53.

Gunkel, H. (2010), *The Cultural Politics of Female Sexuality in South Africa*, New York: Routledge.

Hark, S. (2005), 'Queer Studies', in C. Braun and I. Stephan (eds), *Gender@Wissen: ein Handbuch der Gender-Theorien*, 285–303, Köln: Böhlau.

Hess, S. and B. Kasparek (2017), 'Under Control? Or Border (as) Conflict: Reflections on the European Border Regime', *Social Inclusion*, 5 (3): 58–68.

Hübner, K. (2016), 'Fluchtgrund sexuelle Orientierung und Geschlechtsidentität: Auswirkungen von heteronormativem Wissen auf die Asylverfahren LGBTI-Geflüchteter', *Feministische Studien*, 34 (2): 242–60.

Hucke, V. (2021), 'Sexualities and Borders: Differential Movements of Queer Migrants within the Borderland', in Y. R. Zhou, C. Sindig and D. Goellnicht (eds), *Sexualities, Transnationalism, and Globalisation: New Perspectives*, 19–31, London: Routledge.

Karakayalı, S. and V. S. Tsianos (2007), 'Movements That Matter: Eine Einleitung', in Transit Migration Forschungsgruppe (eds), *Turbulente Ränder: Neue Perspektiven auf Migration an den Grenzen Europas*, 7–17, Bielefeld: transcript.

Kron, S. (2010), 'Grenzen im Transit: Zur Konstitution politischer Subjektivitäten in transmigrantischen Räumen', *PROKLA*, 40 (1): 121–37.

Landau, L. B. (2019), 'What's behind the Deadly Violence in South Africa? The Attacks on Immigrants Are Neither Irrational Nor Spontaneous', *New York Times*, 16 September. Available online: www.nytimes.com/2019/09/16/opinion/south-africa-xenophobia-attacks.html (accessed 19 September 2019).

Lewis, R. A. (2013), 'Deportable Subjects: Lesbians and Political Asylum', *Feminist Formations*, 25 (2): 174–94.

Liinason, M. (2020), 'Challenging the Visibility Paradigm: Tracing Ambivalences in Lesbian Migrant Women's Negotiations of Sexual Identity', *Journal of Lesbian Studies*, 24 (2): 110–25.

Luibhéid, E. (2002), *Entry Denied: Controlling Sexuality at the Border*, Minneapolis: University of Minnesota Press.

Luibhéid, E. (2004), 'Heteronormativity and Immigration Scholarship: A Call for Change', *GLQ*, 10 (2): 227–35.

Luibhéid, E. (2008), 'Queer/Migration: An Unruly Body of Scholarship', *GLQ*, 14 (2/3): 169–90.

Luibhéid, E. (2020), 'Migrant and Refugee Lesbians: Lives That Resist the Telling', *Journal of Lesbian Studies*, 24 (2): 57–76.

Manalansan, M. F. (2003), *Global Divas: Filipino Gay Men in the Diaspora*, Durham: Duke University Press.

Manalansan, M. F. (2006), 'Queer Intersections: Sexuality and Gender in Migration Studies', *International Migration Review*, 40 (1): 224–49.

Marnell, J. (2021), *Seeking Sanctuary: Stories of Sexuality, Faith and Migration*, Johannesburg: Wits University Press.

Marnell, J., E. Oliveira and G. H. Khan (2021), '"It's About Being Safe and Free to Be Who You Are": Exploring the Lived Experiences of Queer Migrants, Refugees and Asylum Seekers in South Africa', *Sexualities*, 24 (1/2): 86–110.

Mathers, K. and L. B. Landau (2007), 'Natives, Tourists, and Makwerekwere: Ethical Concerns with "Proudly South African" Tourism', *Development Southern Africa*, 24 (3): 523–37.

McKnight, J. (2008), 'Through the Fear: A Study of Xenophobia in South Africa's Refugee System', *Journal of Identity and Migration Studies*, 2 (2): 18–42.

Mthembu-Salter, G., R. Amit, C. Gould and L. B. Landau (2014), *Counting the Cost of Securitizing South Africa's Immigration Regime*, Brighton: Migrating out of Poverty.

Mezzadra, S. (2010), 'Autonomie der Migration: Kritik und Ausblick', *Grundrisse*, 34: 22–9.

Mezzadra, S. (2011) 'The Gaze of Autonomy: Capitalism, Migration and Social Struggles', in V. Squire (ed.), *The Contested Politics of Mobility: Borderzones and Irregularity*, 121–42, London: Routledge.

Mlilo, S. N. (2019), *Xenowatch Factsheet 1: Incidents of Xenophobic Violence in South Africa: January – September 2019*, Johannesburg: Xenowatch. Available online: http://www.migration.org.za/wp-content/uploads/2016/07/Factsheet-1-Xenohopbic-violence-incidents-in-SA_-Jan-Sept-2019.pdf (accessed 10 January 2021).

Moulier-Boutang, Y. (1992), 'Interview mit Yann Moulier-Boutang: Aus: razza operaia, Padova edizioni, Mai 1992', in S. R. R. Straße (ed.), *Thesen zur Rassismusdebatte. Strategien der Unterwerfung/Strategien der Befreiung*, 28–55, Berlin: Schwarze Risse.

Nyoka, N. (2020), 'Amended Refugee Act Restricts Fundamental Rights', *New Frame*, 16 January. Available online: www.newframe.com/amended-refugee-act-restricts-fundamental-rights (accessed 31 August 2020).

Oliveira, E., S. V. Meyers and J. Vearey (eds) (2016), *Queer Crossings: A Participatory Arts-Based Project*, Johannesburg: ACMS.

Palmary, I. (2016), *Gender, Sexuality and Migration in South Africa: Governing Morality*, London: Palgrave Macmillan.

Pott, A., C. Rass and F. Wolff (2018), 'Was ist ein Migrationsregime? Einleitung', in A. Pott, C. Rass and F. Wolff (eds), *Was ist ein Migrationsregime? What Is a Migration Regime?*, 1–16, Wiesbaden: VS.

Reddy, V., S. Monro and Z. Matebeni. (2018), 'Introduction', in Z. Matebeni, S. Monro, and V. Reddy (eds), *Queer in Africa: LGBTQ Identities, Citizenship, and Activism*, 1–16, London: Routledge.

Ross, E. and R. Rapp (1981), 'Sex and Society: A Research Note from Social History and Anthropology', *Comparative Studies in Society and History*, 23 (1): 51–72.

Salter, M. (2011), 'Places Everyone! Studying the Performativity of the Border', *Political Geography*, 30 (2): 66–7.

Sandoval, C. (1998), 'Mestizaje as Method: Feminists-of-Color Challenge the Canon', in C. Trujillo (ed.), *Living Chicana Theory*, 352–70, Berkeley: Third Woman Press.

Scalabrini Centre (2020), 'New Refugee Laws Undermine Human Rights of Refugees', press release, 10 January. Available online: www.scalabrini.org.za/news/press-statement-new-refugee-laws-undermine-human-rights-of-refugees (accessed 10 July 2020).

Schwenken, H. (2018), *Globale Migration: zur Einführung*, Hamburg: Junius.

Shivji, N. (2020), 'Change to the Refugees Act Moves South Africa Much Closer to Donald Trump's America', *Daily Maverick*, 4 February. Available online: www.dailymaverick.co.za/article/2020-02-04-change-to-the-refugees-act-moves-south-africa-much-closer-to-donald-trumps-america (accessed 31 August 2020).

Tamale, S. (2011a), 'Introduction', in S. Tamale (ed.), *African Sexualities: A Reader*, 1–7, Cape Town: Pambazuka Press.

Tamale, S. (2011b), 'Researching and Theorizing Sexualities in Africa', in S. Tamale (ed.), *African Sexualities: A Reader*, 11–36, Cape Town: Pambazuka Press.

van Klinken, A. (2019), *Kenyan, Christian, Queer: Religion, LGBT Activism, and Arts of Resistance in Africa*, Pennsylvania: Pennsylvania State University Press.

Yuval-Davis, N., G. Wemyss and K. Cassidy (2019), *Bordering*, Cambridge: Polity Press.

Zomorodi, G. (2016), 'Responding to LGBT Forced Migration in East Africa', *Forced Migration Review*, 52: 91–3.

Chapter 12

DEBUNKING THE LIBERATION NARRATIVE: RETHINKING QUEER MIGRATION AND ASYLUM TO FRANCE

Florent Chossière

In the late 1990s, France – along with other Global North jurisdictions – began to consider asylum claims involving persecution based on sexual orientation and/ or gender identity (SOGI). It increasingly came to recognize sexual and gender minorities as constituting a 'particular social group',[1] thereby opening up the possibility for the granting of refugee status.[2] In the decades since, queer migration scholars have critiqued discourses that explain the movement of queer[3] people from the Global South to the Global North as a form of 'liberation'. More precisely, they have questioned the framing of queer migration as a journey from absolute repression to total freedom, whereby individuals who reach the Global North are suddenly able to live openly, freely and safely. Although some individuals might describe their experiences along these lines, the migration-as-liberation framing remains problematic, especially when it serves as the primary discourse for understanding queer mobility. Such narratives oversimplify the experiences of queer migrants by erasing new forms of marginalization that they may face (Cantú 2009; Manalansan 2003). These narratives can also fuel neo-imperialist practices by positioning the Global North as the 'protector' of sexual and gender minorities (Luibhéid 2005).

Within the migration-as-liberation framing, queer refugees are positioned as 'mediating agents' whose experiences of persecution not only affirm the supposed superiority of the Global North but also reinforce geopolitical hierarchies (Jenicek, Wong and Lee 2009). This culturalization and externalization of homo/ transphobia often justifies interventionist practices by states in the Global North. This is perhaps best illustrated in Jasbir Puar's (2007) conceptual framework of 'homonationalism' and 'sexual exceptionalism'. Puar highlights how, after the 9/11 attacks, a particular form of queerness was integrated into the United States' nation-making project and imperialist interventions. In the European context, Éric Fassin (2006) underlines how the rhetoric of 'sexual democracy' is used to legitimize xenophobic, racist and Islamophobic immigration policies and practices. Furthermore, the geopolitics of sexual nationalisms obscure the colonial legacies and post-colonial tensions that shape contestations over sexual and gender rights in many Global South countries. Numerous scholars show how hetero-patriarchal discourses inform post-colonial nation-building processes on the African continent, noting that some states continue to frame homosexuality as 'unAfrican' even though laws criminalizing same-sex sexuality were inherited from colonial powers (Awondo 2017; Matebeni and Pereira 2014; M'Baye 2013; Msibi 2011).

Writing in the context of Canada, David Murray (2014) unpacks the dangers of the migration-as-liberation framing, noting how it reduces queer migration to a set narrative arc:

> [F]rom closeted in their country of origin to 'out' in Canada that coincides with unidirectional spatial migration towards the nation of refuge, culminating in the liberating moment of the refugee hearing where the claimant can officially 'come out' to the state who will protect her and allow her the freedom to be openly 'gay' 'lesbian' 'bisexual' or 'transgendered' [*sic*] and expect passive, docile citizenship in return.
>
> (453)

As Murray suggests, the lived experiences of queer migrants tell a different story about countries of reception, suggesting that these locations are far from the 'liberating' sanctuaries they market themselves as. First, SOGI asylum procedures – as with other asylum adjudications – operate as a filtering device, excluding those whose credibility appears questionable (Tschalaer 2019; Dustin and Held 2018; Akin 2017; Giametta 2017; Kobelinsky 2012). Second, the depiction of queer migration as a moment of emancipation and ontological becoming obscures the precariousness that shapes people's everyday lives (Chossière, 2021, 2020; Wimark 2021; Lee 2019). Put another way, queer migrants and asylum seekers can be exposed to new power relations that leave them socially, economically and politically marginalized.

This chapter extends the above critiques by interrogating the complex migration trajectories of queer people from Africa – specifically Algeria, Cameroon, Côte d'Ivoire, Democratic Republic of the Congo (DRC), Guinea, Mali, Morocco, Nigeria, Republic of Congo, Senegal, Tunisia and Uganda – who have applied for, or are attempting to apply for, SOGI asylum in France. Their experiences disrupt categories and discourses commonly associated with queer migration, most notably the assumption that the granting of refugee status is a necessarily liberating moment. They also show how France's increasingly restrictive migration policies can block vulnerable individuals from receiving state protection, even though these policies have been justified in part as a necessary defence against 'fake' asylum seekers (Akoka 2020). In other words, policies nominally designed to preserve the asylum system actually work to limit access for those who may need it most.

Literature on SOGI asylum has focused largely on administrative procedures (usually refugee status adjudications), experiences of exclusion/marginalization and, most recently, the role of organizations or support services (Cesaro 2021). Driving this focus is the conceptualization of asylum as a linear spatio-temporal process – what Murray (2014) refers to as a 'unidirectional spatial migration ... culminating in the liberating moment of the refugee hearing' (453). The dominance of this view means that little attention is paid to what happens in the time and space between a queer person's departure from their country of origin and the lodging of an asylum claim in a reception country. This overlooks how Global North bordering regimes obstruct the movement of the very people that homonationalist rhetoric purports to care about. By examining the lived experiences of African queer migrants before they apply for state protection, I argue that asylum and migration policies represent a continuum of exclusionary practices. Thus, I add to scholarship that views queer asylum as a transnational migration issue (Lee 2019; Murray 2014; Randazzo 2005).

My analysis is carried out in three steps. First, I highlight the disjuncture between political/administrative categories and actual lived experiences by taking into consideration the multiplicity of factors leading queer people to migrate. In doing so I problematize discourses that position 'refugees' and 'economic migrants' as discrete, dichotomous categories. I then focus on my informants' migration trajectories and how they came to apply for SOGI asylum in France, thus emphasizing the non-linearity of these processes. Finally, I examine the ways in which asylum can be mobilized by individuals to build practices of transnational queer solidarity. Embedded within the migration-as-liberation framing is an assumption that, once refugee status is granted, queer persons cut all ties with their country of origin (Murray 2014). Tracing my informants' transnational ties reveals this belief to be false, while also offering a counterpoint to representations of asylum seekers as passive victims waiting for help (Ehrkamp 2016).

Methodology

This chapter draws on ethnographic fieldwork carried out between February 2017 and January 2020 at a Paris-based organization supporting queer asylum seekers and refugees. The organization mainly provides guidance on navigating the French asylum system, but also runs language classes and community-building activities. As a volunteer, I provided assistance to individual SOGI asylum seekers regarding their claims, taught French classes, conducted initial assessments with new clients and took part in social activities.

Volunteering allowed me to meet a large number of queer asylum seekers and refugees, seventy-six of whom became the focus of my study. These were people with whom I had at least three discussions about their life, their migration journey and/or the asylum procedure. The vast majority – sixty individuals – came from African countries, and it is these cases that I draw on in this chapter. This high proportion reflects both the characteristics of the people assisted by the organization and the general demographic of SOGI asylum in France.[4] In addition to this ethnographic and observational data, I conducted interviews with twenty-three queer asylum seekers and refugees (nineteen cisgender men and four cisgender women) between the ages of twenty-one and sixty-three.[5]

Blurring the boundaries of political categories

Since the 'migrant crisis'[6] of 2015, European political and media discourses have propagated a simplistic understanding of migratory phenomena, primarily by reinforcing a hard distinction between 'refugees' and 'economic migrants'. Refugees are presented as individuals who flee persecution and war and are therefore deserving of protection. Indeed, European countries present themselves as having a moral and political duty to welcome such individuals. By contrast, economic migrants are portrayed and treated as undesirable; they are depicted as the world's poor and unemployed, desperately trying to access Europe in order to exploit national welfare systems and access economic opportunities. In such a political context, asylum procedures are intrinsically tied to suspicions about migrants. According to dominant rhetoric, refugee status is reserved for those who 'truly' need protection and must be vigilantly defended from misuse by economic migrants (Fassin and Kobelinsky 2012).

This is only the most recent configuration in a long history of distrust towards migration and asylum. In France, the majority of asylum applications have been rejected since the mid-1980s, following the introduction of increasingly restrictive immigration policies in the 1970s (Fassin and Kobelinsky 2012). The anti-migrant discourses underpinning recent policy shifts have been convincingly critiqued by scholars and activists. Many point to the inadequacies of existing migration categories, highlighting a disconnect between the lived experiences of individuals/groups on the move and the language used to describe them. Rather than being neutral descriptors, these categories have been transformed into political tools that exclude and regulate (Lendaro, Rodier and Vertongen 2019; Crawley and Skleparis 2018; Migreurop 2017). Furthermore, scholars have questioned the notion of an absolute definition for who or what constitutes a 'refugee'. They emphasize the historical, spatial, political and social fluctuations that determine who is worthy of state protection (Akoka 2020; Agier and Madeira 2017; Fassin 2013).

Following these contributions, I intend to blur the boundaries of existing political categories by tracing the complex experiences, identities and trajectories of queer African migrants. In particular, I trouble the notion of singular causality by emphasizing the multiple factors that compel queer Africans to migrate. Héctor Carrillo's (2004) definition of 'sexual migration' provides a helpful framing for this discussion:

> [Sexual migration describes] international migration that is motivated, fully or partially, by the sexuality of those who migrate, including motivations connected to sexual desires and pleasures, the pursuit of romantic relations with foreign partners, the exploration of new self-definitions of sexual identity, the need to

distance oneself from experiences of discrimination or oppression caused by sexual difference, or the search for greater sexual equality and rights.

(59)

Carrillo rightly points out that sexuality may be one among many factors that trigger migration. His definition resonates with the experiences of my interlocutors. Amir[7] is a gay man from Morocco who has now been granted refugee status in France. His trajectory illustrates the difficulty of assigning causality – that is, the danger of reducing queer migration to a single factor. When Amir arrived in France, he was living with his boyfriend, Yanis, who is also from Morocco. They met in Turkey when they were both students: Amir in Morocco and Yanis in France. Before meeting Yanis, Amir tried to go to Canada to find work, but was unable to secure the required visa. Reflecting on his decision to move to Canada, Amir explained: 'It had nothing to do with my homosexuality, but it was already to escape Morocco, because I knew that those problems with my family would one day happen.' After he met Yanis, Amir regularly visited him in France. One day, Amir's brother found out about his homosexuality and started an argument that culminated in Amir being injured. Amir then decided to move to France and apply for asylum. How should we classify Amir – as a refugee, an economic migrant or simply a romantic partner seeking to be reunited? Amir's trajectory does not lend itself to being defined by existing classificatory structures.

Migration trajectories are deeply connected to the socio-economic status of individuals – not all people facing persecution can afford to pay for a trip to France, whether direct or not. In the case of queer Africans, differences in socio-economic status enable competing engagements with heteronormativity. In studying the migrations of gay and lesbian Cameroonians to France, Fred Eboko and Patrick Awondo (2013) identify a form of 'sexual nomadism'. This refers to frequent travel by individuals engaged in same-sex relationships in France, while they simultaneously maintain a heterosexual relationship – and everything that comes along with it (marriage, children, social status, etc.) – in Cameroon. Such an arrangement is inevitably elitist, given that it is only open to those who can afford regular transcontinental mobility. However, this articulation of queer mobility – which foregrounds the interplay between socio-economic status, sexuality and migration – disrupts the perception that queer Africans by default do not have the means to negotiate migration. In truth, some may opt for a circulatory mobility pattern, or even choose to stay permanently on the continent.

Paying close attention to the ways in which socio-economic status and sexuality intertwine destabilizes rigid distinctions between refugees and economic migrants. It shows that persecution and the strategies developed to cope with it often impact considerably on the targeted individual's economic situation. In Arsene's case, homophobic persecution brought economic precarity, which in turn shaped his migration trajectory:

When the situation [in Côte d'Ivoire] became unbearable for me, I stayed there and faced the threats for eight months. But then it came to a point where I was really struggling financially, because I was always having to move – if people knew I was in a certain place, I had to move to live in another one. The hunt was still going on.

Discrimination can be experienced very differently depending on a person's social position and available capital. Applying an intersectional lens uncovers the complex interplay of factors that can trigger and potentially constrain movement. I heard multiple accounts of queer migration being precipitated by the discovery of a romantic relationship. In cases involving couples from different socio-economic backgrounds, it was usually the partner in a lower class position who left, as the following example attests:

Mousa: He [in reference to former partner] is still in Mali, but it's over between us.
Florent: And he didn't face any problem?
Moussa: But this guy, he's a rich guy. He lives in his villa. Who will come to say something to him? If you open your mouth, he gives you money and then you keep quiet. That's the way it works in Mali.

A similar dynamic is present in David's story. When his family discovered he was gay, David left for another town in DRC. He was recognized by someone from his former neighbourhood, who then informed David's father of his whereabouts, leading to a confrontation. At the time David was in a relationship with a local businessman, whom he called Mr John:

I called Mr John. We met; I explained the problem. The first thing he said, 'Did [your father] mention me?' 'No.' … One week later, my father came to intimidate my landlady. He came with a police car. But actually he wanted to know the guy I was in a relationship with to prosecute him. I warned Mr John and he told me, 'David, I will think about this. I think the best solution is for you to leave this country so it doesn't impact my position. I'm also scared. A lot of politicians here are homosexuals. But they hide it. If people know I'm homosexual, it will make a lot of problems. So you have to go abroad.' He asked me to go live with him in South Africa where he had his business activities. But I said no; I knew that it's tough [in South Africa]. And I knew that for him it was a way of getting rid of me. I said I wanted to go to Europe. A few days later, Mr John said, 'Okay, David, you have to go to Europe to erase all traces.'

In the end, Mr John funded David's trip to France.

As these examples demonstrate, the link between persecution and migration cannot be divorced from larger socio-economic factors. For example, low socio-economic status may explain unwanted immobility for some individuals (wanting to leave but not having the means to do so), whereas for others it may cause unwanted mobility (wanting to stay but not having the socio-economic capital to protect themselves). Those with a high socio-economic status, such as Mr John, may have the option of chosen immobility based on their social status and available resources. Recognizing the nuanced nature of persecution, and the varying tactics used to survive it, helps to avoid geographical essentialism. Indeed, obscuring the impact of socio-economic factors on individual experiences of persecution allows for African countries to be portrayed as intrinsically and uniformly hostile towards queer people, in line with culturalist and homonationalist discourses.

Lastly, the pretext for migration can, in and of itself, be an issue for queer people who find themselves having to navigate both European border regimes and heteronormative social systems. Cross-border movement can generate new configurations of disclosure, in that potential asylum applicants are expected to indicate their belonging to and identification with sexual or gender minorities in their home country. To get around this, people may try to fit into limited migration categories that will allow them to reach France, thus bypassing the asylum system altogether and avoiding a forced break with family. Abdel and Mustafa started their relationship in Algeria. After experiencing persecution, Mustafa moved to France, where he was granted refugee status. Abdel sometimes visits Mustafa in France. Abdel's parents, who found out about their relationship, do not know that Mustafa now lives in France.

> Abdel: I love Mustafa so much. I don't want to leave him alone, and I don't
>   know what will happen to me in Algeria. I want to come here with him, but
>   in a configuration where it doesn't get worse with my family. I want to find a
>   solution that does not make my family think that I came to France because of
>   what they discovered about me.
> Florent: That's why you're trying to get a student visa?
> Abdel: To hide behind it. That's the plain truth. … I don't want to stay. It's not
>   a question that I want to stay, but it's a question that I want my family, this
>   image of me, I want my family to erase it.

Abdel's example shows that political categories of migration – which are ostensibly designed to track people's motives and thus regulate their access to and movement within states – often fail to reflect lived realities. The strategies people employ to regularize their presence in France may not be intrinsically linked to their reasons for migrating. Instead, they reflect how individuals negotiate multiple power relationships to adjust their movement in a restrictive context marked both by cis-heteronormativity in their home country and by an anti-migrant border regime in Europe.

Looking closely at the trajectories of queer Africans exposes how rigid migration categories are unable to apprehend and respond to complex motivations and needs. It also disrupts simplistic representations of queer African migrants within homonationalist frameworks, insofar as 'queer refugees' cannot be so simply distinguished from other 'migrants'. Europe's restrictive migration policies can also jeopardize the strategies deployed by queer Africans to manage expectations of cis-heteronormativity. This is evident in Abdel's case, where his failed attempts to get a student visa have placed him in an even more precarious position.

Non-direct paths

The migration-as-liberation narrative is predicated on a negative comparison between the country of origin and the country of reception, implying that asylum is an essential step towards securing freedom. What happens to a person in between these locations is rarely afforded the same attention. In this part of the chapter, I highlight obstacles that queer Africans face before applying for, and potentially being granted, refugee status. The latter is usually considered the culmination of the liberation process, indicating a successful transition from oppression to emancipation.

However, when the complexities of a person's migration trajectory are considered, the migration-as-liberation narrative is shown to be reductive at best and misleading at worst. Examining the complex motivations, negotiations and movements that constitute a person's migration can paint a very different picture. For example, press coverage tends to suggest that any queer person 'deserving' of protection can easily reach an asylum destination and appeal for assistance (Jenicek, Wong and Lee 2009). This type of reporting obscures the ways in which Global North border regimes prevent the majority of queer people facing persecution from ever being granted access (Lee 2019; El-Hage and Lee 2016). The European asylum system presents 'migration exclusion [as] morally defensible' (Bhabha 2002: 161) by perpetuating the myth that targeted assistance is provided to those most in need, despite the fact that those who might be recognized as refugees are subjected to restrictive policies that block or constrain their movements. For example, African citizens wishing to come to Europe can apply for a Schengen visa, authorizing a stay up to ninety days in the common zone. In accordance with the Dublin III Regulation, however, only one EU member state can examine an asylum application. The responsibility for this lies with whichever state issued the Schengen visa. Managing and approving visas remains a competence of each EU member state through local consulates, with each state determining what supporting documentation is required. This harmonization of European visa policies relies on a shared concern about the control of movement, especially from countries considered poor and unstable, and effectively transforms visa applications into the first line of European migration control (Migreurop 2017). The Schengen visa can thus be understood as a strategy for policing movement from a distance (Guild and Bigo 2003). Queer Africans attempting to escape persecution are not exempt from visa systems; they, too, encounter this immediate barrier before entering France, or Europe more generally. This is evident in the two examples below, the first of which is taken from field notes and the second from an interview:

> Moussa invites Mustafa and I to have some tea at his place this afternoon. ... He talks to us about a man he knows in Mali who faces serious problems right now. It's his first boyfriend, who managed to contact Moussa recently. As he has been [publicly] identified as gay, he's often beaten up by his older brother, encounters

difficulties at his job, and no longer dares to go out. He recently applied for a visa to come to France, but it has been refused. He called Moussa in the middle of the night, panicked, to explain the situation. Moussa is thinking about sending him some money at the end of the month, as [his ex-boyfriend] has almost nothing left; he already sold his car and other stuff to pay the guy who was supposed to get him a visa, but it didn't work.

Florent: When you were in Cameroon, did you try to get a visa to come directly to France?

Maurice: Well, I told myself, when the problems started, I told myself that if I initiate a procedure to get a visa, because I saw a lot of people applying for a visa, it took such a long time and it didn't even work for most of them, it didn't work, most of the documents you are asked [to provide] by the embassy, you don't have them. Because they may ask you for an employment contract, you have to be a taxpayer, and show your payrolls, a bank account, all of this, there are a lot of things. And I didn't have [these documents].

Maurice's situation demonstrates how highly restrictive visa conditions are all the more difficult to meet for queer people facing persecution; the length of the administrative procedure and the number of supporting documents required are incompatible with an urgent need to leave. Furthermore, the economic precarity brought about by homo/transphobia increases the likelihood that a queer person cannot meet the minimum financial requirements. Miriam Ticktin (2005) shows how asylum procedures are intrinsically linked to restrictive migration policies as they operate as humanitarian exceptions. Following her observation, I argue that this exception frame can be applied beyond asylum decision-making itself since migration policies actively exclude people from accessing asylum by constraining their movements in the first place.

Similarly, the claim that a quick and spontaneous application for asylum can be lodged once in France needs to be critically examined. The stories I collected point to the myriad obstacles that queer Africans face. Accessing asylum requires a certain amount of knowledge and information. Some people I met explained that when they first arrived in France, they had little to no understanding of the asylum procedure. Those who had heard about asylum associated it with political repression or escaping war, unaware of the possibility of being granted refuge due to SOGI persecution. The dual isolation experienced by queer migrants – many are excluded from or avoid country-of-origin networks, while also struggling to access queer support structures in the reception country – may further reduce their chance of learning about SOGI asylum (Randazzo 2005). However, this does not mean that queer Africans in France remain helpless victims. Rather, they deploy strategies to look for information while carefully avoiding dangerous encounters. In the quote below, Adama describes how he exploited language differences to access information while in presence of heterosexual migrants:

[In an informal migrant camp in Paris] there was a Somali. I borrowed his phone and I typed [in French] because he speaks and writes Arabic, so he doesn't understand. So I took his phone and looked for 'queer organisations in France'. Even in French, he doesn't know what it means. I found the organisation [for queer asylum seekers], noted the address and went there.

Even when they have such information, potential asylum seekers may be reluctant to initiate the procedure, as this means having to interact with the state. Making oneself known to the authorities can be a source of anxiety, particularly for those who entered France with false documents or with no documents. Fatima, a lesbian woman from Senegal, was hesitant to come forward even after learning about SOGI asylum:

I was scared. I was really scared because, I don't know, I've never done this. Is it a good or bad thing? Is it safe? Will they not bring me back to my country? To be honest with you, I was so scared. [My friends] talked to me about this in August. But I was [intentionally] slowing down the process. I was saying, 'You never know what can happen. I can't; I'm too scared.' Until September, when I decided, 'Okay, let's go, even if they take me back to Senegal, never mind.'

Fatima's fears provide another example of the impact of restrictive migration policies on access to asylum. Her reluctance to initiate the asylum process, produced by an acute sense of non-belonging, points to the murky relationship between asylum systems and restrictive migration policies. The insecurity engendered by France's border regime fuelled Fatima's hesitation; she anticipated being met with suspicion and hostility, despite France's endorsement of sexual and gender rights. When one looks closely at the lived experiences of people crossing borders, including potential SOGI refugees like Fatima, it is evident that the 'humanitarian' asylum system and 'regulated' migration system are not distinct, but rather work in tandem to limit access to space and rights (Ticktin 2005).

The prohibition on visiting one's country of origin once refugee status is granted emerged as another concern.[8] This prospect is all the more daunting for people involved in advocacy work. Yves, an LGBT and HIV rights campaigner, used to travel between France and Côte d'Ivoire as part of his activism, but was forced to stop due to travel restrictions:

When I say I hesitated about asylum, [it is] because when you speak about asylum, you speak about not going back to your country. When you talk to me about this, I'm thinking maybe [I will apply], sooner or later, not now, not tomorrow, but, for an activist, staying here is like, well, you have to stop forever. But stopping forever is not my goal. And, at first, I didn't know that after you get the refugee status, you can apply for French citizenship and then go to Côte d'Ivoire. ... So first, for me, it was very hard to accept asylum, because when I started this process, I stopped everything.

The transition between migration and asylum is by no means automatic, nor is it simple and quick. The granting of asylum is framed as a liberating moment in hegemonic narratives, yet Yves' experience shows that it is also synonymous with renunciation and abandonment. For Yves, being 'free' in France is contingent on giving up his direct activism and letting go of key ties with Côte d'Ivoire. Doing so comes at a great personal cost.

Abdel's case reveals similar tensions. Denied a student visa and facing new threats in Algeria, Abdel resigned himself to applying for asylum in France. This meant breaking ties with his family – precisely what he had hoped to avoid. Rather than providing queer people like Yves and Abdel with 'liberation', the asylum and migration systems undermine attempts to negotiate cis-heteronormativity in ways that work for specific individuals. In a context of restrictive migration policies, asylum applications by queer Africans can sometimes represent a last resort; it is an option they hope to avoid because of the potential disadvantages it brings.

Transnational queer solidarities

Writing in relation to Canada, Murray (2014) points out the performative nature of queer asylum claims:

> [T]he hegemonic migration to liberation nation narrative usually ends with the LGBT refugee claimant making an emotional statement relating to their feelings of freedom, relief, happiness and desire to make Canada their new home … In these final narrative moments, there is rarely any reference to the SOGI/ LGBT refugee claimants' feelings about their country of origin and/or family or friends there. The implication is that they are starting anew, being reborn into the liberatory democratic nation-state.
>
> (465)

Yet, as the example of Yves shows, not all queer Africans wish to cut ties with their home country once in France. In this section, I extend this line of critique by drawing attention to transnational solidarity practices. These collective strategies undermine Global North states' self-portrayals as saviours and protectors, while also showing that queer Africans do not wait passively for 'rescue' (Ehrkamp 2016). SOGI asylum, along with the humanitarian apparatus associated with it, is just the latest manifestation of 'saving' queers from the Global South, the logic of which is firmly anchored in Global North sexual politics (Giametta and Havkin 2020). Thus, the formation and mobilization of informal transnational networks can be seen as 'acts of resistance' against restrictive migration policies (Lee 2019).

Following Camille Schmoll (2017), I use the notion of 'transnational social space' to describe 'migratory practices and identifications articulating distant places' (43).[9] After arriving in France and becoming familiar with the asylum procedure, some queer Africans initiate solidarity practices that extend into this transnational social space. These practices can consist of knowledge-sharing and even practical one-on-one support, such as circulating one's phone number through queer country-of-origin networks so as to support recent arrivals navigate administrative procedures. Another strategy is to introduce acquaintances to organizations that support queer asylum seekers. The organization where I volunteered held regular welcome sessions for potential clients. On a number of occasions, Adama brought along new people, providing them with both moral and practical support. He explained why he does this in our interview:

> Adama: I help them to come to the meeting. I go with them, to make them registered, to put them in contact with volunteers. And, like this, I brought nine people to [the organisation]. ... But I always say to them, 'I cannot help you to get papers.' I tell them, '[the organisation] will not give you papers, but they can help you with your procedure. And they will help you in your life; they will help you to be self-confident.'
> Florent: And do you give them, yourself, advice?
> Adama: Yes, I do. I tell them, 'Start writing your story, explain why you left your country and why you cannot go back.' And I explain: 'Dates are important. Places also. When? Where?' I help them as I can, as I did for myself.

More general support can also be offered. Mamadou, a gay man from Cameroon who now has refugee status in France, posts informative videos on social media, using these platforms to share advice based on his personal experiences:

> [O]ne guy said to me, 'If I come to France, what can I do? How can I apply for asylum?' [He contacted me] because, actually, I made a video on my Facebook page explaining to people what asylum is. So then they got in touch with me, gay people, that's it. But I don't recommend France to them, because the system is really not very good. Honestly, I was shocked when I saw asylum seekers sleeping on the street. ... Personally, to be honest, I don't recommend people to come to France ... The big problem in France is housing. ... If you have nobody to help you here, no [don't come]. I rather refer people to Belgium.

These examples complicate the migration-as-liberation narrative in which queer Africans are reduced to passive victims awaiting 'rescue'. Adama's and Mamadou's experiences show how asylum often results from solidarity practices initiated by queer Africans, rather than being benevolently bestowed by Global North states. Queer Africans already settled in France actively share knowledge on how to navigate borders regimes and asylum systems. Disseminating information is a crucial component of solidarity, in that it allows queer Africans to produce new transnational social imaginaries:

> [M]uch of what people actually do transnationally is foregrounded by imaging, planning and strategizing; these must be valued and factored into people's agency. Despite the many advances in the transnational migration

framework to date, the contributions of the social imaginary or 'mindwork' are still largely ignored.

(Pessar and Mahler 2003: 817)

We can thus frame the diffusion of information about SOGI asylum from people in France to people in African countries as a form of collective agency, one that builds a new social imaginary. This transmission of knowledge becomes an important factor in how migration plays out, as exemplified by Abubakar's experience:

> In 2016, Dramane came back to Senegal and he called me. When I saw him, he explained that I should think about my life, about what I'm living here, my sexual orientation, [how] I can't live properly in Senegal, [how] I need to apply for asylum in another country and live my true nature. ... Later, he went back to France. And me, when he told me this, I kept thinking of this, and I started to do everything necessary to leave.

Abubakar's situation emphasizes once again that queer migration can rarely be reduced to or explained by a single factor. It often relies on the circulation of information and imaginaries in order to make mobility a reality. The integration of SOGI asylum into transnational social imaginaries appears as a major form of collective agency deployed by African queer people to navigate normative systems and restrictive border regimes. SOGI asylum results as much from these transnational practices of solidarity as it does from direct homo/transphobic persecution. The potential for a collective dimension to SOGI asylum disrupts the neoliberal logic on which the whole system is predicated; refugee status is normally understood to result solely from individual experiences (Akoka 2020), yet the examples above underscore its collective and often transnational dimensions.

Conclusion: Africa, Europe and the queer migrants in between

The framing of queer migration from Africa to Europe – and to the Global North more generally – as a linear movement towards liberation contributes to a polarized and essentialist vision of the world, one that pits the 'tolerant' Global North against the 'barbaric' Global South. Within this worldview, queer refugees are positioned as the ultimate mediating figures. Yet, these narratives obscure how people move between these two supposed geopolitical monoliths, as well as what happens in the spaces and times in between. Literature on SOGI asylum has worked to trouble this narrative by emphasizing how Global North asylum policies operate as filters, excluding many queer applicants through restrictive understandings of gender and sexuality, and by foregrounding the social and economic challenges facing queer migrants in reception countries. However, there remains an urgent need to look at less obvious dynamics of queer migration.

Examining the various stages of people's journeys reveals the complexities of queer migration trajectories and the obstacles individuals negotiate when trying to reach a 'liberating' destination. It also troubles the perception of a direct, linear path to 'freedom'. Uncovering the complexities of queer migrants' experiences highlights major discrepancies between liberation discourses and the constraining and often violent European border regime encountered by queer Africans. Whereas political discourses present asylum and migration as oppositional, in the process fostering a distinction between 'refugees' and 'migrants', the stories of queer Africans in France demonstrate the continuum between restrictive migration policies and access to asylum, between policing and humanitarianism (Ticktin 2005).

By examining the processes that led queer Africans to leave their countries of origin, I have revealed the disconnect between political migration categories and people's actual lived experiences. Reconceptualizing the movement of queer Africans is vital if we are to move beyond reductive and homogenizing rhetoric. Queer Africans face myriad challenges in seeking protection, ranging from being unable to leave their country in the first place, to having a limited understanding of bureaucratic procedures and/or a fear of state authorities. Claiming asylum is by no means a straightforward or self-evident process. Rather, it results from various strategies deployed to overcome restrictive border regimes. The narratives presented above disrupt the categorizations to which queer asylum seekers are subjected. Administrative classifications work to regulate their movements, while media discourses portray queer refugees as individuals who are reborn, free in a new country and willing to forget their pasts and socio-cultural roots. However, by focusing on what happens in between France and various African countries, one can uncover collective practices of solidarity. These transnational spaces offer opportunities to resist cis-heteronormativity and to navigate border regimes and restrictive migration policies.

Notes

1   According to the 1951 Refugee Convention, a refugee is someone who is unable or unwilling to return to their country of origin owing to a 'well-founded fear of being persecuted for reasons of race, religion, nationality, *membership of a particular social group* or political opinion' (emphasis added).
2   I use the term 'refugee' to refer to individuals who have been recognized as such by a state and 'asylum seeker' for individuals who have lodged an application for protection but are still awaiting an official determination. 'Migrant' is used as a generic term, independently of administrative situations.
3   Not everyone may recognize themselves in the categories of lesbian, gay, bisexual or transgender (LGBT). I use the term 'queer' to cover the variety of gender and sexual identities and/or practices that may not conform to cis-heteronormativity. However, none of my interlocutors self-identified using the label 'queer'.
4   French Office for Protection of Refugees and Stateless Persons (OFPRA) does not provide statistics on the grounds/reasons for asylum applications. However, OFPRA

does indicate that most SOGI applications originate from the African continent. Overall, most of the asylum seekers applying for SOGI are men. Transgender and intersex people remain a small minority among applicants (Pegliasco 2019).

5   Women are under-represented in the general population assisted by the organization (only 20 per cent in 2019). Transgender people are largely a minority. My self-identification as a man also played a role in the dominance of men in my sample. A Ugandan woman explicitly mentioned it as a reason she did not want to be interviewed by me.

6   The term 'migrant crisis' emerged in the public sphere in reference to the influx of newcomers to Europe and to a series of shipwrecks in the Mediterranean in 2015. Migration scholars have been particularly critical of this language, noting the way both data and the media have been used to frame it as a 'crisis' (see Leconte, Toureille and Grasland 2019; Migreurop 2017). Some scholars argue that if there is indeed a crisis, it is a 'crisis of response' rather than a 'crisis of migration' (Lendaro, Rodier and Vertongen 2019).

7   All names are pseudonyms. Interviews were conducted in French and translated into English by the author.

8   People who have been granted refugee status are also provided with a travel document, which is not valid for the country of their nationality. Refugees can apply for French citizenship if they fulfil certain criteria. On obtaining citizenship, they are able to travel as any other French citizen.

9   Quote translated from French by the author.

References

Agier, M. and A.-V. Madeira (2017), *Définir les réfugiés*, Paris: Presses Universitaires de France.

Akin, D. (2017), 'Queer Asylum Seekers: Translating Sexuality in Norway', *Journal of Ethnic and Migration Studies*, 43 (3): 458–74.

Akoka, K. (2020), *L'asile et l'exil. Une histoire de la distinction réfugiés/migrants*, Paris: La Découverte.

Awondo, P. (2017), *Le sexe et ses doubles. (Homo)sexualités en postcolonie*. Lyon: ENS Éditions.

Bhabha, J. (2002), 'Boundaries in the Field of Human Rights: International Gatekeepers? The Tension between Asylum Advocacy and Human Rights', *Harvard Human Rights Law Review*, 15: 151–81.

Cantú, L. (2009), *The Sexuality of Migration: Border Crossings and Mexican Immigrant Men*, New York: NYU Press.

Carrillo, H. (2004), 'Sexual Migration, Cross-Cultural Sexual Encounters, and Sexual Health', *Sexuality Research & Social Policy*, 1 (3): 58–70.

Cesaro, S. (2021), 'The (Micro-)Politics of Support for LGBT Asylum Seekers in France', in R. C. M. Mole (ed.), *Queer Migration and Asylum in Europe*, 216–37, London: UCL Press.

Chossière, F. (2020), 'Minorités sexuelles en exil: l'expérience minoritaire en ville à l'aune de marginalisations multiples', *Urbanités*, 13. Available online: https://www.revue-urbanites.fr/13-chossiere/ (accessed 24 March 2020).

Chossière, F. (2021), 'Refugeeness, Sexuality, and Gender: Spatialized Lived Experiences of Intersectionality by Queer Asylum Seekers and Refugees in Paris', *Frontiers in Human Dynamics*. doi: 10.3389/fhumd.2021.634009.

Crawley, H. and D. Skleparis (2018), 'Refugees, Migrants, Neither, Both: Categorical Fetishism and the Politics of Bounding in Europe's "Migration Crisis"', *Journal of Ethnic and Migration Studies*, 44 (1): 48–64.

Dustin, M. and N. Held (2018), 'In or Out? A Queer Intersectional Approach to "Particular Social Group" Membership and Credibility in SOGI Asylum Claims in Germany and the UK', *GenIUS - Rivista di studi giuridici sull'orientamento sessuale e l'identità di genere*, 2: 74–7.

Eboko, F. and P. Awondo (2013), 'Homo-mobilités du Cameroun vers la France', *Africultures*, 96 (6): 188–203.

El-Hage, H. and E. O. J. Lee (2016), 'LGBTQ racisés: Frontières identitaires et barrières structurelles', *Alterstice: Revue internationale de la recherche interculturelle*, 6 (2): 13–27.

Ehrkamp, P. (2016), 'Geographies of Migration I: Refugees', *Progress in Human Geography*, 41 (6): 813–22.

Fassin, D. (2013), 'The Precarious Truth of Asylum', *Public Culture*, 25 (1): 39–63.

Fassin, D. and C. Kobelinsky (2012), 'Comment on juge l'asile. L'institution comme agent moral', *Revue française de sociologie*, 53 (4): 657–88.

Fassin, É. (2006), 'La démocratie sexuelle et le conflit des civilisations', *Multitudes*, 26 (3): 123–31.

Giametta, C. (2017), *The Sexual Politics of Asylum: Sexual Orientation and Gender Identity in the UK Asylum System*, Oxon: Routledge.

Giametta, C. and S. Havkin (2020), 'Mapping Homo/Transphobia: The Valorization of the LGBT Protection Category in the Refugee-Granting System', *ACME: An International Journal for Critical Geographies*, 20 (1): 99–119.

Guild, E. and D. Bigo (2003), 'Le visa Schengen: expression d'une stratégie de "police" à distance', *Cultures & Conflits*, 49: 22–37.

Jenicek, A., A. D. Wong and E. O. J. Lee (2009), 'Dangerous Shortcuts: Representations of Sexual Minority Refugees in the Post-9/11 Canadian Press', *Canadian Journal of Communication*, 34 (4): 635–58.

Kobelinsky, C. (2012), 'L'asile gay: jurisprudence de l'intime à la Cour nationale du droit d'asile', *Droit et société*, 82 (3): 583–601.

Leconte, R., É. Toureille and C. Grasland (2019), 'La production médiatique d'une "crise migratoire". Dynamiques spatio-temporelles de l'agenda global de la presse en 2015', *Socio-anthropologie*, 40: 181–99.

Lee, E. O. J. (2019), 'Responses to Structural Violence: The Everyday Ways in Which Queer and Trans Migrants with Precarious Status Respond to and Resist the Canadian Immigration Regime', *International Journal of Child, Youth and Family Studies*, 10 (1): 70–94.

Lendaro, A., C. Rodier and Y. L. Vertongen (eds) (2019), *La crise de l'accueil. Frontières, droits, résistances*, Paris: La Découverte.

Luibhéid, E. (2005), 'Introduction: Queering Migration and Citizenship', in E. Luibhéid and L. Cantú (eds), *Queer Migration: Sexuality, U.S. Citizenship, and Border Crossings*, Minneapolis: University of Minnesota Press.

Manalansan, M. F. (2003), *Global Divas: Filipino Gay Men in the Diaspora*, Durham: Duke University Press Books.

Matebeni, Z. and J. Pereira (2014), 'Preface', in Z. Matebeni (ed.), *Reclaiming Afrikan: Queer Perspectives on Sexual and Gender Identities*, 7–9, Cape Town: Modjaji Books.

M'Baye, B. (2013), 'The Origins of Senegalese Homophobia: Discourses on Homosexuals and Transgender People in Colonial and Postcolonial Senegal', *African Studies Review*, 56 (2): 109–28.

Migreurop (2017), *Atlas des migrants en Europe. Approches critiques des politiques migratoires*, Paris: Armand Colin.

Msibi, T. (2011), 'The Lies We Have Been Told: On (Homo) Sexuality in Africa', *Africa Today*, 58 (1): 55–77.

Murray, D. A. B. (2014), 'The (Not So) Straight Story: Queering Migration Narratives of Sexual Orientation and Gendered Identity Refugee Claimants', *Sexualities*, 17 (4): 451–71.

Pegliasco, S. (ed.) (2019), *À l'écoute du monde. Rapport d'activité 2018*. Paris: Office Français de Protection des Réfugiés et des Apatrides.

Pessar, P. R. and S. J. Mahler (2003), 'Transnational Migration: Bringing Gender', *International Migration Review*, 37 (3): 812–46.

Puar, J. (2007), *Terrorist Assemblages: Homonationalism in Queer Times*, Durham: Duke University Press.

Randazzo, T. J. (2005), 'Social and Legal Barriers: Sexual Orientation and Asylum in the United States', in E. Luibhéid and L. Cantú (eds), *Queer Migrations. Sexuality, U.S. Citizenship, and Border Crossings*, 30–60, Minneapolis: University of Minnesota Press.

Schmoll, C. (2017), *Spatialités de la migration féminine en Europe du Sud. Une approche par le genre*, Habilitation à diriger des recherches: Université de Poitiers.

Ticktin, M. (2005), 'Policing and Humanitarianism in France: Immigration and the Turn to Law as State of Exception', *Interventions*, 7 (3): 346–68.

Tschalaer, M. (2019), 'Between Queer Liberalisms and Muslim Masculinities: LGBTQI+ Muslim Asylum Assessment in Germany', *Ethnic and Racial Studies*, 43 (7): 1265–83.

Wimark, T. (2021), 'Homemaking and Perpetual Liminality among Queer Refugees', *Social and Cultural Geography*, 22 (5): 647–65.

APPENDIX

We reproduce below the peer-review guidelines we developed for this project. We share this text as a practical example of how book/journal editors can support queer migration research from the Global South. Our goal in developing the guidelines was to remind peer reviewers of simple steps they can take to address persistent barriers to publication. We recognize, of course, that this document does not ameliorate the power imbalances that privilege voices and perspectives from the Global North. Radical structural reform is needed to address racism, colonialism, heterosexism and ableism within the academe, but there is also great value in adjusting our individual practices as scholars working across borders, cultures, languages and disciplines.

Peer-review guidelines

This collection aims to contribute to existing scholarly debates by bringing together diverse inputs on LGBTIQ+ migration on, from and to the African continent. In approaching its topic from a diverse range of disciplinary perspectives, the collection interrogates what it means to do research with, on and perhaps for LGBTIQ+ migrants, particularly at a time when global contestations around human rights have initiated a new 'scramble for Africa' – this time for evidence of homophobia, transphobia, xenophobia and other markers of 'savagery'.

Queer and Trans African Mobilities is the debut publication of the African LGBTIQ+ Migration Research Network (ALMN) and is the first collection of its kind produced on the African continent. In line with ALMN's objectives and values, the collection prioritizes the voices of African scholars, activists and practitioners, and seeks to provide meaningful opportunities for mentorship.

Information for peer reviewers

In keeping with international standards, each chapter will undergo double peer review before being accepted for publication. As well as helping to guide us as editors, the peer-review process is an opportunity for senior academics to support colleagues with less publishing experience and/or those working in difficult circumstances. Thus, we ask reviewers to approach their task with generosity and patience, while still offering unbiased critique based on their expertise. While we do not wish to prescribe how peer reviewers should approach their task, we do offer the following points as guidance:

- Our contributors come from diverse national and linguistic backgrounds. For many, English is their third or fourth language. While it is important to flag any major concerns with terminology, it is unnecessary to dwell on minor issues related to spelling, grammar, etc.
- Some contributors are working in under-resourced and potentially hostile contexts. It may not be possible for them to access recommended materials such as journal articles. If you have suggestions for additional readings, please attach PDFs (where possible).
- Peer review is a great way for emerging scholars to refine their thinking by considering alternative viewpoints or theories. We welcome suggestions for how the central thesis can be strengthened, but encourage reviewers to remain constructive when drafting comments or assessing the overall quality of argumentation. Remember this is about supporting and encouraging colleagues, rather than reinforcing existing socio-political inequalities.

We thank you for taking the time to support this publication. We know our contributors will be grateful for your expert guidance.

INDEX

www.ingramcontent.com/pod-product-compliance
Lightning Source LLC
Chambersburg PA
CBHW070357270326
41926CB00014B/2593